The Indian Militia and Description of the Indies

MILICIA Y DESCRIPCION DE LAS INDIAS, POR

el Capitan don Bernardo de Vargas Machuca, Cauallero Castellano, natural de la villa de Simancas.

DIRIGIDO AL LICENCIADO PAVLO de Laguna Presidente del Consejo Real de las Indias.

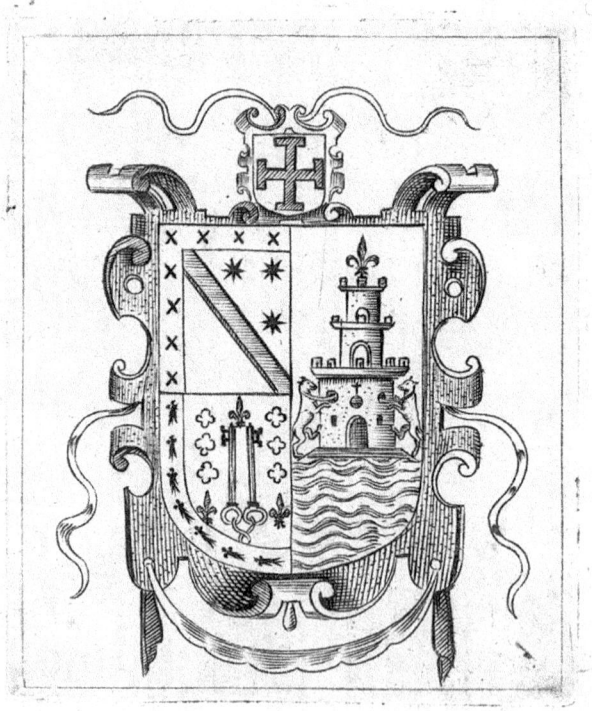

EN MADRID,
En casa de Pedro Madrigal.

THE INDIAN MILITIA
AND DESCRIPTION
OF THE INDIES

Captain Bernardo de Vargas Machuca

Edited by Kris Lane

*Translated by Timothy F. Johnson
from the original Spanish edition, 1599*

DUKE UNIVERSITY PRESS
Durham & London 2008

© 2008 Duke University Press
All rights reserved
Designed by Jennifer Hill
Typeset in Adobe Caslon Pro
by Tseng Information Systems, Inc.

*Library of Congress Cataloging-in-Publication Data
appear on the last printed page of this book.*

THE CULTURES AND PRACTICE OF VIOLENCE SERIES

Series Editors:
Neil L. Whitehead, University of Wisconsin, Madison
Jo Ellen Fair, University of Wisconsin, Madison
Leigh Payne, University of Wisconsin, Madison

The study of violence has often focused on the political and economic conditions under which violence is generated, the suffering of victims, and the psychology of its interpersonal dynamics. Less familiar are the role of perpetrators, their motivations, and the social conditions under which they are able to operate. In the context of postcolonial state building and more latterly the collapse and implosion of society, community violence, state repression, and the phenomena of judicial inquiries in the aftermath of civil conflict, there is a need to better comprehend the role of those who actually do the work of violence—torturers, assassins, and terrorists—as much as the role of those who suffer its consequences.

When atrocity and murder take place, they feed the world of the iconic imagination that transcends reality and its rational articulation, but in doing so imagination can bring further violent realities into being. This series encourages authors who build on traditional disciplines and break out of their constraints and boundaries, incorporating media and performance studies and literary and cultural studies as much as anthropology, sociology, and history.

CONTENTS

List of Illustrations IX
Preface XI
Acknowledgments XIII
Introductory Study XVII

Approvals, Dedications, and Sonnets 1

Book One of the Indian Militia 17

Book Two of the Indian Militia 55

Book Three of the Indian Militia 81

Book Four of the Indian Militia 133

A Brief Description of All the Western Indies 165

Hydrography of the Coasts and Seas of the Indies 213

Geography of the Most Distinguished Kingdoms
and Provinces of the Indies 221

Compendium of the Sphere 229

Declaration of the Proper Names of this Book 235

Appendix One:
A Posthumous Report on Bernardo de Vargas Machuca's
Services, ca. 1622   239

Appendix Two:
Selections from *The Defense of Western Conquests*, ca. 1603   245

Notes   259
Bibliography   281
Index   289

LIST OF ILLUSTRATIONS

1 The Spanish Atlantic in the sixteenth century xix *Maps*
2 The New Kingdom of Granada in the sixteenth century xxx

1 & 2 Philip II of Spain and Bernardo de Vargas Machuca xxv *Figures*
3 Royal Archive of Simancas, Old Castile xxvii
4 Cathedral Square, Bogotá, Colombia xxxiii
5 Royal Treasury, Bogotá, Colombia xxxiv
6 Plaza Bolívar, Tunja, Colombia xxxv
7 House of the governor, Tunja xxxvi
8 Plan of Muzo, Colombia xliv
9 View of Muzo from the south xlv
10 Portobelo fort plans xlvii
11 War canoes from Trinidad and Margarita Islands liii
12 Enslaved African pearl divers near Margarita Island lv
13 Margarita Island in the mid-seventeenth century lvii
14 Cabasset helmet 20
15 Morion helmet 20
16 Helmet with visor 20
17 Halberd 21
18 Harquebus 21
19 Steel sword 21
20 Pike 21
21 Caribbean cacique 22

Figures
22 A Caribbean warrior demonstrates the *macana*, or war club   25
23 Royal Hospital of Simancas   28
24 "The lizards that hang from the churches," Seville Cathedral   39
25 Warrior from Santa Marta, Colombia, with poisoned arrows   62
26 Arrow wound being treated with tobacco   63
27 Wild dogs chasing a boar and a hare, Spanish Caribbean   78
28 Sixteenth-century town square, Villa de Leiva, Colombia   141
29 Basilica of Our Lady of Chiquinquirá, patroness of Colombia   150
30 How emeralds form and are mined   211
31 Armillary sphere   228

PREFACE

Described by the distinguished Hispanist and military historian Geoffrey Parker as "the first manual of guerrilla warfare ever published," Bernardo de Vargas Machuca's 1599 *Milicia Indiana* is in fact the world's first known manual of antiguerrilla, or counterinsurgency, warfare. A longtime veteran of what anthropologists have termed "war in the tribal zone,"[1] its author represented a large and little-known category of Spanish emigrants to the Americas: the luckless conquistador. Thousands of these men, many of them participants in Spanish wars in Europe and the Mediterranean, followed Cortés and Pizarro to the Americas in search of fame and fortune. The vast majority found neither, and many ended their lives fighting Native American *guerrilleros* in the jungles, deserts, mountains, and swamps that marked the outer limits of the Spanish Empire. Unwilling to support costly formal armies abroad given their huge commitments at home, Spain's Habsburg monarchs encouraged such men to defend royal interests in the colonies on their own account, promising them pensions, titles, and even indigenous wards and tributaries in return. Most were baited not by these promises, however, but by variations on the El Dorado legend—the chance at discovering another Mexico or Peru.

As prospects for new conquests dimmed, veteran militiamen and inexperienced greenhorns alike sought new solutions to their poverty as well as outlets for mounting aggression. As a result, by 1599 hundreds of bands of mixed Spanish, creole, mestizo, African-descended, and indigenous paramilitaries roamed the American backcountry from New Mexico to Chile participating in what were often called *castigos*, or "punishments," privately financed police actions against alleged indigenous rebels, thieves, and fugitives. Taking both law and defense into their own hands, the Indies militiamen, sometimes led by petty nobles such as Vargas Machuca, fought pirates, renegades, and even fugitive African slaves. They increasingly saw themselves as a professional class, albeit an often disparaged and officially unrecognized one. Many such soldiers, but more especially their leaders, were literate, and they wrote the king repeatedly requesting compensation in the form of government posts and pensions.

In many ways, Vargas Machuca's *Milicia Indiana*, or "Indian Militia," is an extended autobiographical plea of this kind, known as a *probanza* or *relación de méritos y servicios*. Yet it is much more besides: a list of pointers for the bounty hunter, a primer on field medicine, a taxonomy of tropical plants and animals, a moralistic handbook for Christian commanders, a town-founder's "how-to"—even a compact, geocentric guide to the cosmos. It is also, and perhaps most importantly for historians and anthropologists, a rare account of indigenous ways of life and war in colonial New Granada, roughly today's Colombia. Indeed, it serves as an unwitting testament to the will, ingenuity, and cultural resilience of the many Native American peoples that Vargas Machuca so desperately fought to subdue that his *Indian Militia* manages to be so "Indian."

A manual in four books, *Milicia Indiana* begins with a discourse outlining the ideal qualities of the *caudillo*, or militia commander. Book 2 treats the organization and outfitting of punitive or conquest expeditions, including a portion on how to incorporate priests, and with extended discussions of arms and medicine. Book 3 covers the proper behavior of soldiers, advice on marching through peaceful versus bellicose territories, crossing rivers, bivouacking in foul weather, and carrying out (and beating off) night raids and ambushes. Book 4 treats peacemaking, town founding, and proper treatment of conquered peoples. Appended to these four books is a brief geographical description of all of Spanish America, with special emphasis on the indigenous peoples of New Granada, followed by a very short guide to the southern coasts and heavens. To this we have added a translation of Vargas Machuca's posthumous service record and a brief selection from his unpublished attack on the writings of Fray Bartolomé de Las Casas.

ACKNOWLEDGMENTS

As editor and translator of this, the first English translation of *Milicia Indiana*, we wish to thank the long-suffering staffs of the John Carter Brown Library in Providence, Rhode Island, and the Archivo General de la Nación in Bogotá, Colombia. Thanks also to the staffs of the Archivo General de Indias in Seville, Spain, the Archivo Histórico de Protocolos in Madrid, and the Hispanic Society of America in New York City. We have also benefited tremendously from the general collections and interlibrary loan offices of the Rockefeller Library at Brown University and the Earl Gregg Swem Library at the College of William and Mary. A thousand thanks are also due to Prof. J. Michael Francis of the University of North Florida for his painstaking reading of our first draft manuscript and many pages of valuable suggestions. We would happily blame him for any remaining shortcomings, but that would be unfair to the anonymous readers for Duke University Press who just as kindly let us have it. Special thanks are also due to Professor Hiroshi Kitamura of the College of William and Mary who patiently guided us through the 1994 Japanese edition. We also warmly thank Valerie Millholland and the editorial staff at Duke University Press for shepherding this project through to completion. Finally, we must thank our book's *real* author, Bernardo de Vargas Machuca, who if he were alive today would probably hunt us down and kill us.

Funding for archival research in Colombia during the fall of 2005 came from the Fulbright Commission for the International Exchange of Scholars. Work with original editions of *Milicia Indiana*, *Exercicios de la gineta*, and many other relevant early Americana imprints in the spring of 2006 was made possible by a National Endowment for the Humanities grant administered by the John Carter Brown Library. Research in Spain during the summer of 2006 was made possible by the generous endowment of David B. and Carolyn D. Wakefield administered by the College of William and Mary. These much-appreciated grants made possible not only the reading of Vargas Machuca's words in many forms and contexts, but also the partial retracing of his steps.

KRIS LANE
Williamsburg, Virginia

TIMOTHY F. JOHNSON
Dillon, Colorado

The Indian Militia and Description of the Indies

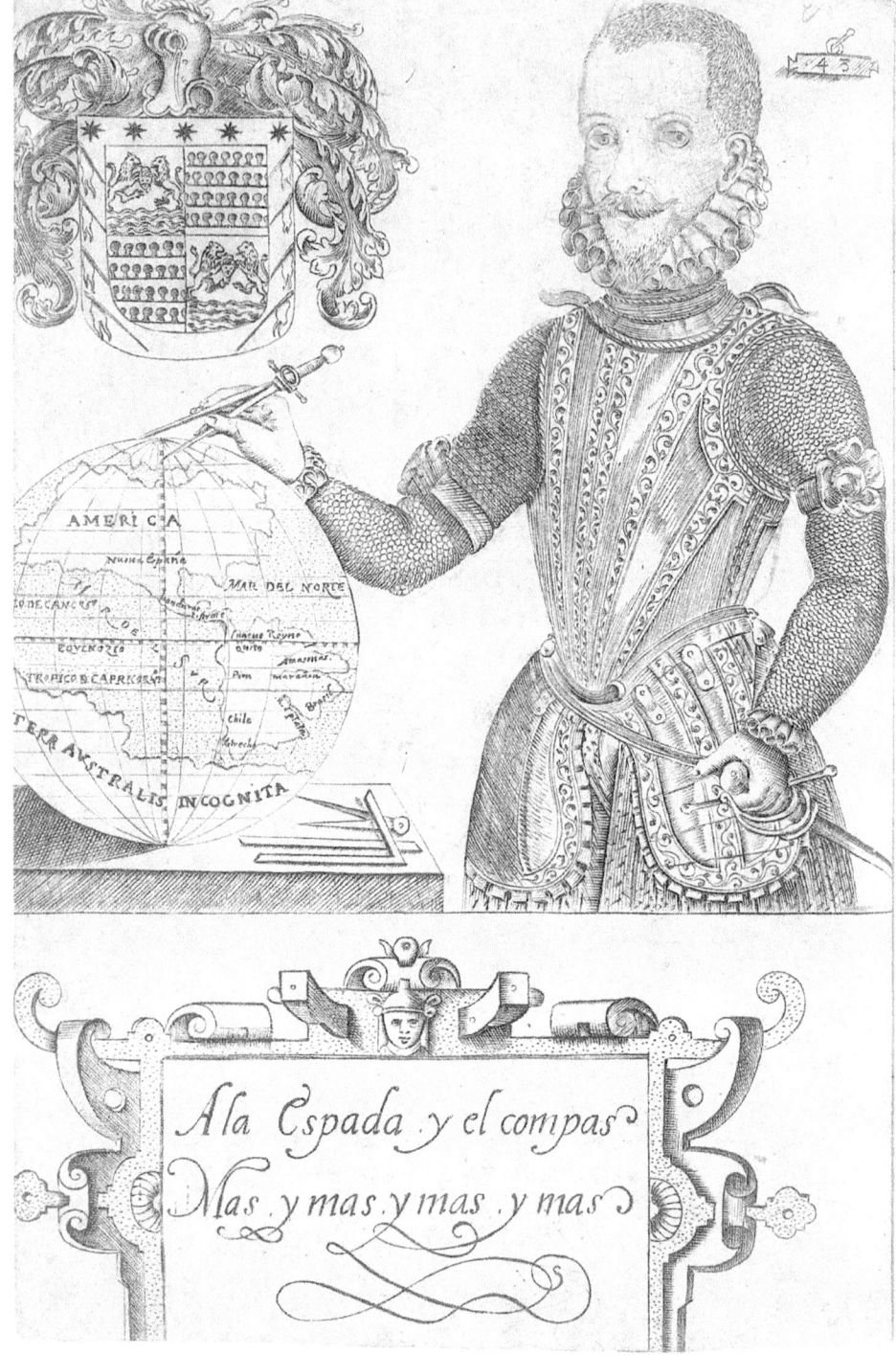

A la Espada y el compas
Mas, y mas, y mas, y mas

INTRODUCTORY STUDY

Kris Lane

It may be only fitting that the first manual of Spanish conquest was published well after the death of the last conquistadors. It was perhaps even more fitting that its author was Captain Bernardo de Vargas Machuca of Simancas, a hapless caballero so out of touch with his times he may well have inspired Cervantes. As he was born too late to be another Cortés or Pizarro, true fame was not Vargas Machuca's destiny. Neither was its opposite, infamy, a specialty of failed conquistadors such as the Basque rebel Lope de Aguirre. Instead, the valiant and loyal Vargas Machuca soldiered on for nearly five decades, unable to either locate a lost empire or contemplate rebellion.

The next best thing was to participate in whatever fight was at hand, be it against rebellious Amerindians, runaway slaves, heretic pirates, or mutinous fellow Spaniards. In short, if he was going to war in the Spanish Indies, Bernardo de Vargas Machuca was destined not for conquest, but rather for "mopping up." By the mid-1590s he had done enough of this, and under sufficiently varied circumstances, to consider himself an expert; hence *Milicia Indiana*. The title is ambiguous even in the original Spanish—hinting as much at Amerindian as at Spanish colonist, or *indiano*, input and content—so we have chosen to translate it directly as *The Indian Militia*. After a five-year wait in Madrid, Spain's grudging Indies Council at last responded to Vargas Machuca's incessant requests for promotion by granting him a minor post in 1602 as paymaster and magistrate of the new fortress town of Portobelo, on the Caribbean coast of Panama.

Why write a manual for something as unglamorous as backcountry "Indian wars"? Was it sincerely meant to help fellow immigrants conquer phantom empires, or was it more likely intended to conquer the heart of the Spanish king, or at least his ministers or courtiers? It is difficult to say for sure, but like many freelance participants in the long and incomplete conquest of the Americas, Vargas Machuca fancied himself a literate soldier with a story to tell. Even in Cortés's day, thanks to the great distances and cultural gulfs entailed by overseas campaigns, one had not only to be tough and resourceful, but also to write well or at least persuasively in order to convince the distant monarch of the value of one's deeds. As the example of Cortés suggests, this was no easy thing.[1] Spain's early Habsburg kings had other, more pressing concerns than the affairs of the Indies, and they were frequently susceptible to the religious arguments of proindigenous priests, most notably the tireless Protector of the Indians, Bartolomé de Las Casas. Only talk of mineral wealth could compete with propagating the faith in pricking up the royal ear.

Vargas Machuca does not fail to mention treasure in his *Indian Militia*, and indeed all but threatens that its continued flow will cease if men like him go unrewarded. Still, he seems to want his book to be judged on its own merits as a neoconquistador's "how-to." Martial arts manuals were in fact common in western Europe by 1600,[2] and this was not Vargas Machuca's only one (as discussed below, he also wrote on horsemanship). Still, *Milicia Indiana* seems not quite to fit the genre, which tended toward highly technical discussions of fencing and other varieties of hand-to-hand combat. Spanish master swordsmen such as Gerónimo Sánchez de Carranza employed the compass not to mark out conquests, but rather for saber sweeps and dagger thrusts. Other experts, many of them battle-hardened soldiers like Vargas Machuca, advised aspiring peninsular cavaliers on wrestling, shooting, and old-fashioned knightly jousting.

Religious self-help manuals were another popular genre in both Spain and the colonies, often drawing metaphorically on soldierly discipline.[3] Against these, *Milicia Indiana* reads something like a colonial gunslinger's version of Ignatius Loyola's *Spiritual Exercises*. The format is standard in its rules and scolding tone; it is the content that is unusual. Vargas Machuca claims to offer nothing more than a collection of precepts and general advice for the frontier commander, but as is evident in the opening epistles and poems, even its contemporary promoters seemed to agree it was something else, a "curious" hybrid. (After all, how many self-help books could claim to teach one how to cure rattlesnake bites with amethysts or make saltpeter for gunpowder from concentrated human urine?)

This weirdness, or "curiosity," of the text raises the question of readership. On whose shelf or in whose saddlebags might one have found *Milicia Indiana*? We know that Thomas Jefferson owned a copy, but what about Spanish contemporaries in the years just after 1599? Would the book have appealed to newly appointed governors? Restless young nobles hoping to reinvent themselves or get rich in America? Aspiring corporate raiders? The title does not appear in Irving Leonard's classic *Books of the Brave*, which catalogues and characterizes the many vernacular imprints heading to the Indies in precisely this period, but certainly a few copies must have reached colonists' hands.[4] Vargas Machuca claims he simply wants to help ill equipped, Indies-bound Spanish greenhorns of any kind to pull up their bootstraps and be done with the conquest once and for all. Yet it becomes clear after reading only a few pages that the author is doing something else, as well: writing an angry letter to the king. In this regard, *Milicia Indiana* is an extended *probanza de méritos y servicios*, a common, stylized boast meant to impress the monarch, or at least the Indies Council (to whose president it is lavishly dedicated). Compensation was expected in the form of an honorable sinecure, at the very least a governorship.

For Vargas Machuca, self-fashioning in a humorless, self-righteous way appears to have been as natural as breathing. Whether in dozens of surviving manuscript requests for promotions, complaints about superiors, recommendations for how to put down indigenous uprisings, or in *Milicia Indiana* itself, the author's tone is the same: that of a short-tempered and arrogant Renaissance pragmatist. What makes him interesting despite his pedantry, at least in part, is how and when he shows his discomfort with a Spanish imperial world that was rapidly changing around him. His confidence alone was an anachronism amid Spain's transition to Baroque reflection—a new sensibility marked by self-doubt, "disenchantment," and bewildering complexity. (Cervantes and a few others responded—after failing to get their own government posts—with irony.) This creeping discomfort—though hardly enough to diminish Vargas Machuca's considerable reserve of self-confidence—emerges in *Milicia Indiana* but finds fullest expression in his impassioned refutation of Las Casas, which he called *The Defense of Western Conquests*, composed shortly after his appointment as castle keep in Portobelo. As if to further vex its author, publication of the *Defense* was suppressed despite support from ranking Dominicans—

members of the same order as Las Casas (see appendix 2 for translated selections).

Part of Vargas Machuca's difficulty in becoming a bona fide conquistador was timing. When he left Spain for the Indies in 1578, might was still right, or seemed to be, and even Spain's enemies unhappily agreed that much of the known world was King Philip II's oyster. Upon Vargas Machuca's return to Spain in 1595, however, things were different; the mood had darkened considerably, and would continue to do so through much of the next century. The king was on his deathbed, the royal treasury was empty, and the multiplying heretic nations of Europe were ascendant.[5] But did not the good knight still get his due despite this changed scenario? In Vargas Machuca's case the Indies Council finally yielded, but not in the desired way. The six-year Portobelo post proved a huge disappointment, and what came next was not much better. Instead of a marquisate or command of a Chilean invasion force, the middle-aged indiano got only a Sancho Panza–like booby prize: the governorship of the moribund desert island of Margarita, off the coast of Venezuela. Booby prize or not, Vargas Machuca ruled it like a personal fiefdom until a few years before his death in 1622.

So why bother to translate and annotate Vargas Machuca's *Indian Militia* if he seems almost a comic loser on the one hand, and an angry, Indian-hating pedant on the other? My own initial interest in the text was as a source for the history of mining and prospecting in early colonial Colombia. As will be seen, Vargas Machuca offers brief descriptions of mineral deposits, mining techniques, and even medicinal uses for gemstones. His will includes mention of an apparently unworked emerald mine. What became clear in reading on, however (and I am hardly the first to notice this), is that scattered throughout *Milicia Indiana* are unwitting fragments of indigenous and rural Spanish colonial history. Perhaps the main gap this book helps to fill, if only partially, is the story of early and unconquered "backcountry" New Granada. For its incidental ethnography alone, *The Indian Militia* seemed a text worthy of translation and annotated study. From a broader perspective it may serve as well, especially when read along with portions of the *Defense of Western Conquests*, as an example of a conservative soldier's understanding of his emerging nation's global empire. Many of the ideas and opinions that Vargas Machuca expresses below in more or less inchoate form would later be expanded and codified by the creole jurist Juan de Solórzano Pereira. Vargas Machuca was in fact al-

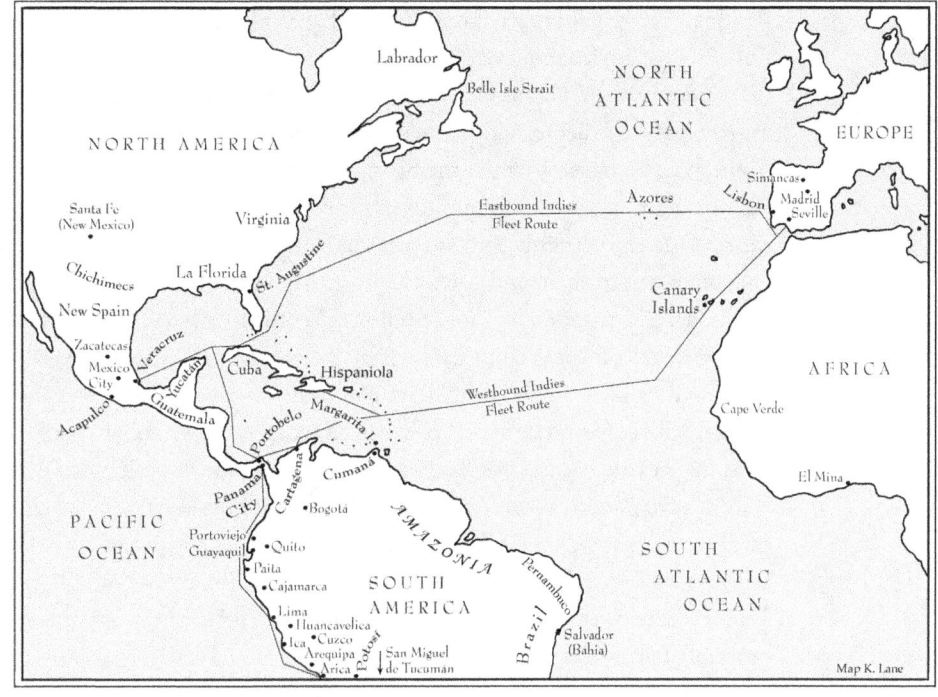

Map 1
The Spanish Atlantic in the sixteenth century

most ahead of his times in arguing for imperial retrenchment. The present book's more narrowly defined value as a neotropical bestiary and manual of field medicine has also been noted, although it is not unique in either case.[6]

Despite its simple format and no-nonsense prose, *Milicia Indiana* is not a self-explanatory text. It begs many questions. Where did Vargas Machuca fit into the story of Spanish American imperial consolidation and indigenous resistance? He was a latecomer, after all, and not a participant in the much better known conquests of Mexico or Peru. Does his text fit into a peculiarly New Granadan model of conquest (or "Indian policing"), or might it reflect a certain moment or step in a larger hemispheric or even global process of imperial consolidation? If the author's main contribution relates to indigenous matters, how does one see and understand colonial Colombia's nonstate native societies through the distorted mirror of a foreigner bent on destroying or at least profoundly altering them? What was the role of so-called friendly Indians, Vargas Machuca's constant allies and fellow soldiers, in these backwoods police actions? Were they really "friendly," or were they simply pursuing their own agendas by allying with the Spanish? Finally, to what extent was what Vargas Machuca repeatedly calls *his* sage advice in fact *theirs*?

As will be seen, Vargas Machuca was as often admiring of indigenous arms, tactics, medicine, and perseverance as he was hostile or dismissive. To be sure, he never doubted the Spanish "right" to rule over indigenous Americans, nor did he ever question the need for a heavy hand. Was he a racist? One can certainly come to that conclusion after reading this book, and much more so if one reads his no-holds-barred refutation of Las Casas (again, see appendix 2 for selections). Yet the label, so full of modern connotations, attaches clumsily to even the most unabashed sixteenth-century European imperialist. "Barbarity" for Vargas Machuca was the natural and unfortunate result of environmental circumstances coupled with inadequate education—bad leadership, really. He is hesitant to declare Native Americans inherently inferior or naturally servile. Still, he is quick to stereotype and judge in the often contradictory, sweeping, and self-serving style of later racists, and he proclaims without reservation that Native American cultures have virtually nothing to offer European settlers beyond a few wilderness survival tips.

Thus, while the possibility of "going native" was the furthest thing from Vargas Machuca's mind, he was nevertheless an indiano through and through, an "American" (but not a creole) and proud of it. Vargas Machuca's life-changing experience as an Indies militiaman, rather like Don Quixote's delusion by way of books of chivalry, had the unexpected consequence of rendering him not a hero but a misfit when he returned to Spain. Like so many imperial outliers, and so many war veterans in general, he was a man who knew too much—about the blunt violence and tough choices that defined politics at the edge of empire. For all its hardships, however, the wild frontier was a simpler place that seemed to suit Vargas Machuca's gun-toting, equestrian, take-charge personality very well. The more subtle machinations of the center, the knowing winks and nudges of prudent King Philip's court, seemed to escape him. Thus, despite the glowing praise of his supporters (who took great pains to declare him famous when hardly anyone, even in New Granada, knew his name), the hard-bitten veteran's frustration shows through like a beacon in both the *Indian Militia* and the *Defense of Western Conquests*.

Vargas Machuca has recently drawn the attention of literary scholars interested in the substantial corpus of "late," ignored, and otherwise obscure chronicles of the Habsburg imperial enterprise, particularly those produced by colonists amid the uneasy transition from Renaissance to baroque ideas and tropes. This transition, which some scholars prefer to label a crisis brought on by early modernity or proto-globalization (or just too much money), was not a simple or complete one. The task of disentangling its complexities and contradictions from the American side has in fact only begun, even as debate on materials produced in Spain rages.[7] Why the delayed attention? In part it is only reasonable that these lesser, often clumsy and derivative indiano works have emerged slowly from the long shadow of Cervantes, Lope de Vega, and other hugely talented contemporaries. (It has also taken a long time to plow through some of them, including Rodríguez Freile's disorganized and unfinished but fascinating anecdotal history of New Granada, known today as *El Carnero*, and Juan de Castellanos's *Elegías de Varones Ilustres de Indias*, to date the longest poem in the Spanish language.)

To take but one of the many questions raised by scholars of Golden Age indiano literature: What role did Indies militiamen and neoconquistadors such as Vargas Machuca play in reshaping imperial narratives that since at least the mid-sixteenth century had been dominated by priests and nonparticipant, peninsular-born Spaniards such as Cortés's chronicler, López de Gómara? And even if they dared to challenge Las Casas, as Vargas Machuca rather brazenly did, was anyone listening? Whom did they really hope to convince? What literary conventions or philosophical models could they now draw on to make their case for a unique, Spanish American heroic?

Treating a somewhat earlier period (ending around the 1566 death of Las Casas), classicist David Lupher has asked how various colonial and peninsular writers' visions of the Spanish Empire in relation to antiquity, specifically the Roman Empire, changed between the period of conquest and royal consolidation. Had the Spanish outdone the Romans, at last? If so, in what specific ways had they bested the ancients? Where did Native Americans fit in a New World "republic" (a term Vargas Machuca repeatedly uses)? Were Amerindians going to be citizens or permanent wards of the state? How were rebels to be treated? Should they be enslaved? Exiled? Annihilated? *Milicia Indiana* is a good test case for such inquiry in the years following Las Casas's death.

A third reason for translating Vargas Machuca is to situate his manual in the larger context of European military history. Given the overtly martial focus of the work, this theme affords many avenues of exploration.

Not being military historians ourselves, however, translator Tim Johnson and I have chosen just three angles we felt at least partly competent to explore: (1) Vargas Machuca's notions of warfare in relation to the so-called military revolution taking place in sixteenth-century Europe; (2) the Indies militia compared with early modern notions of what are today called counterinsurgency and paramilitary conflicts; and (3) where Vargas Machuca's "how-to" fits within the early modern European tradition of the martial arts manual. To this last theme we have added (again, despite our lack of special expertise) observations on the book's potential value to the history of medicine. A significant part of it purports to be a tropical militiaman's first-aid manual.

We address these and related themes following a brief foray into historical background, both global and local, and also a short biographical sketch of the author. Throughout, we feel it should be kept in mind that, as editor and translator, Vargas Machuca's story disturbs us. He lived in the midst of, and actively participated in bringing about, the most precipitous population decline in world history. Many of the indigenous groups he fought were soon after annihilated by disease and abuses not unlike those condemned by his nemesis, Las Casas. Worse, some of Vargas Machuca's own deadly attacks were described by contemporaries as unprovoked or misdirected, and he himself admitted participating in what would today be called war crimes. Our intention is not to judge or moralize. Still, as is no doubt already obvious, we could not help but wince as the evidence about our book's apparently troubled and frustrated author accumulated. In sorting through hundreds of handwritten testimonies and autobiographical musings that more than amply proved Vargas Machuca's fondness for terror as the surest means to make a point—to kill even children in order to save his men—it was difficult not to wonder if paramilitary violence, like economic underdevelopment, was yet another Latin American, or just plain American, colonial legacy.[8]

BERNARDO DE VARGAS MACHUCA IN A CHANGING SPANISH EMPIRE

I remember having read that a Spanish knight by the name of Diego Pérez de Vargas, having broken his sword in a battle, tore a heavy branch or trunk from a live-oak and with it did such things that day, and crushed so many

Moors, that he was left with the nickname "Machuca" [The Smasher], and thus, from then on he and his descendants were called Vargas y Machuca.
—Don Quixote to Sancho Panza following an especially painful attack on a windmill, CERVANTES, *Don Quixote*

When he wrote *Milicia Indiana* in the late 1590s, Bernardo de Vargas Machuca was both an indiano and a *perulero*, that is, an old Indies hand trying to make good on his deeds abroad in Greater Peru—which at this time encompassed almost all of Spanish South America—while cooling his heels at court in Spain.[9] The figure of the perulero, lovingly skewered by Cervantes in his exemplary novella "The Jealous Extremaduran" was not a rare sight in late sixteenth-century Spain.[10] Almost by definition, such men had been born on the Peninsula rather than in the colonies, and nearly all had trouble gaining respect upon their return; their claims on nobility were usually tenuous. Many were more merchants than soldiers, besides (the term *perulero* eventually became synonymous with "Portuguese merchant"), which did not help in a culture that clung obstinately to knightly ideals regarding wealth and status. To add to the insult, courtly attention was now lavished on indigenous or part-indigenous nobles such as "El Inca" Garcilaso de la Vega, author of the widely read *Royal Commentaries of the Incas* (1609).[11] Nostalgic native voices such as Garcilaso's meshed perfectly with the new culture of *desengaño*, a kind of winner's regret that also found expression in verse and on stage. Other indigenous nobles trekked to Madrid from Peru and Mexico to assert their claims. Peru's Guaman Poma de Ayala sent an extraordinary, illustrated letter of over 1,000 pages denouncing Spanish colonialism and arguing for creation of an allied but functionally independent neo-Inca state.[12] Though hardly true, to some it seemed almost easier to be an Indian in Spain than an indiano.

From the point of view of Spain's large and underemployed class of nobles, wealth gained in the Indies was déclassé from the beginning, probably stained (as indeed much of it was) with Amerindian blood, and won by provincial characters of dubious birth. The bastard Francisco Pizarro of Trujillo, conqueror of the wealthiest empire in the Americas (if not the world), was the classic case.[13] No matter what they claimed, for all anyone knew men like Vargas Machuca were nothing more than *pícaros*—low-born charlatans, swineherds, or street hustlers—who had somehow gotten lucky and remade themselves as hidalgos. Such comeuppance was tolerated only in novels and plays, where it could be safely laughed off. In life, fame and infamy could not yet be confused (although that time would come sooner in Spain than elsewhere in Europe).

As it happened, the Indies-bound rogue was at the heart of Spain's new and probably most famous literary genre, the picaresque novel, immortalized in the same year as Vargas Machuca's *Milicia Indiana* by Mateo Alemán in *Guzmán de Alfarache*—a pioneering book that clearly *did* make it to the Americas, and in quantity, despite the repeated attempts of censors to stop it.[14] Of course the "smashing" petty noble, Vargas Machuca, would have deeply resented any comparison with the footloose, amoral Guzmán or with Cervantes's jealous, penny-pinching merchant of Seville, but there was no denying that the Indies left an indelible mark on all who ventured there. Indeed, Vargas Machuca and his heirs appear to have been all but cursed by the indiano stain.

The fabled era of conquistadors was ancient history by 1599, just as Spain's literary golden age was dawning. Had it all been a dream? It is impossible to say if Vargas Machuca spent time contemplating the relationship between art and life either in Spain or the American backcountry, but surviving evidence suggests an unflinching soldierly simplicity and sternness that sustained him to the bitter end. His writings demonstrate a strong preference for Plutarch's exemplary *Lives* versus "fluff" works of romantic fiction like *Lazarillo de Tormes*, or even *Amadís of Gaul*. Reflection not aimed directly at improving performance (the goal of each conquest or "punishment" being assumed righteous and self-evident) was not only useless, but a sign of softness. Who then could Vargas Machuca be, if not another Marquis of Valle, a new Cortés?

Always flexible in the face of material limitations, Vargas Machuca appears to have fancied himself a special type of turn-of-the-century councillor when he wrote the *Indian Militia*, not only a professional soldier but also an "Indian" mirror of the just-dead Prudent King, Philip II. Vargas Machuca's title-page portrait (see figure 2) reinforces such a robust self-perception, posed as he is like the young and optimistic Philip in St. Quentin battle gear. And more so the inscription below: "With sword and compass, more and more and more and more"—not three "mores," but four. Indeed, as was said of Philip, the world was not enough.

Though not to be confused with the modern, or even absolutist, nation-state, Spain under Philip II was the most centralized and globally active monarchy in Europe. American treasure, most notably at this time the vast

1 & 2
Philip II of Spain, ca. 1557, and Bernardo de Vargas Machuca, ca. 1599.
Courtesy Patrimonio Nacional, Madrid

silver deposits of Potosí, had financed Habsburg consolidation and expansion throughout Europe and the Mediterranean.[15] The conquest of the northern Philippines in the 1560s and the 1580 annexation of Portugal and by extension its vast overseas holdings made Spain the world's first truly global empire. In the midst of all this excitement and change, the imperial impulse, first felt in earnest under Philip's father, Holy Roman Emperor Charles V, opened up whole worlds of possibility for Spanish subjects hoping to advance their personal aims. Most were young men and some, like the mythical Guzmán de Alfarache, were bona fide pícaros out for adventure and a quick piece of eight. Many, like Guzmán and Cervantes, never got past Seville.

For people of honor, however, or at least honorable pretenses, fortunes could only be consolidated through marriage and family formation, so noble, creole women, as Vargas Machuca quickly learned upon his arrival in highland New Granada, were at the center of any attempt to build an indiano dynasty. Studies in both Spain and the Americas have shown that throughout early modern times, when weak government and perennially absent men were the norm, women's economic importance and political power increased. This was most marked among the higher social strata, which for a time included indigenous elites.[16] Not all ranking women found their dream mates. Having married the colonial equivalent of a knight-errant, the two wives of Bernardo de Vargas Machuca managed only to bear a few children and watch their dowries disappear.[17]

Along with opportunity, imperial expansion generated new social, political, and economic problems, among them noble resentment of imperial authority, colonial tax revolts, rampant contraband trade and piracy, and innumerable Indian wars, usually at the ranching, mining, or mission frontier. In short, there was a lot to keep track of when the sun never set on empire, and thus it is no surprise that even the most loyal and competent subjects might fail to receive their just desserts as Spain's domain bloated to the point of overstretch. Vargas Machuca was hardly unusual in "falling through the cracks" despite his years of loyal service, and was in fact lucky to get anything at all. But what really sets him apart from countless other writers of service reports is his special plea from the beginning of *Milicia Indiana* that the new defenders of the Indies, unlike the old freelance conquistadors, be recognized as a professional, soldierly class.[18] As it was, he complained, the Indies militiaman got no respect.

Spain was on the defensive by 1599, but hardly crippled. Peace was signed with the French on the eve of Philip II's death in 1598, and it followed under Philip III with the English in 1603 and the Dutch (albeit for only about a decade) in 1609. The Ottomans were a somewhat reduced maritime threat after the 1571 Battle of Lepanto, although North African corsairs aligned with the sultans kept Mediterranean and East Atlantic shipping unsafe and frequently threatened Spanish presidios all along the Maghreb. Throughout the Mediterranean, piracy and hostage exchange were the order of the day just as Vargas Machuca was coming of age in Simancas, an old fortress town just outside the Old Castilian city of Valladolid, where his father served as paymaster of the newly established royal archives.

In the colonies, challenges to empire were equally abundant. This was true despite the fact that by the mid-sixteenth century loyal Spanish subjects and administrators controlled nearly all the significant population centers, strategic ports and waterways, vast tracts of fertile land, and rich mines of precious metals. As was to be expected, the problem with a so-called *Pax Colonial* was not holding the center but expanding the periphery.[19] Native American peoples carried on unconquered all around the fringes, particularly in densely forested, mountainous, and desert regions. For them, of course, center and periphery had entirely different meanings. However deadly for each side, borders, or contact zones, were sites

3
Royal Archive
of Simancas,
Old Castile.
Photo by Kris Lane

of cultural genesis. This was the "tribal zone," a space of regrouping, where things (including germs) and ideas interpenetrated, yielding unexpected combinations or hybrids, "new" tribes.[20] Indeed, many tribes later considered by colonial authorities, missionaries, anthropologists, and even their own members as primordial or deeply rooted in some specific terrain were in fact forged in this outer-edge crucible of war, material exchange, and missionary endeavors.

Among the most daunting and attractive of the "conquest frontiers," at least in sixteenth-century Spanish eyes, were greater Amazonia and what is today the U.S. South and Southwest. Newcomers and old-timers alike felt there just *had* to be treasure and empires hidden in these vast and rugged regions. Indigenous informants claimed as much, usually by pointing excitedly in the direction of their worst enemies. There were many other less promising frontiers, including deserts such as the Gran Chaco of Bolivia-Paraguay, the Guajira Peninsula of northeast Colombia, and the windswept pampas of South America's southern cone. Then there were jungle and swampland zones such as the Maya Petén, the Florida Everglades, the Orinoco and Mississippi Deltas, the Colombian Chocó, and the Mosquito Coast of Nicaragua. The list could go on to include rugged mountain zones such as Mexico's western Sierra Madre, the Guyana Highlands, and Colombia's Sierra Nevada de Santa Marta. In short, what Spaniards claimed in the Americas and what they controlled were two very different things in 1599.

In Vargas Machuca's time, one region stood out as the epitome of the untamed Amerindian frontier: southern Chile. Beyond the Bío-Bío River to the south of Santiago, a loose confederation of indigenous groups dominated a fairly compact and temperate region not unlike northern Spain. In this lushly forested belt of rolling hills between about 37 and 42 degrees south latitude, frontier warfare took on a special character. The Mapuche, or Araucanians, quickly embraced horses and firearms, which they acquired by raiding or barter for captives. When it came to war, however, rather than adopt the standard Spanish practice of daytime engagement of matched forces on an open field, the Mapuche kept to their traditional methods of night raids, ambushes, kidnapping, and sudden withdrawal: in short, what would today be called guerrilla warfare.[21] As a result, the Spanish soon found themselves stalemated despite massive spending on arms, fortresses, and garrisons, a situation that lasted throughout colonial times. More than even the conquest of Mexico, the Mapuche wars would prove to be a gold mine of indiano epic literature; the drama never ended. While at court in Madrid in 1599, the year of a great Mapuche uprising, Vargas Machuca proposed to end the conflict by leading a crack invasion force of four hundred handpicked soldiers, two hundred from Spain and two hundred from the colonies. They would establish a base camp in the interior and then head out in sorties to harass the enemy night and day in groups of ten until the Mapuche were simply so worn out they would be forced to yield. In return for his services, Vargas Machuca asked to be named governor-general of Chile.[22] His plan was not pursued.

There were also fugitive Africans who had escaped slavery living throughout Spanish America, sometimes accompanied by indigenous and European refugees. Unlike the Mapuche, Shuar, Navajo, and other indigenous peoples who flourished well beyond the contact zone, these rebels against colonialism's harsher aspects survived by preying on nearby plantations or mining settlements, or in the case of Panama, Cartagena, and Orizaba (Eastern Mexico), proximity to major trunk lines or ports. These were not guerrilla insurgents like the Mapuche, for the most part, but rather a more parasitical type of rebel, people happy to partake of the spoils and even some of the trappings of empire, just not on the empire's terms. Maroons universally rejected servitude, of course, but they sometimes accepted Catholic priests. All happily consumed imported material goods such as textiles, tools, and weapons. Some maroon groups had formed more by accident than rebellion, as at Esmeraldas, in northwest Ecuador. Like the so-called Black Caribs of the Caribbean's Windward Islands, the Esmeraldas maroons' existence was traced to early colonial shipwrecks; such castaways formed new "tribes."[23] Although it remains unclear if Vargas Machuca was sent out against them prior to his stint in Portobelo (see the biographical sketch below), maroons were a constant security concern in his New Granada.

One such maroon fighter and contemporary of Vargas Machuca was Captain Luis de Angulo, lieutenant governor of the province of Antioquia, in what is today northwestern Colombia (Vargas Machuca would be named governor of this district just before his death in 1622). In his service report of 1608, Angulo claimed to have headed up and outfitted a punitive expedition, or *castigo*, that went after a band of fugitive Africans menacing the gold mining camps of Zaragoza, an isolated town on the upper Nechí River northeast of modern Medellín. According to Angulo and other witnesses, by 1604 these maroons had formed a lasting community by kidnapping or persuading enslaved African women to join them when they went out to pan for gold or fetch water. Angulo's fight with the Zaragoza maroons lasted a full four years, after which he proudly claimed to have opened new gold mines and put the captured maroons to work in them. The violent frontier quest had come full circle. Slavery and precious metals were deemed a natural pair at the imperial fringe, both yielding, in the words of this neoconquistador, "great service to God and Your Majesty."[24]

More troubling for the crown was the fact that some maroons living in strategically sensitive areas allied with northern European interlopers in exchange for weapons and other goods. In Vargas Machuca's day the foreigners were English, French, or Dutch corsairs, along with a few freelance pirates, seeking plunder. At times they organized themselves to the point of attacking major ports—Cartagena, Santa Marta, San Juan de Puerto Rico, Havana—but mostly they remained a danger to straggling ships and smaller, unguarded coastal settlements. Men such as the English West Country merchant John Hawkins and his cousin, Francis

Map 2 *The New Kingdom of Granada in the sixteenth century*

Drake, also sought to trade luxury commodities and enslaved Africans for gold, silver, and other products of the Spanish Indies, but this was a dangerous business with harsh reprisals for those who got caught. Spanish mercantilism was built around monopolies, so anything approaching free trade was criminalized, often punishable by death. Vargas Machuca in fact claimed his first job in the Indies was to help chase Drake as he made his way around the world via Spanish America's vulnerable coasts in the late 1570s. Vargas Machuca's last two American posts would be similarly pirate-oriented in that he was to staff and expand the fortresses of Portobelo, in Panama, and then defend the island of Margarita, both perennial objects of foreign looters' and contrabandists' desire.

How to respond to all these challenges in an era when European wars were draining Spain's reservoir of young men as fast as its treasury? In the Indies, as Vargas Machuca argues at length in *Milicia Indiana*, loyal colonists were not only expected but obliged to create militias: ad hoc, self-financed "defense" forces with broad powers to roam dangerous frontiers and even suppress urban riots. Ideally led by veteran soldiers, civilian militias of this kind fought pirates, put down traitors such as Lope de Aguirre, and also tracked and captured maroons, renegades, and apostates. Most of all, however, they fought fringe-dwelling indigenous peoples identified as "rebels" (*alzados*) and "bandits" (*salteadores*).

What was in it for the loyal militiaman besides a good chance at getting maimed, killed, or saddled with a terminal infection? In truth, not much. Indigenous captives could under some circumstances be enslaved and sold for profit, as happened in Chile, New Mexico, and parts of New Granada late in Philip II's reign and afterward, but most often this was not the case, and no Spanish soldiers seem to have gotten rich from the Indian slave trade. More often rewards were, as in the initial conquest era, given to faithful soldiers in the form of *encomiendas*, quasi-feudal grants of indigenous labor and tribute. As another aspect of the crown's "expansion-on-the-cheap" policy, encomiendas continued to be allotted at the fringes long after their disappearance at the center. In the case of New Granada, if one was lucky Amerindians held in encomienda could be made to work in gold, silver, or emerald mines, yielding cash tributes. Others wove textiles, raised livestock, or harvested cash crops.[25] It is telling that Vargas Machuca, for all his fighting and writing, never won title to an encomienda.

THE END OF EL DORADO: LATE SIXTEENTH-CENTURY NEW GRANADA

By 1599, there were few encomiendas to be had anywhere in the Indies, and the so-called New Kingdom of Granada, the core of which had been conquered some sixty years before, was no exception. New Granada was reminiscent of old Granada, in Andalusia, a rugged yet rich land populated by pockets of rebellious non-Christians. Although probed by Spanish interlopers a few years before Mexico and Peru—and quickly discovered to be rich in gold, emeralds, and pearls—New Granada did not live up to the expectations of many El Dorado seekers. Conquistadors Gonzalo Jiménez de Quesada, Nikolaus de Federmann (sponsored by one of Charles V's German banking families, the Welsers), and Sebastián de Belalcázar did become fabulously wealthy in land and tributaries, as did several dozen of their most loyal followers. Most of these "colonizer" dynasties proved difficult to sustain, however, and even Jiménez de Quesada went on looking for El Dorado in old age.[26] This was due largely to indigenous population decline, which quickly reduced tribute income and access to cheap labor, but also to the fact that the several dozen indigenous ethnic groups living in what is today Colombia recognized no overarching sovereign; there was no analogue here of the Aztec-Mexica or Inca Empires.[27]

Most north Andean indigenous groups preferred instead to make periodic war on one another, a tendency that persisted well into colonial times. Those who inhabited New Granada's many and interpolated jungles, cloud forests, and hot, scrub-forest lowlands were reputed to be cannibals, besides, compounding an already fierce reputation. Evidence for this practice of "man-eating," however misunderstood, is substantial and widespread. Headhunting was also practiced in several regions, as was human sacrifice.[28] No common language was recognized, and the closest thing to a native empire was the Muisca paramount chiefdom of the high savannas east of the Magdalena River basin. Having conquered these highland agriculturalists after a short and brutal campaign, the Spanish under Jiménez de Quesada established a defensible capital abutting a steep cordillera at Santa Fe de Bogotá in 1538. In honor of Jiménez de Quesada's homeland, the surrounding highland region was dubbed the New Kingdom of Granada.

For a time, Bogotá would vie with Tunja, a colder, higher town about 140 kilometers to the north, for control of the early colony. Under mer-

4
Cathedral Square, Bogotá, Colombia. Photo by Kris Lane

chant pressure an *audiencia*, or high appeals court, was established in the former city in 1549, securing Bogotá's future significance. Tunja and the nearby Villa de Leiva nevertheless continued to be home to most of the old *encomendero* elite, and they were still surrounded by the most populous indigenous settlements as late as the eighteenth century. Technically subject to the Peruvian viceroy at Lima, New Granada nevertheless remained all but autonomous for reasons of distance, forming closer ties with Spain via the Atlantic ports of Santa Marta and Cartagena than it ever did with Lima. Interior regions such as Antioquia (near modern Medellín) and Popayán (near Cali) developed in relative autonomy as well, and jurisdiction over Venezuela remained split between New Granada, Santo Domingo, and New Spain. Thanks to trade with Peru, tiny Panama was independent enough to boast its own audiencia, and remained totally autonomous from New Granada until the early eighteenth century.

New Granada's economy in 1599 was based largely on the export of gold, and to a lesser extent emeralds and pearls, but these industries were already suffering from the twin effects of indigenous population decline and exhausted deposits. As suggested by the case of the Zaragoza maroons above, in many mines enslaved Africans already outnumbered native workers.[29] Highland tributary populations were also disappearing with alarming speed, leaving the encomenderos of Tunja, Leiva, and Bogotá with few

INTRODUCTORY STUDY

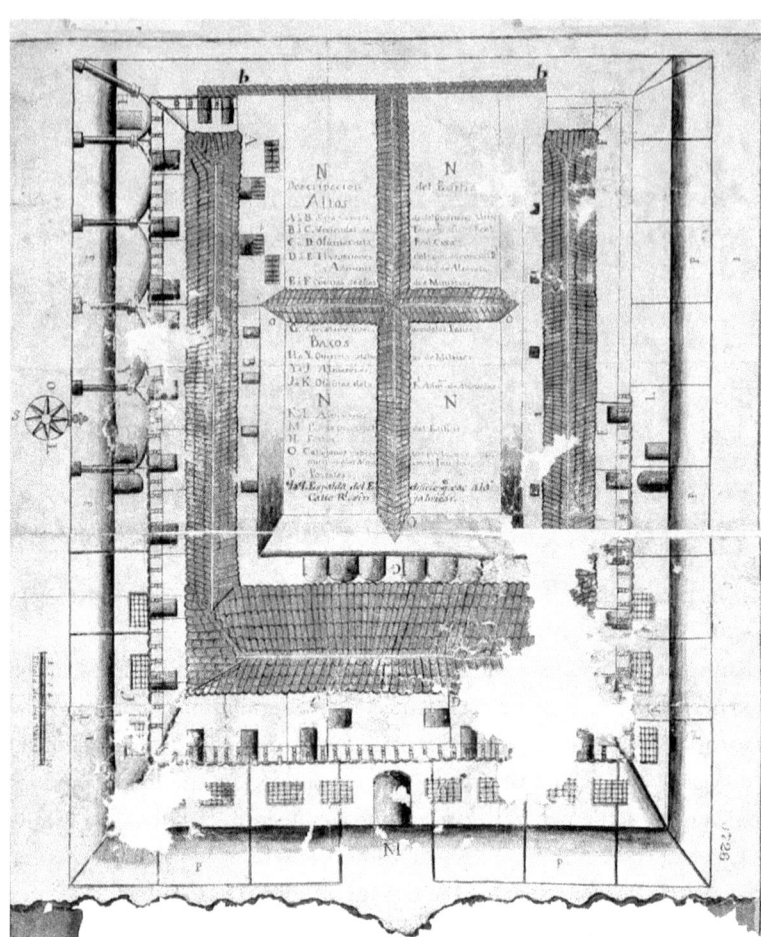

5
Royal Treasury,
Bogotá, Colombia.
Courtesy Archivo
General de la Nación,
Bogotá, Colombia

sources of income to sustain their regal lifestyles. In part for these reasons, coupled with continued immigration of footloose and gullible Spaniards such as Vargas Machuca, belief in the lost kingdom of El Dorado (called variously "Dabeiba," "Meta," "Xerira," and so on) flourished in New Granada long after it faded in Ecuador and Peru.[30]

If he was not to be found in the cloud forests of the Eastern Cordillera or the jungles of the Pacific Coast, then perhaps the famous gilded cacique reigned somewhere to the east, in the Guyana Highlands or upper Putumayo foothills; as noted near the end of *Milicia Indiana*, Vargas Machuca favored this last possibility. Indeed, it was in the midst of Vargas Machuca's New Granadan apprenticeship in the 1580s that the veteran Tunja-based El Dorado seeker, Governor Antonio de Berrío, met Walter Raleigh near

6
Plaza Bolívar, Tunja, Colombia. Photo by Kris Lane

the mouth of the Orinoco.³¹ Potentially mineral-rich interior regions of New Granada, such as the Central Cordillera held by the indomitable Pijao and Páez peoples, also beckoned, as did the equally rugged and far more wealthy Pacific lowlands.³² If the armies of the King of Spain were too busy or broke, who then would tame the empire's frontiers? Who would reap their treasures? Who would save their untold thousands of wayward souls?

THE FRONTIER SOLDIER: A BIOGRAPHICAL SKETCH OF BERNARDO DE VARGAS MACHUCA

Bernardo de Vargas Machuca was as an especially apt candidate for the role of "punisher." Fortunately for the present study, his appearance in the historical record in both Spain and the colonies is frequent, rich, and first-hand—and perfectly in line with his obvious egotism (of his three children by his first wife, for example, one was named Bernardo and another, Bernardina). Vargas Machuca probably also understood the importance of collecting sworn testimonies and filing multiple copies given his father's experience at the royal archive in Simancas. The problem he presents is one not of scant documentation, although, as will be seen, his résumé

7
House of the governor, Tunja.
Photo by Kris Lane

has holes, but rather of interpretation. How much can we really know about the author of *Milicia Indiana* beyond his own copious works of self-promotion?

In 1952, the president of Colombia's National Academy of History, Enrique Otero D'Acosta, published a short biography of Bernardo de Vargas Machuca in the venerable Spanish journal *Revista de Indias*.[33] In those halcyon days of Hispanidad it was fashionable among historians to celebrate the lives of the conquistadors (a whole volume of the *Revista de Indias* was dedicated to Cortés in 1948, for example). Even late or little-known conquistador types were suddenly of interest, and given the evident triumph of fascism in Spain some patriotic champions of working folk must have felt the urge to chronicle—if only to spite their Communist foes—the contributions of the more common sort of men who had defended the fatherland long after the Conquest. (Many Colombian anthropologists, meanwhile, embraced a Las Casas–inspired brand of *indigenismo*, or proindigenism.)

Thus, Otero D'Acosta began his study of Vargas Machuca by describing him as "a man who in remote times lived many and hard-earned years in our Colombian land, to which he tethered his existence and under whose skies he founded a home; a man who governed with honor cities and provinces, one who, sword in hand, conquered fierce tribes in whose rugged lands he founded and refounded towns; and finally, an exemplary man who, despite his unlucky life, managed to leave us with the fruits of his genius."[34] Today, Otero's encomium reads a bit like the gushing sonnets prefacing *Milicia Indiana*. His use of the word *tizona* for "sword" even suggests a New Granadan Cid Campeador—and most definitely not a deluded knight of sad countenance. Still, even Colombia's top historian had to concede with "unlucky life" that Vargas Machuca of Simancas was not "born in a happy hour."

Although he did not bother to cite it, Otero's main source on Vargas Machuca's career was written by the latter's son by his second marriage, Alvaro Félix de Vargas Moxica (having dropped "Smasher" in favor of his maternal grandfather's equally illustrious surname). First brought to light by Chilean historians around the turn of the twentieth century, this document was a last-ditch petition published shortly after Vargas Machuca's death in 1622. Since it serves as a compact example of the ubiquitous *probanza de méritos y servicios*, or imperial-era merit request, we have placed a translation of this document after the main text (see appendix 1).

As historians Murdo MacLeod and Matthew Restall have argued, these autobiographical documents (although they must be read with extreme caution given the motives of their writers) often contain key factual information and perspectives on events not found elsewhere. More than this, they are loaded with insights on colonial mentalities, especially changing perceptions of what might be called the Spanish imperial social contract.[35] MacLeod reminds us that throughout colonial times *hidalguía*, or the claim of noble ancestry, remained at least as important as deeds done in the monarch's name. For this reason the documents generally began with a genealogical summary (*méritos*) followed by testimonies relating outstanding actions (*servicios*), not all of them military. Already in Vargas Machuca's day probanzas were being written by priests and bureaucrats, a trend he and other soldiers found perfectly disgusting.

In 1991, Spanish historian María Luisa Martínez de Salinas superseded Otero D'Acosta's efforts with a full-blown biography of Bernardo de Vargas Machuca, son of Simancas. This is a highly unusual book given its subject's relative obscurity and modest achievements—especially when measured against, say, a Cortés, Pizarro, or Jiménez de Quesada. Titled *Castilla ante el Nuevo Mundo: La trayectoría indiana del Gobernador Bernardo de Vargas Machuca* (roughly, *Castile Faces the New World: The Indian Trajectory of Governor Bernardo de Vargas Machuca*), this deeply researched and thoroughly documented study was published by the regional council of Valladolid with the illustrious author of the *Indian Militia*'s local origins in mind. In what began as a doctoral dissertation, Martínez de Salinas presents her subject as worth pursuing in such depth as a more or less typical example of the indiano, or Spanish-born "Indies hand," experience. The fact that he was a published author who left behind a rich documentary record of course helped make a full-length biography feasible.

Although almost reverent in tone, Martínez de Salinas's study is far more thorough than Otero's in documenting and situating Vargas Machuca's long professional career in the context of his times. The author introduces her indiano captain as follows: "We are faced with a native of [greater] Valladolid who lived the American reality intensely, and who got to know it in depth; it was not in vain that in the beginning he was a conquistador and later a crown functionary with an important government charge. Through it all, his many years' residency in America did not make him forget his Castilian origins, always so present in him that he reflected them in a permanent work: the foundation of [a town called] Simancas in the New Kingdom of Granada."[36]

It may be beside the point that "New Simancas" failed to survive for more than a few months and its exact location is presently unknown, but this "unlucky" detail may be an apt point from which to launch our own biographical sketch, also based on a blend of archival and published sources. Translator Tim Johnson and I must emphasize that Martínez de Salinas's study has been indispensable in filling in many blanks in Vargas Machuca's life, especially for the two decades or so after 1599. In pursuing Spanish archival material, including Vargas Machuca's 1599 publication license for *Milicia Indiana*, his 1622 will and testament, and the many letters written to the Indies Council from Portobelo and Margarita in the intervening years, we merely followed in her footsteps. As will be seen in the notes, we went beyond these documents in only a few instances in Bogotá. We were also aided by the excellent introductory study to a 2003 Spanish edition of *Milicia Indiana* (also published in Valladolid) by Mariano Cuesta Domingo and Fernando López-Rios Fernández. The text of the 2003 Valladolid edition, like another one published in Bogotá the same year with a short but very useful introduction by anthropologist Carl Langebaek, is not annotated, but the introduction is exceptional in exploring Vargas Machuca's medical ideas. The 1994 Japanese edition includes only books 1–3 of *Milicia Indiana*, but they are preceded by five of the six parts of the later *Defense of Western Conquests*. Editor and translator Aoki Yasuyuki explains this choice in a postscript titled "Struggles with Unknown Soldiers" by asking: "Can one not gain a deeper understanding of the conquistador by comparing both arguments?" The other argument is, of course, Las Casas's.[37]

Bernardo de Vargas Machuca was born in the medieval fortress town of Simancas in Old Castile. His birth date is unknown but appears to have been after 1550. Otero and others have suggested 1555, taking the date of *Milicia Indiana*'s publication (or rather, the year of the manuscript's approval by censors) backward forty-three years. The number 43 appears above the engraved portrait of the author in the book's frontispiece without any other explanation. More certain is the year of Vargas Machuca's death, recorded along with his many debts in Madrid in February 1622.[38]

What happened in between? Vargas Machuca claimed later in life to have been educated in Valladolid, although by whom and to what extent we do not know. Like so many Spanish youths of his time, his interests quickly shifted from letters to arms. After a brief stint against Morisco rebels in the 1569–71 Alpujarras campaigns of Old Granada with his father, the young warrior went off to Italy, where he later claimed to have gained a sense of Spanish militia organization. It is unlikely that he saw much action during these first outings, however (if born in 1555 he would have been only sixteen at the *end* of the Alpujarras rebellion, and little fighting took place in Italy during the decades following the 1559 peace with France). By 1578, Vargas Machuca was off to the Caribbean, allegedly as a member of an expedition sent to catch up with and "punish" archpirate Francis Drake. The famous corsair had left England in 1577 to circumnavigate the world (using a Portuguese pilot) and also to take a Spanish prize or two. Prefiguring later misfortunes, Vargas Machuca's vessel was separated from the others in a storm and ended up sheltering in the port town of Santiago de Cuba, which was promptly hit by an earthquake and a plague of snakes.[39]

Vargas Machuca appears to have reached Veracruz and passed briefly through New Spain before sailing to Panama and then Peru, allegedly to chase Drake again in the Pacific. The period 1579–85 is something of a mystery, however, in part because Vargas Machuca's later merit reports skip these years to emphasize service in New Granada, and also because the bundle of military records pertaining to Vargas Machuca for these years housed in Seville includes several dozen folios describing the actions of one "Hernando" aka "Fernando" de Vargas Machuca ranging from eastern Panama to northwest Argentina. Neither Otero D'Acosta nor Martínez de Salinas mentions these documents, nor do they allege that Vargas Machuca had a brother or other similarly named relative engaged in a parallel career. Furthermore, no Vargas Machuca of this name appears in the Indies-bound passenger lists for the period, either (although many individuals were known to have circumvented official controls).

There are reasons to think these documents relate to none other than Bernardo de Vargas Machuca. First, they were filed in the middle of a pile of service-related testimonies unquestionably in his name from the same years. Second, the main bundle was drawn up by a notary in Lima in 1590, when Vargas Machuca was most likely in New Granada and hence unavailable to correct such an "error of the plume," as it would have been called (the report appears to have been sent directly to Madrid, furthermore, where it was received by an Indies Council secretary in 1593). Merit reports collected by third parties, including old army buddies, widows, and descendants, were not unusual. Third, when Vargas Machuca abbreviated his first name in both text and signatures as Ber^{do} or B^{do}, the crabbed B could easily be mistaken for an F or an H. Besides, both *Fernando* and *Hernando* were far more common names than *Bernardo*—the sorts of names a scribe might guess at if unsure. Finally, Bernardo and "Fernando" both claimed to have served in Italy before coming to the Indies to chase Drake and other corsairs.

This case of potential mistaken identity would be of less interest to us if not for the things that Fernando de Vargas Machuca claimed to have done. Witnesses testifying in Lima agreed that he had served on galleys chasing French and English pirates around Cartagena before heading to the Pacific to chase Drake (as *Bernardo* de Vargas Machuca later claimed to have done). Once back on the isthmus, he joined a large punitive campaign against the maroons of Panama's eastern highlands. The objective was to capture maroons serving an African-born ex-slave named Antón Mandinga who had aided Drake and other corsairs since about 1570. The so-called Bayano (or Ballano) War, named for a nearby mountain range and river basin, was in fact one of the biggest antimaroon campaigns in Spanish American history, although Fernando de Vargas Machuca's role in it was not much to brag about. After being named *alférez*, or ensign, by Captain Pedro de Ortega Valencia, Vargas Machuca claimed in his own summary to have led a troop of thirty men in an attack on a maroon village called San Cristóbal.[40] Since its inhabitants were nowhere to be found, the attackers destroyed buildings and crops of maize and plantains. Vargas Machuca later claimed to have headed off some "black archers" in the service of the maroon "king," but there seem to have been no significant engagements or captures. The young caudillo was then named captain and assigned a small reconnaissance vessel and fifty men to hunt refugees hiding out along remote rivers and estuaries. The vessel was apparently lost in the midst of Panama's notoriously torrential rainy season, and Vargas Machuca and his followers were forced to spend three long months "naked" (*en carnes*), scrounging for herbs. After somehow managing to construct a raft, the group was miraculously saved by a chance encounter with a launch sent out to look for them. Vargas Machuca was commended only for surviving.

After an expensive four-month stay in Panama City recovering his health, Fernando de Vargas Machuca sailed to Peru as part of an escort for the returning plate fleet, then promptly made his way to the silver city of Potosí. Here in the high Andes he joined a punitive expedition against the Chiriguano Indians, which soon led to his being assigned a two-year post in San Miguel de Tucumán, a frontier town in what is today northwest Argentina.[41] Here Vargas Machuca led periodic "castigos," but again with no outstanding victories or conquests to report. For all these services, Fernando de Vargas Machuca generously offered to take any one of a long list of vacant jobs: *alguacil mayor*, or chief bailiff, of either Cuzco or Tucumán; *corregidor* of Huamanga; or *alcalde mayor* of mines in Potosí.

Overall, this decidedly south Andean trajectory, plus suggestions in the document that Fernando de Vargas Machuca had been in Lima at some point to file papers around 1590 and may have been in Tucumán in the late 1580s, lead one to believe that this was *not* the same person as our unlucky protagonist, *Bernardo* de Vargas Machuca. Interestingly, however, a 1590 filing in the same bundle of documents clearly signed by the latter also asks to be considered for vacant posts in Potosí and Huamanga, and the countless wild horses of Tucumán get brief mention in *Milicia Indiana*. Finally, one of Vargas Machuca's earliest supporters in New Granada, Alonso Ruiz Lanchero (a fellow native of Simancas whose daughter would later marry one of his sons and file petitions for recognition in Madrid in 1622), claimed in 1586 that before arriving in Tunja Bernardo had served in Panama and Peru.[42] Meanwhile, an obscure novelist working as a clerk in Seville filed his own probanza in 1590 asking to be named accountant to the royal treasury in New Granada or corregidor of La Paz, king's choice. His name was Miguel de Cervantes Saavedra, and he had no more luck than Bernardo (or Fernando) de Vargas Machuca.[43]

There is another possibility. Otero D'Acosta, Martínez de Salinas, and others have suggested that Bernardo de Vargas Machuca spent some part of the early 1580s in Chile. They have argued that given his apparently inside knowledge of the local situation in his 1599 proposal for an invasion of Chile, he must have had a chance to form an opinion of how the rebellious Mapuche fought, and how they ought to be countered. We have found no evidence of either Bernardo or Fernando de Vargas Machuca serving in Chile, but Tucumán was at least somewhat close, perhaps close enough for him to have spoken with veterans of that most difficult front. For now, the period between 1579 and 1585 remains an unclosed chapter in Vargas Machuca's biography.

Fortunately, we are quite certain that the next stop was New Granada, where the roughly thirty-year-old Bernardo de Vargas Machuca was likely attracted by the glow of El Dorado. By this time, the early 1580s, large expeditions in search of the gilded cacique were setting out from Bogotá and Tunja, mostly in the direction of Venezuela. These missions, several organized by an early Vargas Machuca patron, the madly adventurous Governor Antonio de Berrío, focused on the great plains of the Orinoco and foothills of the Guyana massif. It appears Vargas Machuca just missed participating in a disastrous 1584 trip, only to have to sit out what would have been a much larger—but equally fruitless—one the following year. As his (now unequivocal) service record states, he was recruited and named captain general of cavalry by Governor Berrío in 1585, but the regional court delayed the expedition's departure and Vargas Machuca ended up heading off in another direction.[44]

Somewhere in the midst of all this, the soldier from Simancas married a conquistador's granddaughter named María Cerón and established a household in the thriving highland town of Tunja. As we have noted, greater Tunja was where much of the indigenous Muisca population was concentrated, and with them many of the original Spanish elite families. Though clearly itching for another chance at military service, Vargas Machuca briefly enjoyed some portion of the rents from his father-in-law's encomienda, which was tied to the village of Motavita.[45] Title to the encomienda would never be his or his wife's, however, passing instead to other heirs and then to the crown. Before long the couple had three children: Bernardo, Juan, and Bernardina. Money was apparently tight, and whatever wealth there was to be found in the Machuca household came from María Cerón's dowry, which included several farms near the village of Chiquinquirá. One of Vargas Machuca's main motives for continued conquests was certainly to gain steady income for his family by winning an encomienda that would then be inherited by one of his sons. At least as important in Vargas Machuca's case, an encomienda would lift the luckless arriviste from obscurity and offer legitimate entry into local elite society.

Vargas Machuca's martial inclination was satisfied by a series of indigenous uprisings and corresponding crown-authorized castigos of the sort routinely sent out against maroons and pirates. In about a decade's worth of such punitive sorties, Vargas Machuca ranged from the sun-baked Atlantic plains of the lower Cauca valley to the rainy headwaters of the Caquetá, tributary of the Amazon. In all, he would participate in at least six expeditions against five unrelated indigenous groups identified as rebels, and in varying leadership capacities. Vargas Machuca's first major campaign took place in early 1586, when he captained part of an expedition against the so-called Carares of the lower Magdalena River basin.[46] Another outing against the same group followed in 1587, this time with Vargas Machuca at the head.

According to Vargas Machuca's several surviving probanzas, two of which are housed in Colombia's National Archive in Bogotá, he was proudest of the second Carare mission.[47] Soon after their return to the highlands, many of Vargas Machuca's soldiers testified as to his effectiveness as a leader, describing how he suffered hunger along with everyone else and did not give up until he and his men had captured and "administered justice" to a band of alleged indigenous delinquents found deep in the backcountry. It is worth backing up to examine these campaigns in some detail, as they would later inform so much of Vargas Machuca's writing, including *Milicia Indiana* and the *Defense of Western Conquests*.

The first Carare campaign set out from the emerald mining town of La Trinidad de los Muzos (today Muzo) under command of the regional governor, Luis Carrillo de Ovando, in December 1585. Vargas Machuca was already so esteemed for his leadership qualities he was named "field marshal," or *maese de campo*, on the way downriver. The plan was to capture and punish a group of hunter-gatherers who had taken to preying upon the large cargo canoes, or *bogas*, that seasonally made their way up the Magdalena River to Honda, port of Bogotá. Most of these craft were by

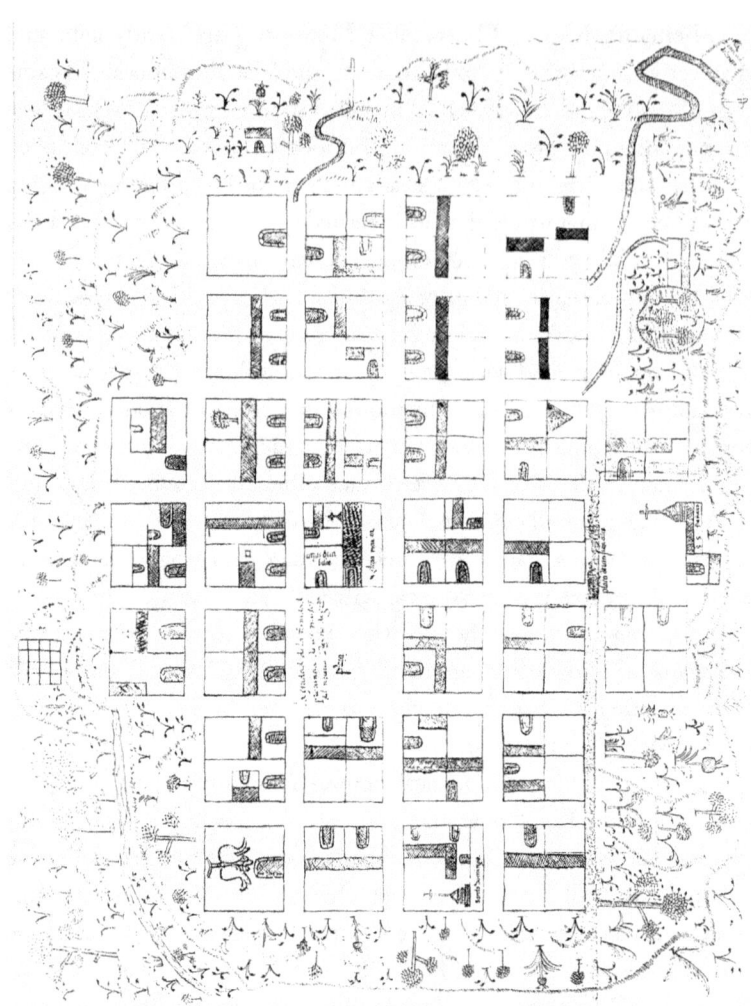

8
Plan of Muzo,
Colombia, ca. 1582.
Courtesy Archivo
General de Indias

this time propelled by enslaved Africans, aided by some Amerindian pilots and a few native polers still held in encomienda.[48] By 1585 the Carares had attacked and captured a half-dozen bogas, killed or taken hostage their crew members and passengers, and made off with an unknown quantity of merchandise, supplies, and arms. Since everyone agreed that the boga traffic was New Granada's lifeline to the Atlantic and hence Spain, the "punishment" of the Carares was given special priority.

The first Carare expedition failed miserably in that not one so-called Indian delinquent was found before the militiamen's supplies ran out and

9
View of Muzo from the south.
Photo by Kris Lane

several members fell ill and died. Spanish-led forces, including those commanded by Vargas Machuca, were not only made fools of, but were also left in broken health and facing financial ruin. The second sortie, which left Muzo in January 1587, was different. Apparently highly motivated, perhaps by revenge, Vargas Machuca proved himself a quick study in counterinsurgency tactics. He returned to the hot hill country surrounding the swampy lower middle Magdalena with a handpicked force of forty-six men. After several weeks' nonstop marching, they located a Carare settlement, attacked and destroyed it, and "administered justice" to alleged ringleaders.

On this expedition Vargas Machuca appears to have adopted the indigenous practices of traveling light, moving constantly, remaining vigilant at all hours, and showing as much resolve and as little mercy as possible. A thirty-year-old participant from Muzo named Juan de Porras testified that he and his fellow punishers traveled "fast and light and without food" (*sin comida*, meaning without herding along live domestic animals, an old conquistador practice described in book 2 of the *Indian Militia*).[49]

Here along the mighty Magdalena is also where Vargas Machuca committed what then, as today, would be called atrocities. Although the dozen or so witness testimonies he gathered and sent to Spain openly mention his personally setting fire to indigenous dwellings, an act resulting in several of their occupants being burned alive, there is no hint that this was considered unjust or excessive at the time; if we are to believe their testimonies, Vargas Machuca's men saw it as an act of valor done in the heat of battle.[50]

They claimed that at the entrance to the Carare village, Vargas Machuca had shouted the standard plea for submission, or *requerimiento* (this was done in Spanish, witnesses said, "lacking an interpreter"), before ordering his men to attack. From their "fortified huts, large and small" the Carares responded with "great fury" and a rain of poisoned arrows, four of which hit Vargas Machuca's followers, one of them an Amerindian ally. In response, several militiamen testified, their caudillo put his shield in front of him and went alone into the fray to torch the dwellings. In the aftermath an allegedly "old and fat chief" was found among the survivors ("un yndio viejo grande de cuerpo," f. 941) and hanged as an example to the others.

The first recorded suggestion of impropriety in this particular castigo comes several years later, from Bogotá audiencia judge Luis Enríquez. In his 1601 report to Spain's Indies Council on continuing attempts to punish the Carares (they would remain a problem well into the seventeenth century), he implied that Vargas Machuca's 1587 burning of some of their dwellings had bordered on criminal and was at best misdirected (this group had not been connected with hostages or stolen merchandise, as a careful reading of the probanza testimonies also strongly suggests). Still, this later summary of Vargas Machuca's most important expedition confuses several key details.[51]

Was it a crime to burn rebellious natives in their dwellings while fighting for one's life in a "castigation" of this kind? Some people besides Las Casas certainly thought so. For example, an expedition leader in Colombia's Sierra Nevada in the 1550s was sentenced by the high court in Bogotá to be drawn and quartered for similar acts, although he broke out of jail and disappeared.[52] Prosecution of similar "excesses" was relatively common in the sixteenth-century Andes, although sentences were rarely carried out. Whatever its legal implications, the Carare house-burning incident appears to have weighed heavily on Vargas Machuca for much of his life. He returned to the matter in his *Defense of Western Conquests* (ca. 1603) to argue that it had been a shame, but was in fact the Indians' fault:

> It happened to a commander that having gone out on a punishment of Indian bandits called Carares, for great robberies and murders they had committed

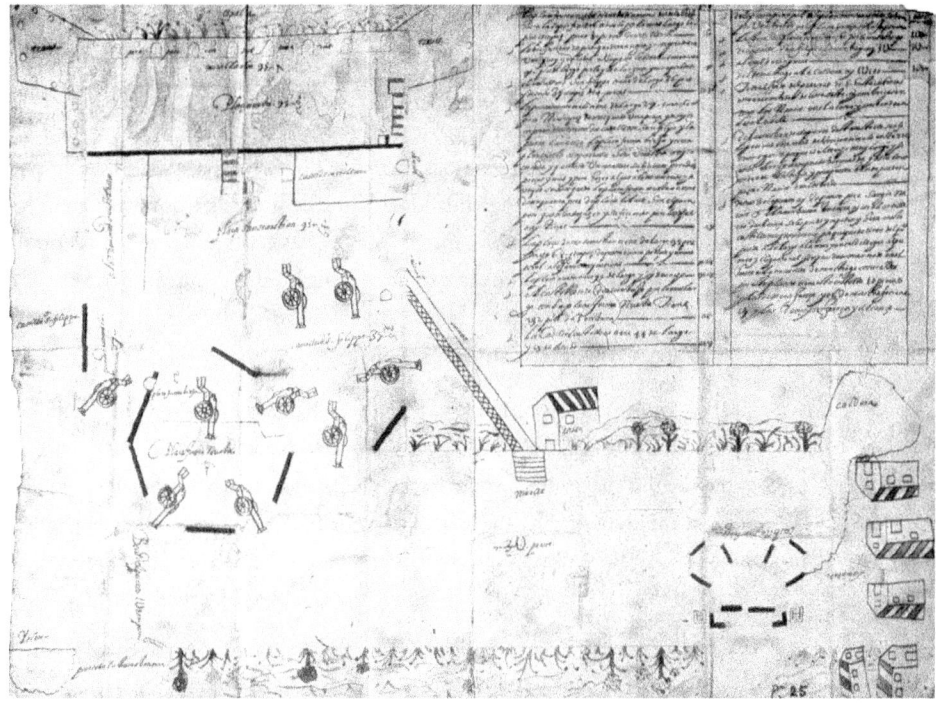

Portobelo fort plans, ca. 1602. Courtesy Archivo General de Indias

against Spanish soldiers and traveling friars who were going up the great River Magdalena ... and having searched for them with a small number of soldiers, he came across them without being sensed, finding them in the midst of a great gathering and drinking party in two large huts with a plaza in between. They fortified themselves and fought valiantly through embrasures [small, protected openings], because the soldiers later took the plaza and surrounded the dwellings, and as the Indians could see well through the embrasures they took their aim with bows and arrows and found their mark with most of their shots, and as they could not be seen, those who shot could not be countered, leaving the majority of the soldiers wounded with a pestiferous and mortal poison. So the commander, seeing the ravages they did and the little effect of his soldiers and *harquebuses* [primitive matchlocks], and that if they did not defeat them soon then they would all perish, and more than this knowing that relief would soon arrive for these adversaries since there were other villages nearby and that they could not wait since these would soon get word either from an Indian who had not been among those surrounded or because they might hear the reports of the harquebuses, he decided to set them on fire, with special advice from his own men.[53]

Or so he remembered things fifteen years after the fact. Much more troubling was an incident not mentioned anywhere in the caudillo's various service records. Again, in the *Defense of Western Conquests* we find Vargas Machuca relating an event from the 1587 Carare *castigo* of which he was the sole leader and principal investor. He says that after burning the dwellings and hanging the alleged cacique, he and his troop were marching away with a number of captive indigenous men and women through the bush. While camped near a river one night, the group's sentries heard rustling in the woods and realized that Carare warriors had surrounded them. Vargas Machuca continues:

> There were six or seven Indian women who had recently given birth, with infants at the breast, and these, sensing that their people were near, and wishing that by this means they would be liberated, began to harshly pinch their children; and these, feeling the pain of the pinches, raised such a great clamor and outcry that the lookouts and crouching sentries who had been posted lost their ability to hear and responded, saying "the enemy is entering, and we cannot stop them properly unless this noise is quieted."[54]

Vargas Machuca claims he was then counseled by a trusted indigenous ally, a Christian cacique, to take one of the women's babies and drown it in the river. "Then you will see how the others calm theirs," the cacique is said to have added. Vargas Machuca ordered it done, although he claims the murdered child was first baptized. Either for this or for some other unknown reason, the Carares retreated. Vargas Machuca believed he had saved the expedition by this sacrifice and adds as proof, "This commander communicated the incident to a theologian, and in the confession was absolved." The priest told him it was "permitted to take a life in order to avoid so many deaths."[55] In part three of *Milicia Indiana*, Vargas Machuca refers to this incident obliquely in a bit of advice to readers.

Atrocious or glorious, Vargas Machuca's dramatic punishment of the Carares would be all but brushed off by New Granada's greatest historian of the early period, Fray Pedro Simón. In his multivolume 1625 monument to the winners and losers of the conquest, he summarized the second Carare outing amid a string of failed punishments: "Things went a little better in the year 1592 for Capt. don Bernardino de Vargas Machuca, who entering Carare Island from the city of the Muzos captured several of the highwaymen and hanged them on the banks of the Great River [Magdalena], which stopped their robberies for a little while, although soon after they resumed."⁵⁶ Even if his name, the year, and even the precise location of his most notable military action were incorrectly recorded, at least Bernardo de Vargas Machuca had finally made history.

Next was a campaign against the just-mentioned Muzos, the indigenous inhabitants of Colombia's emerald district, in August 1587. This time Vargas Machuca moved even more quickly and efficiently and had a cacique named Guazará and a number of other alleged ringleaders hanged. The lightning-fast punishment was justified, he said, due to the many crimes these Indians had committed against Spaniards, including armed robbery, murder, and so on, but also crimes against their own people, including cannibalism. The cannibalism charge was a common one in New Granadan geographical summaries and service reports throughout colonial times, and Vargas Machuca's tone with regard to it is typically casual. He elaborates on cannibal "crimes" in *Milicia Indiana* and more so in the *Defense of Western Conquests*. Interestingly, Vargas Machuca appears to have had no real interest in mining emeralds in Muzo, although he demonstrates familiarity with the processes used in *Milicia Indiana*, and the inventory of his 1622 will alleges that he owned rights to several emerald mines.⁵⁷ He appears always to have been after another sort of treasure: recognition.

In the meantime, we know from notary records filed in Bogotá that María Cerón died in the course of her husband's paramilitary ramblings, and that Vargas Machuca began to sell off the family estate soon afterward.⁵⁸ Who took care of their children in the meantime is unknown, but the aspiring captain seems already to have been planning his return to Spain to personally beg Philip II for some sort of governorship. He would leave New Granada for good after a series of back-to-back rescue and punishment expeditions north and south of Bogotá between 1590 and 1594.

The first outing took Vargas Machuca to the town of Altagracia, in the rough territory southwest of Bogotá occupied by the recently conquered Sutagaos, neighbors and probably ethnic relatives of the Pijaos, New Granada's equivalent of Chile's Mapuche. A 1591 spin-off campaign took Vargas Machuca, along with several Spaniards and mestizos and 150 "friendly Indians" in pursuit of a Pijao band under a cacique named Dapué, who was captured and executed in the upper Magdalena foothills. The incident is related in some detail in *Milicia Indiana*. Dapué was said to have been responsible for attacks on the Sutagao, and also on Spanish settlers at Altagracia. A few prisoners were taken to Bogotá, where they were presumably sold. This was a standard, crown-approved practice with those alleged to be Pijaos at the time, and they were sold as far away as Quito.[59]

Vargas Machuca then signed on to a campaign to put down an uprising in distant Antioquia, on the lower Cauca, but it never materialized. The next job, in early 1592, was northeast of Bogotá, where he participated in efforts to rebuild the towns of Santiago de las Atalayas and Medina de las Torres, both recent mining camps overrun by rebellious "Cusiana" bands held in encomienda. His method of justice-by–speedy terror now well established, Vargas Machuca searched out and had hanged an alleged rebel cacique named Coná and a dozen "ringleaders." Near Medina de las Torres, when no rebels could be found, their dwellings and maize fields were burned until they sued for peace.[60] Mine owners were encouraged to keep digging by a flurry of tax breaks issued from the royal treasury in Bogotá.

The next enemy would not be so easily subdued. The Pijao campaigns, which carried on through the first quarter of the seventeenth century, began in earnest under Governor Bernardino Mujica (or "Moxica") Guevara. Wisely, the bankrupt and widowed Vargas Machuca managed to marry the governor's niece, which yielded access to an 8,000-gold-peso dowry. He joined his new father-in-law under the title of lieutenant general and set off to punish the Pijaos. A brief sidelight appeared when news of Quito's 1592 sales tax revolt arrived in New Granada along with a warrant for the arrest of one of the alleged conspirators (Vargas Machuca called him the "prime mover" in his 1604 service report). This man, Esteban Polo Palomino, was said to be hiding out in the gold mining town of Almaguer, midway between Popayán and Pasto. Vargas Machuca managed the capture and sent the prisoner off to Quito to be tried.[61]

While in the vicinity of Almaguer, Vargas Machuca decided to do what any bona fide Spanish caudillo longed for sooner or later while tramping through the Indies: he founded a town on the upper Iscancé River, a tributary of the Caquetá, and named it Simancas, after his birthplace. This was in June of 1593. Biographer Martínez de Salinas describes the process in detail, having located the official incorporation documents. Vargas Machuca fondly remembered it, too, in book 4 of *Milicia Indiana*. Literary critic Luis Fernando Restrepo has even analyzed this remembrance in terms of its power symbolism.[62] Yet the town was not to be. Like so much else in Vargas Machuca's life, New Simancas simply did not work out. In fact, despite the pompous ceremonies of raising a pillory and delivering invigorating speeches to the hopeful first settlers, it was abandoned within months. There is some suggestion, though no proof, that the local Andakí Indians attacked and destroyed it.[63]

Reminiscent of his relations with wives and children, Vargas Machuca was not around to sustain his new creation. He was quickly drawn off to fight the Pijaos, well to the north. A series of skirmishes near the Saldaña River went badly for Vargas Machuca and his mix of creole and indigenous campaign mates, proof that the Pijaos, like the Carares, would not be conquered even by a resolute and resourceful Spanish commander with long experience. By early 1595 the veteran caudillo was on his way to Madrid to seek compensation for his many sacrifices and valiant deeds. Looking back, the 1590s castigos were not all failures, but for Vargas Machuca nothing matched the fiery defeat of the Carare "bandits" in 1587. Although the vast majority of Carares remained unconquered, and a permanent presidio would have to be built on Carare Island in the Magdalena River to protect the canoe traffic, this experience would be forever idealized.

Philip II's court was crowded in 1595, prompting Vargas Machuca to write up his varied experiences in the Indies in a new format. He called it *Milicia y descripción de las Indias*, or *Milicia Indiana*, for short. Instead of yet another testimony of personal hardship and valor in the king's name, he offered up a manual for the next crop of young and restless strivers with a passion for arms. As if to prove that this was not intended to take away from the traditional, equestrian culture of the caballero, Vargas Machuca quickly followed with his first manual of horsemanship, *Exercicios de la gineta*, which came out with the same publisher as *Milicia Indiana*, in 1600.

Even with these books, and apparently a number of prominent friends, including the banker Alberto Fugger, Vargas Machuca could not get what he wanted. The plum posts were going to men of another kind, not hard workers, as Vargas Machuca complains in the text below, but sheltered, incompetent sycophants. To add insult to injury, a petition to join the knightly order of Santiago was instantly shelved without even so much as a response. That a noble and famously named Spanish veteran with a passion for tilting could not get a knighthood in 1599 was in itself a telling fact, one not lost on Cervantes and other "ignored genius" contemporaries.

Eventually, advisers to the new king, Philip III, decided that this descendant of Vargas the Smasher might be useful in helping to defend the Panamanian Isthmus against the next generation of Drakes. Vargas Machuca was made *alcalde mayor* and paymaster of the three fortresses of Portobelo, said to be one of the sickliest, most pestilential towns in the Indies. When he arrived in March 1602, it had just been attacked by English corsair William Park, and things had not gone well for the poorly armed and disorganized locals, most of whom were merchants, not soldiers.[64] Portobelo was the site of the annual trade fair linking Peru and Spain, and was thus of great strategic importance to the empire. The town's stone defenses had been recently designed and hastily built under the direction of the celebrated Roman military engineer Giambattista Antonelli.[65]

Unfortunately, as in so many things, Vargas Machuca was on the down side of the curve. The great silver mines of Potosí were in decline and trade was shifting away from Panama and Portobelo to favor Veracruz, Acapulco, and Buenos Aires. Worse, Antonelli's forts were already crumbling or sinking into the mire, and the judges of the Audiencia of Panama, among other local officials, took an instant dislike to the busybody from Simancas. As documents in the Archive of the Indies amply reveal, these older and wiser men more than managed to contain him.[66] Martínez de Salinas adds that between the demands of fort upkeep and bureaucratic wrangling, Vargas Machuca almost never got his full salary across six years' duty in one of the colonies' most expensive locations. His incessant complaints to the Indies Council bear this out. Virtually all provisions had to be imported, and the periodic influx of Peruvian silver drove prices, especially for much needed medicines, through the roof. To add insult to injury, Vargas Machuca's paymaster job was deemed superfluous after only two years, further eating away at his salary.[67] As a result, the hapless conquistador left Portobelo more or less in a rage, having composed his *Defense of Western Conquests* in his spare time, part of which was spent in jail during his own *residencia* (investigation of his tenure by the incoming replacement). As if things could not get worse, he claimed the manuscript of this heartfelt, one-hundred-page response to Las Casas was stolen while on its way to a publisher in Lima. He would have to rewrite it.

Vargas Machuca's next post, which came after a shorter but still excruciating wait at court, was even more decadent: governor of Margarita Island, in the eastern Caribbean. Sunny Margarita was starkly beautiful, to be sure, and much healthier than Portobelo, but it was already well past its glory days and very low on Spain's list of imperial priorities. Pearl

War canoes from Trinidad and Margarita Islands, ca. 1586. Courtesy Pierpont Morgan Library

fishing all around the island and nearby mainland dated to Columbus's time, with some significant booms and busts on the smaller islands of Cubagua and Coche occurring through the 1570s. The island had also been briefly famous when it was seized by the Basque rebel Lope de Aguirre in 1561. By the time Vargas Machuca arrived in early 1609, a few more than two hundred Spanish heads of household had managed to hang on, mostly through illegal sales of tobacco to foreigners. The characteristically impatient new governor immediately demanded that the Indies Council enlarge his pint-sized jurisdiction (they refused). He also wasted no time alienating a number of local elites, who he claimed were already conspiring against him.[68]

According to Vargas Machuca and his predecessor's reports to Spanish authorities, the island's indigenous Guayquerí population was severely reduced, totaling perhaps one hundred when he took up his post in 1609. Native inhabitants from outside were somewhat more numerous. In a 1610 report, Vargas Machuca claimed refugees from the mainland and captives from the Windward Islands—the vast majority ethnic Caribs from Dominica—numbered about 550.[69] Regardless of origin, most native islanders lived in either real or quasi-slavery (*encomienda* or *depósito*), working as domestic servants and common laborers for the small Spanish-creole population. Enslaved and free people of African descent constituted the clear majority of Margariteños by this time, with a population perhaps as large as 2,000. Vargas Machuca would soon find a new enemy—along with a few allies—in them.

The approximately five hundred adult men among the enslaved African population of Margarita were nearly all pearl divers, heading out in groups of fifteen to twenty each morning before dawn in caravel-like sailing vessels and returning after sunset. In a boom era in the 1570s and 1580s, several slave ships a year stopped at the island on their way to Cartagena to replenish the pearling workforce. The boom did not last thanks to overexploitation of the fragile *ostiales*, or oyster beds, and between 1600 and 1618 only two slave ships came legally to Margarita. Meanwhile, smallpox ravaged the remaining slave crews and their families, with a major outbreak occurring in 1610.[70] The pearl bust left the surviving enslaved Africans with little to do but grow a bit of tobacco and move about the island like free people. Tobacco cultivation had been outlawed in the region since a 1605 crackdown on contraband, but under pressure from local elites Vargas Machuca asked that slaves be allowed to grow just enough for their own use, since "they are people of such a cold nature that without it they work much less than before and risk their lives by suffering more illnesses, more so when they spend all day under water, where the depths are so cold."

Slaves may have had a right to smoke (since it was thought good for business and followed the dubious health claims of the time), but Vargas Machuca's response to black mobility was less generous. He established a curfew within a year of his arrival, employing a new brand of citizen's militia to monitor the nighttime movements of any person of color. He then demanded that several thousand copper coins be sent from Santo Domingo to stop desperate slaves from bartering precious pearls for food. Like other elite Margariteños, the new governor reflexively blamed enslaved black inhabitants for the island's economic decline, social unrest, dangerous exposure to foreigners, and every other sort of ill. His only seemingly charitable act toward an enslaved African during this period was to ask in June 1610 that the Indies Council free one "Francisco, of the Congo nation" in return for his aiding the Spanish against the Island Caribs. He had been held captive since boyhood, apparently on the island

12 Enslaved African pearl divers near Margarita Island, ca. 1586. Courtesy Pierpont Morgan Library

of St. Vincent, and would serve Vargas Machuca as a valuable translator and guide.[71]

This odd, and in fact more self-serving than generous, petition arose in the context of an Indian militia-style "punishment" of the kind Vargas Machuca had been itching to launch since his days in Panama. In early 1610 he outfitted two large pirogues to hunt Island Caribs. These perennial enemies of the Spanish were said to be threatening a major attack on the good citizens of La Asunción, capital of Margarita, an unlikely scenario given the distances involved and established raiding patterns.[72] The Caribs of Dominica, in particular, were actively engaged in chronic, piratical wars with the Spanish on Puerto Rico, where they often kidnapped enslaved Africans like Francisco Congo. Those of St. Vincent and the Grenadines, though closer at hand, were generally less belligerent. Since the crown wished its governor to stay put on the island should it in fact be besieged,

Vargas Machuca chose to send out his son, Juan, to command the two large canoes. When young Juan de Vargas Machuca returned to Asunción emptyhanded, his father not only reproached him but also summarily exiled him to the war in Flanders, roughly Spain's equivalent of the Russian Front. Local elites, although impressed by Vargas Machuca's lack of favoritism (he had also had one of his own slaves hanged for murder), complained that his bellicose ways and iron fist were driving away the few remaining Guayquerí and interfering with the (technically illegal) tobacco trade.[73]

Restless as ever, Vargas Machuca threw himself into the task of rebuilding Margarita's tiny capital, which to this day stands as a rough-hewn monument to Spanish aspirations at the edge of empire. Margariteños still honor Vargas Machuca for organizing construction of the island's cathedral church, the main portion of which was finished in 1619. Well before his term ended, the man from Simancas boasted of all sorts of public works improvements, ranging from an aqueduct to a slaughterhouse to a pirate-proof fortress named, perhaps coincidentally, for St. Bernard. He even managed to draft island slaves and house servants to construct a stone-enclosed equestrian parade ground, or *carrera*, a no doubt vital necessity for the many caballeros inhabiting this tiny coral island. As in Portobelo, however, Vargas Machuca consistently clashed with entrenched locals, particularly commerce-minded members of the town council whose interests did not match his. The situation differed from that of Portobelo, however, in that by calling attention to the island's woes in his repeated letters to Spain and more or less successfully reconstructing the town center he appears to have won over a loyal faction that could be called upon to write favorable letters from time to time. He would need them for his next promotion.[74]

After five years of unsung improvements on his desert island, Vargas Machuca faced the dreaded residencia.[75] The investigation ended with his owing the crown 800 pesos in fines, a trifling sum for governors and audiencia judges in rich districts but a genuine hardship here at the cash-starved fringe. Vargas Machuca was still in Margarita in 1616 begging his few friends for loans, most of which were still outstanding upon his death six years later. Not content to sail in a standard Indies Fleet galleon like an ordinary passenger, the outgoing governor purchased a small vessel on credit to accommodate his entourage and sailed independently to Cartagena. There he traded up to a caravel called the *San Francisco*, the debt

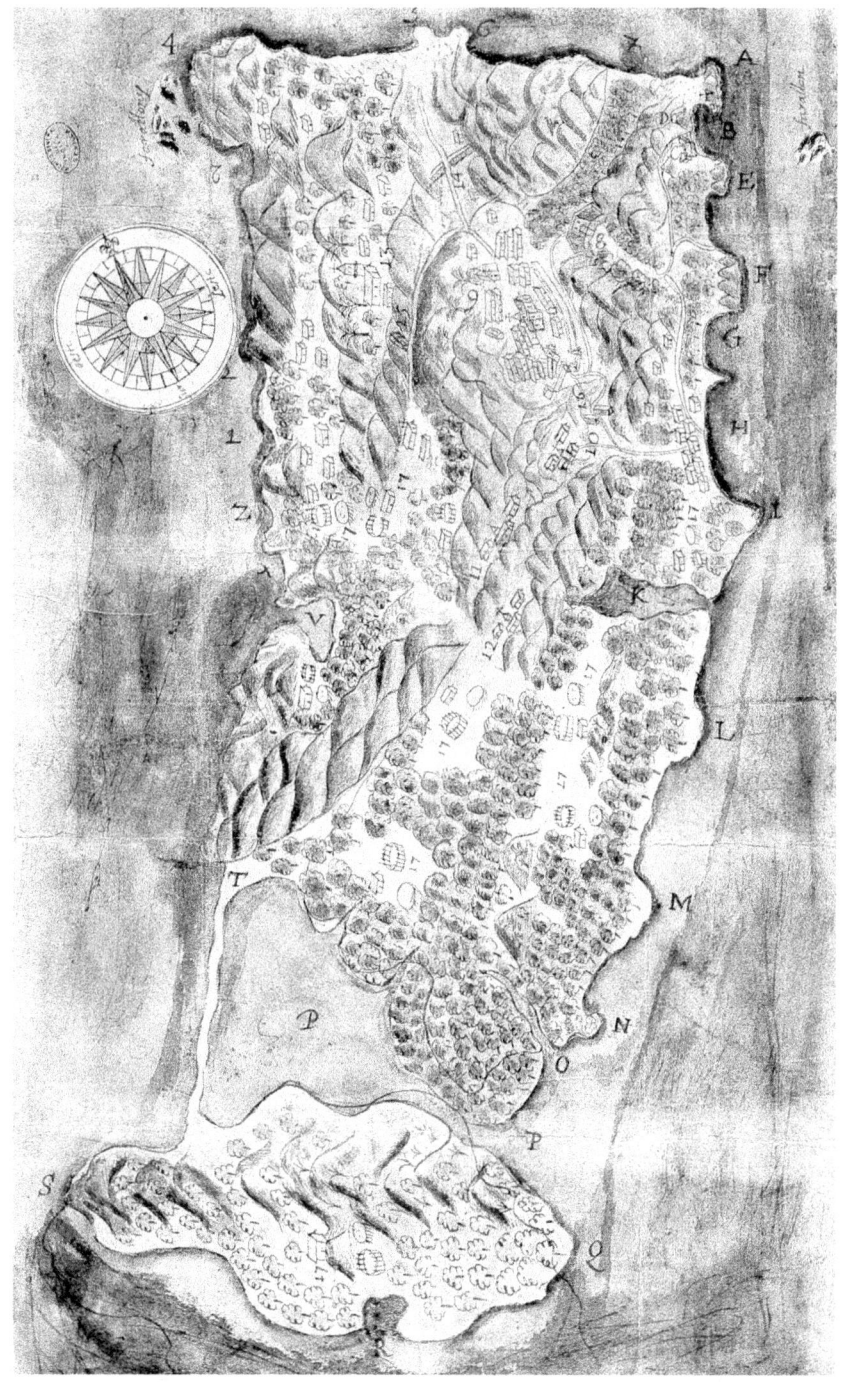

13   *Margarita Island in the mid-seventeenth century. Courtesy Archivo General de Indias*

for which also outlived him, and left with the fleet for Spain to seek yet another promotion. Still unlucky after all these years, Vargas Machuca was caught in a storm somewhere in the North Atlantic and was separated from the fleet. The battered *San Francisco* barely reached Lisbon for repairs, and when it finally crossed the bar at Sanlúcar its owner was whisked off to jail in Seville under suspicion of contraband trading while in Portugal.

The equally broke and indignant Vargas Machuca was soon freed, and after borrowing still more money in Seville he made his way to Madrid to try his luck again at court. While waiting to hear of a promotion, he updated his popular manual of horsemanship, an illustrated edition of which came out in 1619. A second volume of this, his one successful work, was published in 1621. Finally, just after being named governor of Antioquia, one of New Granada's several declining gold districts, Vargas Machuca died suddenly in Madrid of an unknown illness. He was buried in February 1622, so poor his son Alvaro (author of the service report in appendix 1) had to petition for aid to help cover funeral expenses. Along with "the fruits of his genius," he left behind at least a thousand pesos in debt, some of which was liquidated by a brother, Bartolomé, now living in Margarita. An appeal was also made to Vargas Machuca's two daughters, Bernardina and Ana María, Conceptionist nuns in Panama City, to say masses for their father's departed soul every Day of the Dead for the rest of their lives.[76]

A ROMAN IN THE NEW WORLD?
ANTIQUITY IN *MILICIA INDIANA*

Milicia Indiana is a curious book in several ways. One is its author's encyclopedic urge to squeeze in everything from ethnographic anecdotes to reflections on the cosmos. This tendency is made stranger by the book's brevity, a seeming reflection of Vargas Machuca's military discipline. In addition to advising the green caudillo on how to act with subordinates and native American enemies, *Milicia Indiana* summarizes military history since remote antiquity, speculates on imperial politics, compares New and Old World medicine, and lists plants, animals, fish, insects, rivers, lakes, and volcanoes, often with personal observations inserted to add authority. It is a treatise on natural history; then a pilot's rutter, or port guide, presumably meant for lost sailors; and finally a late medieval cosmographer's "compendium of the sphere." Although unusually concise, this kind of miscellaneous, quasi-scientific jumble was common to books by Renaissance men of Vargas Machuca's ilk.[77] Also basic to their "interdisciplinary" rambling was a strong dose of classical references.

In *Romans in a New World*, David Lupher has shown how in the wake of the conquests of the Aztecs and Incas, Spanish authors grappled in several ways with antiquity, particularly the legacy of imperial Rome as it compared with the much larger transoceanic empire of Spain.[78] One way of using the ancients as a touchstone was to compare Roman and conquistador military achievements. Unsurprisingly, many American conquistadors, and at least some of their admirers back home, came to the quick conclusion that theirs was the greater deed. By comparison to Cortés's brilliant amphibious siege of the Mexican capital of Tenochtitlan, Scipio Africanus's taking of Carthage seemed a minor victory.

Another Spanish Renaissance line of argument used the Roman imperial heritage to compare styles of governance. Some looked to Cicero and other statesmen for pointers on how to govern conquered peoples in a just yet rigorous fashion, and also how to justify their conquest. A third stream of thought centered on the question of indigenous civilization in comparison with that of ancient Rome. Were the Incas and Aztecs truly imperial peoples, too, or simply barbaric tribes who mimicked civilization thanks to the Devil's tricks? Could peoples without recognizable systems of writing, much less iron tools and long-distance sailing ships, be called civilized? Had the peoples conquered by the Incas and Aztecs been subject to tyranny, or were they governed by consent? What of nonsedentary or pastoral peoples? Were they to be treated differently, as the Romans had done with refractory mountaineers and desert nomads? In these several ways, then, Spaniards in the first half of the sixteenth century measured themselves against a known yardstick.

Or rather, mostly known yardstick. As Vargas Machuca reveals in his frequent references to Roman and other antique personages and events, there was often a great distance between sixteenth-century Spaniards and original sources in Greek or Latin. Popular glosses of classical works in Spanish were far more commonly read in Vargas Machuca's time, although as Lupher points out, learned writers such as Las Casas often demonstrated profound knowledge of even the most obscure (usually Latin) sources available at the time. Not being classicists, translator Tim Johnson and I have not attempted to exhaust the possible sources from which Vargas Machuca must have drawn, but his sometimes confused sense of ancient history suggests only a superficial reading of such standard authorities as Herodotus, Livy, and Plutarch, along with a variety of later digests.

Although with the exception of his plan for Chilean conquest he does not go nearly as far with Roman references as his fellow Tunjano the poet-historian Juan de Castellanos, Vargas Machuca does occasionally offer comparisons that would have pleased the conquistadors, juxtaposing Pompey with Cortés, for example, or Marcus Aurelius with Jiménez de Quesada. His point is that to be a good leader, the Indies caudillo must learn from the great leaders of the past, both distant and recent; in short, however one felt about the Romans, like the Indians (and even the Ottomans) you could learn from them. Vargas Machuca prepares himself mostly with arguments derived from his and his fellow conquistadors' experience in the Americas, not ancient history, for the task of refuting Las Casas. As Lupher has shown in detail, Las Casas used the Romans mostly as a foil for his own generous appraisal of the "civilized" (i.e., orderly, urban, imperial) peoples of America, the Aztecs and Incas. Focusing instead on nonsedentary forest and desert dwellers with a fondness for guerrilla warfare and herb venom, Vargas Machuca sidesteps this matter altogether.

Classicist and Andeanist Sabine MacCormack has also explored the Roman heritage as an influence on early Spanish Americans, mostly on the ground in Peru. She argues that here in the heart of the former Inca Empire, Roman history and culture (including memories of the Romanized Spanish landscape—its aqueducts, milestones, and temple ruins) served as a lens through which newcomers such as Pedro de Cieza de León saw both native Andeans and themselves.[79] This classical heritage, as Lupher also argues, was not a static yardstick in the minds of Spanish observers, but rather a malleable and even slippery thing in its own right. The long and short of it was that Spanish experience on the ground in Peru changed the way many Spanish colonial subjects, and not only creoles, understood Rome. Experience in a "new" world of seemingly limitless fecundity—where multiple crops could be harvested in a year and whole mountains seemed to consist of precious metals and stones—made observers question even the unfathomable wisdom of Pliny.

As MacCormack demonstrates, it was not only Spaniards such as Vargas Machuca who engaged in this "conversation" with the ancient past, but also native lords, including El Inca Garcilaso de la Vega and Felipe Guaman Poma de Ayala. Like Vargas Machuca, all these authors worked hard to explain why Catholic Spain, in particular, had been fated to bring these worlds together. The native lords saw the Spaniards themselves not as civilization-bearing Romans but as unwitting (and dim-witted) tools of God, a mix of self-styled saints and slobbering scourges. Viewed in this millenarian, Andean Christian way, conquest marked both the glorious arrival of the True Faith and the start of the greatest test of it that could be imagined. Vargas Machuca's view, on the other hand, was more sober, perhaps something like that of a Roman soldier on the Celtic frontier. He was not particularly interested in the fate of indigenous populations, and saw it as his duty simply to subdue recalcitrant ones with force, found cities where they could be properly watched and governed, and then continue on, sword in hand, into the realm of chaos—"más, y más, y más, y más."

HANDBOOK OF THE BRAVE: *MILICIA INDIANA* AND THE SKULKING WAY OF WAR

In what must rank as the first manual of guerrilla warfare ever published— *The Armed Forces and Description of the Indies* (Madrid, 1599)—Captain Bernardo de Vargas Machuca dismissed as irrelevant the entire pattern of European warfare, with its hierarchical tactical units, linear formations, and permanent garrisons. Instead he advocated for the Americas the creation of commando groups to carry out search-and-destroy missions deep within enemy territory for up to two years at a time. The good leader, according to Vargas Machuca (who had a lifetime of experience to draw on), knew as much about planting survival crops and curing tropical ulcers as about laying ambushes and mounting surprise attacks.

GEOFFREY PARKER, *The Military Revolution*

Vargas Machuca would no doubt have been flattered by this glowing characterization of his favorite book, acknowledged at last as a true innovation in the history of arms. It is equally likely, however, that he would have been at pains to disagree with Geoffrey Parker on one essential point: his use of the term *guerrilla warfare*. As noted above, this term has traditionally been reserved for ad hoc, home-based resistance, or native-soil "freedom fighting," not paramilitary raiding by outsiders on behalf of an imperial state. (The term *guerrilla* was in fact first used to describe Spanish and Portuguese civilian resistance to Napoleon's invading forces circa 1810, although the phenomenon is of course much older.)

If there was a first for Vargas Machuca, then, it was in composing a manual of counterinsurgency warfare; a state-approved style of fighting that borrowed copiously—and with occasional acknowledgments—from the unwritten handbook of the true guerrillas, in this case mostly Native Americans and fugitive Africans. So to qualify Parker's assessment even further, Vargas Machuca might have added, if pressed hard enough to admit it, that if there was anything new in *Milicia Indiana* it had come from the Indians themselves, either as enemies or allies of Spaniards. What else was new in the world of early modern warfare circa 1599?

It has been widely argued that the Spanish from about Columbus's time to Philip II's were at the European forefront in developing new tactics and methods of warfare. They were equally quick to adopt innovations from abroad.[80] Key conflicts included the conquest of Granada (1485–92), Italian/Valois Wars (1494–1559), and the long series of attacks, sieges, stalemates, and retreats generally summarized as the Dutch Revolt, or Eighty Years War (1568–1648). Many naval and marine battles also carried Spanish forces to North Africa, the Eastern Mediterranean, and (disastrously) to England. Judging from pension requests and similar documents, it was apparently not unusual for an individual Spanish soldier to have fought the French in Belgium, the Dutch in Holland, Ottoman subjects in North Africa, and Morisco rebels in Andalusia. One Spanish innovation in this era was to field tens of thousands of soldiers at a time. Many such soldiers, among them Vargas Machuca, subsequently migrated to the Americas to seek a better life by carrying on the armed struggle.

According to Geoffrey Parker, and before him Michael Roberts, the Italian Wars revolutionized siege warfare, at least to some extent, with the growing use of heavy artillery partially neutralized by polygonal fortifications in the starlike *trace italienne* style. This trend in part revitalized open field warfare and expanded its scale. Here the Spanish seem to have contributed most, mixing light cavalry (Vargas Machuca's *jinete*, or *gineta*) and compact infantry units (the famous *tercios*) to great and terrible effect.

Contemporary and modern commentators have also noted that the Spanish seemed to excel in the realm of command. Spanish generals in Italy, particularly, were renowned for their courage, intelligence, and discipline; they moved seemingly unwieldy units like chessmen. Most importantly, unlike the French and their allies, they were not above altering the rules to win. Such illustrious men were, like the great Greeks and Romans, Vargas Machuca's role models. Spanish troops did not always win, of course, however brilliant their commanders, but one discovery was that heavily armored knights were vulnerable to handgun fire. Pike men were now paired with musketeers to face the mounted knights of old, and they soon removed them from the field, to be trotted out only on ceremonial occasions. Light cavalry units were deployed for speedy, surprise raids in a more Arabic style. Here, as in the Indian militia, was the new ethic of speed and lightness.

Spanish men in the sixteenth century were thus immersed in a world of "armed forces" operating on a large scale; Vargas Machuca knew it well. Although equally deadly, this was a different sort of game from that of the American backcountry, what early Englishmen in North America described as the "skulking way of war."[81] Where *Milicia Indiana* seems to compare best with this manner of guerrilla warfare aside from its smaller scale and hit-and-run tactics is its emphasis on high moral purpose plus on-the-ground pragmatism. Although a more removed time and context may not be imagined, Che Guevara's 1960 manual of guerrilla warfare bears some comparison with *Milicia Indiana* on this point. Guevara's guerrilla captain, like Vargas Machuca's caudillo, was to conduct himself with utmost reserve, but also maximum flexibility. Both authors celebrate improvisation, in tools as well as tactics, as an art form. Both argued that sorties fared best when carried out "fast and light," leaving little trace. Finally, improvised field medicine, Guevara's specialty, holds pride of place in both texts.[82]

But Che Guevara was an insurgent, not a counterinsurgent. For Vargas Machuca, fighting Indians in the forest demanded a style and, as he calls it, "praxis" only recently advocated by writers of U.S. military manuals: adopting the insurgent enemy's tactics while abhorring "his" supposed lack of moral scruples.[83] Such tactical convergence has been noted in many recent conflicts, from Vietnam to Afghanistan, but how was one to fight like one's allegedly vicious, immoral, cowardly enemy without becoming similarly vicious, immoral, and cowardly?

FAST AND LIGHT, WITH HERBS: PUTTING INDIANS BACK IN THE INDIAN MILITIA

Although he frequently uses the term *republic*, Vargas Machuca's world was not that of a nation, or *patria*, but rather a lumbering goliath just starting to be called the Spanish Empire. Among the empire's many enemies were refractory indigenous groups, found everywhere from the Philippines to Florida. New Granada's Carares, Muzos, Pijaos, and others rightly equated subjection to Spanish rule with irreversible loss of autonomy in most political, economic, and religious matters. As has been seen, however, none of these groups was entirely separate from the colonized world around them; they could not live in total isolation. Often in response to conquest *entradas* (expeditions) organized by settlers and regional governors, they raided colonial ranches, mines, ports, and small towns and also benefited materially from goods stolen along the Camino Real, much-traveled rivers such as the Magdalena, and other trade arteries. Parasitic banditry paralleled modern guerrilla warfare in many ways except for one: the bandits were no longer proposing, or at least expecting to witness, permanent expulsion of all Spaniards and their descendants and auxiliaries.

If indigenous resistance was thus neither unified nor revolutionary, how might it be countered in a geographically and culturally complex region given the technology and accumulated military knowledge of late-sixteenth-century Europe? For Vargas Machuca, what anthropologists have described as "war in the tribal zone" was eminently winnable. To prevail, however, one had to learn to "think like an Indian," or at least to practice a certain amount of mimicking. War of this kind, as Vargas Machuca describes it, was an act of translation as much as bloodshed, and it was very much an *act* in the theatrical sense. Certainly each native group had its own subtle language of warfare, but Vargas Machuca was probably justified in generalizing about the importance of displaying courage, or unflinching resolve, despite being greatly outnumbered. The Indian militia, much more than that of, say, Italy, required a constant show of fearlessness, even in captivity. In an indigenous American way of war, he says, to show *any* weakness was to invite a quick and certain death.

In the rugged forests, deserts, and swamps of New Granada, there were other lessons to be learned from native warriors. One was the need to strip equipment and other supplies down to the bare minimum, and to take along only handpicked, experienced men. Anti-insurgency or police actions were to be undertaken, as Vargas Machuca says, "a la ligera," which may be translated as "fast and light" (to borrow from the language of post-expedition-style mountaineering). Traveling and fighting in this way had its own risks, of course, but in a land where distances were great and geographical obstacles monumental, deep penetration and quick retreat all but mandated a stripped-down survivalist approach. This was especially true given the lack of support available to sustain armed invaders. They could not expect to be relieved or rescued, and thus had to move like their native foes, often traveling nonstop for days on end with no horses or heavy armor.

Another major point of convergence, and one that has drawn far more attention from readers of Vargas Machuca than his advice on searching out and destroying enemy villages, was medicine. References to herbs, wounds, and restorative foods are scattered throughout the text, but Vargas Machuca devotes a whole section of book 2 to field medicine, offering in a very small space a dizzying array of remedies, most containing a substantial "Indian" component, either as an ingredient or procedure. As Saul Jarcho, Mariano Cuesta Domingo, and Fernando López-Ríos Fernández have pointed out, Vargas Machuca's book offers no major insights into the theories underpinning renaissance or even indigenous South American medical arts, but it is a unique field guide, or *vade mecum*, written specifically for unschooled conquistadors. Vargas Machuca's approach is straightforward and pragmatic, all but brushing aside the importance of correct diagnosis. He praises the efficacy of Native American herbs and remedies, but the principles guiding his applications are strictly Galenic, emphasizing balanced humors and timely purging of toxins. Certain indigenous medical practices overlapped with Western ones, especially when it came to purging and even bloodletting, but indigenous shamans differed from their European counterparts in seeing malefic magic behind nearly every illness.[84] Vargas Machuca throws in a few tips on field surgery as well, with toasted maize flour added to traditional European field antiseptics such as gunpowder, corrosive sublimate of mercury, and salt. His guiding principle seems to have been: "If it looks like it might work, try it."

Like martial arts and spiritual self-help manuals, vernacular medical texts were popular in both Spain and the Indies by the time of *Milicia Indiana*'s publication in 1599. Cuesta Domingo and López-Ríos Fernández note that a 1555 Spanish edition of Dioscorides's *Materia Médica* circulated widely and was probably known to Vargas Machuca, as were the surgery manuals of Pedrarias de Benavides (1567) and Bartolomé Hidalgo de Higüero (1584).[85] Two contemporary manuals, including Alonso López de Hinojosos's *Suma y recopilación de cirugía* (1578) and Agustín Farfán's *Tratado breve de medicina* (1592), were published in Mexico City and were thus fairly common in the Indies. Both listed indigenous remedies, particularly purgative and diuretic herbs, alongside traditional, Western ones.

The trend was not new. Scores of curative New World plants and minerals had already been catalogued in Spain by the physician Nicolás Monardes, whose *Historia medicinal de las cosas que se traen de nuestras Indias Occidentales* (1565–74) was even translated to English in 1577 under the title "Joyfull Newes out of the Newe Founde Worlde."[86] Some novel, American drugs proved joyful indeed, although not without side effects and drawbacks. Monardes, as it happened, was in large part responsible for touching off Europe's tobacco craze.

Although disparaged by some European physicians and apothecaries, remedies deriving from American products or therapeutic procedures developed by indigenous peoples spread quickly in the Old World. Syphilis remedies were an early favorite, as this disease seemed to have come from America. Vargas Machuca warns against taking along syphilitic soldiers, who were presumably not uncommon. Scientific interest in such things in fact peaked during the reign of Philip II, who commissioned his chief physician, Dr. Francisco Hernández, to carry out a wide-ranging natural history expedition to both New Spain and Peru in 1570. Although he never got past Mexico, Hernández returned to Madrid seven years later, after having catalogued and noted the therapeutic potential of over 3,000 plants.[87] The American backcountry, as Vargas Machuca repeatedly notes, was a place of many dangers—one could die a thousand ways. Yet this "new" land was also blessed with special remedies, not only countless herbs and counterherbs, but also rare curative minerals such as amethysts and bezoar stones. Indeed, more than anywhere in *Milicia Indiana* or his other writings, it is in this brief section on medicine that Vargas Machuca unequivocally acknowledges and promotes Amerindian knowledge. Years of field tests revealed to the old soldier that the Indian militia required an Indian medicine.

WITH SWORD AND COMPASS: THE MARTIAL ARTS MANUAL IN VARGAS MACHUCA'S SPAIN

In the Villa of Madrid, first of January 1599, there appeared before me, the scribe [Juan López Magarra], and witnesses, on the one part Capt. don Bernardo de Vargas Machuca, resident in this court and native of the Villa of Simancas in Old Castile, and currently citizen, he says, of the city of Santa Fe de Bobotá [sic] in the New Kingdom of Granada in the Indies, and on the other part Juan Rodríguez, merchant, citizen of this villa [Madrid]; and they said that this Capt. don Bernardo de Vargas Machuca had been given license and registry by Your Majesty to print, as they are now printing, a book he composed titled *Milicia yndiana y discreción de las yndias*, to be sold in all Your Majesty's kingdoms by him or by the person or people to whom he gives power of attorney for ten years.

Archivo Histórico de Protocolos de Madrid, Signatura 2508

If he had difficulty getting permission for his refutation of Las Casas, Vargas Machuca seems to have found some success as a writer of handbooks for men at arms. Fortunately the typesetters of *Milicia Indiana* knew its subtitle was "Description" rather than "Discretion" of the Indies, a curious and repeated slip of the public notary's pen.[88] Vargas Machuca's *Exercicios de la gineta* (meaning, roughly, "Principles of Horsemanship") published by the same house in Madrid in 1600 and dedicated to the German merchant prince and banker to the Habsburgs, Alberto Fugger, was revised, expanded, and reissued twice more before Vargas Machuca's death in 1622. This pocket-sized book, aimed at peninsulars and indianos like himself (the author is called such on the title page of the 1600 edition), *Exercicios de la gineta* turns out to be far more technical than *Milicia Indiana*, and may have been composed while the author was awaiting approval for publication of that other, clearly for him, more important book.[89] Why were these military how-tos so popular?

In the most comprehensive study of early modern martial arts manuals to date, Sydney Anglo stresses the important fact that most men of any status (and not only Europeans) were at this time constantly armed with deadly weapons. It was thus urgent they know how to use them. The fact of daily armament, added to the growing popularity of the printing press and general rise in literacy, gave birth to a vast range of how-to books devoted to what Anglo calls "ritualized personal violence." Fencing, in preparation for the inevitable death duel in protection of one's honor (or the honor of slighted loved ones), was most popular. As in other aspects of war and fighting, Spaniards were for a time out front.[90]

Consider, for example, a classic work by the Spanish fencing grandmaster and contemporary of Vargas Machuca, Luis Pacheco de Narváez. Bearing the unwieldy title *Libro de las grandezas de la espada, en que se declaran muchos secretos del que compuso el Comendador Gerónimo de Carranza en el qual cada uno se podrá licionar y deprender a solas, sin tener necesidad de maestro que le enseñe*, it was published in Madrid in 1600. Although its complex mathematical formulas and geometrical illustrations are virtually inscrutable, as Anglo points out, Pacheco de Narváez appears to have written the first fencing manual for autodidacts. His inspiration and main source of "secrets" was Gerónimo Sánchez de Carranza, a towering figure in the history of fencing whose 1582 manual, *Libro que trata de la philosophía de las armas y de su destreza de la agresión y defensión christiana*, set the standard for the Spanish "mathematical" style. Although somewhat fond of high-sounding scientific talk, especially in his chapter on the earthly sphere, Vargas Machuca would probably have scoffed at such stylized forms of fighting in the context of the Indies frontier. No amount of fancy footwork could stop an Indian's dart tipped with the "twenty-four-hour herb."

Pacheco de Narváez added a chapter on horses in his next treatise, *Advertencias para la enseñanza de la filosofía y destreza de las armas, así a pie como a caballo*, and in this regard he most closely resembles Vargas Machuca's *Exercicios de la gineta*.[91] Though consciously adapted to a lighter sort of horsemanship than that practiced by the knights of yore, Vargas Machuca's sections on jousting with canes hark back to a range of Spanish works, most notably Juan Quixada de Reayo's 1548 *Doctrina del arte de la cavallería*. Spanish light cavalry, as Vargas Machuca himself noted, was a Berber inheritance, but one with the potential to revolutionize European warfare when combined with equally disciplined musketry. In writing such technical manuals, then, Vargas Machuca appears to have been very much in line with, if not ahead of, his times. What about content? Is there anything American or Indian about his treatise on horsemanship?

Aside from the similarly gushing sonnets and dedications that introduce the work and its author, *Exercicios de la gineta* resembles *Milicia Indiana* most closely at the end, where Vargas Machuca discusses the art of choosing and caring for horses. To judge from his writing, he must have been a genuinely expert horseman—he mentions in a 1590 probanza always maintaining two or three horses with arms at the ready at his house in Tunja, and we noted above his construction of a parade ground on Margarita.[92] In a typical passage, he advises the reader ("el Caballero") not to punish a spooked horse, but rather to reassure it and bring it if possible to know the thing that had scared it. He also strongly advises against spurring, giving the example of an enslaved rider in Bogotá who was sent out by his master to show off a prized animal by jumping it over an obstacle. Vargas Machuca relates the incident:

> Having received good news about a horse from a friend named Luis Gutiérrez, an alderman in that city, and having wanted to see it run for some time, one day as I was on my way to a shrine [*hermita*] outside town, I ran into him just as he was about to punish his horse, having just returned from a bad outing. I asked that it be given another run, and to please me he ordered the mulatto who was already mounted on it, an experienced horseman, to run and jump a tamped-earth wall that was off to the right. When coming back over it, from the left side, the horse bolted, approaching with such speed that I began to say "God save you, God save you." And not even halfway there the horse, with face and body distorted, leapt clean over the wall, landing with such a crash from the racing flight and the force it carried, that they went rolling and doing somersaults, horse and mulatto, mulatto and horse, such that it seemed like something from a dream. The master, seeing this great fall, turned to me extremely upset and said, "Look here, this is the fault of your mercy." And I responded, "No, it was the spur of the mulatto." And so it was, as we arrived and found on the horse's left side a great spur wound, and on the other side no mark. The horse was lame, having broken a leg, and the mulatto was almost dead. It was a miracle to find him alive, and wounded we took him to his home, where they cured him. (103–4)

Vargas Machuca of course does not wish to link this unfortunate incident to his own perennial bad luck, but rather sees in it an object lesson on excessive spurring: "The caballero must use extreme caution with the spur." Some readers may find it surprising that such a disciplinarian as Vargas Machuca would recommend, over and over, the lightest touch in dealing with horses (the conquistador as horse whisperer!). Yet in fact Vargas Machuca was very much in line with his predecessors in this regard, as likely to humanize their horses (and dogs) as they were to dehumanize their Native American enemies.[93]

There are other examples in the *Exercicios de la gineta* drawn from Vargas Machuca's personal experiences in the Indies, mostly recommending caution in the course of bull baiting ("be sure the bull is dead before turning your back to celebrate") and tilting with canes ("try not to kill bystanders, as so often happens"). In the section on veterinary care, Vargas Machuca describes in great detail the best methods for regulating a horse's humors, including bleeding to cool and applying hot bricks to warm. Cures most likely derived from Native Americans include blowing tobacco snuff into the nostrils to ease congestion and applying toasted maize-flour plasters to various types of wounds. "And lacking this wheat of the Indies, use flour from here in Spain, although I cannot assure you of a good result," he writes (111v). A few other remedies employed maize, but Vargas Machuca's core veterinary ideas basically matched those of European contemporaries.[94]

CONCLUSION

Bernarndo de Vargas Machuca was in many ways atypical of the late-arriving, frustrated Spanish conquistador in the Americas. He managed to publish several books, after all, and he was granted three administrative posts as compensation for his services. We even have a picture of him. Still, these unusual characteristics could just as easily be ascribed to quirks in Vargas Machuca's personality: he seems to have been possessed of that rare combination of egotism, single-mindedness, and boundless energy nowadays associated with populist dictators and corporate CEOs. He was rare not for his loyalty, bravery, or wide-ranging career path but rather for his exceptionally dogged persistence in the face of an imperial bureaucracy even Kafka would have had difficulty imagining. In this regard we may compare Vargas Machuca with Cortés's similarly "forgotten" contemporary, Bernal Díaz del Castillo.[95] These good and loyal soldiers who had conquered the Indies (at least in their minds) for a distant monarch were by the later sixteenth century as disillusioned as any modern war veteran. They felt used, even betrayed, and desperately hoped to set the record straight while reiterating their claims on what they regarded as proper rewards.

Both Díaz and Vargas Machuca were quick to acknowledge that fighting in the Indies was fundamentally different from fighting in Europe, yet the "Indian militia" or conquistador way of war was, they emphatically added, nothing less than the real thing. In Vargas Machuca's estimation it was *more* real, or at least more challenging, in that it was not staged in the fashion of a massive, afternoon chess game but rather resembled a treacherous 24/7 hunt in the wilderness with the Spaniard himself as prey. The only way to fight Indian "hunters" in his view was to fight—and hunt—like them. Díaz, whose experiences in the conquests of Mexico and Guatemala were distinct and less concerned with poisoned arrows and long-term guerrilla campaigns, wrote up his "corrections" using the classical trope of prose history. Others, like Juan de Castellanos, chose epic poetry.[96] Vargas Machuca was odd only in selecting a more obscure literary form, the martial arts manual, to tell his tale and drive home his main point: that even second-rate conquistadors deserved better.

Bernardo de Vargas Machuca's *Indian Militia and Description of the Indies* is a curious but in the end not quite unique artifact of its times. It makes most sense if one takes into account the context of its production: geographical, personal, literary, and historical. In the course of his various sorties into the wilds of South America, Vargas Machuca inhabited a world unimaginable to most European readers, including his king. He would try to bridge that cognitive gap in the *Indian Militia* with a wide range of detailed descriptions, several of them borrowed from other authorities. Easier to imagine, at least for some, was the author's personal journey, from the parched battlefields of Old Granada to the rain-drenched tropical ones of New Granada. Many Spaniards had an uncle, nephew, son, or husband with similar tales to tell. The format of the self-help manual was well established at this time, too, whether for strong-willed housewives or knights in training. Readers apparently enjoyed being scolded in print. Harder to grasp even in Vargas Machuca's own era, perhaps, was the shifting and ambiguous course of Spain's imperial juggernaut at the end of Philip II's reign. Where some contemporaries such as Cervantes saw irony amid the smoke and confusion and resignedly embraced it (after failing to get their own merit requests approved), Vargas Machuca and many others saw collapse and crisis and argued for massive retrenchment. Vargas Machuca went so far as to attack (although too late for a reply, of course) Spain's most important internal critic, Bartolomé de Las Casas. Whatever we may think of him, Vargas Machuca's other main point in *The Indian Militia* is an important and only recently appreciated one: not only was the conquest of the Indies far from over in 1599, it was also unlikely to end.

A NOTE ON THE TRANSLATION

In grappling with Vargas Machuca's compact yet refractory prose, translator Timothy Johnson and I found ourselves sympathizing with Borges's Pierre Menard, "author of the *Quixote*." Many an hour was spent diligently scribbling what we hoped were "the very same words as the original author," yet we had to believe that "but for the passage of time [we] found in them a meaning that was infinitely richer."

Although recently translated into Japanese, *Milicia Indiana* is no *Don Quixote*, and Vargas Machuca was no Cervantes. Yet he did have a style. What we have tried almost as desperately as Menard to do is remain faithful to the author's voice, however strained, shrill, or wooden. When Vargas Machuca strings yet another idea to an already too-long string of ideas with a comma and another *y*, we mostly try to follow suit. Only when the meaning becomes hopelessly confused have we resorted to semicolons, colons, and whole new sentences or even paragraphs.

In trying to make the translation a more perfect mirror, we have also avoided adding words or phrases we felt Vargas Machuca would not have used, even if they were common among his contemporaries. Spellings of most place names, however, have been standardized according to modern usage for ease of location. Vargas Machuca's classical references seem to have derived mostly from Plutarch's *Lives*, of which there were several Spanish versions available in his time,[97] although he also cites Plato, Thucydides, Livy, Sallust, and Cicero. On natural history, he usually cites Pliny. Vargas Machuca's knowledge of Latin appears to have been (thankfully) as sparing as our own. In these and other matters we have chosen to footnote only those references that seem unclear or equivocal, and we have tried to provide citations that can be easily followed up in popular editions of classical works. Biologists familiar with the New World tropics will no doubt be stunned and saddened by our limited knowledge of the dozens of beasts, birds, bugs, and plants that Vargas Machuca briefly describes, but we have done our best to attach Linnaean names and brief descriptions to uncommon organisms. Thus far we have been unable to confirm the existence of griffins in the jungles of Guyana or miniature cattle in New Mexico, but on these and a few other things even Vargas Machuca had doubts.

APPROVALS, DEDICATIONS, AND SONNETS

ASSESSMENT

I, Juan Gallo de Andrada, scribe of His Majesty's Chamber, of those who reside in his Council, do certify and testify, that a book entitled *The Indian Militia and Description of the Indies*, composed by Captain D. Bernardo de Vargas Machuca, having been seen by his lords who appraised each page of the said book, with five left blank, which has fifty-six pages for each of the five blank which comprise the said book, at one hundred and forty *maravedís*, to be sold on paper; and gave license so that at this price it may be sold. And they ordered that this price be placed at the beginning of the said book and it may not be sold without it. And for the record, I gave the present [declaration] in Madrid on the third of April of the year one thousand five hundred and ninety nine.

Juan Gallo de Andrada.

APPROVAL

MOST POWERFUL LORD:

By those of your Royal Council, I was ordered to see and examine a book entitled *The Indian Militia*, made by D. Bernardo de Vargas Machuca, in order to correct it where necessary. I have seen this book, along with the *Description of the Indies and Compendium of the Sphere*, noting, with all care, what it may have needed of censure and emendation, and by the much experience I have with the said militia in question and extensive knowledge of those parts and the rest contained within it, I find that it is written with great care and labor, and the efforts of this captain to put it into practice, and to abbreviate such diffuse and important material as he has done, would have been no small thing. And so it seems to me that it would serve God and Your Highness to give him license to print it, because of the great usefulness it will have for all the Indies, being such a good mirror for those in that militia to make use of, and for those in these parts as well, because of the curiosity and notable things that it contains.

D. Juan de Mendoza.

APPROVAL

I have carefully examined, by order of the lords of the Council, the discourse of *The Indian Militia*, composed by the Captain D. Bernardo de Vargas Machuca, divided into four books that contain many and varied things for the war and conquests of those kingdoms and the expansion of the Royal Crown and universal good. Some things are flawed, such as written errors of the quill; once these are removed, it seems to me that one may print and expect, by way of its advice, good results. [Signed] in Madrid on the nineteenth of October, 1597.

D. Diego Vázquez Arce.

APPROVAL

LORD

By order of Your Majesty I have seen the book entitled *The Indian Militia*, composed by the Captain D. Bernardo de Vargas Machuca, who should be thanked for what he has done in this work, having done it while attending to his aspirations in this court: and with the things that have been emended, it seems to me that it may be printed, being Your Majesty served by giving license for it. [Signed] in Madrid, 8 of August of the year 1598.

D. Antonio Ossorio.

APPROVAL

By order of the lords of the Supreme Royal Council, I, Friar Francisco de Ortega, of the Order of Saint Augustine, Visitor General and Apostolic of his order in the Philippine Islands, have seen this book entitled *The Indian Militia*, divided into four books, and *A Brief Description of the Indies* and a compendium and part of the sphere, composed by the Captain D. Bernardo de Vargas Machuca, and before I state my sentiment and opinion, by the much experience of more than forty years that I have in the Indies, I say that in that New World there are three sorts of Indians, some who have not given their obedience to Your Majesty, nor have been subjected to Spaniards, nor have been baptized, nor have come to the knowledge of God Our Lord, nor have seen the ministry of the Gospel which preaches and shows his divine law to them, and so they remain with their idolatries and infidelity, quiet and peaceful, where God created them, without leaving their land to offend or do evil to our Spaniards. There are others who, after having given their obedience to Your Majesty and to the Church, and having been baptized and converted by the preaching of the religious ministers of God, have been altered and raised up against our Spaniards, and returned to their pristine idolatries, apostatizing their faith, doing all the evil they can. The other class of Indians are those who have given neither obedience to the king our lord, nor to the church, nor have desired nor desire peace nor friendship with us Spaniards, and without our offending them or doing evil to them, they come to offend us and to do the greatest evil that they may, as are some in New Spain, which are called Chichimecas, who go in many places, divided in groups of two and three hundred and sometimes more, with their bows and arrows and other arms, and they come to rob and kill the Spaniards who go from Mexico to the mines of Zacatecas, which have the greatest abundance in New Spain, and are like the mount of Potosí in Peru; and so it is necessary to gather many Spaniards together, arming them and their horses with cotton blankets three fingers thick, so that they may trap the arrows shot by the Indians: and in other places the Indians do the same. And eight years ago they entered a monastery of my order, in a village called Chapuluacan, and they robbed it and tied a friar priest to a tree and there they shot him with arrows like St. Sebastian, and there he died a martyr. There are other Indians similar to those in the Philippines, on the island of Luzón, twenty-five leagues from the city of Manila, and in Peru and the kingdom of Chile, and in the New Kingdom of Granada and in other parts, that have done and do many and greater evils. And considering this, I say that the first class of Indians I mentioned above must be pacified and conquered by the Evangelical ministers with the arms of the Gospel and divine words, procuring with all gentleness and good works to bring them with peace and love into the union of the Church and knowledge of our true God, so that they may be saved. And if they should not wish to receive the peace and friendship asked of them and offered to them, to leave them without making war with them nor causing them any harm, that if there are some who have been predestined in the divine mind of God, He knows how and when they must be brought to his divine knowledge and service. So considering this, and that the author of this book has neither composed it nor ordered it for these Indians, but for the other two classes referred to, I say that the book has nothing against our holy faith, nor does it contradict our good customs, but rather it contains much and is a good example, curiosity, and advantage for just wars, and that the author shows himself to be a valorous soldier and experienced captain, cautious and wary with the advice and warnings he gives; and he is worthy of praise for having composed it and for how greatly he has served your Majesty in those parts; he is deserving of much grace and may the lords of the Royal Council give him this by granting license for this book to be printed and brought to light. This is my opinion and I sign it in my name in San Felipe de Madrid, on the fourteenth of December, in the year one thousand five hundred and ninety six.

Fray Francisco de Ortega.

THE KING

Inasmuch as by your part, Captain don Bernardo de Vargas Machuca, resident of the city of Santa Fe in the New Kingdom of Granada of the Western Indies, it was related to us that you had composed a book entitled *Indian Militia and Description of the Indies*, with which you had occupied much time, and the said book was of much usefulness by addressing within it enterprises of importance to our service and the welfare of the Indians native to that land; you asked and implored us to grant license and authority in order to print it and to have this privilege for thirty years or as our grace wished: Which, seen by those of our Council, inasmuch as with the said book formalities were followed according to decree, ultimately made by us over the printing of books, it was agreed that we should order to grant these our letters patent to you with said reason and we consider it good. Thus, to show grace and goodness to you, we give you license and authority so that you or the person within your power and none other, may print the said book entitled *The Indian Militia and Description of the Indies*, mentioned above, in all these kingdoms of Castile, for the time and space of ten years counted from the day of the date of this our letter, under penalty that the person or persons who, without your power, should print or sell it or cause it to be printed or sold should lose the printing that he made, along with the forms and their matrices, and incur the penalty of fifty thousand maravedís each time he should do so; of this penalty, the third part shall be for the person who should accuse him and the other third part for our Chamber and the other third part for the judge who should sentence him: wherewith every time that the said book be printed, during the time of the said ten years, you shall bring it to our Council together with the original seen by it, being each page signed and sealed to this end by Juan Gallo de Andrada, our Chamber secretary, of those who reside within it, so that it may be seen if the said printing conforms to the original, or you shall bring testimony, in public form, of how the said printing was seen and corrected by a corrector named by our mandate, and printed according to him, and that the errors printed are noted by him for each of the books printed thus, so that the price for each volume is appraised and set. And we order that the printer who should print the said book shall not print the beginning or even the first page of it, nor give more than but one book, with the original, to the author and person upon whose cost it should be printed, nor to any other, in order to make the said correction and appraisal, until the book is first and foremost corrected and appraised by those of our Council: and once completed and by no other manner, the beginning and first page shall be printed, placing this our letter and approval, appraisal, and misprints in succession, under penalty of incurring the penalties contained in the laws and decrees of these our kingdoms. And we order those of our Council and any other justices of these our kingdoms to guard and keep this our letter and that contained within. Dated in Madrid on the second day of the month of October of the year one thousand five hundred and ninety eight.

I THE KING.

By order of the king our lord,
Juan Vázquez.

THE CAPTAIN

D. Bernardo de Vargas Machuca, to Doctor Pablo de Laguna, President of the Royal Council of the Indies.

When Hernando Cortés, Marquis of Valle, famous and first commander in the Indian regions, began the Indian militia, making immortal fame of his valorous arm, he was so pursued by the enemy that he chose, as the correct recourse, to make for that great and famous Mexican lake, imitating the Egyptian king Menes when he was pressed by his hosts and sought refuge at the famous Lake Moeris, where his life was spared. As the Marquis recognized the favorable refuge, and with more admiration than that of Menes, he gained an invincible spirit, securing his labors and reaping innumerable fruits from it. Well, I consider myself to be in no less dire circumstances and danger, laid in ambush for the material in this book, the first discourse of the Indian militia, which I have composed in the time before I am ordered to take up my arms again, with Royal service my aim when unoccupied by my aspirations [of the reward for my services], after twenty-eight years that I have been employed in pacifications in the Indies, except for six that I spent on expeditions in Italy. As the work of envious detractors has always been to pursue similar labors, generally fearing their undertaking (with reason) and normally pursuing things of greater study, I am forced to follow and search for similar refuge, and throw myself into the waves of the protection of Your Lordship, a lake of greater and more assured safety than Moeris was to him of Egypt and that [lake] of Mexico was to the Marquis of Valle; for there is no doubting your favorable shelter to those who value such a generous hand, for with it I am assured new determination and spirit to face all evil intentions. I beg Your Lordship, as supreme governor of those kingdoms, to protect and favor this work, as it is produced in the service of the Royal Majesty and for the common good of those provinces, opening the path of theory to some, and to others, that of the practice required by most who govern in times of peace as well as war, for even when there is sufficient [knowledge] of some things, it is advisable to have compiled all that memory may have lost. To this cause I believe this work will be well received, principally with the protection of Your Lordship, whose valor shines with such excellence in our time.

PROLOGUE

When the totality of the power of a clock is considered with reflection, it must bring pleasure to the soul: but if it is divided into parts, taking but one piece in hand, one could hardly keep from throwing it into a corner, judging each piece alone as a useless thing. Curious reader, books bear a great similarity to this clock, in that by reading their entirety, their craft and doctrine can only bring pleasure; but if they are read in parts, one must also be forced to throw them into a corner and judge them useless. I do not expect not to be judged, nor do I wish to ask that he who would be a judge of this book spend twenty-eight years in this school, as I have done, so that the judgment may be true, or that after such experience he write and compose another, in such a calamity of three years of aspirations such as I have had. I must beg him, however, before he makes any corrections, to read the whole book, so that each part is included in its intention, for I hope to God that in its examination, each will find the complete clock and it will seem good to him: not only he who has experience in that which this book addresses, but also he who understands the theory of it. The principal reason that obligated me to write this book was to serve the Royal Majesty, encouraging that militia which is so weakened, as well as to give instruction of it to many commanders who begin conquests and pacifications in those parts without any knowledge of it, for they are the reason that so many of our Spaniards are needlessly lost. Likewise, I was obligated by my fondness for this art of the militia that I have had since the day I first drew sword, following it in Italy, and in the navies and the Indies where I began with the duty of Field Marshal; and as I became Commander General, all the expeditions and conquests I was given, which were not few, were my own account and risk. As to the manner in which I created this book, I named it *The Militia and Description of the Indies*, dividing it into four books, placing an exhortation at the beginning in order to move and illuminate its purpose, and adding the description of the Indies at the end. I was forced to do this after seeing how some books that address this encompass little and, as they are written as accounts, have many errors; and also so that those who live in these parts [*i.e.* in Spain] may understand what happens there with the same truth. Likewise, I added a brief compendium of the Sphere, as the discourse with which I address all things in the Indies required it, addressing, however, only that which was necessary, as that was not my intention; and also to encourage those who join that militia, who lack so much [knowledge] of its composition, to study it, making use of Sacrobosco[1] and other serious authors. *Fin.*

PERSUASIVE EPISTLE

from Captain Alonso de Carvajal, native of the city of Tunja, in the New Kingdom of Granada, to the wise and prudent reader.

Where the arrogant Indian
Wished to spread his empire,
Don Bernardo de Vargas y Machuca,
Exalted and martial Spaniard,
Has placed his bellicose arms upon a point so high
That no captain has ever surpassed.

With glory and triumph and fame of Castile,
Has the name of God ever been celebrated,
Forcing the indomitable Indian to yield,
With no less art than Julius Caesar,
Nor Hannibal nor Scipio nor any other warrior
Who conquered kingdoms with great renown.

May the heavens and planets that influence
Such fierce antipodes bear testimony,
That I am a true witness to this story,
That labor has been his companion,
Drawing from talent and experience,
Another military way, new and necessary.

Like Ptolemy, he gives heights to the Indies,
Courses through the sea, lands distance,
He is Aesculapius[2] with trees and herbs,
Animals and fish. Chronicler

Of rites and customs of the Indians,
Crops and mines and riches.

As the native I am of Tunja, I affirm
That this is the discipline of import
To the empire of our Catholic King.
Just as Cato was important to the Romans
To bring mines, vassals, kings, and provinces
Under his sacred scepter.

A Spaniard has been so honored,
That he has justly conquered much,
And has newly founded another Simancas,
An imitation of that in Castile,
Where his good father, Juan de Vargas,
Served as alderman with that same strength.

Whoever wishes to know how to tame
The arrogant or unyielding cacique,
What force, what valor is necessary,
What skill, what craft, what prudence,
Shall here in the most pure and precise form
Know that art and discipline.

Arms and quill take flight,
Talent and the arm have joined in league,
The wise man who should read this, feel your way,
For valor and prudence fly high,
And he who should fail this exercise in India,
Beware, for he loses the name of soldier.

DOCTOR TRONALDOS OF TOLEDO

to the author

SONNET

None such as you, illustrious Bernardo,
Shows the noble Spaniard in the southern part,
How to tear down the barbarous standard,
Either on the open field or in wild scrub.

How he shall make his squadron resound,
How he shall light it with the fury of Mars,
How shall the valor of his art aid him
If he be set upon in unequal battle?

For such high instruction, Spain owes you,
The possession of a world, by my judgment,
More than to Columbus, discovering commander,
For how much more glory is such a deed,
When it is a greater enterprise to conquer it,
Than to discover it at first sight.

PEDRO LIÑÁN DE RIAZA

to don Bernardo de Vargas.

SONNET

Expanding the limits of Spain,
Fulfilling the high augury of the *plus ultra*,
He conquers, writes, and takes with his steel,
Strength and command over the heathen rebel.
    The barbarous disorder disentangling,
The first who knew how and could subdue,

Warrior Caesar and Ulysses inform and advise
His prudent exercise.
  Don Bernardo de Vargas, fame and glory
Of Spain, in the remote antipode,
Rare deed; he has done so much, I tell you.
May the future age honor his memory,
May the present age prevail with its vote,
And they shall have war and peace, prize and punishment.

CAPTAIN DON LUIS BRAVO DE ACUÑA

to don Bernardo de Vargas Machuca

SONNET

The name of the Latin so praiseworthy,
From the frigid zone to the torrid,
Whose power the most remote people felt,
Subject to the miserable yoke.
  The incomparable strength and valor,
Of the Macedonian astonishment of the Orient,
The most brave and excellent captain,
Worthy of eternal and everlasting fame.
  If by talent and skill you were not aided,
Famous Vargas, you would have never gained,
That which you won on your own.
For you clearly show in your rare story,
To all the world, the method and manner
With which one must defeat those you defeated.

THE CAPTAIN AND SERGEANT MAJOR LÁZARO LUIS IRANZO

to the Author.

SONNET

He brought light to the colorless region,
With fierce Mars, with Minerva and Apollo
Don Bernardo de Vargas, for only to him
Was granted the authority of heaven.
    Nature was made better,
And one pole made envious of the other,
Neptune, Jupiter, and Aeolus made happy,
That they allowed passage and gave strength in the campaign.
    His labor arrived at the point of desire,
Those barbarous Indians he humbled
For Philip the Second, with no second:
Because of him, fame raised up a trophy,
That above the Antarctic is fixed,
And they call him sun of the new world.

THE DOCTOR FRANCISCO DE LA TORRE ESCOBAR

Native of Santa Fe, of the New Kingdom of Granada, to the Captain don Bernardo de Vargas Machuca.

SONNET

The Spaniard who found the new land,
Over wide sea and great misfortune,
Took pleasure in the gold that the hard ground
Encloses hidden within its bowels.

And if the opinion of the people be not mistaken,
Exalting the pure faith of Christ,
The spoils assure he was victorious
[In] the most uncertain and difficult war.
   Only thee, to whom went the greatest portion
Of this immortal triumph, proof hast thou made
That this treasure was thy plunder,
Here thou givest us the art of conquering,
Virtue which in a noble, honored breast
Is valued more than silver and gold.

THE DOCTOR CIPRIANO DE LA CUEVA MONTESDOCA

to don Bernardo de Vargas.

SONNET

If the celestial order that inclines itself
Towards thee with blessed influence be not mistaken,
The new arms of the Indian war
Shall be a rare design of immortal valor.
   The envious earth has not consumed
The ashes of the Phoenix that produced thee,
That if to the yoke of Faith the Moors reduced,
Thou [shall reduce the] barbarians the new orb encloses.
   Pure blood returns to its authors,
And this, with living example ignites the breast
That attempts deeds so lofty in its virtue:
May the victorious and wise hand emend,
Errors of sword and quill and their praises,
Of themselves both celebrated and at fault.

THE DOCTOR GONZALO MATEO DE BERRÍO

to don Bernardo de Vargas Machuca

SONNET

So as not to leave without prize the holy zeal
With which Cortés, spurning gold,
Gave to the Sacred Choir so many courtesans,[3]
And such lofty flight to the royal eagle,

The just heavens did not reveal in his time
The great treasure of thy militia
To which it would give immortal reverence
With which his fame increased throughout the land.

Likewise Bernardo, to him who dares,
And to him who mixes advice with the sword,
Thou art a guide in that which is prudent and that which is bold.
And thy book owes thee another militia,
Which, with breastplate and helmet,
Is armed for thee against envy and time.

D. JUAN DE TASSIS Y PERALTA

to don Bernardo de Vargas.

SONNET

Glory and honor of the Indian West,
Prudent and brave knight,
Valorous in the battles of Mars,
And eloquent in the acts of Pallas.

Fortunate are you, whose invincible brow
Bears the blossom of the victorious wreath,
Owed in court to the famous writer,
As to the valiant general on campaign.

And more fortunate is the Spanish empire,
For your rare valor and arm so skillfully hold
In military art and glory,
That which is necessary in the Antarctic hemisphere
To imitate the blows of his lance,
Obeying his style as master.

FROM CAPTAIN HERNANDO DE MENA

SONNET

Achilles parts from Greece to Troy,
Ulysses from Troy to our Spain,
Homer celebrates each deed,
Neptune makes one and fierce Mars the other.

Bernardo, with labor, strength, and art
Travels over most of the orb
Bypassing no mountain, plying the seas,
Running the campaign; a Golden Age, at last.

Enduring drowning torrents,
Eating herbs, only fighting,
With many cruel, fierce, and enemy people.
And in this book proves and writes
How the Indians must be conquered,
And what is to be esteemed, he tells us.

BOOK ONE
OF THE INDIAN
Militia Which Addresses The Qualities Of Which A Good Commander Must Be Composed

EXHORTATION

THE DIVISION OF THE CELESTIAL and elemental orbs and their composition are well-known things among all classes of people, and particularly among those upon whom God wished to bestow reasonable talent and discourse. The earthly machine, being considered, will have been found divided by its zones, parallels, meridians, major and minor circles, and horizons. And the people who inhabit this machine each have their corresponding antipode, *anteco* and *pirieco*, *piriseo* and *anfiseo*,[1] each with its corresponding influence, quality, and location according to its distance from the Arctic and Antarctic poles and from the equinoctial line. And the seas and abundant rivers, kingdoms, provinces, cities, towns, and villages will likewise have been considered; the mountain ranges and level plains; the hot valley, the temperate midland, the cold highland; the number of peoples; the natural, divine, and human laws; the sects, rites, and ceremonies; and of the persons, their factions, colors, statures, moods, understandings, and inclinations; the attire, customs, and nature of arms; and in the seas and rivers, the magnitude and variety of fish, almost with the same division as the land, distributed in their different places according to their classes, which cause the artifice of fishing them to vary. With these considerations, I think, should any good republican classify and examine, having knowledge of any and all things, in order to govern his republic with courtesy and proper order; making watchful care commonplace in it; for it is not with mere decrees that kingdoms, cities, and smaller towns are governed even though they should serve the army under a law both divine and human; for these are similar in part, but not entirely. And so we see that for each republic the laws are adapted; for poorly one governs Seville with the laws of Madrid, or Burgos with those of Bilbao, or a village with those of a populous city. And so the prince should govern his lands differentiating the royal decrees, adapting his motives and qualities. It would be, then, advisable for the prince, like his governors, to have experience and knowledge of them, generally and specifically, wherever they keep and govern kingdoms and provinces, expanding them more each day, without too much labor. And therefore, as all things differ according to their causes, it is thought that wars as well should have different modes and practices, as diverse as the lands, the peoples, the spirits, and the arms with which they fight according to their invention.

Romans And so we know that in their ancient wars, the Romans made use of crossbows, javelins and bucklers, shields and cabassets; as well as cuirasses, vambraces, and greaves,[2] bows and slings, and their squadrons were arranged according to similar arms.

Greeks The Greeks used pikes and certain arms of the Romans.

French The French when mounted on horseback used arrows, while those on foot used bucklers and rapiers; in the attack they issued great shrieks and yells.

Africans The Africans made use of camels, as the Orientals used elephants, upon which they constructed strongholds, and used projectile weapons.

Spaniards Our Spaniards used great wagons of fire and projectile weapons; and those now used commonly in parts of the Levant and in our Spain, which are the pike, halberd, and the sword invented by the Swiss [i.e., the baselard, or pikeman's shortsword], as well as harquebuses and corselets.³ The pikemen and the men at arms bore armor and thrusting lances; the horsemen bore lance and leather shield [*adarga*]; they use heavy artillery and precise musketry [*mosquetería*], advantageous weapons; and in the forts they use walls and trenches; and to explode them with fire the enemy makes mines and those inside defend themselves by making their countermines.

In parts of the Indies they used crossbows, coats of mail, cuirasses, and a few harquebuses, as well as bucklers at first. Nowadays, however, with long experience and recognizing the best and most useful arms, they use hackbuts, hauberks made of cotton,[4] broadswords,[5] poleyns and helmets of cotton, and bucklers; and those on horseback use lances and in some parts coats of mail, and buff coats[6] and mesh visors. Some use trumpets. These arms, both on foot and horseback, are adapted to the fury and arms of the Indian, to the ruggedness or flatness of the land, to the heat or cold, and according to the devices with which the Indian fights. And thus they divide and arrange their people and camp (as will be stated later), striving to move with the movement of the Indian; for he changes so much that from one valley to another, and within ten leagues of latitude or longitude, they discover a new manner of arms. Therefore, it is advisable that our Spaniards adapt as well, and often the aid of dogs is taken advantage of, having found how important they are for defense and sentry duty in the army camps and for discovering ambushes.[7] Not all of these arms are used in one kingdom, but rather as the lands require. In New Spain some will be employed, but not all. Likewise in Peru and the New Kingdom of Granada; and even within each of these kingdoms, their provinces differ. However, as now is not the time to examine this, I pass succinctly in order to address the Indians and their inventions of arms.

Arms used in the Indies by Spaniards

The Indians, historically as well as in our time, have used and still use lances up to thirty spans long and made of palm wood, the tips burnt, and in hardness no different from a bone. Others use iron weapons won and traded for from our Spaniards, a thing most worthy of exemplary punishment as it is almost a sort of treason, for even though they are traded to peaceful Indians with healthy intentions, harquebuses have passed into the hands of their enemies, with which they have taken many lives of our own (a thing to be looked into and prevented, and

Arms of the Indians

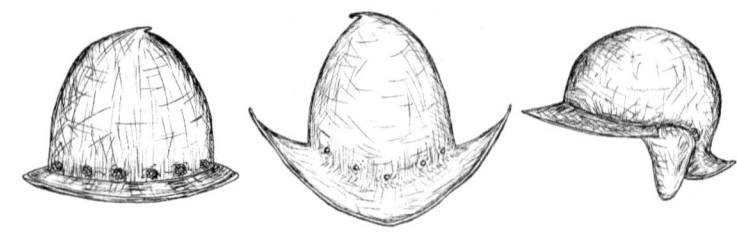

14–16
Cabasset helmet.
Morion helmet.
Helmet with visor,
or celada.
Drawing by Kris Lane

punished by the governors). They also use cudgels of palm wood like two-handed or bastard swords, wielding them with two hands. They use arrows tipped with flint and ray quills, which are quite venomous, and others with palm tips coated with twenty-four-hour venom.[8] Javelins and shields, helmets and corselets of bull hide (these are used only by those of Chile). Other Indians use the blowgun with poison darts; others, spears and dart throwers, quills, spikes, pits, traps, stones, and false bridges. They also use slings, a damaging weapon, and often lay ambushes. They attack with great shouts and shrieks.

Indian manners in war   Some wear their hair long and untied, like women, others wear it braided, others, cut and shaved. These latter are the best warriors, for they escape when they come into the hands of the Spaniards, who make prisoners of them; and since they have no hair and are naked, they slip away with no manner to lay hold of them by hand. Every nation makes use of some of these weapons according to their application and the lay of the land.

The Indians paint themselves to go to war   They go out to their wars naked, the face and body highly painted to appear more ferocious. They paint themselves with *vija*, which is the color of henna, and others with *jagua*, an ink made of fruit, which does not come off for nine days.[9]

Jewels of the Indians— The Indians' use of animal tails   The most important of them wear varied feather-work and laden with jewels of gold in their manner, such as nose plates [*caracuries*] in the nostrils, chest plates [*chagualas*], ear pieces, half moons, and bracelets and beads. They wear the paws of lions and tigers on the head, and from around the waist hang the tails of these animals.

They use instruments to raise their spirits, such as shells, flutes [*fotutos*], drums, and horns. And in the mountains, to gather and warn

*17–20
Halberd.
Harquebus.
Steel sword.
Pike.
Drawing by
Kris Lane*

each other from afar and to call to arms, they use great drums played with sticks.

They are people who, if they begin to flee in the course of their wars and battles, are routed with ease, with no hope of being able to turn about and re-form, regroup, or become stronger. *Flight of the Indians*

The world has no better warriors than these who pursue the victory once recognized, for they may pursue a target three or four days without eating or resting, sustaining themselves only by the coca they chew.[10] *Victorious Indians*

All of their fights are founded upon betrayals, except when they enter into a *guazabara*, which our Castilian calls "battle." Confident in the strength of their people and in the appropriateness of the site, they will enter the open field, having scouted and prepared an escape. They are similarly guarded in their ambushes and assaults, for without this precaution they are not a people who take risks unless the case and *Indian precautions when entering a fight*

BOOK ONE OF THE INDIAN MILITIA

21
*Caribbean cacique,
ca. 1586.
Courtesy Pierpont
Morgan Library*

occasion require it, whether on the clear savanna or in the high, craggy mountain.

Agile Indians They are agile because of the habits and customs they have, and thus may catch a deer with their strength of spirit, and there is no dog quicker nor more unhindered in the chase, be it in the scrublands of the high plains, the marshes, or the thick forest, that better follows the trail of people who have passed, even if it is eight days old, along roads, paths, or streams of water. They keep their dwellings very much like warriors; those who pursue war have them in the hills, divided by families; each family has its recognized head, although they respect him very little.

When they must meet or give some warning, this is understood by way of the aforementioned drums. And when the distance is great, such that the echo of the drums will not reach, they make smoke in such a manner that a messenger could hardly make the idea better understood. The watchtowers of the coast of Spain send word in a similar way; others have them in lakes in a thousand various ways. And the conquests of the people who live in this manner have lasted and will last (as experience has shown) some years longer, as we will later address, than those who have been and are found united as a republic; they have been and are conquered with ease.

Manner of warning Indians in war

They are all a leaderless and disorderly people, with neither a sense of merit nor valor, and thus, if they find themselves imprisoned, they let themselves die miserably in two days. And if there have been any notably valiant ones who have demonstrated strength amid their misfortunes, there have been and are but a very few, such as that Araucano told of by Alonso de Ercilla[11] who, before and after having his hands cut off by us Spaniards, promised great harm (telling them with great opprobrium) if they left him with life, as it so happened—something the commander should avoid, leaving without limbs he who does not directly deserve death, but to the deserved, give it with the law in hand; and to him who should be released, oblige him to friendship with good deeds, for he whose strength is cut from his hands will multiply it in his tongue—that being seen so wounded, anyone well knows how to persuade and move those of their band to courage and pity, as was well seen in this case of the effect he made with only his tongue; that with his speeches and exhortations he gained for that nation so many victories and renown, so much to our ruin and damage. There have been other valiant ones, but they have been few and unpersuasive, and following their false religion they are taken by a barbarous rage. And if that famous Lautaro demonstrated discourse and valor with such memorable deeds, it can be attributed to the time he spent among our Spaniards serving us; and among such a great number of people, not many are found, such as I have encountered during my conquests and expeditions.

Valor of an Indian— Persuasion of an Indian

BOOK ONE OF THE INDIAN MILITIA

THE INDIES WERE INTRACTABLE
BEFORE OUR SPANIARDS

Returning to our purpose, I say that there being such a difference between us, in arms as well as other things, that we will be forced to have in those parts a different praxis [*prática*] and militia, and differently will our Spaniards comport themselves with this people who after God created the world had no communication with parts North,[12] or, that is to say, returned to them over so great a distance from one part to another. And [I add] that the Indies are all one island in whose body are embraced Peru, the New Kingdom of Granada, Brazil, Tierra Firme, and New Spain, and also Florida and New Mexico, lands that were always savage until our Spaniards tread upon and discovered them.

The Indian uses only his invention of arms

If it is true that the apostles came to preach the Holy Gospel (as I believe, and we have found signs of that, although there is no scripture divine or human where one can prove that the apostles went to the Western Indies, but piously one may believe),[13] they would not have shown them devices of arms or methods and training of war, but rather addressed only those things of our holy faith. And so it remains proven that they are defended only by their inventions of arms and instinct, and that our Spaniards also will have adapted to the same land and to that which its nature demands, and for this purpose they will have made new discourse and new practices, setting aside those of Italy for the most part, not for lacking them (for among such a number of people one would well believe that there passed soldiers who were able to practice them), but as they are not completely advisable for use against those [Indian] nations in their conquests, they are not addressed.

Until now there has been no discourse on the Indian Militia—Because of the lack of knowledge and training on the part of the commander or governor, problems remain

It is good that when some Spaniards confront other enemy nations on the coasts,[14] they take any advantage (and not because some precepts cease to apply, as this example will reveal), but the thing is that after the Indies were discovered, none have wanted to nor have made discourse or school of this [style of warfare], though it is of such great importance and not less worthy of being known than any other. [This discourse] is the Pole Star for the soldier, the captain, and the gover-

22

A Caribbean warrior demonstrates the macana, *or war-club, ca. 1586.*
Courtesy Pierpont Morgan Library

nor, as he who governs without experience and training must govern by theory and knowledge of things, even if they are not present, so that he may resolve matters with alacrity and certitude. Those who have written [about this] have only addressed the conquests, the deeds and the famous captains and soldiers, the qualities, lands, and locations, without revealing the method and practice of the militias our Spaniards have formed there, which now results in many poor choices with troublesome results, and yields many who lack all training and theory; and it is like sending many blind men instead of two who might have some sight, so that when these finally open their eyes, they have lost the opportunity that one cannot take hold of with one's face averted.

In the Indian Militia the prince does not assume the cost—In the Italian Militia duty is distributed

So then, we know that there is no government today in all of the Indies that does not participate in wars and pacifications, and if not all, most of them, and with proper care a million problems will be avoided as long as they know the [war's] cause in order to choose [correctly]; and some will manage to serve their king and lord and he will honor his most deserving commanders and settlers with respectable awards. For in this militia the prince does not assume the cost, because the captain or commander who takes the opportunity gathers the people and sustains and pays them, and supplies all that is necessary, providing arms and munitions, without the intervention of royal paymasters; for when the time for work and danger arrives, it is always him first, and hunger always passes first through the house of the good commander before sleep and rest. The soldier has a defined time for work; the commander never, for during the time that is left after work he is vigilant over the health of his camp, for all depends on him. In the militia of Italy the work is distributed among the general, the field marshal, the sergeant major and his assistant, and between the captains, their lieutenants and sergeants and squadron officers, and other ordinary and extraordinary officers.

In the Indian militia all the duty rests upon the commander

But in the Indies, everything is under the charge of the commander, although it is true he names some officials; but this is mere formality [*propter formam*], for he governs, punishes and composes and measures; distributes his people like a sergeant; and, above all, pays them. He is also, at times, doctor and surgeon, and is the first to help carry the sick or wounded, taking on the office of father, and sometimes it happens that he removes his shoes and goes barefooted on the road in order to shoe the soldier and remedy a greater need than his. Well, I would like to know what prize is owed to the commander who attends to so much? And much more than this example will reveal, since it is with great faith and love of serving his king that he waits for a just reward; [it is] he [the monarch] who has leave to grant it or not, as no salary is spent on it, something the captain or soldier of Italy could not do unless provided by the pay they have received or by other emergency measures, and so at times they serve more by force than willingly, of which I am a witness by having seen and considered it closely, that that militia has cost me my years. So if they lack their payment, we know that a mutiny is engendered and the camp is altered, such that you may not be able to verify who acted as instigator and agitator.

And if we were to consider this against the profit that the Indian militia brings us and what is owed to it, we find that year after year many millions in coin, silver, and gold enter our Spain through the mouth of [the Guadalquivir River at] Sanlúcar [de Barrameda], and this wealth is a result of the labors of her people and of the valor of her swords; for this has been and is the beginning of everything. These conquerors who have acquired so much wealth to adorn our land, her sons and heirs, what will we say comes of them? They will tell me that they all die, and I will acknowledge that it is true. Yet none will deny that most do not even die in the hospitals.[15] And since nowadays they do not die in them, they die in their poverty, a right piteous thing and worthy of remedy. For whoever went to win the land would surely govern it as well as any other, and even better according to his training, commitment, and knowledge of the law, without favoring new people naked of all merit in those parts.

Wealth of the Indies

If they were to tell me that they [i.e., Indies veterans] lack talent, I would have to confess that perhaps some lack it, but not all; and he that should lack it to govern would not lack it to eat of the favors that his king would provide him for his or his ancestors' service. Great evils have resulted from some governors not taking this into consideration, and the prince does not suffer the blame; for so Christian-like has he arranged and ordered everything, yet many governors cause him harm by lacking knowledge of things, and thus they are easily deceived and persuaded by pleas and favors, or they are moved by other particular ends, taking from the deserving and giving to the servant or favorite, to the merchant friend or to another official; and by this the worthy are angered. If only they would consider that they are going against royal decrees and the damage that could result, they would not do it, nor would the conquerors be discouraged, for we all know how important it is to our Spain that they not miss the regular arrival of wealth from the Indies, and it is such that if the fleet were missing for one year, Spain would be afflicted not only in a particular way, but in general.[16] And come what may, more is needed to sustain so many ongoing

Those who take the prize from the worthy, wound.—Spain is troubled if it lacks the tribute from the Indies

*23
Royal Hospital of
Simancas, built late
sixteenth century.
Photo by Kris Lane*

wars; and one could hope for this growth, rewarding the settlers and encouraging them so they might discover new peoples to better serve Our Lord God.

THE QUALITIES A COMMANDER IN THE INDIAN MILITIA MUST POSSESS— AND ALL THOSE OF WHICH HE SHOULD BE COMPOSED

In order to expand the monarchies, conquests have been necessary.—The kings of Spain took fortune away from the Romans.—It is right that the commander keeps what he settles.—The judgment of the commander must be according to the good qualities he possesses

In order to extend and amplify monarchies, discoveries and conquests have been necessary. For it is because of them that monarchies have been expanded and princes have become powerful and gained esteem and renown; and their vassals have become noble and with their valor states have grown, leaving perpetual memory, and this benefit has been common to all republics. Now, in order to enjoy this bounty, it was necessary that the princes were suitable, and in those parts that managed to have them, this good luck was enjoyed all the longer, for the prince is he who casts the die and makes the good soldier, and who instills true resolve and engenders good subjects. Those who have most shown this were the Romans, for they had the wheel of fortune fixed for long years, until the Catholic Kings of Spain darkened and tore down their name from the summit where they stood, by their government and sword, taking from their hands the fortune they held so hard, taking it for themselves, spreading wide the wings of fame for their famous deeds, such that never was seen a monarchy that spread them so far, embracing all parts and the most remote regions, in such a manner that four thousand leagues from our Spain the Holy Gospel is received, and her flags and standards are waving. And the cause has been the great and valiant princes we have had and do have, having produced great and famous commanders and captains who in their conquests and settlements have shown great strength, which they should hold and conserve in those places that are settled as well as in those that will later be settled. And they should not abandon, due to negligence and carelessness, that which has cost so much (as we have already seen something of the sort in parts of the Indies), and so that this may not happen, it is good that they elect the governors with care, as well as the commanders, finding them suitable in the most possible ways, without deference or other obligations, for it is a great pity to see what happens now in those places because of this, as will be addressed later. Opportunity, time, and the service of God and king are lost by lack of fair election.

Our commander must be composed of these qualities: first, a good Christian, noble, wealthy, generous, of good age, strong, diligent, prudent, affable, and determined. Other qualities that stem from these I should like to declare, for he who should join or address this militia observes that the commander must be happy, discreet, cautious, resourceful, and honest.

Qualities of a commander

The commander possessing all these qualities should know that it is a special gift of God and may securely pursue conquests and settlements, and he who is chosen with more of these qualities will produce greater effects, not he who is naked of them. The Greeks and Romans observed well this mode of election according to qualities.

The commander who has the most qualities will produce better results.—Election of the Greeks and Romans

HOW OUR COMMANDER SHOULD BE A GOOD CHRISTIAN

The commander should be a good Christian.—Nothing raises the spirit like being right with God.—Advice of Plato

The leaf in the tree moves not but by the will of God, and if He is with us, who will be against us? Thus, there may be no good thing where there is no fear of God, nor may there be victory but what God gives, for only He gives it and He may take it, allow it and hinder it, and only to Him should one turn. And what thing is there that may raise the spirit of a commander but turning to His divine providence, placing all his thoughts and works in His hands so that the effects thereof are favored, as Plato advised us, in grave cases as in the easy ones? For in all things, and particularly in cases of war, a happy end follows a good beginning.

The preparation of David

David never went to war without knowing first if he went according to divine will.

Constantine carried the cross as his standard.—Victories of the Theodosians by prayer—When Joshua fought, Aaron and Moses prayed.—Before the commander goes to war, he makes his sacrifices.—The commander brings a priest

When Constantine went forth, he carried the cross as his standard. The ancients affirm that the victories of the Theodosians[17] came about more from their prayers than from their armies. And when Joshua fought, Aaron and Moses prayed. And so it is seen that turning to God produces good effects; and so that God receives the one who turns to Him, the commander should, above all things, and before leaving for his conquests, perform the duties of a Christian, with sacrifices and prayers. And so that this may continue over the course of his expedition, for him as well as for his soldiers, it is necessary to take priests with them, with the reverence we will discuss in its time, so that they may be cleansed of their sins and bring the grace of God. This greatly inspires and gives them hope of victory and they go forth certain of it.

Religion of the Romans

The Romans had religion as a principal article of their government and did not permit it to be violated; and they never addressed things of the Republic or war but by first procuring the grace of their gods and giving them thanks for the benefits received.

The commander should avoid swearing

So that the sacrifices and prayers that the commander makes to God are better accepted, he should avoid swearing by His holy name, for, according to St. Augustine, of all things, one must keep from swearing, for by doing this from time to time it then becomes a habit and as such gravely offends the majesty of God.[18] And so the commander should refrain from it, and also as an example to the soldiers, for it is true that they must imitate the head in good or in evil, unless [the soldier] is someone virtuous whom evil does not corrupt, or [whose will] is not defeated by the communication of his commander.

Swearing is so abominable that Socrates permitted the captain or the soldier to swear but in two cases: when they were forced to free themselves from some evil suspicion received in their dishonor, or to free a friend from some danger. And to this I say it must be swearing the truth, and there has been much reform among old soldiers, so that now it is only done by those with little experience in war.

Permission of Socrates in the oath

In the same way it is important that the commander does not have illicit relations, nor permit any soldier to do so, for in addition to being harmful to the soul, it is for the health, due to the poor quality of the land, as we will state later in detail. Procure to avoid the harm that often presents itself on such excursions, and most importantly, observe the divine cult and veneration of the priests, and thus all will be well.

The commander should not have illicit relations

Pompey the Great showed this well after having won Jerusalem: when the High Priest (now dressed as Pontiff) went to him, he did not refuse to worship him. [Instead, he acted] like many other ancients, who carefully observed the religion of their false gods. With all the more reason are Christian commanders obligated to observe their own [religion] and hope for victories even more famous, with more prosperous outcomes, placing the object of their desire in the hands of God, from whom comes true redemption and happiness.

Example of Pompey— Submitting all to God has a good outcome

HOW IMPORTANT IT IS THAT OUR COMMANDER IS NOBLE

Now that we have said how important it is that our commander is a good Christian in order to have great success, it will be good to say how important it is that he also has nobility, for after being a good

Nobility is very important to the commander

Christian, this quality is also very important, more so in the Indian militia than in any other.

The militia is held in low esteem.—Virtue is its own reward

Though it is true that the militia ennobles the one who comes from low lineage, exercising arms in the service of his king and loyally serving him, this most sublime and honored of all arts is in disfavor these days. There is hardly a citizen now who does not laugh at him who joins the militia and not only laughs but deems him lacking in judgment. But they are mistaken, for when there is no other prize than that which imparts its own virtue to him who joins it, it is good to join and serve his king and lord.

Nobility is more important in a commander than wealth.—Little respect is the cause of destruction

Returning to the purpose, I say, that in order to command and govern, it is good that the commander comes from nobility, for he will come to use it often, for there is nothing that has destroyed a campaign more than dissent engendered by the little respect given to [militia] commanders. This arises, on most occasions, from the low condition for which they are known; and this nobility is more important for the service of the prince than the commander being a man of means. Evil and harm have been avoided because of respect for a commander.

Rarely does the prize match the meritorious.—Governors choose without consideration

It would be much better to have both [wealth and nobility], but the occasions when this happens are rare due to the small rewards one gains nowadays from the governors who distribute them. In executing the royal will, they have the obligation of distributing prizes among those deserving, conquerors and their sons, but they, in order to evade this obligation, sometimes choose low persons to elevate from their trades and vain earnings and grant them the title of captain, which is like the wings of the ant that are grown only to be lost. And worst of all is that they are lost and cause so many to be lost, and the royal service is forfeited.

The presumption of soldiers of the Indies

This is why it is said that in the Indies there are many soldiers but few heads [*cabezas*], and they say the truth; and it is a great shame that noble and experienced people are not directly chosen, for there are many. But lacking either one or the other [i.e., noble or experienced people] is bad, for one cannot hope for success, but rather much harm, born of the presumption by soldiers in that [Indian] militia that anyone can be trusted and given the responsibility of the government of the Indies and of giving their vote. And so it is that in this militia they all have it.

And when the opportunity presents itself for the soldier to say what he feels, it should be allowed, sometimes because of the advantage that results from it and sometimes because of duty, the commander doing what seems best. Such liberty requires the respect of nobility, for without this one cannot take advantage of the respect of love nor of fear; it would be a pane of glass that breaks at the first knock. And apart from giving deserved respect to this nobility, one can expect the commander to follow the values of his ancestors; just as one seeks good breeding in a dog and the same in a horse, all the more carefully should one search for these qualities in a commander. For we know that clear thought engenders high spirits and high spirits, valor, which never shies from adversity nor retreats from what he once attempted honorably, until he sees the end and achieves it with honor by the valor passed on from his parents. This nobility is accompanied by virtues, for it does not only consist of being high born.

The commander takes advice and makes the best choice.—Clear thought engenders high spirits

Plato said there were four types of nobility: one inherited from just and good ancestors; another from powerful, princely parents; another born of fame and opinion of deeds done in war; and the other acquired by greatness of spirit, with the help of none but virtue.

The maxim of Plato

Marius bragged about this and often said: "My nobility is new, which I value more having engendered it, instead of being corrupted by receiving it from another."

Boasting of Marius—Nobility created is more esteemed than that received from one's ancestors

Virtue and nobility correspond, for many ancients have been judged to be descendants of gods simply by their virtue; thus was born the opinion that Theseus was the son of Neptune, Romulus of Mars, and Alexander of Jupiter. If this nobility that our commander should have is accompanied by virtue, it is certain that it will never be out of place.

Theseus, Romulus, and Alexander were taken for gods.—Nobility accompanied by virtue will never be out of place

HOW IMPORTANT IT IS THAT OUR COMMANDER IS WEALTHY

Wealth is useful for all things

Wealth is a gift used for as many things as may offer themselves to a man, to spend it as he likes, for one attains glory knowing how to utilize wealth. If a man is rich, he is powerful, discreet, beloved, revered, and served; if he has enemies, he subjugates them; if he commits crimes, he is freed; if he wishes to be a mediator, he reconciles everything with ease; and if he knows how to distribute it with discretion, the whole republic is his.

Because of wealth Hernando Cortés conquered Pánfilo de Narváez.—Because of wealth great kingdoms are discovered, and are conquered for it

And in effect wealth levels all, for the strong castle and the most experienced infantry surrender to it. In our times, Hernando Cortés vanquished Pánfilo de Narváez with it.[19] For it the soldier labors, as do those of the other estates, below and above. So many lives are risked and sustain themselves over so many and varied paths because of it. One crosses the sea and the equinoctial line for it. We have gone to find our *anfiseos* and *antecos* and antipodes for it.[20] And with it entails estates are established, and new estates reached, and condition and nobility are gained through marriages. And because of wealth, today we see our Spain so surrounded by enemies.

The commander uses his property and wealth to sustain the militia

And finally, because of wealth we have seen and will see many victories and great conquests and discoveries of great empires that were hidden from us, as is seen each day, by commanders who, with royal powers, have thus occupied themselves, wishing to show themselves serving their king and embarking on campaigns of great risk, labor, and expense, spending their wealth with the help of no one. For, as has been said, it is he who gathers the people, the arms, pay and sustenance, and because of this it is important to be wealthy.

Wealth of Croesus— Lacking the means to sustain the militia, it collapses

I do not say one must have the wealth of Croesus, just sufficient means, for to gather soldiers in those parts where things are so costly there is a need of it. For apart from supplying them with all that is necessary, untangling them from debts (which they never lack), he provides each one with what is needed for horse and saddle, sword, blankets, sandals, and cloth with which they make clothing for the campaign; arms, harquebuses and bucklers, black powder, lead, and match[21] and the provisions with which they will sustain themselves according to the time the campaign will last. For until they have settled and the land, once distributed, has given benefit to the soldiers, the commander must provide everything for them, in such a manner that if anything is lacking, this edifice crumbles away until all is on the ground.

In addition to this he must sustain regular, salaried priests and their vestments and regularly bestow upon the Indians gifts, presents, and rewards in order to incline them toward trade and friendship with the Spaniards. In like manner, it is necessary to always have medicines on hand to cure the sick, and all types of implements, for carpentry as well as other necessities; and neither should the expense of introducing livestock be forgotten, as required by royal decree.[22]

With gifts are the Indians swayed to trade with the Christians

Oh! Poor commander (for so I would call you even if you were rich), for after risking your life and perhaps your soul as a matter of course, your risk, your work, and your spending do not move the governor (sleeping in his soft bed, eating when he wishes and in complete safety, multiplying his wealth as quick as he may) to have mercy upon you or favor you with anything, without, for his personal ends, sending his servant or lackey, or grocer, or merchant, or some other of higher or lower quality, to remove your sweat, going against royal decree, evading such by three or four thousand leagues of water.

The commander, though he may be wealthy, always becomes poor.—The governors reward the conquerors poorly.—They favor the unworthy over the worthy

May God remedy all—and give us another Peasant of the Danube[23]— so that by kneeling at the royal feet we may have spirit and language with which to describe the great evil that happens in this manner; and so that every point be remedied, ordering the encomiendas and positions to be given and distributed to those deserving, according to royal writ and according to their qualifications, for though it is so ordered, they are neither observed nor kept.

The king gives reward

And returning to my proposition, I say that it is necessary for the commander to be sufficiently wealthy for all these expenses and so that the soldiers follow him. And by following him they should have great success, which, with prudence, should cover the expense in such

The commander should spend and withhold

a manner that he, after having worked at a loss (as is often the case), is left with enough to find a piece of bread to eat when he goes out, and enough to go before his prince and ask for his just rewards.

HOW IMPORTANT IT IS THAT OUR COMMANDER IS GENEROUS WITH HIS SOLDIERS

Wealth should be distributed according to what Aristotle said.— One should know how to use generosity

Since we have seen how important wealth is to our commander in order for him to provide for his campaigns, it would be good to examine whether this wealth alone will be effective or if it is necessary to accompany it with another quality, generosity, in order to use it well. And indeed it is necessary, because of what experience has shown us, in that militia more than in any other. For wealth without generosity would be like a body without a soul, avoiding the extremes of avarice and prodigality, according to Aristotle's conclusions, noting the way one gives. And this must be done in such a manner that what is given does not harm the receiver, nor does one take from one to give to another, or offend by measuring another's means and strengths, [always] considering the person and quality of him to whom it is given, having respect for the merits of each one. It [i.e., a reward] must be given when deserved and not out of ostentation or to gain fame as one generous, as one would be taken instead for a blind and foolish prodigal.

The opinion of Agesilaus[24]

And by distributing his wealth with such care, the commander will have justly fulfilled his obligations and name as one generous with his people. As Agesilaus said, "Enriching his camp more than himself is the charge of the good captain." For the commander in those parts, it is more natural to give than to receive.

The maxim of Alexander the Great

Alexander the Great was once asked where he had his treasures, and he replied, "In my friends." And if they had asked me this when I was commander I would have said, "In my soldiers," for with this answer the commander encourages his people and wins them over, and each one tries to satisfy his generosity and spirit; and he will often have all the camp devoted to him.

This generosity should not be used sparingly, but rather as a matter of course, and in all sackings and settlements one must maintain the same responsibility and moderation, not desiring to possess entirely his share nor count it out; and if he should receive it, it should be with a demonstration that it is held in deposit so that it may be used to relieve the needs of his soldiers who deserve it; for he who gives to the deserving, in giving, receives.

He who gives to the deserving, in giving, receives

Vespatian showed this well. Flee also from being greedy, for among soldiers this is a most loathsome quality; one cannot expect a greedy man to do what a brave man would. As Sallust says, it weakens him and his body, and it is a worm that takes hold in his bowels and is the cause of all evils. And so it has been in the treatment of the Indians, for because of [Spanish] greed they have been obliged to rebel, killing a great number of people, sustaining war for many long years, thus sentencing to death many soldiers, all this born of a chaotic greed that kept them from using generosity with the Indians. There is no command more urgent, as if we had trusted some goods to them; and it could be said that he who desires all, loses all, as we have seen in the havoc wreaked by the Indians because of it; such that our greed is the principal foundation for rebellion, and the thirst we have for silver and gold is such that it has been poured melted into the mouths of the Christians on occasion, telling them to get their fill of gold, as happened to Valdivia and to other captains.²⁵ And so I say that the commander should be generous and not greedy, using this generosity with as much caution with the surrendered and vanquished Indian as with the victor, so that all may be protected.

The opinion of Sallust—Because of the greed of the Spaniards, the Indians have rebelled.—He who desires all, loses all.—The Indians have made some Spaniards to drink melted gold

HOW IMPORTANT IT IS THAT OUR COMMANDER IS OF GOOD AGE IN ORDER TO BEAR THE COMMON RESPONSIBILITIES

For all that has been said thus far the work to which the commander of the Indian militia is subjected will have been recognized as one that requires a comfortable age in order to carry out the insufferable labors that pass day and night, with no resting point. In order to prove this,

The commander needs to be of good age

there is no necessity of examples or authority, for everyone has it to consider, requiring a competent age, enough to be neither very young nor very old, for to the young respect is lost, and to the old, strength. And in order that he is of appropriate age, such a commander will be between thirty and fifty years of age, for these twenty years are for service and may be passed and welcomed by him in good account, for having fewer, he would lack the experience to make decisions, and having more, he would lack the fortitude for success. In the Italian militia, it is not important if one has more years, but in this one, where one must work with bodily strength, it is most important that one is not older than the above-stated age.

Duties and risks of the commander To make this more evident, I would like to examine closely that to which the commander is subjected: and so I say that he must be of an age to walk night and day through the ravine, mud, and mountain range in winter and in summer, where the sun offends, the land being under the equinoctial line [i.e., the celestial equator] and [within] the tropics; and through this great heat, laden with arms, suffering a tempest or downpour, which are very common in those parts, arriving wet to the mighty river, where it is necessary to swim across because of the currents, helping to pass his people and baggage across, as will be told later. What occurs from this is a chill or a cold or other sicknesses, for the night offered to them is also laborious, tired and wet, with no protection whatsoever. Speaking of the calamities that occur on such a campaign, they are many, such as: constant marching, night and day, stumbling in one part and falling headlong into another; receiving a wound and walking on with it so as to not lose any opportunity; constantly sleeping clothed and shod and armed during the entire campaign; and on one foot like a crane, keeping the dawn watch every night, which he cannot avoid, for at this hour the enemy is always near. And if the commander neglects his watch, a great misfortune can be expected. Apart from this, he is the first to work, making the fort, opening the path into the jungle,[26] making the bridge and boat in the river to be able to cross, for doing so encourages his people. Thirst and hunger also afflict him, and being an honorable commander he must experience these as much as the least of the soldiers, being the cause of infinite deaths as will be said later. He is also troubled by the mosquito

24
"*The lizards that hang from the churches*," Seville Cathedral. Photo by Kris Lane

day and night, and the sudden sting of the wasp, which exist in those jungles in droves, and other vermin, such as ticks and worms that grow in the flesh; ants whose bite causes a fever lasting twenty-four hours. Arriving at the settlement of the Indians there are fleas and chiggers that cause many to lose their feet, for they burrow into the flesh like a spit and they grow bigger than lentils, and one is freed from this evil only by their careful removing and by washing oneself.[27]

There is also the risk of serpents called rattlesnakes, like vipers in our Spain, of which there are many in those parts; they are most dangerous, for whomever is bitten lasts but twenty-four hours. And in the rivers there is the risk of caimans, which are [like] the lizards that hang from the churches.[28] Also, in the ravines and rivers that are crossed, there is no lack of thorns that pass through the foot, and these are so venomous that there is no pain more acute. Also, after this, the risk of the [Indian] trap, of the spike, of the thorn, and of the stone when one proceeds unwarily. And particularly the venom with which they rub their arrows and other arms, which is so bad that by drawing one drop of blood, causes a raging death.

Sustenance in times of hunger   And if they [i.e., militiamen] are routed and lose, there is the work of carrying one another because of sickness or wounds, and carrying all the clothing and arms because of a lack of horses or beasts of burden, eating the snake, the dog, the monkey, the parrot, and other worse vermin, and if this were all it took to get to the promised land, it might not be so bad to go through, but sometimes they lack favorable weather. As it [the land] is often largely uninhabited for two hundred or three hundred leagues, more or less, many people die of hunger along the way, going with less and less spirit, that in such times there is neither friend nor brother worth anything. For all these burdens it is necessary that the commander be of the stated age, and that he plead with God that with it [i.e., his age and experience] he may bear them and arrive at his salvation.

HOW IMPORTANT IT IS TO HAVE FORTITUDE FOR DUTY AND CALAMITIES

Without interior strength, the exterior is not sufficient   I wish to reduce fortitude into two parts, which are strength in the exterior and in the interior, so that our commander may better know how to make use of them, accompanying one part with the other, for as we say that wealth without generosity in a commander is like a body without a soul, so would be exterior force without interior force; for no labor would reach its end without it, being crippled beforehand. Interior force is the guide of exterior force in this militia, for the labors involved are great and excessive; therefore he must be gifted with this quality of fortitude in order for all to end well.

Strength of Columbus   Columbus showed exterior strength as he navigated on his voyage of discovery; but if he had lacked that force of spirit with which he assured his people amid such torment and peril, from the sea as well as from malevolence, all would have been lost without doubt. And thus when they were not lost, by turning back they could have lost, by chance, the New World, given to us by his interior force of spirit.

Strength of Hernando Cortés   Hernando Cortés, Marquis of Valle, showed this as well, scuttling the ships and sinking them, placing hope only in victory, like a strong man.[29] Well do we know that he did not have sufficient forces for such a great number of peoples [i.e., the Aztec-Mexica and other foes], and if he had only possessed exterior strength, lacking interior strength, he would have returned and lost the empire, so great and so rich, that he won by strength of spirit, as can be seen in his story.

The deeds done by Francisco Pizarro in Peru were also due to the persistence of interior strength, until he reached the desired end, giving us such innumerable riches.

Strength of Francisco Pizarro

When don Gonzalo Jiménez de Quesada discovered the New Kingdom of Granada, what was it that placed such a distinguished and wealthy kingdom in his hands? Interior fortitude, for although with exterior strength he broke through so much forest undergrowth and suffered innumerable labors, at the end, force of spirit fed this strength in such a manner that he never lost heart amid such adversities and deaths of many of his soldiers from hunger, with the lengthy navigation of rivers and path finding. Thus, when he entered the Kingdom [i.e., the highland region surrounding the Sabana de Bogotá], finding himself among such a great number of people, being so many that our men called them flies,[30] and he having taken so few, only a surplus of fortitude of spirit displaced the small force he brought with him.

Strength of don Gonzalo Jiménez de Quesada—A surplus of spirit displaces a lack of corporal strength

It is necessary that these two strengths or qualities go together, for they correspond. But if our commander were to lack one, the most advisable would be to lack corporal strength, for in the end, without it, one can still succeed with the spirit, which is interior force, because with this one eliminates all cowardice, both for the attack and in awaiting unknown events, breaking through all difficulties and labors; and if to corporal strength we do not add this other part we call interior strength, what has been said will occur.

Spirit drives away cowardice

It has happened to me, having taken giants of great strength on my conquests, that whoever lacked interior fortitude surrendered to labor, wounds, hunger, and even the enemy. And so that this does not happen, one should be a strong man in order to bear labor and hunger and other necessities, and with this expect victory and secure the camp with patience.

Work defeats him who lacks spirit

Valor of Caius Marius   Caius Marius patiently bore Pompey's long siege.³¹

Strength of Alexander   And Alexander, in the Cimmerian war,³² where he fought alone against them with strength of spirit and mortally wounded, did not falter, for as his blood flowed out, his strength grew in order to seek the one who had wounded him to kill him, which he did; and so will our commander do in all such battles.

HOW IMPORTANT DILIGENCE WILL BE TO OUR COMMANDER

Diligence is the mother of good fortune   Diligence is the mother of good fortune and the commander who makes use of it will enjoy success and he who is negligent will have misfortune, for the soldier will be no more diligent than his captain.

Saying of Alexander   Alexander was asked how he had conquered so much in such a short time; he responded, "Accomplishing today all I could, leaving nothing for tomorrow." Thus was the dictum of this great prince, valorous and wise.

Diligence is necessary in the Indian Militia more than in any other   And if any militia has the highest grade of perfection in this matter of diligence, it is the Indian one, for he who is careless will die or lose, without any doubt.

The great care of Alexander   In other wars one might forego success and fail to achieve an objective and still keep one's life, but in this one, all will be lost [without diligence]. Alexander, it is said, slept with a ball of iron in his hand and with his arm out of the bed, and underneath, a brass basin, in order to wake up by the noise if the ball should fall.

The Indians are like nocturnal birds.— Diligence of the Indians in times of war   The quality of the Indians is like nocturnal birds, who travel all night without resting a bit even when they carry arms in their hands, and in this respect there is no nation in the world who can defeat them, nor, can I say, equal them, for their commander walks on air [*anda en el aire*] when he prepares for the things of war; he neither eats, nor stops, nor sleeps; and his soldiers even surpass him, for among them was never refused any command from their cacique and captain, nor were any orders to work and take a risk, for the first to come upon it occupies himself with it. They are such that, if a sentry is placed, he is left for two days and nights and in all this time does not sleep, obeying, standing or sitting, chewing a leaf of the tree called coca and by its other name, *hayo*, lacking nothing in his barbarous way. And this should not seem an exaggeration, for there are many who have seen it. They are a people who walk in the dark of night, with thunder and lightning, in order to warn their neighbors and prevent affairs of war, bothered neither by the ruggedness nor the undergrowth of the land, nor the long road, the great flood, the mighty river, nor thirst, hunger, fatigue, or work, breaking through everything, passing everywhere, counting our steps, always keeping us in sight, day and night, noting the carelessness into which we fall.

There being, then, on the part of the Indian, this diligence and caution, which will stop the commander who should sleep or be negligent, the health of his camp is charged to him alone, and if he should be careless, there is no one else to correct him. And if he lacks assistance when there is need of it in difficult times, and if at some time he is defeated and regroups poorly, all his people are at risk; for the Indians are people who know well how to chase victory, and they reach it with neither hindrance nor weariness, and all is born of the diligence and spirit they have; in this they seem gifted and chosen. I believe that their diligence should make their opponents diligent, and so it seems to me that the commander is obligated to be diligent in order to have success, corresponding to the enemy. In addition, in all wars the captain must be like thunder in the preparation, and in the execution, like a lightning bolt.

The risk he who is careless runs.—The diligence of the Indian is great

Asking Marcus Cato how he had conquered a Spanish city, a seemingly incredulous thing given the speediness of its surrender, he responded, "Making a journey of four days in only two," in which was shown his diligence.

The diligence of Marcus Cato

In his poetry, Homer called Achilles light of foot not because he was a runner or jumper, but because of his great diligence and promptness in commencing and finishing a duty.

Consideration of Homer

The Indians are surprising — Our commander should be the same with all opportunities offered to him in this militia, for the natives are surprising in their actions, as will be stated later.

HOW IMPORTANT IT IS TO OUR COMMANDER TO BE PRUDENT

Prudence is the key to everything — In addition to those parts that we have already applied to him, no less a necessity has our commander than that of being prudent on all occasions offered to him during his expeditions, for although it is true that one rarely finds a man so perfect that he is gifted with all these qualities, experience shows us some who, by lacking some of these parts, did not have good success.

Maxim of Boethius — Others have been seen who, although lacking these qualities, have succeeded in their attempts, for as Boethius says, there is no mortal without sin, nor has there been any famous man who has not had some fault noted of him; they are even found in natural things. My aim is to choose a commander for the militia in question composed of the aforementioned qualities, as well as others yet to be offered; such that when he is not found so perfect, he at least will be found, if one searches, to have some of the appropriate qualities, and that what he lacks will not be notably harmful; and if on the contrary he is selected [i.e., the perfect commander], it will be great luck to hit the mark. So I say that our commander must be prudent in that which he desires to attempt, looking first at the difficulty, and what may happen, and if his enterprise will go well, for no less than his own life and those of his whole camp depend on it.

Prudence is the key to the other qualities — Prudence is the key to all the qualities we apply to him and is most excellent among them; it is like the sun among the planets, by means of which their light and influence is communicated to us. Cicero says, "It is the principal virtue."

He who repairs the small evil, does not see it become large.—Secure the acquired — And so, with prudence he will repair the little evils, in order not to see them become great and harmful. And with it also he will see how to take charge of important enterprises, and how much time each one needs, without overburdening himself with too many, and securing right away each undertaking, conquest, and acquisition; for to do otherwise would pull the edifice to the ground.

With prudence he will take the advice of his most skilled and experienced soldiers, not delaying the execution of the work, for if it is detained one bit, the opportunity will be lost; for foresight must go paired with action, and it follows that in the execution one must be as a lightning bolt. With prudence he will put his heart into work and danger, for if he flees he will be surrounded by a million dangers, and they will land him in too great a predicament.

Take advice without delaying the work

With prudence he will put his heart into any disturbance and will avoid showing partiality, either toward one group or another, for this would engender a mutiny in the air that would give birth to an uprising, causing the loss of him and of everyone.

The commander does not show partiality

With prudence he trusts no one, for even the closest friend wounds if he is offended for some thing, as has been seen in those parts in uprisings and deaths that have happened.[33] With it, he avoids entrusting a deed to one who would have manifestly contradicted him.

None trust the reconciled friend

With it he will watch how peace is secured and he will not be obligated to yield his arms from his hands.

Peace is no assurance to lay down arms.

With it he will know how to obey time and also take advantage of it.

Prudence is knowing time

With it he will know how to gather his people and choose them, as it is not an undertaking that one can do twice; for in those parts, fifty soldiers who care to keep a friend and weaken the enemy are more valuable than two hundred.

He who knows how to gather people will have made many from a few

With it he will know how to march without making war in peaceful lands.

And with it he will know how to affirm peace in the land of war and, in its time, settle it and divide it without offending anyone, conserving both republics. He who founds with prudence, secures what he gains.

He who founds [colonies] with prudence, secures his deed

Disturb the enemy and discipline the friend.—He who knows how to enjoy triumph forces the enemy.—The prudent is preferred to the robust

With it he will calm the friend, working and disciplining his people without letting them become sheepish and weak. With it he will trouble the enemy by knowing how to enjoy triumph and victory; and on the other hand, win over the vanquished with good deeds. With it he will be shielded from all adversity, as Thucydides[34] says; the prudent man is to be preferred to the robust, for with strength he prepares for present affairs and those yet to come.

Experience is sufficient to create skill

With prudence he will know how to take advantage of the experience of others, and also build upon his own with that which he should newly discover. As Aristotle says, prudence alone is sufficient to gain expertise [*hacer arte*] and knowledge of universal things.

OF THE CONSIDERATION IT WILL BE THAT OUR COMMANDER IS AFFABLE

A commander, being affable, endures.—Affability is found in lords.—Poor upbringing is found in the low-born

It is also of great importance that our commander and captain is pleasant with his soldiers, for a man has no better thing in him than to be affable and well-mannered for his conservation, with which he captures the hearts of everyone. And those who have good understanding and discretion should use it at all times. This is seen more in the great princes and lords than in the low-born, in whom we find arrogance, poor upbringing, conceit, pomposity, and vanity when they are granted some honorific post, whereupon they never execute their intentions well, nor make a good name for themselves. And if they have some fault, though it may have disappeared many years before, they refresh and discover it, for which they lose respect, and because of this they lose fathers and grandfathers.[35]

The father should show the son how to be well bred

One of the most important things that a father should impress upon his son is to show him good upbringing and affability, for I think that it is a step to winning people over and rising always to a higher position and dignity and conserving what one has. And if all varieties of peoples are obligated to this, all the more should our commander be, especially in those parts [i.e., the Indies] where the soldier thinks himself as good or better than him, and where the limits and jurisdiction of justice are still unknown because the land is so new. And it follows from this that each one earns the respect he sets out to claim. And if such a commander were not to have these mentioned talents, he would not make good soldiers of his men though he may recruit many; for we know that in the Indian militia, the soldier is not obligated to join any campaign, for there is no soldier, no matter how miserable, who does not have at his disposal a horse and saddle, a garment and blanket on which to sleep, and someone to give him food. And if such a commander finds soldiers that follow him, he will win their love and friendship because of his affability.

Pliny says that in order for enterprises to have profitable outcomes, this quality is necessary, and although it is true that commanders spend much money preparing themselves and in preparations for their expedition, they do not spend anything compared to what they would spend were they alone to pay their people, as they do in Italy.

Pliny says that for great success, a man must be affable

And though it is true that one soldier in the Indies is paid more than ten in Italy, considering the expenses and cost of living of these lands, he earns less. It remains proven that one hundred soldiers in those parts cost more than one thousand in Italy, and even with this they are not entirely paid; for where and how could a commander cover this expense, helped not even by the royal coffer, nor with recompense for his expenses? And so whatever is lacking in the payment should be surpassed with good treatment and affability, so that he is followed with love and gains fruits and does not waste his time and expense.

What the soldier lacks in pay should be surpassed in his treatment

We know that Marcus Cato treated his people so graciously that he ate and drank with them to win their hearts, doing this particularly with those of his galley. By not following this path, as we have seen, many uprisings have been engendered, many camps routed, and many opportunities lost. And when there is none of this [graciousness], once the land is settled and established, it often happens that enemies bring him down; thus we have seen them cause a thousand deaths of valiant captains along with the toppling of others from their deserved positions.

Example of Marcus Cato—Uprisings and other harm have befallen some for lack of courtesy

BOOK ONE OF THE INDIAN MILITIA

Enemies broke apart the Columbus brothers.— Affability shone brightly in Hernando Cortés

As an example of this, it will be sufficient to bring to mind those valiant Columbus brothers who, because of their inductive reason [*discurso*] and valor, discovered another New World, so enlightening and enriching our Spain; though they performed such notable services and governed with the title of viceroy, there were enough enemies to destroy them, and if they had been loved they would have survived, as did the good Marquis of Valle, Hernando Cortés, whose camp always had love for him. And to prove this, what happened to Pánfilo de Narváez is enough; it [i.e., Cortés's victory] was caused by the love his soldiers had for him and the great fame he had abroad for his affability.

Alexander the Great was affable with his soldiers

Of Alexander the Great it is said that while seated before a fire, a soldier of his passed by, penetrated by cold, and seeing him, Alexander called to him and bade him to sit in his own chair to warm himself and said to him, "If you were from Persia it would cost you your life, but being Macedonian it is permitted." Suitable words from such a prince. I know that the famous captain has a need for strength of spirit, for prudence in his enterprises, for severity in command, for good fortune in his deeds, and for theory and praxis [*ciencia y prática*] in the militia, in addition to the other qualities related to them, as has been said and will be said later. But in order for these parts and qualities to each have their unoccupied seat and be safe from the jealous tooth, one should send forth the safe conduct of love, born of good upbringing and courtesy, for with these two things it later takes very little to sustain oneself in healthy peace.

The love his soldiers had for the Marquis of Pescara

So the commander of the Indian militia, directed by our objective, will be careful to win his soldiers over with deeds and words, for after such innumerable labors that pass, what prize is left to them but to beg for some part of the great misfortune they have suffered? It takes little to honor his people, and with this they will respect him, and this is what most makes the soldier fight beside his commander until death, as was seen in Pavia, in the time of the imprisonment of King Francis, how much some soldiers fought out of the love they had for the Marquis of Pescara.[36] One in particular showed this who, having been wounded two times and having retreated and wanting to die, asked that they summon the Marquis in order to ask his pardon for being absent in such circumstances. Such love as this would the commanders in the

Indian militia cultivate in their soldiers and with all the more reason, for we know that they neither go nor are followed to war out of special interest; it is not even considered.

HOW IMPORTANT IT IS THAT OUR COMMANDER IS DETERMINED

Fortune favors the bold. Julius Caesar used to say that great and dangerous things should be undertaken without too much consideration of the difficulties offered within them, for they produce glory and renown, which is the reward for the labor. But I would like to think that those are the things that, lacking all remedy, should be left to fortune, betting all the rest on valor and spirit without showing any kind of fear. *Saying of Julius Caesar*

Many captains with determination, together with prudence and good order, had victories over great but poorly organized armies with but a few people. *Victory is won with prudence and good order*

When Alexander the Great attacked such a great number of people in Asia, small was the number he took with him. *The attack of Alexander the Great*

Commanders in the Indies should make great use of determination, for they will find themselves in difficulty at every step. As a barbarous people, there is nothing that cows the Indian more than seeing good determination, though the people are few and their numbers quite unequal. They seem to naturally respect the Spaniards; and we have seen that, for the most part, the more one has made use of determination, the better his attacks have fared. *Determination cows the Indian*

The Indians lack prudence and strength of spirit, the two pillars upon which war rests; they govern only with bodily strength and appetite, and these both have limits. *Indians lack prudence and spirit*

One could easily call to mind examples of many valorous and determined commanders who have gained victories, with but a few soldiers, from such a great number of Indians that there were five hundred to one; but I will mention only some that one cannot forget, such as when *The victory of Francisco Pizarro*

Francisco Pizarro, at Cajamarca, waited for the battle that Atahualpa gave him, from whom he won the victory and did so with such few people.³⁷

Victory of Hernando Cortés

And Hernando Cortés, with fewer than a thousand infantrymen, vanquished such a great empire as New Spain, all because of determination.

Victory of don Gonzalo Jiménez

Don Gonzalo Jiménez de Quesada, with 170 Spaniards, conquered the New Kingdom of Granada. Our commanders are advised that determination is very important for the Indian militia, that without it they will not gain celebrated victories or profitable outcomes, but instead will place their campaigns in danger.

THE REMAINING PARTS TO BE ATTRIBUTED TO OUR COMMANDER, BEING ADVISABLE TO THE MILITIA IN QUESTION, WE WILL STATE BRIEFLY

Fortune is very important

Though it is true that he has been given those advisable qualities so that his discoveries and campaigns are successful in every way, as we have stated in previous chapters, it occurred to me to apply the remaining qualities to him, which, in my opinion, are necessary, such as being happy, discreet, cautious, ingenious, and honest. These qualities are as advantageous as one could imagine for the organization of his enterprises, and so it is that our commander has need of them; and particularly having the good fortune [*dicha*] to proceed with what he would attempt, for without it there is no affair that has an end or perfect finish, but rather one weak and frustrating.

A commander doing his duty is not unworthy because of misfortune

And though it is true that one should not have a commander unlucky in his dealings, undertaking them with determination and the other qualities that should accompany it, in order to have fortunate outcomes, neither skill nor experience show him; although he who has more qualities would be closer to hitting his mark and gaining renown as a fortunate man. And when he lacks this, he is not unworthy of being called a good commander, but it is of some consideration that he should be fortunate, for by being so, the soldiers fear no storm, nor retreat from any encounter. It appears to them that their commander has fortune by the hand, which is like a happy doctor having gained renown in the republic: the sick rise from the bed by the faith they have in him, that which he applies being perfect health. And so should one consider this circumstance when choosing him, by the many advantages it brings in its wake.

Caesar said that good fortune is necessary in all things, and more so in encounters between enemies, the events in war being so variable that however great a squadron may be, it cannot be assured victory. And thus he who with only the favor of virtue seeks to achieve his desired ends, must do so entirely at his own cost and risk; that much and more than the profit gained in the victory. However, helped by good fortune or luck, he will abundantly fulfill his desires. *Opinion of Caesar*

The Romans deeply venerated Fortune, adored as a goddess, by building many and varied temples to her. And they esteemed and honored the fortunate captain with great attention, so much was his fortune important to them. *The Romans made temples to Fortune*

Pompey, aided by fortune, conquered innumerable and great armies with little damage to his own men. *Fortune of Pompey*

This good luck and fortune was always known of Julius Caesar, and he himself boasted of it, as he did in Brindisi while riding out a storm. Caesar noticed the boatman was afraid and said to him, "Fear not, for the luck of Caesar goes with you." *Fortune of Julius Caesar*

This good fortune comes from heaven, and God gives it to whomever serves him in his undertakings, sometimes by the virtue of the captain, sometimes by that of the republic, sometimes by that of the prince. They are his secret judgments. *Good fortune comes from heaven*

Whoever would consider Hernando Cortés, in such dire straits in New Spain, would find him fortunate that Pánfilo de Narváez arrived in time, with whom he re-formed his camp. And in the arrival of *Saying of Hernando Cortés* the Tlascaltecas,[38] who favored his side; God assisted him these two ways.

Fortune of don Gonzalo Jiménez One would also consider the good fortune of don Gonzalo Jiménez de Quesada, finding him fortunate when he discovered the New Kingdom of Granada by following the Carare River on his right hand, opening the way to the kingdom; that although he found Indians, they came out peacefully, being domestic [i.e., sedentary farming] people, and they took him in and gave of their sustenance; and if he had happened to travel with the river on his left hand it would have been impossible for anyone to escape, because of the difficulty of the terrain as well as the great abundance of warlike Indians and the twenty-four-hour herb venom that they use. This was fortune sent from heaven; and all the other incidents in those parts go primarily accompanied by good fortune more than strength of reason [*fuerza de ciencia*].

When a commander is chosen, one should consider the fortune he has And this part is of consideration when choosing the commander who would carry out difficult conquests, for his good fortune will promise to give them a successful conclusion.

Secrecy never caused harm.—Opinion of St. Augustine Secrecy is of great advantage to the captain in order for the thing attempted to be free of problems or hindrances along the way toward its expected execution; and thus, one should reveal an important secret to no one, unless forced to do so. As St. Augustine says, "A secret known by more than one can be considered divulged." And our commander in those parts and conquests should live with great caution not to manifest what he may have in his heart, not only because he would risk his person and attendants, but all the people in his camp.[39]

The esteem in which the Romans held secrecy The Romans, on one of their flags, displayed a Minotaur in a labyrinth, meaning that the secrets of the captains must be as guarded as the secret of the labyrinth. This quality, in affairs of war as well as in those of peace, is very important as it facilitates the execution of the designs and the control of the venture; things revealed cause great accidents and difficulties. But if the commander is not so experienced as to resolve and execute [his secret plan] alone, he must communicate it only to another person of his condition, for the secret cannot last long among many.

Tiberius Caesar took pride in nothing so much as being discreet. [During Charles V's Italian Wars,] Naples rebelled while Don Alfonso, the Duke of Calabria, was in Lombardy, because of the punishment they thought he would carry out upon his return. If this secret had not been revealed, it would not have been known in Naples nor would the rebellion have happened. And whoever does not guard a secret gives arms to the enemy, with which he kills and offends.

Tiberius prided himself on secrecy.—Rebellion in Naples

No less advisable is it to our commander to be cautious, which greatly animates the soldier, for it appears to him that the enemy will not reach him and the chances he takes are more certain, being neither precipitate nor hasty, badly risking the lives of his men. Caution weakens the enemy and forces him to consideration and friendship, and thus, the tricks the commander would use in his battles and encounters should be done with caution. He also has need of it to retain his soldiers in such great undertakings and dangers; and with it he receives peace from his rival, for peace has always been given cautiously. He would do well to understand it and countermine it to avoid the damage the enemy can cause. The commander must watch cautiously, marching with his camp along the river as well as other places of danger, strengthening himself, laying his ambushes and guarding himself from those of others; and if they [i.e., enemy Indians] come into his hands, he must skirmish, or give battle, improving his position.

Our commander will be cautious

Though our commander could be partly exempt from being inventive, due to the little construction this militia has to do making fortifications for castles, mines, or countermines, and other machines of war [*máquinas de fuego*], he still has the need to be so, for there is always an opportunity to cultivate his ingenuity and have need of it. Since the Indies are lands of so many and different powerful rivers, from time to time he may have the need to make as yet unimagined rafts and bridges, as well as the boat and canoe, where many times he will find himself without materials; and with his skill and resourcefulness, he will fabricate them in order to supply those necessary things which seem humanly impossible to do without, as we will later see. Apart from this, a million things will be presented to him along the paths where he would proceed, making forts in which to gather and resist the enemy and his fury, as the first impulse is great.

The commander will be ingenious

The commander will be honest   An advisable thing it is to be honest in all his dealings and discussions, for one must be an example to all his soldiers, avoiding dishonest and idle conversations, which is one thing that truly destroys authority and respect, for nothing else is more quickly lost on the soldier. And thus he should separate himself from being dishonest, especially in illicit relations, for, apart from being harmful to the soul, the body walks in great danger and all he touches will fall apart, for he who walks in mortal sin is certain to fail, and the soldier will lose all respect for him, causing everything to have a terrible end.

BOOK TWO
OF THE INDIAN
Militia Which Advises As To The Manner Of Making Soldiers And Preparing Priests, Medicines, Arms, Munitions, Tools And Stores

PREPARATION FOR MAKING SOLDIERS

NO STONEWORK BUILDING in the world has been made nor attempted today without addressing, before the edifice is begun, which mortar will be best and most appropriate so that it may last, consulting with the architects. And afterward, those who created the work throw themselves into it with a determined spirit, certain of success with their construction. I would first like to consider that the prince has made a wise choice, as is necessary for his royal service, laying the foundations for this militia and purposefully choosing a governor and captain general. He likewise has known how to choose the proper captain and commander, so that the edifice and machine addressed in this militia does not fall to the ground; for if this choice is off the mark, precepts and warnings will be of no use, and I will have tired myself out. For although theory may be sufficient to make a selection, the captain general and his commander, who must knead the dough between their hands, must rely on the weight of experience. Assuming then that this is clear, I say that our commander, before raising the flag and beating the drum, should consider the allies he has most appropriate to his intention, with whom he will address his enterprise with some care until he has discovered the depths of their hearts and they have pledged their assistance in the expedition. Each one plays a part in stretching the net and raising the spirits of his friends such that when the flag is hoisted, the people are almost gathered in secret, for someone has given a good name to the expedition, selecting his officials from among the most diligent, who are named according to what needs to be done and the demands of the occasion.

Officers for the conquest — If it is an expedition to conquer a new area and the governor and captain general are backing it, its lieutenant general and field marshal, captains, and sergeant major, second lieutenant and field constable will be named; and the number of captains will be such that fifty soldiers correspond to each, as sufficient a number in this militia as two hundred are in that of Italy.

Expert and seasoned people are necessary.—Greenhorn soldiers are a risk — If it is an expedition aimed at relief, punishment, pacification, or rebuilding, its commander will be named, who will in turn name his lieutenant and sergeant and gather the necessary people with care and, if possible, all should be skilled and expert, for it would be a great inconvenience for the soldier as well as the commander to take newly arrived Spaniards, for as they are not made for the climate of the land, nor for its foods, they become ill and die, and with this the commander loses what he has done and is ruined. But those who are first subjected to the climate of the land can, with the discipline and schooling of a good commander, easily and in a short time become good soldiers.

Syphilitic people should not be admitted into this militia — One should take care not to take sickly and obviously syphilitic people, because of the many rivers and swamps there, and the need to walk almost always wet. Skilled though they may be, they will be of no use.

Age of the soldier — Also be aware not to take soldiers more than fifty years old or less than fifteen, the work being unbearable.

Fat men are of no use — One must keep from receiving fat and clumsy men, for they are of no use for walking and sustaining the labor.

Avoid agitated soldiers, for it will be more important to the commander to enter his expedition with ten fewer, rather than take into his camp one who stirs it up and incites, for men such as these cause an uprising or mutiny just when he thinks all is secure, unless he is forced to receive someone like this because he [i.e., the agitated one] has a few good soldiers attached to him, as often happens; but by various means and artifices the commander may do away with him and win over and capture those who relied upon him; that these same are happy to see him thrown out and dismissed at a time when he could cause no damage, disturbing quiet spirits. With this foresight will one avoid mutinies in his camp and he will avoid hanging anyone, as it is a great misfortune for a commander in those parts to need to do this, because of the harm that results from it, as we will speak of later. He must [likewise] avoid taking cowardly people into his camp because of the damage that results. The valorous captains have always held valor in higher esteem than the throng.

One should not receive the agitated soldier

Alexander the Great subdued the entire Orient with 30,000 infantrymen and 4,000 horses.

Alexander the Great subdued the Orient with very few people

Hannibal, crossing into Italy, dismissed 7,000 Spaniards for having sensed in them some fear, judging that by taking them they would sooner harm than be advantageous.

Hannibal dismissed useless soldiers

Giovanni di Medici, with the soldiers he always chose, greatly distinguished the Italian militia.

Giovanni di Medici selected ordinary soldiers

I also advise our commander to avoid taking women for the service of his soldiers, unless they are going to settle, for in all other occasions it is a great bother and intolerable labor is spent on the road with them, apart from the commotion of the camp and the sickness caused to the soldier; for where there is no health there is no strength. They are also a great nuisance when marching, causing very worthy projects to be abandoned; and as an example of this and to oblige the soldier not to take one, one must start with oneself, persuading the soldiers of it because of the risk they knowingly run, by the frailty of the women, and because of their inability to sustain the work. Apart from this,

Women should not be taken on the expeditions

they are the cause of disturbances and deaths, as has been seen already many times.[1]

PREPARATION OF PRIESTS

Priests must be venerated

We have already stated the care that our commander must have in selecting and preparing his people, and now it would be good that we address the necessity of taking a priest with him for the health and good success of his expedition and the consolation of his camp. He should be of good age, in order to endure any misfortune and labor, and above all he should be virtuous and a good example. And it seems to me that friars [i.e., members of the regular orders such as Franciscans] are most suitable, although concerning this one must proceed according to the devotion of each [priest], prepared with vestments and the other things of the divine cult. And such a priest will carry, if going to settle, the title of magistrate, in order to take possession of the churches and rural parishes being made and who, as priest and vicar, would administer the sacraments and know of the crimes over which he would have jurisdiction. The commander will take particular care to hold him in all reverence, and the soldiers should do likewise and show respect. By demonstrating this in all public acts, the commander will be an example for all to imitate, and for he who does not follow, the punishment will be just. But I see this respect so lost among many commanders who join this militia that they treat their priests as if they were ordinary soldiers, overruling them on very light occasions, as if they had jurisdiction over them and as if they were soldiers. And though they appear as such by being participants in the labors [of the expedition], they should not be counted thus, for they are mediators between God and man and restorers of souls. If one reveres him who cures the body, how much more care is owed to him who cures the soul, whom God calls his Christs. One commander, whose name is not important here, kept this poorly on one expedition, marching with his people in search of some land, and discovered that the friar chaplain he took along had tried to incite some soldiers to mutiny in order to escape with them to a peaceful land. The commander captured him and made him kneel at the foot of a tree and, placing rope around his throat and a garrote, ordered that they turn it to choke him. There was none who wished or dared to commit such a deed. And while this was happening, the good friar, with many tears, asked and implored him to look and consider that he was a priest, that if what he were charged of were true, he should pardon and forgive and not take his life so roughly and suddenly. And though the commander showed himself very severe and cruel, the persuasions of the people of his camp softened him, and he freed the friar; and in a few days our friar, with license from the same commander, left the land.

On the day this happened, say his soldiers, such a strange thing occurred that it is considered to be a miracle. While they camped beside a brook, which had water in abundance, it ran dry in such a manner that not one soldier was able to find a way to drink, an occurrence that filled all with fright. Oh! Secret judgment of God, who in this way wished to show that He was offended by what had been committed, promising future punishment if the sinner did not fill it back up with his tears and return the waters to their stream with contrition! Oh! Greatness of God, to some You give water from within a flint-stone and from the jawbone of an animal; but from others You hide it and divert it from its own veins and natural course. It seems to me that one could not have hoped for anything in that expedition to end well. *Miracle*

Oh! Good Marquis of Valle, how well you knew to please God, from whose hand you received reward in this world and in the other, according to our faith; and well your surname of Cortés harmonized with your works, for they too were in reverence to God and his ministers, among us as well as among the native Indians, on whom it was stamped, so that today such respect for the priests lasts and will last. For along the roads, bearing their burdens, they release them to kneel on the ground and kiss his hand, and they do this so naturally and he is so received among them that although they are occupied with their sowing and labors, they leave everything and gather to him and hold him in great honor, learning from this teacher who, after showing himself to be such a great warrior and so brave, showed himself so Christian, teaching doctrine to both republics;[2] such that every time he happened upon a priest, he dismounted to kiss his hand, pushing his knee into the ground, reverence for which he was repaid by God, making him so fortunate, placing at his feet such a great number of people, kings, and lords with such great riches, giving him the title of *The respect the Marquis of Valle had for the priests—An example well worth imitating*

Marquis, with such fame and so many victories, helped by the blessed Lord Santiago, our patron saint; and he who deserved this deserves to be placed among the famous, whose renown is well extended over all the world, whom all the commanders should follow in valor as well as in reverence toward priests.

Concern of the commander with his people and camp in the service of God

Leaving this to the consideration of each, I return to my path and say that the commander will take the priest in his company and at his table, as a gift to him as well as for all to respect. He will recite the *Salve Regina* every day, even though he is traveling, and his people will confess in their time and there should be full account kept of this. He will prevent the soldiers from swearing and blaspheming and will make an effort to punish them for it.

The care the commander will have in attracting the Indians to our faith

He will take great care, likewise, when the Indians make peace, that the priest works with the highest ranking caciques and that they receive holy baptism, moving them with preaching and other holy things so that they are moved [i.e., converted], honoring well those who receive it, rewarding them and giving them gifts; and the commander will seat some of the most important at his table with some ceremony and demonstration that they are given those favors for being Christians, so that with this incentive may the rest be persuaded. But there are some priests so scrupulous about baptizing without being catechized that they sometimes cause harm. I confess that it ought to be like this, however, an exception should be made for the most important chiefs, so that they shall interact and become accustomed to being with us; for they are so barbarous that if they were made to work on the Catechism they would become angry and withdraw. Every commander will work to surpass himself in this exercise.

PREPARATION OF MEDICINES AND THEIR APPLICATION

No less care should the commander have in the preparation of medicines, along with his surgeon, for the treatment of his soldiers for the sicknesses and wounds that occur from time to time on such expeditions, so that with care and good preparation all evil and risk are intercepted.

Regarding the first, the surgeon will carry several mild cathartics, such as *mechoacán*,[3] castor oil, and other herbs and roots known for that effect. He will carry the chamomile flower, tobacco, sugar, and incense resin [*anime*]. He will carry raw, sublimated quicksilver [*solimán crudo*, "corrosive sublimate"], verdigris, and the herb for buboes, balm, alum, herb poultice, tallow, milkweed, sulfur, stone of Buga, bezoar stone, *caraña*[4] resin, white salve, antivenin, and his carrying case with all provisions. These things should require only minimal preparation, for they must be speedy cures due to the scant convenience of the field. And in order to apply the useful medicines, I will state the illnesses that most commonly occur on such excursions.

First: wounds, with and without herb poison, chills, fevers, sores, diarrheas, swelling, ray stings, fire, venomous herbs in the food, impetigo, stitches, eye diseases, earaches, headaches, pain in the body, spleen, tooth diseases, tightness of the chest, and altitude sickness [*la del monte*].[5] Now that the illnesses have been stated, it will be good for the surgeon, or the person who is to do it, to apply the remedy here referred to with great diligence.

If it is a wound from herb venom, the best and safest cure is to cut away all the flesh affected by the wound; be warned that this cure must be done as quickly as possible. And for this, those commanders who are shrewd order the surgeon to always carry a fishhook and a knife in his bag in order to lift the flesh with the hook and cut it with the knife, as it is correctly done, taking care not to cut the nerves which, once the flesh is cut away, if the wound should affect them, should be scraped with the fingernail and cleaned later so that they do not remain infected by the poison; the friendly Indians know well how to do this. And for this cure he should carry a prepared mixture of toasted maize flour and gunpowder, salt, ash, and charcoal. And with this mixture, according to the hollow of the wound, he will make a ball and place it inside and bandage it, even though much blood may escape from the cut veins; he will cauterize and staunch the blood later. And if, beneath this ball and mixture, he introduces another small one of tallow and raw quicksilver sublimate, of four parts fat, the cure will in every way be certain, for one restricts the blood and the other kills the venom; along the same path that the poison takes, the quicksilver mixed with the tallow follows, and with as much and more violence reaches it and kills it.[6] And once repaired with this cure, he will be advised to give

25
Warrior from
Santa Marta,
Colombia, with
poisoned arrows,
ca. 1586.
Courtesy Pierpont
Morgan Library

him the antivenin, and, lacking this, the juice of the milkweed is good; also a choice antidote is ground river clam dissolved in water or maize beer [*chicha*], as well as the juice of *guama* shoots. The [antivenin] *Ambire de Santa Marta*[7] is a choice thing, a thing to drink little of, as its strength is great. All these things are admirable against venomous herbs, as well as the juice of *cordoncillo*[8] root; and when all should fail, refer to the ordinary and approved antidote. Likewise, beware that the wounded does not drink a drop of water, for it interferes, and in such a case, they usually expire by drinking, so in order to remedy thirst he will be given thin porridges of maize flour and milk, called *poleadas*, which serve as both drink and food, and he should not eat any other thing for at least twenty days. Also, he will be given certain good odors [i.e., smelling salts or concentrated fragrances] to detain the swelling

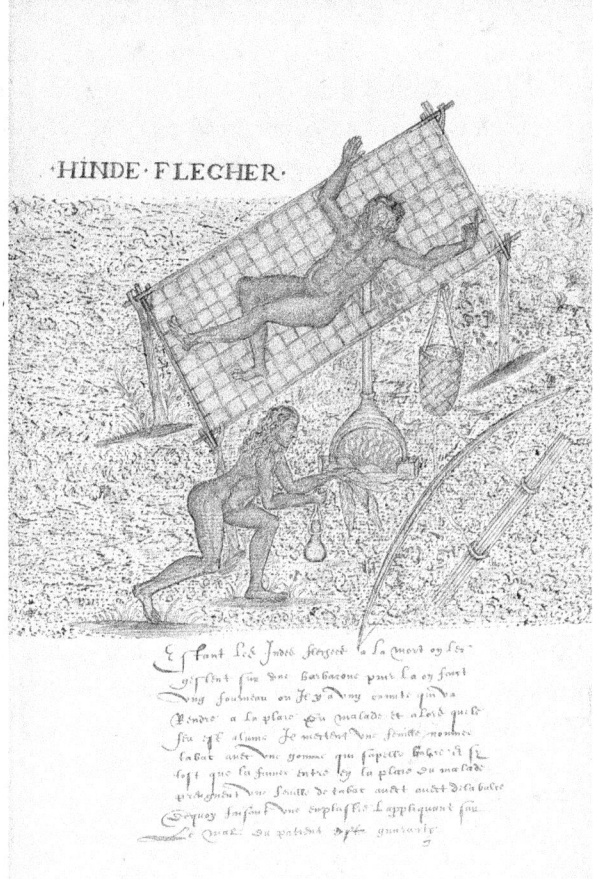

26
Arrow wound being treated with tobacco, ca. 1586.
Courtesy Pierpont Morgan Library

of the brain. The bezoar stone is good, and if there is any, make use of it. And beware that if this care is not taken with the wound, he will die a raging death.

And as it comes to suit this purpose, I will recount a case that was certified to me of two soldiers who were wounded by venom in the city of Mariquita, having retreated from the war of Guali.[9] One was called Antonio de Herrera, a native of Plasencia in these parts, who for his gallantry was called the Brave Spaniard. Each one was in his own bed, but all were in the same room, and one companion was so pitiful and complained with such intolerable anger, that the Brave Spaniard, being in the same agony, arose from his bed and went to that of his friend, encouraging and reprimanding him with very rough words, as

The bravery of a soldier

BOOK TWO OF THE INDIAN MILITIA 63

if he were ready to take up arms, telling him that the world was not conquered with such soldiers, encouraging him and attending to him and preparing his bed and turning him from one side to another; and with much valor and arrogance asked him, "Are you well?" and the other responded, "Yes." He spoke to him again, saying, "Well, then, stay with God and may he give you strength and life, for I am going to die," and returning to his bed, instantly expired and the next day the friend died. Venomous herbs have this quality, such that the end comes with much talking and raving.

Let us go to wounds without venoms, which are to be burned with balsam, tallow, or oil, and if they are bleeding from cut veins, the mixture of maize mentioned before should be used, until they are stanched and afterward use crushed green tobacco. And in fresh wounds, crushed gunpowder is good; and the stone of Buga is a good and miraculous thing, for it restricts and tightens and closes the wound with but a little material; note that one must first wash the wound with hot water. And if paralysis should occur with such a wound, heat should be applied where the loss of movement is felt; and if this paralysis advances, the patient will drink one spoonful of powdered sulfur in honey or in wine or in chicha, or in an egg, having first heated the nape and the neck, spreading the fires with hot tallow; and this must be done during the night, in order to better conserve the heat; this same effect will be achieved for any pain of knee or shin, for it consumes and relieves the pain.

No illness is so common in the soldier in this militia than the common cold [*resfriado*], for he often suffers from it, for the land where he goes is so hot and the soldier is on foot and since he is forced to sweat, as well as to drink from every stream he comes to, and since he arrives so hot and with exposed flesh, he catches cold. This happens crossing rivers or from the ever-present downpours. These chills often paralyze or cause one to faint or cause some pain; this should be treated by heating the part where the pain is located and by giving him sulfur to drink at night, as mentioned, or giving him water cooked with chamomile, a bowl of it, adding bee honey while cooking, and drinking this water as hot as possible and wrapping him up; so that with this he will be restored, adding tobacco smoke, for this greatly hinders the chills that any excess may cause.

Concerning fever or high temperatures, everyone is already skilled, in the absence of doctors, in knowing how to bleed and make comfortable with the syrup that may be available or preparing and giving a purgative, that there is no reason to dwell on this. I would only like to give a notable remedy for a confirmed tertian or quartan [i.e., malarial] fever, which is taking the skin of a serpent, of those that shed their skin, grinding it sufficiently into a powder, and passing it through a cloth (rather than a sieve) and into a broth, wine, or chicha. The patient will drink the weight of a dram of it and will be wrapped up, and on the third time that he takes it while the chill is upon him, I assure you with the grace of God, the humor which causes his fever will surrender. Once covered, if a light purging should be desired for the patient, without having purgatives or syrups for that purpose, he should remain in bed; a bit of tobacco will be cooked in water, and once it is quite strong, a little cooking oil will be added to the water; and while somewhat hot and stirred-up, the patient will drink half a bowl of it. This he will do while fasting and with it the cholera and phlegms will be vomited out in such a manner that he will be purged.

If he should suffer from sores, a mixture of fat and verdigris and toasted maize flour will be made, for it is good; also, the powders made from the shells of crabs, as well as potato leaves, crushed and hot; and milkweed powder, to eat away the bad flesh. And so that the sores grow scabs, powders from the buboes herb,[10] being careful to first wash the sores with very hot water and treat them often.

Bloody diarrheas are quite dangerous in torrid lands and weaken greatly if they are not stopped carefully; and for this, if they are caused by cold humor, which is the most usual, place a poultice on the stomach of caraña or anime, and he will drink powders of the Buga stone, with an egg, wine, or chicha or honey, and in water if these are lacking, while fasting for three or four mornings. Powders of myrtle, laurel bark, and pomegranate peel are also good. A poultice made from guava or quince jelly mixed with powdered rosemary, mint, incense, and mastic resin, and placed on the stomach, is also good. This poultice is a marvelous thing for relaxing the stomach from purges or vomiting or any other thing preventing the retention of food; and if it is from cold humor, it is good to heat the stomach. Drinking juice or powders made from the peel of the teasel is also good; fresh horse manure, where available, is good dissolved in wine, chicha, or broth, and in water if these are lacking, straining it beforehand and drinking it over three mornings while fasting. I warn that one should not hold back the diarrheas, until they have been purged for eight days.

Inflammation ordinarily occurs in two places on the soldier, either the backside [*los supinos*] or the legs. If it should happen on the backside, a poultice of thick maize porridge will be made and left to sour or be mixed with an equal amount of *mazato*[11] and applied once made. And if it is necessary to walk, the poultice will be covered with a cloth so that it neither falls off nor hinders. He will have this poultice until it reeks strongly, and then he will remove it and wash with jagua juice every day or as many times as possible, which, I assure, will restore his humor. And it will be better if it is possible to bleed and purge him first. And if his legs become inflamed, wash them by night with hot brine or seawater, if available. If supported, the legs will be rubbed with jagua juice, as the Indians use it.

These inflammations occur from much traveling by foot, and after stopping for one day, the humor hangs low.

The bite of the serpent happens often because of their abundance in torrid lands, and because the soldier walks mostly at night when the serpent is most often about, for they move little during the day—although it is more dangerous [i.e., to be bitten during the day] because of the heat; and this risk is run most by the servant Indian, being continuously in service of the camp. The most venomous bites are those of the rattlesnake. The remedy for its bite is to cut open the same bite with a knife or lancet so that it bleeds and exposes the flesh beneath; then suck it with a straw or small horn, in the same manner that the blacks use a cupping glass.[12] And in the hollow of the incision, which will have been made in the form of a cross, insert a small ball of fat and the powder of raw sublimate of quicksilver mixed together, and bandage it and, afterward, give the patient cordoncillo juice or milkweed or the powdered peels of their roots to drink. Jagua juice with ground river clam is good as well, drinking a portion of the powders in water. This remedy of quicksilver sublimate and fat is an extraordinary and miraculous thing, for though the patient is quite inflamed and taken by the venom, he is removed from danger. It is also good, after cutting open the snakebite, to place a stone of amethyst there and bandage it; this is not sufficient on its own, however, and the patient will make use of good odors [i.e., inhalants] for its reduction.

When rivers are forded, if they are flat and sandy, rays often sting, as they are found commonly in these parts, causing a pain so insistent that while it lasts the soldier rages and suffers perturbed fevers. And its remedy is to cut open the sting and soak the foot in water as hot as can be endured, always adding hot water so that it does not cool, until the pain is broken; and afterward take the foot from the water and clean the wound and place a ball of fat and quicksilver sublimate into the incision, as mentioned with the bite of the serpent. If the soldier should burn himself with fire from gunpowder or in any manner, take soap mixed with oil and make an unguent, rubbing it on him morning and night until nine days have passed.

The Indians often add some bad and poisonous herbs to the foods and drinks they offer, in powder as well as juice, and they also do this when they abandon their settlements, leaving these toxins and venoms in the food; so before laying a hand on these foods, one should test them, for since the soldiers arrive hungry, it has happened that some have died before sitting down. The remedy for this is—if the soldier feels any pain or other disorder—to vomit, provoking himself to it by chewing green or dry tobacco and swallowing it; and if it is possible to drink a jar of warm water beforehand in order to mix it up, he will do so; and having vomited, he will be able to drink oil and jagua juice and this is good.

And if the soldier should happen to eat some strong manioc[13] and feel its effects, he should procure to vomit and later dissolve a bit of salt in water and drink it, with which its bad effect will be made safe.

If he should suffer from impetigo and it is a land where dock (*romaza*) can be found, rub him often with the beardlike sprouts of it and a marvelous thing will be seen. And if it is possible to make a water of quicksilver sublimate, vinegar, and vitriol, wash him with it, for it is also good. Also, spread the impetigo with any kind of resin after having scratched it, and dust it with ground sulfur and place combed cotton over it. Another easy remedy is to take some coals and drown them at once with water, and over the smoke place anything made of iron, and rub him with the sweat of the water that congeals there; but above all of these remedies is that of dock.

If he should suffer from side aches, take several crickets and toast them, grind them well, and take a half spoonful of them with wine or chicha; and it will help to take the smoke of tobacco. And if the urine is impeded, take some garlic and crush it and cook it with wine and strain this and drink it. Drinking hot olive broth with oil is also good. Note that with either of these two potions, one should wrap oneself up and sleep it off.

If he has an accident and sickness of the eye, and it should be from a cold or aqueous humor, put a bit of ground tobacco in each corner of the eye, with no other preparation, for though it may burn a little, a good and quick cure will be seen. If the accident is of a hot humor, he should be bled, and one will place a few drops of sour lime in the eyes with a feather that is fresh. Warm wine and dissolved sugar of lead[14] is also good. A very small grain of verdigris dissolved in egg tincture (*aceite de huevo*) is also good.

If he should suffer from pain in the ears, at night he will insert wicks smeared with hot balsam, not too much, and sleep on this, having fumigated himself with the same balsam.

Most of the soldiers already know that tobacco in powder and in smoke is good for the head, and when the pain is confirmed to be of a cold humor, he will rub a peeled clove of garlic behind the ears; and, if it is of a hot humor, it is good to fumigate oneself with the recovered smoke from sugar thrown on coals. And putting defensives of watered-down vinegar on the forehead is also good.

If he should have pain in the leg or arm or another part, caused by cold humor or a blow and this has altered him, fumigate it and if by the second day it is rebellious and does not surrender, take some garlic crushed with fat and make a poultice and put it on the pain at nighttime, which it will not be able to bear for twenty-four hours, and though the humor may be removed from him, fumigate it over fires, applying a poultice of soft incense resin or caraña or whatever one has on hand, and with this will the pain be vanquished however rebellious it may be. The quickest and best poultice for pain is spreading hot virgin bee honey and sprinkling ground mustard powder on top of it and covering it with cotton, wool, or burlap.

If he should suffer from spleen illness, he will drink his own urines with honey while fasting for nine mornings, rubbing the spleen with a bit of soap moistened in urine before arising those nine days, and it will be completely dissolved. It is also good to apply a plaster of *diapalma* or diachylon,[15] heating it and taking care to often clean the water removed by it.

If he should suffer from tooth illness, caused by rheumatism, make use of a few perforated olive pits placed on the neck in place of beads of amber, the approved thing; and if it is possible to take, when a deer is killed, a nerve that goes from the left ear to the heart, which is as thick as a large guitar string, and place this on the neck after it is dry, this is an admirable remedy. And if it is a rheumatism from a cold humor, chewing tobacco and sleeping with it between the teeth will be enough to take away the pain. It is also good to cut a few little nerves that go to the ears, which can be seen by pulling the ears, and later burning them with something made of gold to cauterize them. This is with the understanding that the pain is not caused by a damaged molar; if it is, the best remedy is to remove it.

If he should have a tight chest from a cold humor, it is good to fumigate it and smear it with fat, drinking sulfur at night, as mentioned. And if the tightness is from phlegms and congestion of the blood, bleed him, and make a broth of blackberry shoots and take a bowl of that water and half a bowl of urine and another half of bee honey and, bringing it to a boil, make a syrup, and he will drink it bit by bit; and if he should finish it, prepare another, whatever is necessary, and a notable cure will be seen.

And if he should suffer from altitude sickness, take a jar of water, almost boiling, and let it drip over him little by little, as much as he can bear, and do this often for four or five days, and, God willing, the sickness will be taken without fail. In all of these wounds and cures, if one should use the holy incantation [*santo ensalmo*],[16] it will be very good, for with this, miraculous things have been done. In my expeditions I have made extraordinary cures and have tried out all these medicines, some learned from the Indians, great herbalists that they are. And I have acquired others through experience, as each one may do [in the field], discovering new medicines, being a new inventor of them through experiment as well as with good philosophy, for the health of his soldiers. Where there are no doctors, we must all make a choice. And even where there are [doctors] this [new medicine] calls for careful study because of the simplicity of the medicines we apply, using no compounds.

PREPARATION OF ARMS

It is reasonable that we now turn to that which is more to our purpose, as we have distanced ourselves from it so, although everything has been very important to our intention: the end and aim of the Indian militia and the misfortunes and labors, hungers, and dangers to which our Spaniards are subjected. We state, then, the care our commander will take in preparing and supplying himself with horses and arms, making first a list of his soldiers and knowing which arms each has and providing what is needed, having for that effect some part of it gathered, in such a manner that later in the expedition he should lack nothing. Supposing that there are two manners of expeditions: one of savanna and flat lands and the other of mountain and thick forest; in one land horses are useful and in the other no, owing to the roughness and undergrowth. In flat lands, where horses may be taken, they will be used. Whatever the nature of the expedition, it is advisable for all of the soldiers to be harquebusiers if possible, for being so doubles the number of people, for if they are one hundred, all hundred have effect, each one carrying his small buckler at his back, with his neck harness in order to make use of it as the occasion offers. Likewise will he take four reserve muskets,[17] more or less, for each fort. The harquebuses will be short so that they may be wielded better on horseback or on foot, for considering the distance that an arrow or dart may reach, which is the weapon used by the enemy, any harquebus of four spans in length reaches farther. And for the dense forests [*montañas*] they are not so awkward as long ones. It must be understood that these harquebuses will be carried by the soldiers who know how to shoot them or have the inclination, and the rest who lack it or do not know how to handle them will carry large, circular bucklers, for they must protect themselves and the harquebusier assigned to him. The harquebusier, as required, will not be exempted from carrying his buckler, for many times the harquebus may slip from his hands, as will be seen in the course of this book, and it is best that he be found with a shielding weapon.

Some commanders have the ill habit of permitting the harquebusier to not carry a sword because of its awkwardness, but this is wrongly done, for we have already seen in sudden ambushes the inability to ignite the match, because of humidity or haste, and other times, though they are ignited, the powder does not take the fire or, having taken it, the harquebus does not fire because of the humidity of the powder; and cut short by this, they turn their backs because they find themselves without arms, and it is a cause of being routed and losing everything. The soldier does not have the blame in this, but rather the commander, for not taking his people well armed and prepared for the event; for the soldiers who go prepared take strength and spirit. In such circumstances, each should consider the difference from one to the other, carrying arms with which to fight and offend the opponent, or being run off for the failure of a harquebus. He will do his duty, doubling in the steel of the sword that which he desired to show with the harquebus, and this occurs in soldiers of esteem and honor. Being valiant and doing one's duty is born from this. The commander should keep to this, selecting soldiers for such cases, because they will often be presented to him. Braggarts and brigands serve not but to agitate the camp, and in times of need we have seen them cut down, being of no use.

And returning to my purpose, I do not deny the encumbrance of having the sword in the belt, because of the roughness of the land, but I say that in its place should be worn half-swords, cutlasses or scimitars, machetes or long mountain knives, of three or four spans in length, which will serve the same purpose with the buckler and without encumbrance, carried on the neck harness; and the soldier should not tire of carrying it, though the commander may not have ordered him; for when it does not serve him directly against the enemy, it will serve him because of the risk he runs among the very same friendly Indians who accompany him, such that upon seeing [the soldiers] prepared, none will dare take them on, for after all they are Indians. In general, all will wear their hauberks [i.e., battle tunics] made of blankets and cotton. The best are tabards of two skirts, like the capes from Biscay, with their peg buttons on the sides, or ties that overlap one skirt upon the other, so the side is not uncovered. These tunics should be wide in order to remain hollow, hindering the arrow or dart; these are more effective than others for a sharp weapon. Apart from this they serve as mattresses to sleep upon, and without danger. They are best worn on the body, for they produce the same effect, which is to impede the humidity of the ground. To each of these tunics one should not add more than six pounds of cotton, which is sufficient for an arrow; and note that the stitches need to be long and loose so that the tunic is loose. If it reaches to the knee, add eight pounds. These will be used where there is venom. And when serving on horseback, they will be split in front and in back, for the sake of the saddletree and so they cover the thigh. The soldiers will avoid getting wet, if possible, for the cotton compacts and is easily pierced by an arrow, dart or lance, though others are of a different opinion. And if it needs to be light and carry little cotton, make a thin board and pass it lightly over the garment and the stitches will loosen so the cotton may be removed. Those on horseback will wear their helmets with earpieces made of cotton or bull hide, with visors of mesh to cover their faces so that they are not wounded in battle, for one cannot always guide the horse and shield oneself at the same time. Besides, an arrow flies without being seen and it is good that the face is protected, for that part is in greater danger. Many do not use shields and so those that are brought should be small and light and he who can should bring a harness with bells; this is very good, for they strike fear in the Indians as well as greatly encourage the horse. Short-stirrup saddles will be used and long-stirrup saddles not permitted, for a river is forded with less risk to the rider and they are faster to saddle and they make horsemen.[18] The horses wear their chest, head, and flank armor made of the same cotton, and a dozen horsemen among one hundred infantrymen will be sufficient.

In the belt all soldiers will wear a butcher knife, which is a fine weapon. The horses are good and advantageous among the infantry, even if the number of opponents is great. And I advise them to carry their bucklers and harquebuses of the recommended size, for they will carry them to places where the horses are of no use, and it is good that they find themselves ready to fight. The spurs should be sparrow-beaked, for prick spurs are very dangerous.

The commander will be careful to carry a few reserve lance heads, so he should not lack them when they are needed, and if even these are lacking, there are enough to be found in the woods. Arms increase valor, which is why the poets in their fables pretend that the gods made them for the persons they have celebrated. Horses are a sort of weapon, by whose strength many victories have been won, and for our purpose they are quite good in the land where they may tread. And of the soldier who may be opposed to carrying arms, one may presume he places more hope for his life in his feet than in his hands.

PREPARATION OF MUNITIONS

I confess that some of the captains and soldiers of the Indies do not ignore necessary things for their expeditions, but to prove my point, it is necessary to place them here and closely examine them, in order to better take note of the necessity of all of them. And so firstly, I state, the harquebusiers will carry extra locks and screws, which is of great foresight and advantage, one being a flintlock and the other a matchlock, if possible, and if not, both will be matchlocks, for they are better and more certain. They will carry their files and molds, ramrods, cleaning rods, scouring rods, and reams. They will carry matches; they will carry their jackets or bags and packs in which to carry the ammunition, on their shield straps or sword belts, for they cannot make use of pockets because of the tunics, upon which some use small pockets, sewn on the outside, for the ammunition; but the packs are better. They already know to carry their cartridges made into paper tubes, for the powder flask is not to be considered. The shield bearers and harquebusiers will wear their hauberks and helms without earpieces when they enter the fray, for having the ears covered hinders hearing the voice and orders of the commander; they hinder those who wear them, except where there are slings, in which case they are necessary.

It is good foresight that the soldier knows how to make his own munitions and goes well prepared with them; it is a thing of good soldiering, and they should be skilled in shooting; they will carry their awls and needles to make sandals, their butcher knives, hatchets, and machetes to make clearings at bedtime, and to make bridges over rivers and marshes in order for horses and baggage to cross. The commander will carry enough lead, which he will distribute in its time and with good account; he will carry the ladles so that the soldiers may melt the lead and make their own munitions; he will carry the best gunpowder possible in earthenware jugs covered in sheepskin, the wool to the outside and the mouths stopped with spelt wads and tied atop with cloth. In these jugs the powder is well protected, even though the land may be quite humid, and it travels secure from water and fire. Cotton will be carried in balls in order to make matches when needed by the soldier. Large quantities of hemp sandals will be carried to aid his camp in time of need, and any fiber that may be found in the land

Munitions

should be made known in order to make rope and sandals when necessary, and when it is lacking, note that the *maguey* or *cabuya*[19] may be used for the match, crushing it well and cooking it with ash; and if this should fail, *amahagua*[20] can be found, good for producing the same benefit; matches can also be made quickly from cotton blankets. Blankets, canvas, hats, and fishhooks will be carried in large quantities to aid his people. For the Indians he will bring trading goods, which are the first means of conquest,[21] such as hatchets, knives, machetes, needles, fishhooks, combs, mirrors, Turkish horns, bells, colored caps, and hats. The commander will bring knee guards made of cotton and strong sandals, if the land has thorns. He will carry a large quantity of sulfur, for if he should have the opportunity to make powder, it can be done in time of need.

Saltpeter He will, however, first take and obtain saltpeter by collecting earth from humid or dry niter fields and ash deposits, which are near the huts of the Indians or where cows sleep, and put this earth or whichever of them into large, earthenware bowls, where the Indians brew their drink, making a hole in the bottom and covering it with a cloth.[22] Place in the bottom of the vessel a handful of cabuya or maguey [fiber] to serve as a colander and on top, a layer of sticks placed in their order, so they make a base, and upon them another bed of straw, and on top of this third layer will be one made of earth. And after filling the vessel with layers made in this same way, as referred, he will pour water on it until it is covered, using rainwater or brackish water if the ordinary is lacking. In this way, this mixture will be like this for twenty-four hours, and later, removing the cloth from the base, all the water in the upright vessel will be allowed to strain into something to collect it. This strained water will be cooked until it is reduced two-thirds, regularly skimming it with a gourd or perforated spoon, for only the purified foam or fat is removed, which is gathered and kept to be added several times to the aforesaid cooking liquid. And in order to know if the saltpeter is cooked, place a drop on a cold iron and if it dries, it is a signal that it is done. Afterward, remove it from the fire and, when cool, pour the water into a separate vessel and leave it for twenty-four hours, having placed some peeled sticks on top in order for the saltpeter to condense on them. After it congeals, the water that is left should be kept, removing it without mixing in the earth [i.e., sediment] at the bottom [of the condensing vessel], since the foundation for the remaining processes must be made with this water, in place of the above-mentioned water; this is better. And note that little saltpeter is recovered in the first cooking but by the second time, following the stated order, a large quantity will be taken. Note also that this water is to be used as a base or mother; when it is old it will not be of use and this will be known when it is very black or greasy. Then prepare another new one, though the last brewing will be finer than any of those others, yet such a large quantity will not be taken from it.

Let us make, then, the powder, that it may be easy and of high quality, making charcoal from wild vine shoots for it, which are in hot lands, or asphodel or orange peelings, or of willow or *ceiba* tree or fig, and grind it in a millstone for maize, with the sulfur as well, in such a manner that it contains no earth, and the same for the saltpeter and charcoal. And these materials must not be humid, incorporating them together, and after they are well ground and mixed, they will be sprinkled with rainwater or last night's urine, and, with milling, made into a paste with the hands like a lump of dough. The ratio of each of these components is one part sulfur and four parts saltpeter, and one part of charcoal. And in order for these materials not to become moist, they will be smoked, for in the sun they lose the saltpeter and are damaged. Lacking sieves for this process, carry a net of string or fiber, the thinnest possible, and square so that between two men it can be drawn tight and framed in the air. And once the said dough is made, take the just-made paste and pass it over the top of the net by hand, always in only one direction, squeezing the mass and lightly passing the hand over it; and have a cloth underneath where the powder will fall, and leave it there to dry and keep it in the earthenware jugs.

Powder

PREPARATION OF IMPLEMENTS

If going to settle in a newly conquered area it is important for the commander to take all necessary implements, such as large and medium axes for making houses, sheds, and clearings and bridges; as well as machetes, flat and curved adzes, flat and curved mattocks, to make canoes where needed; and washing pans for panning where there are signs of gold; and for the service of the inhabitants, drills of all kinds, weeding hoes, small and medium bars, saws, chisels, hammers, and tongs; implements for shoeing horses, horseshoes and nails. And above all he will carry a complete forge with his blacksmith in order to maintain all these tools and make the rest as needed, taking steel and iron. And one or two yokes [*corrientes*] with their collars should not be forgotten, for they are very important, for with them, the prisoners are not so restricted and yet they are secure. Carry some leg irons for soldiers, for I am of the opinion that the collar should not be placed on any of them, for there is nothing that so embitters and rightly offends them.

PREPARATION OF STORES

We have addressed the munitions of war and other things related to it, and so we should state which stores must be taken, as they are of such necessity. If it is a land where horses may be introduced, carry the stores of hardtack upon them, and this should be little, as it is cumbersome. Carry as much toasted maize flour as possible, for it is the perfect provision for making porridges, which is what most sustains and has the least bulk. Carry salt pork, cheeses, garlic, and do not forget salt, which is most essential. And along with these supplies, which are the most important, the commander will take some preserves for the sick, such as guava jam, which is good for diarrhea; and also some sugar. Carry some chickpeas for a necessity, for they greatly satisfy. Take some oil and grease and lard without salt. Take some cauliflower and radish seeds, lettuce and some legumes to plant later if they settle or winter in some part, for they are good crops. Take frying pans of copper or brass, to make their meals. Take gourds full of ground red pepper, which is good aliment [*mantenimiento*], even giving it to the villages. Above all, take milk cows, and these go in a herd, though they are privately owned, with their brands. Those belonging to the commander will be very numerous, for if necessary everyone will rely on them for salvation. Take bulls to multiply, and so that the cows may be comforted. And of the latter, procure ones that are gentle and have given birth, so that they do not stray and are led with less work. Avoid bringing porcine or ovine livestock until fully settled, for these are troublesome and laborious.[23] And if horses are unable to go on the expedition, even less will cattle be, until villages are populated and roads are opened. And the commander should note that the reserve stores taken for the community should not be used until times of necessity, and that the soldiers have first used their own. All that is stated in these chapters concerning preparation, more or less, I leave to the discretion of the commander who will have the pertinent things present.

It will be good to add, as a dessert to this book, the important help of dogs in the defense of our Spaniards in their expeditions in those parts, for they have been of such an advantage. There is great experience with this, as has been seen in the pacification of Costa Rica, Veragua, Santa Marta, Muzo, Guali, and Antioquia, which is where they have most been used, for the Indians have been very bellicose and treacherous, particularly in Muzo, where they used the twenty-four-hour venom so much and ate human flesh, with which they finished many of ours. There would have been many more if it were not for their being taken by great fear of the dogs, for at the same time they entered the land, ours were ready to abandon it, which had already happened other times, as with Pedro de Ursúa, and so it was until Captain Luis Lanchero settled [the town of Muzo], which survives to this day and will endure long years hence; and the same has been experienced in other pacifications.[24]

Help from dogs

They are great help when there are skirmishes (armored, due to their love of [chasing] arrows) if loosed properly.[25] The Indian greatly fears the horse and the harquebus, but he fears the dog more, such that upon hearing their bark, the Indian does not stop.

The Indians also make use of them and bring them along with them; and they take advantage of their vigilance. To catch and follow a scent, one needs only to loose the dog; later it finds the Indian without the soldier going with it, and there it is until the people arrive, having the Indian cowered. They reveal an ambush from a great distance, for they smell it. They are very advantageous and I would not go on an expedition without them.

In order to see the effect they have, I will recount a deed done by a dog named Capitán. Many days after the land of Muzo had been occupied by our Spaniards, a soldier named Luis Rodríguez, who had been my soldier on certain expeditions and whose dog it was, told this story to me and made it public in all the said land of Muzo. He had found himself twelve leagues from the city in an uninhabited land, alone with

The luck of a dog

27
Wild dogs chasing a boar and a hare, Spanish Caribbean, ca. 1586.
Courtesy Pierpont Morgan Library

his dog at a fishing hole they made along a river, surrounded by over one hundred Indians. His dog was tied with a straw plait [*tramojo*] in the clearing that he had made to sleep in while fishing for a few days. He was by the bank of the river, unconcerned and unarmed, for he had them in the clearing, trusting in the peace of the Indians and feeling safe from the betrayal that they had arranged for him, which was to kill him and throw him in the river. Upon seeing such a fine opportunity, the soldier unarmed and his dog tied up, they agreed to carry out the act, delivering a blow with a club upon him (which is the weapon that they use, as has been said), from which he fell bewildered. As they were taking hold of him to throw him into the river, the soldier, with the rage of death, began to struggle and cry out. The dog heard the noise and the voice of his master and forcibly broke the plait, rushing upon the squadron of Indians, biting and knocking them down such that they, with the sudden assault, ran over each other in flight, leaving the soldier be and removing themselves from the danger, most being unarmed since they thought the dog was tied and the soldier unarmed, therefore needing none themselves, as would have been true if the strength of the love that the dog has for his master had not come to his rescue. Such is the great instinct of dogs that he understood the danger his master was in, and felt that he alone should liberate him from this danger amid so large a squadron, and then after routing them, returned to him. The master, having come to and recovered strength from such a rescue, arose and rushed to his clearing, without abandoning his dog, in search of his arms. And taking up his sword and buckler, the soldier, with the dog at his side, renewed and struck up the fight and routed them in a short time and they fled, leaving dog and master alone. Afterward they took the road to where there were Spaniards, for they had already been given up for dead because an Indian servant of the soldier, who fled while all of this was happening, had said he was dead. Dogs such as these can well be taken on similar enterprises and should be highly esteemed, for they are such good companions, with all care for their comfort, giving them their rations as to any soldier. Take those that have a good stature, but not too large, for these become fatigued, sore-footed, and a hindrance in the jungle [*arcabuco*]; and those to be taken should be young, testing them first by firing the harquebus near them, and if the dogs flee a long distance from the report, it is no use laying a hand on them, for they will never be tamed nor be of use, for they have a thousand problems; and train those that pass this test not to quarrel with each other, making them brotherly, for if they are not so, they will cause harm before they are useful. I will not address everything I could say on this matter, for I leave it to the discretion of the commander and soldier.

BOOK THREE
OF THE INDIAN
Militia Which Addresses The Duty Of The Soldier, Leading People Out From Peaceful Lands, Marching Through Warring Lands, Crossing Rivers, Being Quartered With Strength, Giving And Receiving Night Attacks, Ambushes, And Battles.

ONE OF THE MOST principal virtues that pleases God is humility, a buttress for all things great, medium, and small, and without it, none may correspond to their duty; and so the soldier must make use of this virtue more than any other person, for if, due to disobedience, an opportunity is lost, it is impossible to return to collect it, and in losing one, it is likely that others that follow in succession will be lost.

The duty of a soldier

And thus, [Titus] Manlius Torquatus ordered his son beheaded for not being obedient in following orders, though he returned from his battle victorious and laden with plunder;[1] and many others have served as epitomes of its importance, and we keep them in our eyes every day as examples.

Example of Manlius Torquatus

The soldier should recognize this duty, being obedient to the mandates of his commander, a thing the soldier of the Indies keeps quite poorly, with such arrogance that he believes he knows as much as his commander and that, being skilled, has no need of one to govern him; and confident of this, they commit a thousand errors worthy of punishment.

He that does not follow the order of his commander loses his reputation.—The soldier follows any order that he may be given

I warn you of one thing, and that is that every time they do not follow the order of their commander, they lose much reputation and credit, and will justly lose the post they have been given and another may occupy it. For in war, the valorous soldier is always offered many opportunities to prove himself; for this reason he is obligated to guard the post wherever his commander may place him, even though it may seem to him that there is another, better place to distinguish himself. It suits the soldier well to be humble, for upon humility fall the other virtues, like enamel upon gold, and thus will he gain all reputation and not with vain appearances or boasting which is easily done.

The soldier who keeps secrets will be esteemed.—The soldier should not avoid work.—The soldier should be trained in arms

The soldier should avoid being a bully and a talker, resolving this by being quiet and well liked and in all things discreet. From this, the commander will recognize his fortune and be forced to entrust many things to him, trusting them to show his value, and to befriend him on important occasions, a thing earned only by fulfilling duty honorably and with courtesy. This he will have in always doing the work of his commander, placing his hand where it would be placed, and he will gain fame and win over his commander (otherwise, idleness leads to a million vices), procuring to always train in arms so that when the occasion should present itself, he may find himself with all confidence and alacrity.

The soldier should not sleep on sentry duty

Also, if the soldier who has been entrusted with sentry duty, which is the health of an entire camp, does his duty, he does what he must and fulfills his obligation, whereas he who sleeps loses honor and risks his life and deserves the death penalty, and in this I would have no qualm in taking [his life] from him. And when, for some reason, one should have mercy upon him, he should be given a terrible punishment, and I believe that no good commander would refrain from allowing him to die for the betrayal he commits, for everyone places their honor and lives in his hands and are remunerated so little for things so important.

Epirates, while in Corinth, came upon a sleeping sentry and killed him, and in our times we see this deed every day; but if the soldier understands honor, it is certain that he will avoid all of this, not being rebellious nor a gossip, so terrible that many evils and ills are brought forth, and all that is drawn from it is a poor reputation. These vices most often engender a mutiny, which generally causes harm in such a manner that though one may not be among those involved in it, he may participate by his poor name, for if it is discovered that he keeps such company, one may presume to judge. Satisfying everyone is no small thing and there is no better nor honored satisfaction to the soldier than earning acclaim; may he be a friend to the honor of his commander and of his friend and comrade, not consenting that any should speak ill of him and reprimanding them, favoring reason and duty; and if he lacks this, he will be bound by what he owes to the virtue of a good soldier and friend; and if he does not have speech nor condition nor spirit to attend to this, may he turn his back, for if he is not an honored defender, he is an infamous complaisant; and whoever falls into this infamy and later goes to gossip to his commander or friend, reveals his fault, and his spirit is offended in such a manner that he will forever be an enemy in his heart, for he who would recite a verse to you may also use it to insult you,[2] and if one does his duty as an honorable soldier, may others say so.

The example of Epirates—The soldier should not be a gossip.—The soldier should flee from mutiny.—The soldier must be defender of the honor of his commander and comrade

The soldier will be obligated not to consent to any mutiny nor take part in one, nor cause one, for apart from being a disservice to God, it is one to the king; and it is a form of betrayal for which he risks his honor and life. In this should he live most vigilantly, for here is where conspiracies and revolts are born.

The soldier is obligated not to permit a mutiny

This is a stain that spreads; to remedy it he will keep from evil company, and if he feels set upon or that they would capture him, may he flee from it, remembering to give warning to the commander in time and with discretion, for if he finds out from another, he will run the same risk as the others.

The soldier should be loyal to his king

This should the soldier keep secret, and in doing so he will keep the title of faithful supporter and serve God and king; and he is so obligated to this that he will not show his face to his own comrade if he sees that he is against the king.

An occurrence between two comrades

As this comes so appropriately, I will recount a case that occurred but a few years ago, when the Governor Antonio de Berrío was searching to discover El Dorado, more than three hundred leagues from the New Kingdom of Granada, from whence he set forth.[3] In his camp were two soldiers who were comrades [*camaradas*] and had been friends and brothers for many years, so much so that one knew not what to do without the other; and thus, together, they went on this expedition, one being a captain in it. One was called Pérez and the other Chacón. Chacón, due to some quarrel between him and the governor, or because the Devil reigned over him, wished to kill the governor. So he consulted with his comrade, Captain Pérez, who reprimanded him repeatedly and tried to prevent such treason. He pressed him in such a manner that, upon seeing that he was not able to dissuade his comrade but that Chacón was determined to go through with it, Pérez communicated it to the governor, who, having satisfactorily verified the case, garroted Chacón, with which all was laid to rest. And this punishment was deemed correct in all the places where it was announced, and thus Captain Pérez did his duty, for with this he prevented many deaths and damages.

Swearing is ill seeming to the soldier

Following our purpose, I advise and say that the soldier, as a custom, should not swear. I truly believe that there is no necessity in giving precepts to good soldiers; however, for those who have not such experience nor live with such care, it is fitting that they know that swearing much and displaying it as gallantry is a great fault, and may a plague be upon his house.

It is well seeming to be an honest soldier

And if one must also be honest, it is right that he is virtuous, for swearing much does not fit with being honest. This virtue suits a soldier so well, for the commander holds him in high esteem and everyone respects him.

It is ill seeming to be a gambler, having it as a trade [*oficio*], for it brings with it many vices. I am not saying that one should not play nor enjoy oneself, but rather not to call attention to it in the camp, bringing cards into the chapel, or wagering his sword and clothing, for this is ill-seeming and one cannot attend to his duties well.

The soldier should not gamble much

There are some despicable soldiers who cheat other soldiers of their service. This is base and should not be permitted, for many grievances are born of this; and may the commander leave such a soldier wherever he wishes.

It is bad to wheedle inappropriate service from another

It could well be omitted here to say that the soldier should be assiduous in his arms and munitions, carrying them all cleaned and readied, for it is his trade and he has a duty to it. But I have seen some soldiers quite remiss in this, which has moved me, and it is good, apart from doing his duty, that the time he may have free he spends to the benefit of his arms. And the commander knows them well [i.e., those who maintain their arms] and takes a liking to them and always takes care to make use of them in serious matters.

The soldier should be assiduous in arms

And I warn that it is most important that the soldier at his post does not give false alarm, but that he discerns well before he gives it; and if he is doubtful, may he quickly advise his commander or the first soldier so that they may be alert, so that when he confirms it with the harquebus, the people are already prepared and ready with their arms. And it seems to me that, if the attack is not sudden, one should customarily give the alert in silence before giving it with arms, for with this, one takes advantage of much territory, as we will state later.

The soldier should not give false alarm

The soldier has no less a need of spirit and courage when opportunity falls into his hands, for one of these would be sufficient for many men; and the commander who senses the opposite in someone should eject him from his camp, for he does more harm than good.

The soldier, given the opportunity, should show spirit and courage

It is known that after observing the orders of his commander, the good soldier, in courtesy, has the duty of sending to his commander part of what he may hunt and shoot with his harquebus and other meals he

The soldier should share with his commander

should acquire, for after doing what he should, all the commander has is for everyone.

There should be much peace among the soldiers.—The soldier should not mock

And it seems to me that soldiers, one and all, should have much peace and brotherhood, as they all go to achieve a common end and must live together, remaining in the land as neighbors, avoiding all sort of quarrels and disputes, and above all, insults, for these can become serious, and usually offend, a truly reprehensible thing in all the militia. There is great carelessness in this among the Indies soldiery, and among some commanders in the remediation and prevention of it, whose concern is the health and peace of his entire camp.

THE METHOD OUR COMMANDER MUST HAVE IN LEADING HIS PEOPLE OUT OF PEACEFUL LANDS WITHOUT HARMING THE NATIVES

Marching without causing harm in peaceful lands

Now that we are about to march with our people, it would be good that we have a good beginning, for with this we may expect for our expedition a similar ending. If it is lacking, a good ending will be impossible. And so we should lead these people who are determined and prepared for war out of peaceful lands, causing no harm or offense, as usually occurs, taking the son, the wife, or the daughter, and taking from the neighbor the services most freely given, such as use of acculturated [*ladino*] Indian servant girls and boys, taking horse or mule from their owners along the road or from the field, and causing harm in the farmhouses where they eat, raping and committing many other offenses, disrupting everything, bringing upon themselves a million curses. What may one who would go forth with this footing and principle expect but ill fortune? And clearly the commander neither desires nor gives permission for this; however, the bad and pernicious soldiers commit these acts with no fear of God or justice, confident that they are soldiers and that they go to serve the king. Shame upon those whose lack of consideration causes them to commit such unmerited acts, lacking honor and not considering the risk they run, so soullessly they throw themselves into committing robbery, rape, and abuse.

In order to remedy this, I wish to give my thoughts, for it is proper that the commander remedy and put a stop to it without risking [the loss of] his soldiers, which is to be feared; for if he should wish to settle these outrages by punishment before they set forth, he will be left with few soldiers. Commanders should know that to depart in an orderly manner, prepared and supplied, an encampment must always be chosen at the farthest reaches of the peaceful territory. Here the camp will gather and everyone will congregate and be supplied with all that is necessary for their journey, such as meat and maize flour. And here also they will complete the preparation of arms and munitions, and arrange equipment and give orders. And it is of great importance to stay at this location; and it is good that it is done thus. The commander will signal the captains and soldiers to this purpose, and according to the number of people, they will be divided so that they go to this place in squads, maintaining the orders given to them, charging them with all seriousness to cause no sorrow to anyone wherever they might pass, neither to the citizen nor to the traveler nor to the Indian, warning them that this is the reason they are sent forth, with the people assigned to them, trusting them in a similar manner. And in the presence of each of these officers, he will give the soldiers a brief speech, obliging them to follow him, placing his honor before them, and promising to gain their esteem by honoring them and rewarding them in due time; and he who would do the contrary will never be their friend and will be abandoned by them. And with this will he charge them to follow the orders of the officer; and he will stay behind until all are dispatched, leaving with the rearmost squad, having provided for the people in the said encampment meat and maize to be eaten during their stay so as not to use up their stores, as well as to be newly resupplied. And afterward, these actions taken, before leaving the town where the people were gathered, an edict shall be issued that all the denizens and any other persons who have received some offense from the soldiers may pursue it and make it known, and amends will be made on every point. This will be done with great account and care, returning to each what belongs to him, for if it is not done in this way, the commander would remain obligated to make restitution for everything and with a besmirched name; and with this, he will have fulfilled his honor and duty, so that if they do not ask, it will not be his fault.

Remedy for causing no harm upon leaving.— The men should march through peaceful lands in squads to avoid damage

The commander makes amends to the offended

So having come what may from these claims, he will then take action with all discretion and, finding the guilty parties, will reprimand them with no commotion and make amends; and if it is necessary to go and pay in order to satisfy, he will do this in such a manner that they take leave of him satisfied and speaking well of him, and that he may not be left indebted to them.

A turbulent river benefits the fisherman

And I must note that in these gatherings, there are many thieves who take advantage of, as they say, a turbulent river, charging the soldiers with everything, registering a million complaints that, upon verification, show that the soldier has done no such thing; and with regards to this matter, the commander should proceed with moderation. Having taken this action and satisfied everyone, he will take great care with the camp stores, gauging the uninhabited areas, taking reserves for whatever might occur.

A man prepared has fought half the battle

Likewise, the commander will be sure that every soldier gathers and prepares his weapons and munitions, making lists of them and their arms, inspecting them personally, in such a manner that when they set forth from there [i.e., base camp] they do so well armed and prepared, lacking nothing, because of what is said about the prepared man, for on the trail no inns are to be found where one may rest and recuperate. And with this, having done the things of a Christian commander, and the priest having said mass and blessed flags and standards, the camp will depart with the care that we will discuss in the following chapter.

Warning

And I warn that it is important that the commander visits all the comrades and does not permit more than four in each dwelling [*rancho*], for having many at one table creates many inconveniences worthy of remedy. The commander knows well that he must take his translators and guides, the best he can, and that trumpets are required in the camp at all hours.

THE CAUTION WITH WHICH OUR COMMANDER WILL MARCH THROUGH WARRING LANDS, ALWAYS LEADING HIS PEOPLE IN ORDER

Now we are at the time when our commander must demonstrate the qualities we have attributed to him and the soldiers must do their duties; up to now, all has been peace and what has been said and prepared for is what is left to us; all will be war and stratagems for it. As each day offers many discoveries in the Indies, my purpose and the labors I have taken are nothing other than that the commanders and captains know how to serve and keep order such that the natives of those kingdoms do not destroy everything, at a loss of so much work, and for what they are going to do, which is to convert souls; and for this it will be necessary to discuss quite extensively all the particulars and precautions, even though it may appear tedious to the old soldiers and conquerors; in the end, if they were to return to work, they would follow these footsteps, and so beginning, I state:

In warring lands, the commander has a duty to go in the vanguard upon entering it; and upon leaving, in the rear guard, for the greatest danger is always found there. He gathers up all the people who march out of order along the way. And so, upon departing, he orders his trumpets to play, so that all may ready themselves and tie down their loads. And being an expedition with horses, he divides his people into two squads, the number of harquebusiers equaling the number of lances and scythes [*dalles*]. One squad will take the vanguard and the other, the rear guard; and distinguished soldiers from these two squads will be positioned among the equipment, and the rest likewise, changing their positions each day, so that they may go forth from the camp in silence, one and two harquebus shots away, discovering the land, in such a manner and with such account that they have no impediment to their returning to camp, not allowing too narrow a path to come between themselves and the camp, nor a river they should be forced to cross by a bridge of reeds or a boat or swimming, not straying so that they may hear the report of a harquebus and may investigate with no offense, careful to always make a stop along the way until the camp

The commander should enter the land in the vanguard and leave in the rear guard.—Sound the trumpets upon marching

arrives and begins to occupy the spot. Afterward, the scouts advance to a vantage point, where they come to a halt, having their sentinel positioned in order to give warning, and commencing to march back to the camp after having avoided a difficult passage or river, they will return to their pathfinding.

Livestock always walks behind

Livestock that must be taken will always go behind the rear guard with extra soldiers taken from the rear guard, in order to guide them along the path that the camp is opening; and these should be soldiers experienced in this and of such account that they do not lose sight of the camp. And they will take several Indian cowherds for their help.

Method of carrying equipment without horses

If it is an expedition by foot, where there are no horses or livestock because of the roughness of the terrain, the commander orders the Indian porters to be placed among the soldiers in this way: the camp must be made into three squads, one for the vanguard, one for the rear guard, and one for the battalion. The porters will be distributed to march one by one between soldiers, for their protection and defense as well as so they do not flee and leave their loads. Great care must be taken in this, for, like barbarous people, they do it at any moment, not considering the harm they may receive. These three squads must pair the harquebusier with the shield bearer, who should know his harquebusier; and for this to be so at all hours, the comrades should be paired in arms, shield bearer with harquebusier. And extras will likewise be placed ahead, with the order and care mentioned. Our commander is advised to place two shield bearers and two harquebusiers before him; and in the rear guard, two shield bearers will remain behind the field marshal, if he is positioned there, or behind another in whose charge it may be; and may these be among the best. And these two should be the hindmost, for if the enemy should harass, they need only to turn around.

The soldiers should march with their arms

The soldiers should march with their arms and the commander should not consent to any other thing, for even though it may not be necessary on the first sorties, having not yet arrived in the destined lands or because they have not been seen, it is good for them to grow accustomed to it, for when there is danger, the hare jumps out when least expected.

They will always carry burning fires with the vanguard, as well as with the battalion and the rear guard and scouts and those who control the livestock, their coils of matches prepared; and where there is a dangerous passage, all will be lighted. Do this always in settled terrain, for in a sudden ambush, it is usually lit poorly; and because of this every soldier should carry his steel and flint in his jacket, for at any moment the need may present itself to the harquebusier. It is also good preparation that the soldiers wear their two-skirted capes to resist a downpour, particularly the harquebusiers, for beneath them they protect their harquebuses and powder; and those who are conscientious should carry several oilcloths wrapped around the locks to better keep the embers from wetness.

Lighted matches

Our commander is advised that silence is of great importance while marching, for with it, detection is avoided and our soldiers will detect the enemy (whereas ordinarily they create a great murmur wherever they may be), and the order given by the commander will be understood.

Silence while marching is of great importance

It is advised to take great care in not firing any harquebus before being noticed in the terrain, so that they are not forewarned and take up arms in their villages. And because Indians ordinarily go hunting in the fields and cross through them on their raids, if one should hear a harquebus, all the land will have warning in a short time and the result of this will be ambushes made against our people. Our not being perceived will give us strength against them, allowing us to take some for translators and guides and peacemakers, which shall shorten the time and the effort. Likewise, keep from playing the trumpet until they are perceived and discovered in the land.

The harquebus will not be fired until being sensed

The commander should march with much account and reason, making halts and finding out if the people are breaking ranks, and if the rear guard is rested; for it is important that the soldiers refresh themselves where there is water, so that they do not become fatigued. And this will be done in such a manner that the rear guard always posts a sentinel on the path in view of the water supply or stream, and the vanguard will place its own on the path at their position. And the commander will see to it that the porters are refreshed and fed, for there is often

Always march with halts so that order is not broken.—It is good to refresh the people

much carelessness and cruelty in this regard, making sure that the load is not too large, for with no consideration, the soldiers often burden the porters as if they were horses and kill them in four days.

Large loads are quite damaging The comfortable load is two *arrobas*,[4] and more should be neither suffered nor permitted, so that the porters may take heart and bear the work.

Alertness upon marching The scouts must always march with great alertness, as the vanguard will do, being wary of and avoiding the trap and pit, the barb and dart, which are their [i.e., the Indians'] combat devices. Whether marching through forest or mountain, they will keep watch and proceed carefully, for the enemy makes use of one tree with another as a trap over the path, positioning a great log or timber with such artifice that with but one fine reed it is sustained in the air among the branches, and this reed is strung across the path so that stepping upon it causes [the log] to come down like a steelyard, a trap that often does great damage, more by night than by day. For this it is good to send friendly Indians ahead to reconnoiter. On the savanna and flat terrain, they make very large holes and drive great stakes inside, subtly covering these pits with branch and earth, such that inadvertently stepping upon it the soldier falls in and is left stabbed and dead. For this, friendly Indians that are taken along may be sent ahead, discovering them with ease; and if there are none, a soldier will find the pit by beating the ground with a half lance. They also use barbs or fine spikes placed unseen among the low branches over the path, and usually by striking the branch, the soldier may pass through.

The friendly Indian, sent ahead with his war club, proceeds by striking branches to discover traps; likewise the soldier with his sword. This is done on narrow and close paths. Where there are venomous thorns, the Indian is not sent ahead, due to the risk he runs, but rather soldiers with their gaiters; in such a way that they always proceed by dragging their feet and in a line across the path, for they strike the thorns and sweep everything away, and as they go uncovering the thorns, they pull them up and make piles in order to burn them, so that the Indians may not take advantage of them in case they find them.

Also, I advise the commander to leave no road he comes upon without following it in order to discover if there is a population close by or if he is able to take an Indian for a guide, coming to a halt until he discovers what it is. And the same will be done on the path or trail, assigning light soldiers to it and with such diligence that they do not hinder the primary goal.

Roads should be reconnoitered

So that he proceeds advised of everything, I say, the roads the Indians follow are different from each other, as some are paths, tracks, streams, rivers, straight paths, and their shortcuts. The paths in dense forest are broken branches on small trees, and upon finding a broken branch, looking straight through the break, another break will be seen ahead, and another ahead of it, and in this manner they will follow this trail until they find the open and trodden path. Only the Indians are able to make use of the trails, but our soldiers may if they are skilled in the terrain as well, for the Indians walk marking one hill or another, and a river and trees. It is difficult to find the path along a stream, but if a trail has brought them to it, it will not be lost even if the Indian goes in the water, for sometimes footprints will be found on a rock or on some islet of sand; apart from the fact that, since the Indian goes confident that none else should enter there, he may cut a large leaf upon which to sit, and rocks where he places his foot will be found washed clean and flat; and this trail should be followed, for later it will give onto a road, as little lasts long in the water. The hilly path is continuous, for as it rises the path is seen, by which the Indians mostly communicate; and these roads are better in order to find a village, but only at nighttime; and one must march along them with great care, because of the large stones, cliffs, and dangerous paths that may exist; on these roads the Indian always takes his rest and recovers. On the river, the Indians commonly have dealings with each other in canoes or rafts or swimming on loose logs; and if our commander should come upon this trail and wish to follow it, rafts or canoes should be made and launched downstream, advancing between both shores with care, searching the ravines on either bank until coming upon roads or populations. And be advised to go with all the people in order, being aware of the waterfalls that often exist, these being where parties are usually lost and scattered. They also use shortcuts, which, it seems to me, should not be followed

Indian roads

unless one finds oneself trapped, for they are rugged and difficult and uncertain, unless one has a guide who is sure.

Dangerous paths While marching, the camp may also discover dangerous paths where they may be harmed by ambushes. It is the responsibility of the commander to personally clear these trails with the people he sees fit, bringing the camp to a halt and avoiding ambushes before coming upon them, opening the road on one side or the other. And if he does not wish to do this, he will take a dozen harquebusiers and walk ahead and, before entering the passage, they will go on one side and another between the mountain and the edge of the savanna, firing the harquebuses, for if there is an ambush, the Indians will rise up, giving their cry, and will leave the passage, and afterward it may be safely passed. And this method of securing the passage from ambushes will be used when our soldiers have been detected in the land; for if they are not discovered, it is not right that they, in doubt, are discovered by firing harquebuses. And in order to resolve this doubt it is sufficient to release a pair of dogs so that they discover the ambush if there is one, even though they are risked, for it is certain that the Indian will kill them except in a fortunate case. And likewise on other occasions, particular care should be exercised in knowing whether to release them and at what time, so that they are not killed but rather are advantageous and helpful, always leading them tied and positioned among the vanguard, main battalion, and rear guard, and among the scouts and in the squadron that would bring the livestock to a halt if there is one. And may they know how to honestly make use of their help, to our defense.

Dangerous paths should be reconnoitered It is also important to identify a passage where Indians may offend the camp [by rolling] large stones [down upon it], for they may often destroy much with them and even more if they attack from below with an ambush. To avoid this, one of two things must be prepared for: either take the high ground with harquebusiers and shield bearers as soon as the entire camp passes; or pass this way with the people divided into squads of four or six, so that the stones wreak no havoc, for small numbers are better prepared and retreat easier. To me, however, it is safer to secure the passage by taking the high ground, being able to do so without too much labor, taking care to follow and ascend along the sharpest ridge, for on it, though many stones may be set loose, they cannot cause harm, for they cannot be guided well and soon fall to one side or another. Knowing how to choose this ascent, they will ascend free from harm with their shield bearers ahead because of the arrows, slings, and darts; and the harquebusiers firing in their order if the ascent is defended. They will have this opportunity to take the high ground on a thousand occasions, upon which the commander, according to the occasion, will choose the people to take it; and this secures much and is quickly concluded, as will be stated later.

The commander will be prepared with a large tent, for if, in the land through which they are marching, the Indians use lances and darts, the tent will be of use, raising it in a downpour as protection for the harquebusiers; for the Indians who use these arms do so at close range and accurately, and if the harquebusiers, because of the rain, are unable to fire their arms, they will receive much harm, and be ruined; for the buckler is no arm to resist the fury of many lances together and the Indians know well how to follow the camp until they see an opportunity, which they diligently take advantage of, seeing that the harquebus is of no use with the water; and with the defense offered by the tent, these problems are secured against, raising the tent high, placing all the equipment between the openings and on the sides, and shield bearers for the protection of it. A few of the lances that the Indians and servants carry will be very important here, as it is a fine arm and its own defense. And at this time the shield bearers will make use of them for it will have a great effect. They will also avoid the archers in this way, for the water is also harmful to them with respect to their bowstrings that stretch and prevent straight shooting. And when they close in to fight hand-to-hand the Indians use their clubs, an inferior arm to the sword and buckler.

Good preparation

This tent, as has been said, is useful in terrain where lances are used and where our men may not make use of horses, for where they may use them they assure and defeat all. Apart from what has been said, it is good for the commander to order the captain in charge of the rear guard to advise his soldiers that if the Indians attack the vanguard, our men should continue marching without leaving their posts, halting the vanguard with care; for if the ambush be answered with an attack in the rear guard, they should be at the ready, and with this care and order they will arrive to the place where the vanguard is fighting, being careful not to leave any equipment behind. And he who is in charge of the battalion, at the same instant he hears the alarm, will make a pile of all the equipment and make the porters sit among the loads; and the shield bearers and harquebusiers of the battalion will surround them in order and keep this position until the skirmish or battle passes and the camp begins to march again, each one assuming his post. And if the ambush is begun in the rear guard, the vanguard will come retreating with the same order and care, firing their harquebuses, in case the enemy should attack from the front, in such a way that retreat and fighting become one until, encountering battalion and rear guard, they will rejoin the battle and act upon the orders of the commander, who will choose according to the movements of the fight. In so doing, the vanguard, as well as the rear guard, is strengthened, sword with sword, and the battalion in the middle or to one side. And so that this may come to a good end, the commander should take particular care that the camp always marches in tight formation, in such a manner that where one soldier lifts his foot, the other places his, both on these occasions and on suspect passages when such a commander may have been careless in clearing the passage or taking the high ground, as said before.

Opening roads The need to open roads in order to continue will often present itself. And for this, if it is dense forest, the machete wielders will go ahead, opening the path, changing places often so that everyone works and does not receive so much damage to their hands, for they usually become blistered. And in order to safely open the path on a mountain or in dense forest, the camp will halt at a comfortable place, until a good stretch has been opened. Here they are safe from ambushes, for the Indian will not reach his objective in their direction. And if the Indian should come following the camp and they desire to lay an ambush on the road they are opening, he will fall into it without a doubt.

A [compass] needle is greatly important in this opening of roads, marking the terrain; for with it they will open the path straight and reach their destination; but on the contrary, if the sun is clouded over, they may make a thousand turns and not improve their road and labor in vain; this happens more on flat land.

All that has been said in this chapter consists of proper order and discipline, for if it is lacking it will be impossible to accomplish anything, unless it is by chance, for the strength of an army lies more in its order than in its numbers or in any other thing. Experience has shown us in these places that with proper order, twelve soldiers have beaten and scattered a squad of two thousand Indians; and because of disorganization, fewer than thirty Indians have routed seventy Spaniards, killing and carrying off several in their hands. And the commander who would have his enterprise come to success follows two things: proper order and caution, for with these I can assure you fine success with divine favor.

METHODS OF CROSSING WIDE AND MID-SIZED RIVERS

Rivers are the most dangerous passages that our commander may have in his expeditions and discoveries; therefore, he should fear and prepare for them with particular care, for it is a thing to be watchful of; for if the strength of the enemy damages in one of the aforementioned passages, here it harms with greater strength, for they may be caught naked, unarmed, and separated. And above all, the strength and impetus of the river is what causes the most harm, as we have witnessed many people drown from lack of ability and knowledge, with no way to save them; or the river may carry away the raft with the clothing and arms with no way of retrieving it; or if some escape by swimming, they are left bare and unarmed. So, it is good that all these dangers and risks are prepared for with great consideration, knowing how to choose a given passage; and as this must be assured, it could have been addressed in the previous chapter; however, by examining it and giving more extensive advice on the manners and opportunities often presented, the choice is left to the commander, who will have everything at hand, whereby he may take advantage of that which he sees best suits his purpose.

First, then, and before all other things, regardless of how the river should be crossed, one must secure both banks with armed people, that they may halt on the opposite bank; and until that is done neither clothing nor service will pass. And until all are safely positioned on the other bank, the soldiers who have halted on this one will not pass nor let their arms leave their hands. While the camp prepares to cross, *Secure the river crossings* it is best that the soldiers who secure the opposite bank are swimmers and unencumbered soldiers and hard workers, who, if the river should run deep and cannot be forded, will make a small raft to carry their harquebuses, bucklers, or lances, and keep hold of it while they swim; and in this manner they will cross. Also, each soldier may do without the raft using his own log by carrying it between the legs or under his left arm; and with this he may swim in such a manner that his gunpowder, match, and embers for his harquebus do not become wet. On a raft there is greater security that the harquebus and munitions will not become wet, but none should climb aboard, rather holding to it and swimming. If they use logs, the lancers will tie their lances to it with vines; if they are shield bearers, they will tie their bucklers to their backs with their sword belts and carry their swords in their mouths; and if they are harquebusiers, they will wear their powder charges at their back with the harquebus lengthwise, such that the match and stock protrude above the head and the barrel hangs downward. As they are upon a log, their backs are above the water, and the matches are on their hats or the stock of their harquebus, and the gunpowder in its place. They will carry their knives in their belts and wear their linen underpants and espadrilles and no other clothing, for afterward, the first thing the commander will order them to do upon crossing is to dress. If they are able to pass across a dog or two, they will do this, for they will be good for discovering if there is an ambush, a thing to be feared if following an open road; and if they are opening the passage they may be sure of it, but if it is already open, they should be suspicious. Just as we secure the camp by sending these soldiers to the opposite bank, it will also be proper that we secure them from danger, ordering them to launch their raft or log from such a place that they get out of the river a harquebus shot above the continuance of the path, where they may ready their arms in safety. Order them to scout the entire bank, from wherever the enemy may be feared up to the next pass. The dog or dogs that may have crossed will run loose, and the soldiers, with their arms at the ready, will scout the crossing and surroundings, looking for any trace of Indians. They will position a sentinel on the path ahead, in order to discover any approaching people and give warning and ambush them; and they will remain there with such caution until the camp passes. And if upon crossing these soldiers should encounter people lying in ambush, they will defend themselves in good order with their harquebuses, firing as able, always having the river for refuge, and with the objective of securing the beach so the Indian does not take the river crossing from them. And the commander will encourage them from this bank, joining them with harquebuses, sending them help with swimming soldiers. And if they are unable to sustain the attack until help arrives, because of too many people, they will throw themselves into the river and return to the camp, and they will make boats or canoes or bridges in order to cross with greater strength, for at this point the land will have already been warned.

If the river is clear and slow, and along the shore or close to it there are logs for making canoes, these are the best things to make, lacking a bridge. These canoes are of great service in many undertakings; the logs for them are cedar, *caracoli*, and *ceiba*; and two canoes tied together may be loaded heavily and with safety; and alone, launched with wooden outriggers so that they do not capsize, they sustain a great load. *Canoes*

Also, if the river is easy with no falls or rapids, rafts are quite good and secure; they should be made of logs called *balsa*, or *rumos*, and of *guadua* bamboo; these materials trap water because their stems swell, and they are easy to work. Rafts may also be made of palm and of reeds or bulrush. They can also be made of gourds wherever they are found; it is the best invention of all. But the best and most common are logs of balsa wood, found everywhere. *Rafts*

But when it is necessary to make a raft, because there is no other remedy, and in order to make it with all precautions, I will comment here on an extraordinary manner of making one. It is to make a framework in the shape of the raft of any sort of thin poles, with thick cross-points; next, attach the bucklers necessary to make it solid, tying them to the frame by their handles, procuring to attach as many as possible. If it is made with two layers of bucklers, it will be higher and the clothes will be safe from getting wet; and if it is of one layer, place brushwood atop a rack of reeds. These bucklers are to go with the concave side down, and upon this raft they will pass the bundles across safely, the river being calm, and they will make use of this in times of necessity. *Extraordinary manner of making rafts*

The best method to make a raft is in an equilateral triangle, the sides of equal length, for it is directed and guided with any of its three points and they are quite safe in this shape, for if they should hit something in the river, be it a log or a stone, one of the other two points will come around, escaping with no risk. This shape is not good for the sea, for it does not break the water well even though it is under much sail. A raft long in the stem and stern is better for this, as the triangular one is useful only for navigating a river with the current.

Type of bridge It also happens that one arrives at a river with a great many stones, wide and deep, where one cannot make a rope bridge, nor a platform bridge, nor place trees across it, nor launch raft or canoes because it has rocks and waterfalls in it. In such a river a bridge will be made log by log and rock by rock, placing poles across and making the deck with the angular trusses it should require, and poles will be placed in the river as a buttress between it and the bridge so that its poles do not slide, shoring up the deck of the bridge and sustaining it, and in this manner should it be built up until it reaches the opposite bank.

Other types of bridges They may arrive at a river where there is no other way to cross but by swimming; here they will pass across those people who do not know how to swim by passing a thick vine or rope from one bank to the other at a place where the river is slow-moving and the bank is close to the water, tying it from one tree to another, or from one post to another, or log to log. And when all of these are lacking, digging a trench away from the shore, knee deep, and running the cord or vine from it to another trench on the other bank and packing it in with earth, it will be as fixed as if it were tied to trees; and along this may those who do not know how to swim be passed across, placing their entire bodies in the river and pulling themselves along the rope, supporting themselves in the water, and in this manner a few swimmers may cross first, taking a small bundle across. Be aware that the cord must be taut in order to sustain a body, for it must be used and loaded with force. Be aware of this manner of crossing in case such a necessity requires it.

The camp may also arrive at a narrow ravine with no place to cross; they will cross with brevity by cutting a tree so that it may reach the other side, and if it does not reach, they will cut one from the other side, across from it, with which they will have made a bridge, adding the desired or necessary poles on top in order to cross in safety.

At other times they may arrive at rivers that seem to be running high, which they may cross without having to make a bridge, in complete silence, if they are in a populated area. Two good swimmers enter the river to see if they may slip across, and being able, squads will cross little by little and holding together so as not to become mixed up in the current; and from one bank to the other there will be swimmers in the water up to their belts and in the middle to help them. In this manner the porters will cross between soldiers who hold on to them. And they are advised that harquebuses and munitions will be carried on the head with one hand, and the Indians will carry their loads in the same manner, so that they do not get wet. They must keep two things in mind: go with the current, and be sure the crossing is clear with no large rocks.

Methods of crossing rivers

Another manner of crossing rivers uses expert soldiers, with no bridges nor rafts nor ropes, as they are skilled and know everything, and it is this: if the river is waist-deep and quick and littered with rocks, there is great danger among the people to go loaded with so much baggage. Those soldiers who are swimmers will cross the river with the current, not against it, for they are not able to sustain this; but rather, as I say, and holding on to each other from one bank to the other. In this way they will ensure that they go across, soldiers as well as porters and disabled people, holding on to one another by the lower part on the leeward side and in the slowness of the river made by these people who make the bridge; and with this remedy they will pass so that the water neither disturbs nor carries any piece away, having a few good swimmers below with their staves, striving in the middle of the river to save anyone who should fall and save the load should some porter let it escape.

If a river is of such condition that one cannot pass in the said manner because it is deep and wide and with rapids, the commander will order a vine bridge to be strung, giving orders to cut as many and as thick as they may find, passing one across, and from one bank to another, tying it tightly to two trees or, lacking these, to thick posts, and they will proceed building their bridge upon this; the friendly Indians know well how to do this. And until the bridge is complete, with ropes in place to take hold of, no one is permitted across; and once finished they will pass little by little and with wariness, due to the danger.

The commander will occasionally need to send lightly laden people ahead, and these may encounter rivers along the road that cannot be crossed, where rafts cannot be made because there are falls and rapids, and where it would not be good to be hindered by making a bridge of vines. It is good to make a one-rope hauling bridge [*tarabita*], tying a very thick vine or rope from one bank to the other between two trees or thick posts, then attaching a sort of rope swing to it, and the person will sit in it and another vine or rope will be tied to the swing, and they will pull it from one bank, holding on to the rope, and let out rope from the other and allow the swing to travel along the cord to which it is attached; and thus all the people and baggage will quickly pass across. And if the camp should be at such a river for a long time, it may also make use of this ropeway, although for many people it is slow.

If the camp should arrive at a waterfall or rapid whose depth reaches the waist and is fast-moving, and if it is clear, there is no reason to wait and search for a way to make a bridge; but rather, follow the course shown by the current, either with or against the water, according to the space offered by the banks. Everyone holding together in a group, and placing between two swimmers anyone who is not, they will cross with ease, for in this manner they break the fury of the water such that boys will pass with no grief or misfortune. And I warn that none should pass alone, for he will be carried away by the water.

As a final point regarding these bridges and crossings, I wish to demonstrate here something extraordinary, strong and secure, requiring little work, for a lone soldier may make it, helping himself across the same river. It is a bridge that, though the enemy may be on the opposite bank guarding the crossing, can be made without being noticed in less than two hours; by the time the enemy notices, they have already crossed. Measure this river with mathematics, if known, or with a good eye, if the enemy defends it; if not, there is no necessity of it. Once measured, a cluster of guadua bamboo canes will be cut to measure, and if an extension is necessary one may tie one to another, but it is better if they are whole. Once cut, a tree root exposed by the river or a steep point on the opposite bank will be chosen, and in case the enemy defends this place, one will be chosen farther up or down river, making the presence of the camp known to the enemy. And by night at the chosen site, a good stake will be driven into the ground and this bamboo will be tied to it, some by the top and some by the base, placing them along the shore upstream, in the water; and in this manner, as much bamboo as needed, according to the plan for the bridge, will be tied together; and afterward, with a long pole, the bamboo canes should be pushed away from the bank one by one, pushing them into the current, which will take hold of them and carry them to rest at the place chosen on the opposite bank, which is the root of a tree or steep point, and there they will stop and support each other. And having passed them in this manner, they will start at one end of the bridge, tying crossbars across all the bamboo; and thus, two steps by two steps, they will place and tie them with vines until they reach the other side, making it strong and secure, and more so if they attach a handrail and buttress the bridge.

I have not addressed the method of taking horses across, for when one has the opportunity of taking them, crossing rivers is easy; and thus each one will see, having the matter at hand, how to do it, to whom I remit the decision, as with all the rest that has been stated.

What I advise to the commander is that he takes great care with the gunpowder, that it is carried with respect, and that the soldiers carry it in their jackets, as there is usually great carelessness in this and it is important that it not become wet; for when clothing is wet, little is lost, but with gunpowder, much is lost. *Warning*

METHODS OF QUARTERING A CAMP WITH STRENGTH

Nature shows us how important fortification is in all things, showing it to us in our own head and in fruits, encased in a thousand varied manners, such that without this protection it would be impossible to conserve [that which is held] or keep [it] for any time at all; and in the same manner are kingdoms, estates, and cities kept; for however great they may be, even though the enemy lies distant, if they lack fortification, they are never without fear and suspicion; at times they are suspicious of those native to the land, and at others, of their neighbors.

The Greeks always sought shelter, as people of so much government, in a fortress or citadel. The Romans maintained their empire and fatherland with fortresses. *Example of the Greeks—Romans*

The Turk—Persians   The Turk has been broken several times and has repaired himself with fortresses, and with them he has won and secured great lands; but because they lacked them, the Persians have lost campaigns and cities.

No less necessity has our commander in strengthening and securing his camp and settlements, eyes always on the enemy, for though he may not require the castle, the wall, the counterscarp, the moat, nor artillery strength, he will require, according to his manner and weakness, other strengths that in their way are no less important; for inasmuch as strength corresponds to the enemy, it is legitimate strength, and such care should be taken with it as with that which is more tedious, more costly, or more obvious; because it is with this strength that the objective is either claimed or lost, as we have seen in those parts [i.e., the Indies], whatever their importance. And before we speak about the kinds of fortresses needed to resist the impetus of the enemy, we will state that in order for the site to be perfectly comfortable, our commander should have the custom of making camp at three hours after noon whenever he marches, so that the people may make themselves comfortable, arranging their quarters to sleep in that night or pitching their tents; for as tired people, they have the necessity of refreshing themselves and preparing their meals and arms and other duties of greater or lesser importance. And above all, if they plan on making any type of fortification, they should have time for it; for if not, arriving late, they will lack all comfort and place to choose the site and inspect it, and will be left with no form of relief.

Open terrain is good lodging   The ideal quarters or camp is on flat, open terrain when taking horses, for with them the enemy is thwarted when he might attack, and he is better noticed and distance is better judged and there is less risk. Our commander, should he reach such a place, may camp here, mindful that there is a stream of water nearby, which, if the terrain is forested, he will keep at the distance of an arrow shot, so that they cannot be reached. And if it is not wooded, he may place the camp close to the river, for it will be more secure and closer to the service of the water, positioning the river at their backs and posting a sentinel.

Modes of situating the camp   The encampment may be made of one lane with two entrances or in a triangle, with three, or in a square, with four, leaving a commons in the middle, clean and cleared.

The site itself will determine the method, and once chosen, the people will be distributed in their squads; the horsemen in the manner they would be on open terrain, taking care that twelve tied horses, more or less, according to what the commander may deem necessary, sleep inside of the camp, saddled with neither breast strap nor crupper, and with the bridle hanging from the pommel and the spurs of sparrow-beak type tied to the cavalry stirrup, so they are not forgotten nor lost. When the armed soldier goes to his horse, his other arms should also be ready, the lance placed with its end upon the ground close to the horse so that it may be grasped upon mounting. And in order for these horsemen to go forth, the harquebusiers will clear the area near the entrance, to gain space and be able to face the enemy.

And by night, they will not leave nor separate until the dawn is breaking, in such a manner that they all go together in a group. And, the day being clear, they may divide themselves two by two, for they may see and aid one another. And the horses should be gathered together and kept with good grazing close to the encampment, where the cavalry is permitted to go out at night to defend them. During their watches the horses will be gathered by two mounted soldiers, with their lances and arms, so that the Indians neither carry them away nor shoot them with arrows. And once their watch is finished, two more will go out; and if they should come upon Indians, they should hold them off until the rest of the camp arrives.

And take note that none should wear bells by night, for it is quite harmful; by day, on the contrary, they are useful. And returning to the infantry, the camp entrances should be guarded by squads, harquebusier with shield bearer, and at the entrances, the muskets they carry. The camp sentry walk should be clear in order for the sentinels to be able to run and move from one side to the other. *By night, horses should not wear bells*

And if the enemy has much strength in numbers and there is need to rest one day, build a stockade, as it is quite secure. A light defense will be sufficient for one night, but having to rest several days it is best to make a stockade, such as should be done in a wet season; one is required where there are many people, just for meals. *The stockade secures the camp*

Everyone knows that the poles of a stockade must be closely and *Stockade form* deeply placed, two stories high, leaving a few embrasures for the harquebusiers; and, above all, the gates should conform to the design and features of the stockade, such that a man on horseback may enter. At the gate should be built a fore-gate in such a way that one is a lance length from the other, for they are very strong entrances, and the Indian, if he is one of those who use them, may neither enter nor make use of his lance. And note that ropes should not be used around the stockade, for it gives the enemy a way to climb over; the strength comes from burying the poles well.

The best fort against Indians is of tamped earth   And if the land is settled and a tamped-earth [*tapia*] fort can be built, it should be done; it is best and safest. And if a stockade is built due to a lack of clay earth, may it be done in the interim before they have another mode of protection. And the site will determine the manner of fortification. If it is of tamped earth, covered towers will be made over the gates or on the corners, so that the harquebusiers may be of use in times of rain and take advantage of the stone [*piedra*]. These towers have been used but a few times, nor is there much reason to use them, unless it is for a clear advantage or a necessity that constrains them to such a defense.

Defenses on a night of necessity   If the camp or a lone squad should march with an objective and find itself among many of the enemy, unable to build a fort because of the lateness of the hour or because they lack such convenience, it is good to prepare by cutting many thick branches and surrounding themselves with them as fence and defense, for at least that will hamper the enemy and break the fury with which he comes, primarily if the harquebusiers fire in time. Erecting another, second fence and leaving the middle part empty is better. It may be made of guadua bamboo or of spiny palms or wild canes, and it will be strong due to the spines and barbs it has. And lacking all of this, our own trunks and bags can be made into a type of impediment for people with lances; because as they attack in haste, they cross without stopping, to take what they can at one time, and upon discovering the impediment, they will be stopped and defeated as the harquebusiers fire. And the best of all is to make their quarters where they may, joining some with others, situating themselves in the space offered by the site. Single-roofed quarters [*ranchos de agua y media*] are the finest, making a courtyard, for in this way the enemy is hindered and the lodgings are clear and the soldiers may communicate; and take care that the common is clear with nothing that would impede walking. And if it is not convenient to make such quarters, camps may be made of tents in the same way.

For few people, and if it is for one night, another good method is to camp among thick reeds, making a clearing with machete and hatchet, leaving tangled reeds as a manner of fence, and leaving the gate or entrances as the site allows. This manner of campsite serves against the enemy, opening a new path in the morning, and marching toward their objective upon leaving; for if they should leave by an open road, they run the risk of ambush. And if it is a land of arrows, they should be aware of a method of defense that appears a laughable thing but is a very good remedy; first making their clearing in thick forest or vegetation and tangling large and small trees around it with ropes or the chords of the harquebusiers, as if they had fallen in a circle around the clearing. From this, drape the blankets of the porters and soldiers, which are a stature and a half long, and tie all the baggage around their base, leaving the entrances where advisable and quite narrow; and be sure that though the Indians may let fly a great quantity of arrows, they will not cause harm, for because of the trees, they cannot shoot from above, but rather straight on, forcing them to shoot into the defense of blankets and as these are hanging all around, when the arrow penetrates four fingers deep, it stops and is left hanging, so that in no manner may they offend the camp, and this remedy is sufficient.

Artifices for quartering few people

The best site of all, in lands of lances as well as arrows, taking horses or not, is upon a barren height, where the Indian may not offend with arrows and from which the campaign may be controlled; it is quite secure for a few people to camp on high, for though they have no other strength, this is sufficient.

Now that we have spoken of several modes of forts for the defense of our camp, I wish to conclude this chapter by giving some necessary advice for marching either in the rainy season or through a settlement.

Our commander should take care not to permit a soldier to call a false alarm without verifying it well beforehand, and once verified, give the alert first, as has been mentioned, and later the alarm, unless it is so sudden that it cannot be avoided. I warn of this because there are sol-

Advice for the commander

diers who, being very inexperienced or fearful, upon hearing a fruit fall from the tree, or a stick, or a monkey making a noise, or a tiger or lion or other beast, fire their harquebus, calling the alarm, raising the camp for no reason, and unsettling everyone for the rest of the night.

Likewise, be sure to order the sentinel not to sit or rest upon anything, so that he does not sleep, nor walk too much, though the watch is clear. For they are so subtle, the Indians, that in one turning of the sentinel, they come in, dragging their bellies upon the ground and when they see that he is returning, they stop. They use all these deceits in order to give a sudden assault; and with the sentinel standing at his post, looking out from one side to another, they will not do it and they will be noticed. Doubling the sentries will be all the more secure. And likewise, do not permit the mounted watch, who patrols the surroundings and the camp, the livestock and horses, to wear bells, for at night they are very harmful and detrimental.

Take heed not to permit any soldier to sleep naked or unshod; and for this, make it customary to inspect those soldiers with whom he has not been satisfied, and if he should arrive wet and desire to change his clothes, warn him that he must sleep with shoes on, as they are essential if an alarm should find the soldier barefooted, for he is unable to walk well through the confusion of logs, spikes, and rocks, which, with his hemp sandals, would not hinder him at all.

Be advised that in times of doubt, none should disarm, but rather sleep in their coats and with the harquebuses at the ready, for it is a slow weapon in an attack. Here, lances are of great help in holding back the impetus of the enemy while the harquebusiers fire.

Be advised to frequently examine the arms of the soldiers so that there is no carelessness with them.

Our commander is advised in times of danger to double the sentries in order to cover that which a lone sentinel might overlook, and they should be a harquebusier and shield bearer.

Be advised to avoid murmuring in the camp, particularly among the rabble, and even more if there are Indians with children among them, for these often pinch them so that they cry, all to impede the sentinel from hearing so that the enemy may better enter; and great care must be taken in this, and quickly, for if there is no silence, the sentinel will carry out his duty poorly, and in not doing it well, poor is the security.

Our commander is advised that in any assault that the Indians should give, by night or by day, the camp should not be abandoned until the supplies and baggage are carried away with great order, for damages will occur. Thus, it is best to leave by day, accounting for everything.

Be advised to have fire in the camp all through the night, partly so that it is not extinguished if it rains, and also that near it none should sleep; and the sentinel should take his watch there, for it usually happens that two Indians come alone in the hills only to shoot their arrows at those they may see. And if it should rain and they find themselves with no covering branches, camp, or tents for the fire, shelter it with whatever means possible; and the sentinels will attend to it so that it is not extinguished. And if there is too much water for a fire, light matches so that they have fire for the harquebuses.

Be advised to always secure the captives' chain, placing it around a tree; and if they are on the savanna, drive a good stake into the ground for this purpose and place a guard at it, for security is of great importance.

Be advised not to permit, by night or by day, anyone to leave the camp without orders, for in this there is great carelessness in some commanders and great harm occurs.

And likewise take care not to permit Indians, those of service as well as allies, to leave the camp in dubious lands for water or wood or palm fronds for tents or to fish or trap, without soldiers who can make them halt, due to the risk they run from the enemy; for sometimes misfortunes occur, and with this precaution the Indian will not flee.

Take heed not to permit the soldier to wager his arms nor his clothes, for the commander is obligated to supply the soldier with what he needs, and with a little care taken in this they are supplied and remedied.

Be advised in lands of war, that in the interim between the time they arrive at a site and begin to camp, make several soldiers halt with their arms, so that the enemy does not attack and find everyone separated and unarmed. Also, upon striking the camp to march, take the proper precautions, that those whose turn it is to be the vanguard for that day should halt while the camp ties and loads.

Also, the commander is advised, if he finds himself in a predicament with but a few people, to make a demonstration of making camp with many bright lights, and as the night closes, to march on, if the night be suited to it; and if it is not, to detour his camp, laying an ambush in a place where they may later be relieved.

Be advised that in all places where the enemy is near, after offering peace to them and having made many offers, if they do not wish for peace, cut them short, procuring to ruin their plans, for it is a sign that they are awaiting help. To prepare for this, one of the prisoners taken [in the standard hostage exchange] will be pressured to declare where help is expected, so that they may lay an ambush along the path.

Be advised that as soon as his [i.e., the captain's] people are at leisure, he should teach them and practice all things concerning arms and agility, being a good teacher; for the captain should be so in all things, so that with this he does his duty and avoids idleness, which is the teacher of great evils and evil thoughts.

The commander must work so that the enemy does not glory in taking loot.—Example of Julius Caesar

The commander will not cease to work, such that the enemy may not rejoice in having taken some plunder. Julius Caesar did this well and showed it when he was defeated by the Alexandrians; diving in to swim the river Nile, he crossed while armed, taking the *Commentaries* in one hand and swimming with the other, carrying his clothing in his mouth.[5]

The commander should attend to all important matters in person.—The soldier is to be punished with the sword

To all matters of importance the commander should attend in person, trusting no one, if he wants them to transpire prosperously; for he runs a great danger of losing his honor, earned over many years, in but an hour if the enemy finds him unorganized; and also, for the soldier who does not obey his order, a punishment with the sword in the hand is just, for with this he is punished and honored. And if it is a small thing, a reprimand will be enough, placing him under guard, according to custom.

The commander must not write against the soldier, unless it is to take his life for treason or mutiny.—If the commander allows gossip, his command will rot and be lost

And abstain from making proceedings of any kind, unless it is that he cannot avoid taking a life because of mutiny or conspiracy; to ease his conscience he should procure to avoid gossip, not permitting it, for it greatly corrupts those who give orders and creates great evils. And he should always foster friendships so that there are no divisions, being a father to all, without showing partiality.

THE METHOD OUR COMMANDER WILL HAVE IN NIGHT ATTACKS

There is no wound so straight and true as that given by your own blade, and with reason should the one that gives it be called skilled, if in order to give it he has prepared his means proportionately and knowledgeably, for with this he will be assured success; and this occurs likewise in arms as in the other wiles of war. And as my aim and purpose is to advise upon all the features of this militia we are considering, it being so different from the others, it is necessary that we also discuss extensively all the manners of attracting to our communication those people who, under orders of our lord king, will go to pacify, and procuring their conservation. Because many commanders may ignore that which is so necessary for them to know, I will speak about night attacks, and how fundamental they are, and at what time and occasion they will be given, and how they should be made use of, being the best and most advisable artifice for acquiring that which is desired. Because of the labor this requires, the awaited prize will be claimed, which is to see the land peaceful and the natives domesticated; and in addition to this it redeems much of the war they often give to us, being rested and comfortable, for all their war is night attacks, and as they are a treacherous people, this is their manner of arms. And thus have they struck us with many lances, taking us unawares; and it is a good remedy to give them the same wound so that they do not worry us, but rather fear us; and most importantly, in order to take some of them to secure peace, I believe the commander should make much use of these night attacks, not permitting unjust damage to be inflicted; for with this, weary and fearful, they will make peace and be calmed. Treat them thusly, corresponding to the enemy's every intention; for there [i.e., in the Indies], only the greatest diligence and speed wins, because the most important hour of their war is the nighttime, as they are nocturnal birds; and so the same path should be followed, for by doing so, their intentions are ruined and all their thoughts and strengths are severed. Make use of these night attacks according to the opportunities presented, marching the camp in silence before being noticed; for it is good advice not to show oneself until the prey is captive. Thus the commander will send ahead a squadron of people by night, so that they awake in the village,

Night attacks are important.—Method of night attacks

in order to make note of the language of the land; and having done this, they will speak to the Indians they take in their own language, making them understand their coming; and until the camp arrives, if it is necessary, their position will be fortified. This night attack is given with a guide, either by smoke seen by day, marking the land, or by following the fire by night.

A night attack should also be given in a pursuit, following the tracks by day, and by night, the firelight; then the assault is given quite securely.

Why a night attack should be given and at what time — An attack should also be made when the province has rebelled, breaking the peace they may have made. This night attack must be made with the greatest possible speed and with great pronouncements and care due to the uproar and vigilance the Indians are sure to possess, fleeing from the punishment they expect.

Another method of night attack — Attacks should also be given during one of the frequent drunken gatherings of the Indians, in order to disrupt it and give them no place for their alliances or conspiracies; for it should appear to them that we are over them at all times, and that they know this regardless of what they attempt or do; this is easy to make them believe, as they take us for children of the sun and call us that in the new conquests.[6]

An opportunity to give a night attack — Night attacks should also be given in a retreat if the land allows, as has been stated, leaving fires made while marching in silence in order to deceive the enemy, the soldier placing his foot where another has stepped. And in doing this much will be revealed, for in silence any word or order is heard.

Caution — Note that the rivers that must be crossed on rafts or by any other artifice, such as when there is no bridge or secure crossing, should not be crossed at night unless there is moonlight, and unless they cross in canoes and all the people go together and safe from all harm.

An attack on a rainy night is the best — Note that in order to be effective, the best night attack of all, though requiring more labor, is on a rainy and tempestuous night, for this provides two assurances: one is not being noticed, and the other is that the Indians are all gathered inside their huts or hovels. On the contrary, on a pleasant night they sleep outside their houses at the doors and covered with branches; and in the countryside they sleep near fishing holes and in the fields; and with a rainstorm, as they are not ready for war, fewer Indians walk about by night.

The commander is advised that the soldiers on these night attacks must carry their matches lit, and guard the tubes in which they are carried, so that they are not extinguished, nor wet with water or dew, nor seen. *Warnings to the commander*

Be sure to lead the dogs on leashes and not to step on them, for in a night attack, with respect to this risk, this usually causes damage, for should they be stepped upon they bark, and by night this carries far and wakes the people if they happen to be near, and so one must caution the soldiers to take great care.

The commander and soldiers should beware that if anyone falls and rolls down a hill or precipice and hurts his head or receives any other injury, he should not cry out; nor should those who see him fall or stumble, even if it is the commander himself. For no advantage can be gained from this, and the opportunity may be lost by being noticed either by some sentinel or from some farmland that lies near, or from a village that happens to be close, for there are always people. Two risks are run by anything being noticed: one is losing the prey and the other is that they mount an ambush before reaching the village. This is bad, but much worse if by night, for if one should stumble, this is made loud in the silence, and he who is closest will help if necessary. If, however, they are quiet, though the noise of the shield is heard, they believe that it is some stick that fell in the hills or forest and are reassured. And the soldiers will march with such account and reason that they do not break up nor lose each other, first for strength, but also in order to pass along the word or order in silence, as has been stated as being necessary. *Warnings*

Beware to take much care with the harquebuses, so that they do not get wet, or that a spark from the match falls onto the pan; apart from the danger of killing the man who may be in front or behind, the opportunity is lost by firing, for the report can be heard. And for this, wax cloth or black wax on the priming pan is good for covering the openings, and a tuft of wool between the powder and the pan, for more security, so it not only consumes the humidity in the powder but also contains the fire and does not allow it to come into contact with the powder.

Warnings Be aware that in the rain forest or in dense thickets, if the night is very dark and the people have taken a remote path and are sure that they cannot be noticed (by not taking the straight path), and the guide is following it by marks, they may light some small, rolled candles at times, for the road is made shorter with them. And if they lack candles, use torches made of palm, but few of these and carefully, extinguishing them upon nearing the objective.

Beware that if carrying out a night attack requires walking during the day, they should not make fire, for they will be discovered by the smoke; and if they should stop at night they should not make fire either, unless they are in the jungle; there they may safely do so, because by night the smoke cannot be seen, and by being in the forest, neither can the flame. Note that fire should not be made upon planted clearings, nor any open ground.

Be aware that one must arrive to give the dawn raid before daybreak and for this it is good to arrive with time to spare and wait for the hour somewhat away from the settlement, so that if a noise is made, it is not noticed; sending forth spies to the settlement and making the raid before dawn breaks, for the Indians have the custom of leaving their huts at this time for their necessities and they may notice the people. And this is a good hour, for while they are surrendering, the day breaks and one may see what is being done.

Be well aware when distributing the people, if the houses or villages are set apart, that they all make the attack at the same time, upon the signal. This may be according to the position of the moon if it should rise or set at this time, or, lacking this, by a signal at daybreak. It is not good to sound the trumpet nor fire the harquebus, for if there are other villages nearby that have not been seen, allow time for them and take them unawares. And this division of the people should be in such a manner that they may aid one another, that they are not so far away to hear the signal to regroup; and the commander should position his people before attacking, giving orders to each one as to what he must do. Afterward, a second order cannot be followed, for a dawn raid is different from a skirmish, because with the first order one must succeed or fail.

Be aware that, as has been stated, the harquebus must not be fired, not only so that the nearby villages do not notice, but also due to the risk that our Spaniards run in killing each other, unless it is that they find themselves in dire circumstances and are obliged to do it; but all should be gathered to one side first.

Beware that as men are sent out to the hut or house or fort according to their distribution, they will send in soldiers who are assigned to it, unless the Indians have taken up arms; and if they have, they should not do this until day breaks, surrounding all parts so that the people may not go, guarding the entrances to the huts or forts, where there are usually traps, spikes, and other devices, for by being armed, everything is ready, and by day one sees what is done. But in case they are unaware, the soldiers will approach the entrances, wearing their helmets and their bucklers, protecting their eyesight from the arrow, in case some Indian is so prepared as to seize his bow at the slightest noise, for they sleep with bows in the hammock and bed. Those who enter should then corner the people to one side, without dividing them up, but forming a half moon. And at this time the commander will have taken the doors and sides with his people, as they usually have false doors through which they escape or open suddenly. And beware that there is no hut but that has two principal doors, and when there is no more than one, the other is secret.

Be warned not to release any dogs at this time, for they rush in and the Indians kill them, and to avoid this, order that they be kept on leash. It will also be good that at this juncture the friendly Indians detour around and encircle the camp opposite the Spaniards so that the guilty do not flee or escape, but rather are captured, for otherwise they will cause more damage by bringing together others and stirring up the land against us.

Our commander should note that if they be put on the defensive, they may be persuaded with peace; and so through any interpreters that may be captured, promise them that no harm will befall them, unless they are guilty, for with this they usually submit and turn over the delinquents.

The commander should be aware that before entering the village, all the clothing they are carrying and useless [i.e., noncombatant] people should be hidden in the forest, but not far away so that they may be aided and relieved should something occur.

Methods of night attacks I have forgotten two important methods of night attacks, so it would be good to state them. After having sent forward an interpreter or notice appropriate to the nature of the deed, such as "the Spaniards wish to speak with them," have them gather that night so that the raid may be made upon them. This is taken out upon people who have rebelled and broken the peace, but with new people this should not be done.

Another secure night attack, having taken prisoners and left an area, is to return after two or three days, traveling fast and light [*a la ligera*], for other surrounding peoples will be found in their huts and villages.

Warning to the commander Our commander is advised to give the dawn raid with quickness, gathering up his people if they are scattered; and with the prisoners taken, retreating to the camp or the place from whence they came at double speed; for they run the risk of ambushes. But if too isolated the retreat should not be undertaken with great quickness, but rather by concealing the path they took to make the assault, and taking instead the cleanest [i.e., hardest to follow] paths possible through marshes or difficult passages. This speed is of great importance in all affairs concerning this militia and particularly in saving a prisoner. And all these warnings, and those I will later give, are intended for the greater good, and so that evil may not be done; for as these pacifications are required, it is necessary to know how one is to act in them, procuring our defense with the least harm to the natives.

METHOD OF GIVING AND RECEIVING AMBUSHES

As has been stated, the inventions of war that the natives of those parts use are so many that they have shown us some that we use and that are necessary in order to countermine them. One of the most harmful things that I notice in war and which should most be feared are ambushes, for with all the care that a captain may have, if he is taken by one, they will always cause him harm. And so, in my view, the commander should procure two things: the first, to always ambush the enemy, for it is something that greatly destroys their strength and breaks their spirit; and the other, to flee from them if at all possible; and so for one as for the other, I will give the precepts and warnings as well as I may, charging the commanders to seek out new methods according to the opportunities they may have at hand, for if they are watchful in this, time and opportunity will teach them.

The most ordinary ambush made is on a great, well-traveled road, for the purpose of taking some people as guides or interpreters of the land, or to strike at people who are known to be coming along the road; and if it is a crossroads, the prey will be all the more certain. The method of laying it is that wherever it is to be lain there must be no trace, otherwise whoever is leading the people [along the road] will stop; and from here on, the ambush is set by placing the two columns of soldiers in the scrubland, marsh, or forest; and these take up positions at a distance of a stone's throw; and they should not be too close nor too far, but somewhat set away from the road, so that they are not noticed and the people enter the ambush. And he who is to issue the cry "Santiago!"[7] is to be very close to the road where the trail was made by our people, so that at this moment all the people will be caught in the ambush. Along with he who would give the Santiago, there should be half a dozen good soldiers; and there should be several more gathered at the place where the enemy enters, all well hidden among the branches, making no noise. He who issues the Santiago should have his harquebus at the ready so that he may fire it when the group of people arrives, for this will be the signal to all those in the ambush who will take the road and the flanks with swords and bucklers, so that none should have to fire the harquebus but he who gives the signal, as stated. And with this the people who have entered the ambush will turn back to where they entered and will find themselves surrounded, for the road will have been taken. And the Indians, hearing voices and murmurs, which are the only sounds permitted, are disturbed and cut off. And he who issues the Santiago beware that, if his harquebus does not fire due to some mishap, he is to draw his sword and buckler and give the

Common ambush

Santiago by mouth, all responding to him together as one voice. And beware that, before setting the ambush, the troops should take their useless [i.e., noncombatant] and disabled [*impedida*] people away from the road. The friendly Indians should be armed and positioned among the Spaniards, according to those who are present, for they have a great effect. Several harquebusiers should also be near if the enemy has such tenacity as to reach a position of victory, though this rarely occurs; and at such a time, it will be good that they assist, gathering themselves into squads for more strength. In this ambush, prior to setting it, avoid all murmurings. This method of ambush must be used when expecting many people, for if it is only for taking guides, there is no necessity of going so far or firing the harquebus.

Ambush They may also be laid in ravines, where roads follow, downstream or upstream.

Method of ambush These ambushes may also be laid when they come upon a village without being noticed and find it deserted, the Indians being in their fisheries or maize plantings; it may be set in the very same huts or cabins, letting them arrive and come inside. And if there is any underbrush close to the huts, remove it.

Other methods of ambush It may also be set in an encampment, allowing the troop to go ahead, with orders to halt and maintain silence once hidden; for afterward the Indians come to the huts and shelters to see if anything has been forgotten or if they have buried any dead in order to eat them. An ambush is good there.

Another good ambush is where some justice has been served [i.e., someone has been executed], for later they come to carry away the dead and there they cry, saying a thousand disgraces about the soldiers; and at the moment they are carrying them away it is good to come out in ambush; and there are more than a few who are to be found at this burial.

Another good ambush is near where livestock and horses are kept, for they come to steal them and kill them with arrows.

Another important ambush and remedy is upon a freshly opened path which has been cut to avoid some ambush recognized on the open road; for the enemy sees that the Christians do not enter the ambush that is set, so they rise and follow the [new] path, and there it is good to have one ready, for they are sure to fall into it.

The ambush should also be laid before the camp is settled, at a good distance, in case the enemy should come following our people.

Another good ambush, and the most important of all, when the enemy comes following and harassing, is to lengthen the steps of the camp, which makes it appear to be fleeing; and when this happens, the people are already signaled and positioned in order to give the ambush, which will pass to the vanguard; and in the place where they are to lay it, they will separate [into two columns] according to the aforementioned account and method, and the army will continue through the middle of it. And beware that in the marsh, scrubland, or forest where they must go, they are to leave no trail, and the people of the camp are to pass carefully, without leaving the road; and the camp should stop where they may be aided, if it is necessary.

Another good ambush when taking horses is to show the enemy two dozen mounted soldiers, taking some other Indians on the pillion and making them return. The soldiers remain in ambush and the Indians return with the horses to the camp, dressed so they may not be distinguished from the soldiers and with orders to return to the same place another day in the morning. That night the soldiers must march to make their ambush, close to where they exercise the horses [*hacer la perneta*], and as they have seen the horses again, they come out to the same place, unaware of the ambush that lies there.

The soldiers who find themselves [waiting] in any ambush are advised to let the enemy enter and not to rise or make any disturbance until the Santiago is given by the one who is in charge of it, even though by their movements it is clear that they have been noticed; for they come fearing an ambush and usually say in their language to rise, for they have been noticed already, and they make their movements naturally; and he who does not know this well, or it is not well reported, will be goaded [*le haran picar*] into thinking that they have been seen and discovered; and so everyone should be still until they hear the Santiago, unless the Indian should close on him, for then there is no need to wait. *Warning to the soldiers*

Now that we have said how to lay ambushes and take advantage of them, it would be good to understand those used by the Indians, so *Warning* that they may be guarded against, for it is a very important thing because of the harm it does to our Spaniards.

Customs of the Indians in their ambushes The Indians have the custom of laying their ambushes in ravines or rivers. In the ravine, make use of this invention: a loose squad of soldiers will go ahead within sight of the camp, and with a released dog will discover the ambush outside of the ravine, in the adjacent forest. This must be done where one is suspected; and if they find one, upon hearing the voices or harquebuses, the camp will halt, sending people to the rescue. And if the ravine is such that the vanguard are not able to pass along through the flanks because of its thickness, and are forced to proceed in the middle of the ravine, these should go with all possible care, their harquebuses in their hands, priming pans and two matches lit, with such care that in all difficult passages they halt until the camp arrives. And if it is certain that they are noticed in the land, they may clear the passage with their harquebuses, for the Indians are of such condition that, upon hearing the harquebus, they rise from the ambush in an uproar, and particularly if they feel the striking of the bullet where they have laid the ambush. And in case, even with all this preparation, the ambush is given on all sides, the soldiers will retreat a bit so that the Indians are revealed, in order to have a better effect upon them there, with order and account, as if it were a raid; they will go against them without the shield bearer abandoning the harquebusier. And if the ravine is of such condition that they may not retreat without damages, half of the people will turn to face one direction and the other half to the contrary, strengthening themselves back-to-back; the harquebusiers and their shield bearers ahead of each one, in such a manner that they are positioned in four rows; and when they are not too close it will be better. And if the enemy wields lances, the shield bearers will be lancers, in order to better withstand them, for the buckler is inferior against a lance. And be sure that shots are fired low, for this is always superior; or have the habit, upon lighting the powder or upon taking aim, of lying upon the ground; doing it in this way the shot will not err, unless the harquebusier is already so concealed that the enemy does not see him take aim. Highly skilled soldiers may occasionally take aim with the harquebus without firing, until they think it is time for them to rise and employ their shots thus; and it often happens that the harquebus is aimed without powder or munitions, and [the Indians] are stopped with this, from the fear they have of it.

The harquebusier is warned not to fire his harquebus until his companion tells him that it is loaded; but both need to do this with haste and in the meantime, attack as if they were firing upon them, to hold them at bay.

Warning to the harquebusier

The Indians often lay their ambushes by surrounding a field, for there the soldiers, greedy in searching for food, may be defeated. It is ill-advised to run such a risk for food, for the servants may obtain it; and in the interim it is good that the soldier is ready with his arms, covering them, always keeping as close to one side of the field as possible, avoiding the damages that may come to him from all [other] sides, for in this manner they may be offended on one side only and by closing and quickly thwarting one attack, all the others are thwarted.

Indian ambushes

They [i.e., ambushes] are also set upon a height, or difficult passage, and when the camp arrives, they are quiet until it has descended halfway and then they come out of the ambush, unleashing a great quantity of large rocks and arrows with which they rout the camp; and if the ambush is reinforced from below and the camp is taken by the rocks, it will be lost. For this, the commander, at these heights or difficult passages, should always leave a fourth of the lightest people at the top with their matches lit; and those who remain behind should see that the height is not abandoned until the commander, with the camp, has reached the plain and is beyond the danger of the rocks, for as the Indians see people remaining, they remain quiet and those below do not respond; and afterward, these soldiers descend the hill with all possible haste, as they are lightly laden, for the Indian, though he may come out of his ambush, cannot offend with the stones; and the camp below will halt, so that in this manner they are in my charge if they are offended. And if the enemy should strike those who stayed behind while the camp descends, they should fight and hold their ground, lest some be lost; and the camp should turn back to take the height, making the rear guard the vanguard; and if the Indians respond from below, they should take the height, retreating in good order, joining the companions, and there the commander will choose what is best in order to defeat these people and descend safely; and to ascend a height, the camp will take the precautions stated earlier.

Danger of Indian ambush

It also happens that the camp is traversing a hillside and is ambushed with stones from the heights above and an attack from below; and in order not to fall into this situation and danger, the commander should order some soldiers to take the high ground before the camp begins the traverse. And those who take it ascend with great caution, for in the heights there are often large rocks or shrubberies in which the Indians may lie in ambush, and if they ascend carelessly they will be harmed. And if it is the case that they are unable to take the high ground because the place where they enter is a loose and broken crag and a difficult road, they are to pass four by four, until a good squad is formed on the other side and they may take the height with greater ease; if they do not wish the entire camp to pass this way, or are forced to, this way is better, since four soldiers run less risk than the whole camp together as a troop.

The Indians often lay ambushes close to their village, a bit before arriving to it. Walk here with great caution, matches lit, harquebuses ready; and if attacked from the rear, as stated, fight.

They often lay an ambush after the squad that has gone out to patrol the area has returned, close to the camp or Spanish village, for the land there is already secure and the people do not go with order: one leaving his harquebus behind, another his doublet and another leaving his buckler to his servant boy. The Indians know these habits, particularly the skilled ones, and as they find them so disorganized, they kill and destroy them, taking the prize; and it is very poorly done if the commander, until he is within the camp or village, permits this disorder and does not proceed with much caution, because of what may happen to him.

Ambushes the Indian sets

The Indian often lays ambushes at the water supply, close to the camp or village and in the plots or fields and in the streams where the Indian servants go to wash or where they collect firewood. All this should be prepared for so that everyone is wary, for they often take the servants. And for this, dogs should be taken along, for they discover [the Indians]; and as only a few people do this [type of ambush], they later flee upon noticing the dog. And if the land is marshy or covered with dense forest, everything should be cut and razed, for being clean and clear, the Indians do not dare to approach, so as not to be seen.

The commander is advised that the Indians often position a spy in a tree, close to the road, to count the Spaniards; and for this, always look up into the trees when in a populated land. And they should also be warned that before the camp or squadron arrives anywhere, if they hear the screaming of monkeys or turkeys, they should consider that people have been noticed beneath the trees they are in, and upon hearing them, may guess where. And if it is along the road, they will proceed with caution, looking in the trees. The same occurs when the Indians lay an ambush, so that one should indicate the other. A dog should be loosed for this purpose, so that if it is an ambush, it will be then discovered, and if it is a spy positioned up a tree, by catching his trail, the dog will bark at his feet. And note that it may be thought that the dog is only barking at some monkey [leading the group to] pass inadvertently, and much damage and lost opportunity is the result of this.

Warning to the commander

The commander is also warned that if he should enter a dry reed bed, the Indian often sets one part on fire and attacks from another with an ambush. For this, before the camp enters, a squad of light soldiers should cross this reed bed, and when the other side is reached, the camp will march. This fire is also often set near a village or encampment; if the grass of the savannah is dry, they often set it around the very same camp or village. It is quite advisable to pull up the grass, making a road around the camp, and after it is made, set fire all around so that it meets that set by the enemy. This is called counterfire and is a good technique, but if not set with haste, the fire causes great damage upon reaching the camp, with all the impulse it has, and if there is a village, it burns everything; and the enemy at that time is not remiss, for he attacks after the fire.

The commander who should fall into an ambush unawares deserves great guilt and even pity, unless it is that he enters it for some purpose [*artificio*], warning all his people first (when he should determine to do so), which I do not take to be a good thing, leading his people in silence and in formation, and the harquebuses ready with the matches in the serpentine and the shield bearers and lancers so positioned and ordered, that when the enemy chooses to give the ambush, it may not

The commander who falls into an ambush deserves most of the blame

be called as such, but rather a skirmish; for the ambush takes pleasure in this name because of its surprise and the unwariness with which it takes the opponent.

Warning to the commander The commander is advised to recognize an ambush by the place, and by the odor of the paint the Indians spread upon themselves, for it smells bad. Also by the odor of the maize porridge or chicha they drink, and by the trail they make. And if it is marshy, an ambush is recognized by the broken branch or grass, for up to now no Indian laid an ambush but by first opening and securing an escape. On all these occasions, much is revealed to the commander, etc.

METHOD OF GIVING AND RECEIVING SKIRMISHES, WITH OTHER IMPORTANT WARNINGS ON NATURAL DEFENSE

War more noble than the Indian makes it What has been stated will have brought to light the risks and dangers that befall and have befallen our Spaniards in the new conquests of the Indies, and how much it should be rewarded I leave for its time. We have also stated the techniques that the natives of those parts have to defeat us, all founded upon betrayal and varieties of ambush. Likewise, it has been said how our Spaniards must confront them. What remains now is to declare, and even show, how they must be esteemed in their raids or battles, which are often represented by convening and gathering all the land against us. It often happens that a hundred Indians gather for each soldier [of ours] and most of them suffer the worst, when on our part there is valor and strength in the commander and soldiers, and over all, good order; for as they are a fainthearted people they weaken and retreat upon seeing this. And as we have touched upon everything, according to the chapter for each thing, in this one we will address at length that which our commander and soldiers should do, as it is worth no less than their very lives. And they are now at the time when their hands are needed, for the enemy desires to make a raid upon an open field, which is the most noble form of war that they use, a thing that should be greatly considered, for in it we always or most often emerge victorious, bringing labors to an end, avoiding damages, and settling the land with peace, which is the principal objective. And in accordance with this, it is reasonable to present it with greater care than in all the other stratagems of war.

When it is determined to go forth in battle, our commander should be advised to order each soldier to fight with all his arms, each one remembering to carry his butcher knife, and when they are ready for it, ask all of them to show their knives in case they do not carry them at the ready to be able to take full advantage of them. And when the commander is not able to see to everything in person, place two soldiers whom he trusts in charge of it, that they may see it in order. And having done this, he should then make his parley, making them understand that in the battle that awaits them, fleeing is not permitted, because of the risk they run, for apart from losing honor, they have no other remedy for saving lives, as in other wars.

Advice to the commander—Retreat is not permitted in combat

As an example of this, I will mention Callicratidas, a commander of those from Sparta, in the naval battle he had against the Athenians, whose armada exceeded his with great advantage. When counseled to retreat by Hermon, the governor of his ship, who saw their defeat clearly, he responded that he would do no such thing, to be condemned among those of Sparta, fleeing being the greatest act of dishonor.[8] The best that may befall the valiant man is to win or die. Being honest and acclaimed, this arms us well for this war we are addressing, for in it I find nothing more than death or glory, because our people [i.e., Indies militiamen on campaign] have no place from which to expect relief, nor any place to fortify in the hope of saving themselves. I say, in new conquests where the Indians win the battle or combat but one time and ours are defeated, and by having fled are unable to re-form themselves, the Indians are of such quality that they will follow the trail for ten and twenty days until they find them and kill them; and when they escape from this, they die of hunger; and if each one considers this, they would clench their fists and not fall to pieces, so that the field may be theirs; and when they die, may they die honorably.

Example of Callicratidas

Hannibal, having his soldiers in the middle of Italy, told them, "The time is at hand, we have been left with nothing but what we may keep with our arms."[9]

Saying of Hannibal

The Marquis del Valle—He who attacks may take bold advice.—Good advice secures the victory.—The commander who does not take advice deserves the blame	So said the Marquis of Valle [Cortés] when he sank his ships, which was well thought out in order to encourage his men, making them understand that there was nothing left but to die or win, for whoever does not risk does not win; and whoever attacks may take risky advice, but when one does not attack, it is reasonable to follow advice that is well founded, mature, and least likely to cause accidents, for sound advice assures the victory. The commander, who, through his opinion and deliberation wagers a good or bad outcome, should he have an opportunity to declare it, deserves the blame, even if things turn out well.
Advice of Artabanus	Artabanus advised Xerxes, when he was preparing his armada in Greece, that when he was most satisfied with what he had determined he should do, he should consider it again and consult with others.[10]
He who is experienced in a thing may give advice	And Democritus said that too much haste in an undertaking brings too late regret, for that which is once done poorly, when it is amended, may not return to its initial state;[11] therefore whoever has experience in a thing may give advice, just as he with sharp ingenuity and a willingness to speculate may do so.
It is a dangerous affair when the commander is not resolute in war	Also, it is a very dangerous thing for the captain not to be decisive in war, for it cools the spirit of the soldier and makes him a coward and takes away his will to fight, when all that is needed is that he be called upon for spirit and skill in arms, and that food be ready at any hour so that his commander may order him to march; and thus, resolution and deliberation in preparation fall to the commander.
The known advantage secures the victory	The known advantage in making battle secures the victory, and the commander should take care to procure it always, for though the Indian has the advantage over us in number, we, by our spirit, by our arms, by knowing to choose the place for cavalry or harquebuses, have the advantage and prevail with fewer people.
Why the Turks have had victories	If the Turks have had so many victories, it has not been by coming in close units but rather in open campaign, for the stratagems in war are a great part of the victory; guile is another force and often more is gained with it than with strength.

Hannibal the Carthaginian excelled in stratagems, for nothing ever came into his hands but that he was not greatly helped by skill, making a good choice of the place, the arms, the air, and other things.

Hannibal made much use of skill

The captain, in order to encourage his soldiers to battle, must be confident and possess wit with them and much ability in preparation.

The captain must be confident

Hannibal, in the battle of Cannae, scaled a height to see the enemy, and a friend of his, named Guijón, was startled upon seeing such a number of people. Hannibal told him, "Notice another marvelous thing: that in such a great number of people there is none named Guijón." All those present laughed heartily at this answer and were encouraged, seeing that their captain could be witty at such a time.[12]

The wit of Hannibal

This is brought to light so that the commander, at similar times, may demonstrate bravery and not be troubled. And as it is now time to address that which should be cautioned against before entering in battle, I will state the warnings necessary.

Warnings to the commander

Upon launching the attack he should keep close the comrades and friends whom he most trusts, both for the guarding of his person as well as to have someone [on hand] with whom to entrust those things that may present themselves.

The commander should see to it that no soldier is lost on his account, for he will be seen as a negligent and careless man. And be aware to always know the name of the outstanding soldiers so that they may attend to any necessity and so that those in the battle do not lack munitions or aid; and for this he should have persons of account.

He will order the wounded to retreat to the camp or to another indicated place, taking care that their wounds are cured as has been stated; and if the camp is in formation, he should refresh the posts of the wounded. And beware that he must fortify his camp with falconets or muskets if he has them, and if not, with harquebuses, lances, and bucklers.

The commander is advised that the soldier should not fight with shouts, for it animates the opponents, unless supplies and orders are not understood; and the wounded should complain even less, for they receive no relief and discourage their companions, and it is better if the enemy does not notice this.

Singing victory discourages the opponent	It is of my opinion that victory should be sung out with trumpets, even though it may not be verified, for it greatly disheartens the Indian, as he begins to retreat; it is a thing known to cause them to turn their backs.
Warning to the commander	Beware that when the battle is joined to not distance oneself too far from the camp, because of the strength it imparts.
Battle formation	On level ground, those on horseback will enter first, the horses with their bells, which will break out first; and afterward, the infantry in squads with their shield bearers at the fore. And if the enemy is armed with lances, the harquebuses will fire first from a wing formation, with their shield bearers and lancers forward. The cavalry should not attack until the enemy is somewhat routed, unless our men need them. On rough land the squads will also be used as offense in all places.
Avoid coming to blows	Avoid coming to blows, always offering peace, but when the Indian does not agree to it, apply force, for natural defense is permitted; and once it is clear that coming to blows is unavoidable, go right to them, breaking them where they would be broken, turning upon them to force them into the middle; and the cavalry should break out first if they are not a people with lances, and the harquebusiers will make their volley low, as has already been advised, always procuring that the first shots are employed upon those most obvious. Fray Pedro de Betanzos, being a saint, was of this opinion. On one occasion while going to preach among the Indians, persuaded by the general to take several soldiers with him for company, he understood that the Indians had determined to kill them all. He secured himself within a hut, which they surrounded at dawn, and the good friar, seeing the danger, encouraged the soldiers by saying not to aim poorly and that only because of them would they escape harm. This happened in Costa Rica.[13] Such is the importance of harquebusiers, as they are the ones who defeat the enemy.
Warnings to the commander	I warn the commander that if he has marsh or scrubland behind him or to one side, and the enemy should set it afire in order to offend on all sides, he should pass over them with his people, as has been said,

forcing them to turn about and procuring to drive them back against the fire.

The commander should also be careful to always take the side with dense forest, turning upon the enemy on the level ground, so that the cavalry may offend him first; and after he is defeated, take the place with such care that if relief to the Indian should come out of the forest, they may notice it and face it as well.

Our commander should beware to reconnoiter the countryside where the battle is to take place in order to know the swamps, for they are quite harmful to the cavalry but may provide protection if their location is known. Also, know the ravines and difficult and easy passages, as everything is of great importance. And in all, if the Indian should raise himself to the high ground, it should always be taken, as it is a great advantage. And likewise, be aware that the rest of the camp is better on the high ground, for their defense and strength, as well as to lord over and see the events and movements of the battle.

As a good soldier, the commander is obligated to risk his person, as he will also be obligated to always take the land from the enemy and fight with his sword and buckler, for there he may not use other arms, finding himself always at the forefront, warning and aiding in all parts; with this he will gain renown and embolden his men.

The duty of the commander

With these preparations and warnings, the commander should issue the Santiago, having prayed and summoned the Indian in peace[14] and having made speeches among his men, knowing that persuading builds the spirit of a regiment and fosters opportunity. In the interim, I return to the order with which the Indians enter the battle: [first,] all the people of the land are gathered in such a manner that enemies are made friends for that day, or most of it, in order to resist us, even though they may have their own wars declared. And if some should not enter into this league our commander will procure to ally himself with them, for they join it easily; [second,] those who give battle that day unfurl their pennants with many and varied feathers, bodies and faces well-painted red, yellow, and black, with their animal tails hanging from the waist and on the forehead. The captains wear tiger and lion paws and the flayed head of the lion as a cap, applying all the gold

Order of the Indians in giving battle

they have as jewels: on their chests, plates and eagles; on the waist, a belt of beads of bone and of gold; on the nose they hang golden rings, and in the ears, a type of earring, but larger and of diverse types; on their wrists, their bracelets, and at the neck, beads of bone and gold; and at the waist many bells made of snail shells. They come naked and with long and braided hair, and those who have it cut are the best warriors. And for this day in particular they become drunk, though they are always so, and the most drunk among them is the most valiant. They come making great gestures and boasts, and once the drunkenness ends, so does the battle; and as the field is no longer theirs, they retreat or flee in disarray, as has earlier been said.

Their squads come in their own manner of formation, and their captains, appointed to govern and encourage, always come ahead; and each nation or clan recognizes their commander and obeys him, but the superiority of all the commanders and captains is not recognized among themselves on this occasion, and so once they begin to be routed, they are then lost. These commanders agree with the first one to speak and give voice, following him, and likewise upon fleeing. During the battle they do not cease giving shouts and shrieks; with this they are animated and believe that they terrorize us. The musical instruments that they bring are little trumpets made from tails of armadillos, large snails, horns made of gourds, and drums, so that with these and the voices of so many, our people almost cannot hear one another; and at this time much composure is required.

The weapons they bring are distributed according to formation: if they use lances and shields, they are placed at the front, and behind them are the people with darts and slings; and the lancers crouch so that those with the slings may throw; and if they use arrows, each man brings his war club hanging at his back and his quiver at his side, and while firing their arrows, they close in with their clubs if they have the opportunity. They enter in a half-moon formation, procuring to encircle the Spaniards, for their aim and objective is to capture them by hand. They are so barbarous, and cooperative among themselves, that they bring large mesh bags, in which fit a *fanega* (ca. 1.6 bushels) of wheat or maize, in order to carry away the Spaniards they should capture or kill. After these come many females with gourds in order to carry away the flesh and entrails of our men, which is no less barbarous.

They also bring munitions of arrows for the war, and maize porridge and chicha so their people may drink and be refreshed. In the hills and along the ridges and in the trees there are many people who are watching the fight, as if it were a great and distinguished celebration; and on this day they come from afar to see it and as they are foreign Indians, they are paid for this occasion, for they come to help them in the war; and these people come quite content with the pay, primarily those who eat human flesh. They often boast, for they promise and warn that they shall be ready for the battle on such a day at such an hour.

They are a people who keep formation only at the outset or until the battle is joined, for they later turn about and fight with no order. And if they are a newly conquered people, upon their first defeat they see our men as children of the sun and judge horse and rider as one immortal being. This is only where they have never seen or heard of us. They are a cruel people, so that if they manage to lay hands upon some Spaniard, they inflict a thousand torments upon him, plucking out his eyes and pulling him with a halter through the markets and drunken celebrations, and later they kill him and eat him; and when they use courtesy with him it is by placing him, eyeless, to guard the bags, plots of land, or maize fields, so that he screams at the parrots, and this has been seen with the Pijao.[15] They often impale them alive, as has been seen in Santa Marta, and they hang the heads at the doors of their houses and drink from their skullcaps in their great drunken festivals. They make flutes of the leg and arm bones; the great captains wear these at their necks. And where they eat human flesh, they grind the bones and drink them in chicha. They are quite fainthearted, so that if they are defeated, they flee, leaving their weapons behind and the females leaving their gourds in which they carry meat and the jugs of chicha, and each flees on his own account, such that they will not gather together for a month. And what the captains and chiefs most prepare for is sending their ambassadors to make peace, saying that they wish to serve, and for this they bring some presents of little importance, and the commander should receive them and present them with gifts, regardless of what has happened.

The commander should beware that if the enemy is defeated, those in pursuit should do so in formation, having named a person for this with a squad of soldiers. And this pursuit should be but a short distance, for

Warning to the commander

it is more to frighten than to kill, as the victory should not be taken to its conclusion for two reasons: one is not to be too bloody [*no sea sangrienta*] with those whom we want alive more than dead; and the other, because it is enough that the poor outcome causes them to turn their backs with such confusion.

Opinion of Pyrrhus Pyrrhus always prohibited his men from finishing their defeated opponents.

Opinion of Hannibal And Hannibal was noted for never bringing the victory to its end, being content with forcing the enemy to flee in order to save their lives.

Remedy for poor outcomes.—Saying of Seneca Victory is human, but forgiveness is divine. And if the enemy should defeat our men (which happens rarely), the commander should be neither cowed nor confused, for this will manifest itself in a thousand inconveniences, striking fear into his people. He should first encourage them and remind them of the valor of some captains who, after being defeated, have won great battles, fostering new determination in his soldiers and the certain hope of having an honored satisfaction; placing before them the words of Seneca, that Fortune is the perpetual pursuer of valorous men, which was what Caesar valued in similar difficult circumstances, and Hannibal and other valorous captains. And with this valor and consideration he gathers and returns to the camp with his soldiers, where a fortification is made; and during the interim when they have no relief, they should no longer engage them [i.e., the enemy] on the open field, using rather ambushes and assaults, taking them divided with night attacks and dawn raids, traveling by night and ever attentive, so that they will come out in submission. Also, procure to ally with several paramount chiefs, however far off, for better strength. And in everything, proceed with careful actions, as the skilled commander will recognize, always living wary of those with whom he might ally himself.

BOOK FOUR
OF THE INDIAN
Militia Which Addresses How Peace Is To Be Settled, How A City Is To Be Founded, How The Land Is To Be Distributed, And The Kind Treatment That Is Owed To The Indian, With The Reward For Conquerors And Settlers.

MAKING PEACE WITH THE INDIAN is the primary intention of the prince and with it should one begin. For in peace is the Holy Gospel taught, and in peace the Indian gives vassalage and obedience, and in recognition of it does he give tribute to the prince, though the conquerors are ordained to enjoy two lives to his one, during which they are obligated to their [i.e., the Indians'] administration and to indoctrinate them, the benefit of which justifies their bearing it, and with it and with industry they live and sustain settled areas.[1] However, in order for these peaces to last, it is most important that the commander knows how to settle and protect them with sagacity and keep the enemy from knowing his three objectives, which are: weakening their forces, impeding confederations, and allying and confederating with a different and contrary nation. Knowing how to make use of this [i.e., the following instruction] will conserve peace after it has once been established, carefully tearing down their forts and stock-

Peace treaties

ades, and making them understand that they have no need for them, for the Christians are charged with their defense and that of the land, excepting only the frontiers with enemies who have not made peace. This should not be done in these areas, for they serve as wall and defense for the settlements that are there peacefully. They should also be prohibited (with the same care) from making arrows, bows, spears, and shields, and also herb venom, wherever it may be traded and possessed for hunting, taking it from warring Indians or from some peaceful Indians; for by whatever way and means these arms go, they come into the hands of our enemies whereby we are knowingly offended by them, and permitting them is a bad thing to do. There are many encomenderos who allow this, greedy for their vassals to trade in them in order to better pay their tribute; not warning or putting a stop to this is a great mistake in judgment, both the trading and possessing of arms, for there is no need of them. It is sufficient to leave them their hunting bows, for leaving them even one of those for war is a bad thing, nor any of the other instruments, except (as has been said) to those on the frontier, under the condition that they are not to ally themselves with those whom they are warring against. And for this one must involve them often in affairs, helping them and making them understand that the Christians are moved out of consideration for them, otherwise they would surely be aroused to hostility. And returning to the purpose, I say that it is good to weaken the Indian's force of arms for the security of all.

Example of Caesar   Caesar, when any city would surrender to him and give him obedience, took away their force of arms before any other thing.

It is also quite important to impede their confederations, hindering them from pairing one nation with another; this should be prohibited even in times of much peace because of the many disputes that are engendered among the encomenderos, as well as favoring alliances, for great enemies become great friends. Their drunken gatherings and councils serve as an instrument for this, and it is good to impede these and use dissimulation in such a manner that they are kept separate and know each other always from opposite sides, if that is how they are [when conquered], until the land is settled and the roads are opened and the commerce between nearby cities is established. For as the Indian does not see this, if he is able to gather and make alliances, it is certain he will not correspond to the faith and peace given to him and he will rise up.

Dividing the Indians consists in cutting off the way and desire to gather together, artfully seeding suspicions among them, so they do not dare trust each other. Having spies among them from a different chief's district, bribed for the purpose, is good for this. And whoever is found guilty should be given a brief punishment as this greatly reassures the Indian. And our commander should always ally himself with a contrary band or nation, always making friendships; this is important, for there are no hunting hounds like these for discovering and destroying his opposition.

Spies are advantageous

And what most helps in conserving peace is, with fair means, dispersing the elders who wander about igniting discord; this must always be sustained in order to conserve peace, for it is great happiness to live with it and take pleasure in what is possessed in peace. God loved peace and charged his disciples with it. Republics are protected by peace. Without peace, everything is confusion. In peace are the spoils of war enjoyed, and without it they are consumed and finished. Therefore, it is right that peace is conserved on all occasions; it is as necessary for the body as for the soul. The intention of our conquests is to seek and establish this peace with the natives, showing them its qualities and conditions; for since they, as barbarians, do not know them, it is best to declare them [i.e. the conditions for peace], as well as to avoid the risk of their not keeping them.

Conserving the peace is happiness

And in these peaces, our commander should first consider the quality of the Indians: whether they are a people newly introduced to similar peace treaties, it being the first time they are conquered and discovered, or if they are Indians from before, breakers of peace, destroyers of villages, killers of Spaniards. These, afflicted by the war made upon them, always make peace with a wounded breast, waiting for a good opportunity to turn and rise up, killing and destroying according to their ancient customs (which, upon finding us divided and unguarded, they know well how to gather and wait). The commander should deny them peace, even though they ask for it once, twice, and three times; for they should be cured like old sores, with strong caustics, in such a

One should consider with whom to settle peace

manner that when peace is finally reached, they understand that they must honor it. To peaceful people who have not been conquered or settled, this should be given later, always inviting them with it, but living with as much caution with these as with the others. And however the peace may be offered and accepted by either side, it is to be settled with the authority of a scribe and of witnesses.

Warning given to the Indian   And later the commander, having the caciques and lesser chieftains together, will make them understand, through an interpreter, that this peace which they give in the name of all the subjects and vassals of the Christians and their obedience and vassalage to the king must be honored by all means, neither rising up nor retreating from their settlements, nor taking up more arms to make war, nor assaulting, nor killing Spanish-speaking Indians of service along the roads or in any other place. And they are obligated to keep the same peace with all those Indians friendly to the Spaniards. Advise them that should they be delinquent in any of these things or in any manner that harms us, the headmen as well as the guilty will be punished with all severity, such a punishment having already been justified. Those caciques who will have consented to this and who knew of it and gave no warning will be relieved of their position as cacique, just as persons incur in similar acts of treason. And they will likewise be obligated to attend to all official gatherings required by magistrates. The commander will promise them in the name of His Majesty to guard all peace and friendship, and that he will protect and defend them from their enemies. And as a signal of this declared peace he will embrace every cacique and native lord, and at the same time fire a salvo as a sign of happiness, regaling them and eating with them on that day. And he will present them with the trade items that they esteem, for all they desire is of such little value; there are no children who love toys more, with which they are so quickly contented. And then the caciques and lords will be asked, as guarantors of these friendships, to give up some of their sons so that they may become endeared to us and learn of our good manners and orderliness, and learn the language, warning them that above all other things they must lay down their arms and not take them up again, for the Spaniards are in charge of their defense and protection.

And with these ceremonies and gifts will they be sent back to their homes and settlements contentedly, charging them to see about supplying the camp with local provisions, sustaining the Christians while they sow their crops and settle. And do not trust completely in the peace that would leave behind all arms, as unarmed peace is weak.

Peace without arms is quite weak

THE MANNER OUR COMMANDER WILL USE IN CONSERVING WHAT IS PACIFIED AND SETTLED

Now that we have arrived at this point, which requires so much labor and is so important to the service of God and the prince and the conservation of the two republics, that of the Indian as well as that which is newly settled by our commander, it is good that we carefully present the model and make a discourse in which everything is in accordance with the royal decrees, so that they may remain perpetually in the service of God and king. And may the settlers live quietly and in peace, without debates and differences, and safe from the treason and harm that the Indian is so often planning. Regarding the first, I say, that having need to settle, and it being well considered and determined, it will be done in such a manner that the land should first be surrendered to the dominion of His Majesty; most, if not all of it, by way of good treaties of peace or by other causes that have obligated them to it. On a certain day our commander will convoke and gather all the caciques and lords, for whom will be made a great reception, giving gifts to them and having agreeable words for them.

Manner of settling—In order to settle, the good will of the Indian should be won

And this being ready, they will be told and advised, through interpreters, how the Christians wish to make their houses in order to rest and retire their hands from war; because from that day forward they want nothing more than to be their friends, as they are, and to defend them from those who are not, taking up arms for them and their cause, permitting no one to do harm to their persons or property. They wish to build their houses in a comfortable place, where all people may easily go to visit and trade with the Christians and hear the Christian doctrine. For this benefit it would be good to build in the heart of the land, which, there being no notable inconvenience, should be done by

*Settling in the heart of the land (*riñón de la tierra*) assures much.—The commander should settle on a site with the best comforts*

our commander, for with this he will secure the most favorable means for his soldiers as well their provisions. He will choose the flattest site possible, as long as it is not in a hollow, for it must be airy, dry, and open to the north wind, with the additional comforts of water and firewood if possible; and when they are unable to arrange all of these qualities, they will settle on the site that has the most of them.[2]

Before settling, the native lords give their vote.—The Indian may suddenly forget caution.—Secrecy is kept, but if word gets out, it should be while working

Having decided this with the vote of the lords of the land and their consenting to it, they will proceed to the chosen place, without returning to their houses nor having an opportunity to communicate with each other, for they are a people who suddenly do not recognize any caution, so fickle and easy that once their backs are turned, any word or persuasion offered them turns and transforms them into whatever color the persuader wishes (in this they are similar to the chameleon). And so the commander will always flee from these obstacles, guarding as secret all his designs, and if word does get out, may it be while they are all working together.

So let us suppose that this site has been chosen and consent given by the native lords, along with the other requirements already mentioned and many others that the occasion will reveal to them, as they are joined to our purpose.

The strength to found a city

In the middle of the flattest place a great hole will be made, having cut a great tree trunk sufficiently long that once it is stuck deep into the earth, there will remain exposed one-and-a-half or two statures of length. These same caciques and lords will raise it together with some Spaniards, with no intervention by other Indians. Our commander, having made his parley, will also place his hands upon it, in order for this town to be justifiably created. They will stand this pole in the hole and later tamp the earth around it, leaving it straight and well set.

Ceremony—Declaration

Later, clearing the people away, the commander will take a knife (which he will have prepared for the occasion) and stab it into the pole and, turning to the entire camp, will say, "Gentlemen, soldiers, my companions, and those who are present, I here display the gallows and the knife, foundation and site of the city of Seville," or whatever name he wishes to give. "Long may God guard it, as well as rebuild this town where he may, in the name of His Majesty; and in his royal name, I will guard and maintain peace and justice for all Spaniards, conquerors, householders, [temporary] inhabitants, and foreigners, and for all the natives, keeping and doing justice for the poor as well as the rich, for the small as well as the great, protecting widows and orphans."

And later, armed with all his weapons (being dressed thus for effect), he will draw his sword and will spread the camp wide, among the people, and will declare with choleric passion, "Gentlemen, I have just founded the city of Seville in the name of His Majesty. If there is any person who wishes to contradict me, may he come out with me to the battlefield, where we can fight it out. I assure you of it, for in its defense I offer to die, now and at any time, defending it for the king my lord, as his captain, servant, and vassal, and as a noble knight." (If this commander is not one by blood [i.e., a noble], he is one according to the privilege conceded to such conquerors.) He will say this three times, and all will say and respond each time, "The city is well-founded; long live the king our lord!" And they will make this understood to the lords of the land in their language. *Rite*

And as a sign of possession he will cut plants and herbs from that place with his sword, showing those present why he does this and saying that he hereby makes it subject to this audiencia or to that governorship, or if he is making it a head-town [*cabecera*]. And with that he will sheath his sword. *Possession*

And at that instant he will set a cross made for the occasion at one corner of the square, which will be the place selected for the church. The priest, in his vestments, will plant it and make an altar at its base and will say mass. All the soldiers will approach with devotion and solemnity in order to demonstrate this to the natives and move their hearts, celebrating this day with trumpets, drums, and many harquebus salvos. And the priest will dedicate the church, together with the commander. *Founding of the church*

Once the mass is finished, our commander will take out a list already prepared for the election, in which no one will intervene so as to avoid scandals, jealousies, and coteries. The offices of the town council will be named according to the characteristics of the city, whether it is gov- *Election of the town council* erning or being governed. From the day they enter the land the commander will have named the scribe of the expedition in the presence of the royal scribe, to whom he will give the list and election, signed with his name, and he will sign it in the presence of all. Then, he will take it and, with all his people and camp around him, give the staffs of office to those elected by him. The election should be made with consideration, for the people are appointed for two-year terms. And since it is the first election, may the first administration be chosen from among those persons of greater judgment and trustworthiness.

Oaths And with this account he will call the two common magistrates, to whom, in the name of His Majesty, he will present the staffs, giving one first to the oldest or most noble, for seniority. He will receive the oath from them with solemnity, that they will faithfully use their charges and that they will keep peace and justice in that city in the name of their prince, doing so with all due respect. And our commander will proceed calling aldermen, head bailiff, magistrates of the Holy Brotherhood,[3] attorney general, the stewards of the holy church and city, and the other officials that seem convenient to him, taking the common oath from them as well. Once finished, he will instruct the entire council to assemble at a place chosen for it, where they will name and receive the scribe for the public and the council, who will have made the book of the council. In it they will commence the court record of the settlement, with the day, month, and year, declaring the limits of jurisdiction and to which audiencia and district they are subject, and whether it is a seat or a subject town, extending the jurisdiction without prejudice. And after making this record of the settlement, that of the justice and the town council will be made, chosen, and signed by our commander. Next [comes] their naming, in sequence as they appear in the said council, receiving our commander as captain and chief justice, he giving the standard bonds [*fianzas*], and after him, his lieutenant will be received, with the same bonds.

Edict And once finished, an edict will be issued. All the soldiers and conquerors who wish to be citizens of this city will present themselves at the town council to sign the oath of citizenship and swear to keep such citizenship of that city, obligating them not to leave without just license, protecting it and defending it in the name of their prince. And

28
Sixteenth-century town square, Villa de Leiva, Colombia.
Photo by Kris Lane

once this is done, if it is necessary, our commander will name royal officials until His Royal Majesty provides them.

And once finished an edict will be issued, that all the citizens and inhabitants present will pitch their tents and make their quarters within the town square, so that they do not interfere with the forming of the streets and residences. For security, the garrison will be made in the middle of the square where the soldiers may gather and post their sentinels and guard prisoners, taking up the labor of measuring the square in a right quadrangle, according to the lay of the land, whether it is rough or flat, hot or cold, savanna or forest. And because this is chosen by our commander, who has everything at hand, he must look to see if the proportion of the square should be confined or broad for its defense. Eight streets, level and straight, will lead from the square, leaving a corner between every two, which faces the center, middle, and end of the square; and the rest of the streets will go according to the sides of the square. The most ordinary and well-proportioned measurement of the opposing sides is two hundred feet by two hundred fifty, and the opening of the streets, twenty-five feet. Our commander should decide this.

Measurement of the town to be settled

And after the town square and blocks and parcels and streets have been straightly measured, our commander will take a census, whose original

Census and governance of parcels

BOOK FOUR OF THE INDIAN MILITIA

141

will be placed in the book of the town council, as public record, and he will distribute the parcels according to it, so that at the highest point of the square, on one side, which is four parcels, a parcel will be assigned for the central church, and the second parcel behind, farther along the street, for the priest and chaplain; and the parcel sharing a wall, giving on to the square, will be assigned to the houses of the town council; and the jail will be built upon the quarter that remains. Later, six parcels will be assigned, facing the square, our commander taking one for himself and giving the rest to his lieutenant and the two common magistrates and the magistrates of the Holy Brotherhood; and the parcels behind, to the aldermen and head bailiff. And the citizens will follow behind these, according to how it may suit our commander, having assigned comfortable sites for monasteries and hospitals.

Sites will also be assigned for a butcher shop and slaughterhouse.

Distribution of Indians for building the church and city   This finished, he will take a list of the lords of the land who are at peace and assign their duties, charging some with building the church with the Indians and Spaniards who act as overseers, others with building the houses of the town council and the prison, others with leveling the square, streets, and avenues. Others, as part of a suitable community, will later prepare farmland or tillage in the name of the Christians, sufficient for any people there. This should be close to the town, so that the Spaniards may utilize it.

Warning to the commander   And while these four endeavors are being carried out in the hands of the Indians, our commander will post soldiers on watch who will not take their hands off their weapons, for it must be noted that at this time many great tragedies have occurred; as everyone intermingles unarmed, attending to their daily needs. Since it is necessary for Indians from all over the land to be gathered together, they will at the slightest lapse attack, for they have inventions for concealing their weapons, as I have found, hidden within the fronds they bring to cover their houses. And so, in order to have some sort of security, before the projects are begun a stockade will be made around the garrison, which may prove useful should the need arise.

Preparation   This finished, the construction of the houses of the inhabitants will be addressed, noting that not more than one parcel should be given to each one, for each block is occupied by four householders, which our commander will order to be in communication with each other from within by way of false doors or aqueducts, for if some attack or raid should occur by night, they may gather together in order to emerge stronger in search of the garrison. They should take care at such a time not to leave by any of the four main entrances, but rather jump over the wall or make an opening because of the danger presented by leaving through the doors. And in order to avoid this danger, our commander, after posting the sentinel of the garrison, will order the watches to make their rounds in order to detect and discover; and this will last until the residents have completed their houses, which they will construct with all possible strength. Should they have hardware to build forms, they ought to construct tamped-earth walls; but whatever manner they employ, the Indians will be distributed with their cacique or captain, so that they help in the building.

And meanwhile, take care that the Spaniards are neither divided nor separated in the land. And if forced to move, they should do so in armed patrols with their first officer.

And once the settlement is formed and placed in order and the church is built, the priest will take possession of it in the name of the bishopric or archbishopric to which they are subject or that is closest. Our commander will send a dispatch with all of this and the related court records to the governor or audiencia by whose power it has been settled, so that the prince may be advised of it; and the priest will do the same for his prelate. *Possession of the church*

Then, armed patrols of soldiers with their officers will be sent to explore the land with their guides and translators, and the priest will go with them throughout the provinces in order to take possession of his church and parish, placing its crosses, saying its mass, and baptizing the greater and lesser native lords who may request the water of holy baptism, having his book for this in order to write them down, doing it with account and reason, recording the day, month, and year, and the province, requesting it on the testimony of the scribe, and whose purpose will be declared by the council. *It is advisable to explore the land.—Baptismal water should be given to the headmen who ask for it*

The secrets of the land should always be procured

The officer will also proceed taking possession and requesting it with testimony. He will take a record of the caciques and men who ruled over the land when the Spaniards came, making a description and an account of the Indians regarding their rites and laws, and the lives, quality, and judgment of each of the caciques; the rivers, fishing and hunting, the metals, mines, and notable things they may encounter and discover, noting the boundaries that are ahead and yet to be discovered, with particular care to prospect the land's streams and rivers using pick and pan, so that the Indians will not wish to hide it if it is a land with gold. And with artifice and gifts he will try to learn of all the advantages and secrets of the land, as much in spices as in other things that in time will be discovered, which, out of negligence, some parts have passed many years without enjoying.

Once one part of the land has been explored, giving gifts and treating the Indians well, they will return to the town, from which another squad will set out, until all the land has been plowed up and discovered. And all these accounts and descriptions will be collected, and the original will remain in the control of the town council and the copy sent to the governor or audiencia of the district under whose commission it has been performed, so that they may be informed of all that is being done. And our commander will always be inclined to make more discoveries wherever possible, seeking word of, settling, and making alliance with one province or another.

Note

And when requesting assistance from the lands left behind, [the commander should] procure to send a good account and samples of gold and other valuable things, in order to incline the spirit of the soldiers; and he should do this according to the occasion that presents itself.

Precautions

The officers who have scouted the land should be sure to give names to all the rivers, ranges, hills, and ravines.

Take care before harvesting local food crops, preparing for the occasion and not losing it, and in the interest of others, do not act greedily, showing oneself zealous for the honor of God and serving his prince. The governors should carefully look at which persons they commission for such duties, for if they are not God-fearing, their expeditions are certain to be ruinous failures.

To avoid disturbances, passions, and deaths, which often happen between separate camps, the commander should beware not to enter a different jurisdiction where another has entered before him in order to conquer the land, unless he should find it barren and uninhabited. If there is any doubt, by deferring to his superior to determine it, all of this will be prevented.

Our commander is advised that, when he settles, the land should be healthy and beneficial, which will be noted in the natives, if they are robust and strong-limbed, and that it is well populated, and with many elders, all of which imply health. They will also know this in the farmland and crops, in the domestic animals, in the temperature, not excessively hot or cold. And having to reject one, it would best be the cold, because [it lacks] the appropriate farmlands for sowing and pastures for livestock and good waters and wood for the construction of houses.[4] Consider the convenient entrances and exits by land or by sea for commerce, and also so that they may be used for relief should the need arise.

Likewise, note how the town council makes and proceeds with its orders for the republic, sending them for confirmation to the royal audiencia. He [i.e., the commander] will do the parcel owners the favor, in virtue of his powers, of giving them titles for them and having them measured by a master builder. He will advise the inhabitants at the time of building their houses to construct them in such a way that they enjoy the north and south winds if possible. He will reserve some of the more comfortable parcels for the town itself, where shops shall be built to lease them to merchants who may enter over time. He should have an interest in acquiring these properties, as it is a relief for the republic, having the means to adorn and defend it. All of this, more or less, I leave to the good judgment and consideration of the commander.

Our commander is warned to always beware of the deceit and treason of the Indian, which they often use to destroy that which they cannot with arms. Like Zopyrus, a soldier of Darius, who, with his remarkable tricking of the Babylonians, gave to his king the city that could not be taken by force of arms.[5]

The enemy often destroys more with deceit than with arms.—Example of the deceit Zopyrus used

Also beware that although a province rebels, their crops are not to be cut down, nor their houses burned, so that the Indians are not sepa-

Warnings

rated from their village. In war, he will have more comforts and better means of reducing them.

Be sure that the inhabitants always dedicate themselves to work and are not lazy in their homes or labors, not forgetting their arms and the practice of war, which is important, for by these means strength grows. This is how the Romans became the monarchs of the world, by impeding vices and other dangers.

Agriculture is of great advantage to republics

Agriculture is fundamental to the multiplication and conservation of the cities that are settled.

The Romans—Saying of Queen Isabel

The Romans were very careful with this, and Queen Isabel the Catholic said that for Spain to be enormously abundant, it should be given to the monks of Saint Benedict, as they are great farmers.

Denis, King of Portugal

And Denis, King of Portugal, called farmers [full] members of republics.[6] Our commander should take particular care to do this, favoring those who know how to take advantage of the lands and waters, for the humidity makes the land fat and abundant.

Our commander will also show himself prudent in quickly posting officials of the republic, for the inhabitation of his town is assured with it.

Selim, the first emperor of Turkey

Selim, the first emperor of the Turks, in order to ennoble and populate Constantinople, brought many craftsmen from the cities of Tabriz and Cairo.[7]

Industry is more important than agriculture

Agriculture and the cultivation of the land are good for the growth of a city, but industry is more important and more valuable, and the things produced by the hands of the craftsmen bring a better price. Nature gives agriculture the material and subject; but industry and the art of man give an innumerable variety of things. More people are sustained by art and industry than by the bounty of the land.

Notice to the commander

Our commander is advised that conserving what is thus settled consists of two things: the tranquility and peace of the inhabitants. This [peace] consists of two forms: not having civil wars one against another, and not conspiring against the prince. This is prevented by the commander setting a good example and having a well-earned reputation, for thus they will lovingly guard his precepts and warnings and good advice and follow virtue. But the commander should reward this [obedience] in order to encourage those who follow it and make the rest rightly envious of the meritorious ones, worthy of honored rewards.

One who settles and conquers deserves great renown, but one who holds on and moves settlement forward deserves more.

Custom of the Lacedaemonians

The Lacedaemonians, wishing to demonstrate that conserving is more than acquiring, punished whoever lost his shield in battle and not his sword.

THE CONSIDERATION WITH WHICH THE LAND SHOULD BE DIVIDED AMONG THE SETTLERS

No one is so good that they are not judged by the bad, and our commander should not think that, as he is the only one giving orders, he should be exempt from risk. He will run many risks over the course of his conquests, but these are of little consideration compared to those presented to him at the time he distributes the land, for on this day lies the greatest danger of his conquests as we see that he must divide the land among the conquerors who have worked and sweated. And justly we see the obligation and consideration he must have, accommodating each one according to his merits and quality.

One must also consider the harm done to the natives. On this day he runs all the risks together; today he ventures his life, his honor, his property, his time, his labor, his service to the king, and above all, his soul; for if he is not wise, I do not doubt but that he should encounter all or at least most of these obstacles. And so, to remedy everything he has the example of the royal orders and the advice and example of this militia; may he know how to judge, and to govern, and not sleep, and be vigilant of that which is so important, and not plead ignorance, for this will not save him from sin, with which he would risk everything. And so, as he is served more by the precepts we give than those from outside, may he live carefully, as he should live; after giving him opinion and instruction, may he choose that which seems best in order to effect his purpose, serving God and his prince.

And as it is time to work, he should take particular caution after having settled with the approval of the native lords of the land. The estates that he grants to the Spaniards for planting and raising livestock should not harm the natives. And before distributing and assigning the Indians to their encomiendas, he should have had the land pacified and prospected, made a general description of the lords who governed at the time they arrived, and taken their names on a list, omitting no one; and with artifice and gifts he will make them give an account of all their subjects and elders. They will have made the description (as has been stated) while exploring the land, recording what some caciques say of others. And in the town and city, once the proper procedure is taken, our commander will assign according to provinces, dividing and separating and including in each the men who would comfortably remain there; then he will count the Indians, having counted their leaders, and will then add it together. Once the number has been noted, he will consider the bounties of the land, if there are pearls, gold, or precious stones, or if they must profit only by industry, such as in sugar or textile mills, livestock, cropland, and other things of lesser value. He will distribute the land considering all of this, and assign the Indians more or less according to the products of each province. And once this judgment and consideration is made, with nothing in the land hidden from him, he will appoint and entrust the Indians according to their villages or caciques, captains, and headmen; or by houses, or heads of family, or clans, or valleys, according to the land and its disposition; considering, as well, the quantity and merits of the Spaniards; and so giving to some, more, and to others, less, weighing and measuring the value of each one and the substance of the Indians, as four from one valley may be worth more than eight from another.

Poor practices of commanders—Faith must be guarded at all times

There is one thing practiced by many commanders that lacks reason and conscience, a thing that not only scandalizes the one who bears it and the one who sees it, but also the one who hears of it from afar. And would that I could be the confessor of certain of these men, having seen how they discharge and satisfy this deed, which is this: when they gather people for the conquest, from the greatest to the smallest and most humble, observing the words and the faith that compel them, with God and His saints as witnesses, that He will feed them from whatever may be in the land, be it much or little; with this, the poor, assured soldier sets out on his journey, sells his treasures, using it all up in his preparation, and working the rest of the year; then two or three years later, more or less, in which there is no slave such as him, running a million dangers each day, until, with his labors and sweat, the land is leveled, they conquer and settle. And when this unlucky one thinks about collecting the fruits of his labor, the commander puts forth a decree assigning the land to thirty or forty *Guzmanes*[8] (more or less), persons who have only served as hangers-on and settlement clerks; and the simple and humble soldiers, who are the ones who have labored and who make the conquest, are told, with all liberty, to beg pardon, for there is nothing in the land left to feed them. This is done without remembering the good-faith promise [made to them], which should be kept secretly and publicly, and in both populated and uninhabited lands. Recognizing the witnesses cited and that there is a God, who should permit them to lose all that has been built? The worst of it is that if these soldiers, seeing the injustice that is done to them, should wish to leave the land and seek their own lives, they are not given license to do so, and if they take it, seeing themselves in need and desperate, they are pursued and the one that is caught is hanged with such authority that if it is not to God, there is no appeal. I would like to know why they hang these men. What royal payment have they received? What robbery have they committed? In what mutiny or conspiracy have they been found, and who may absolve such a one as this? After causing them such notable injury, are the laws then used only to take their lives? These poor soldiers have thrived well in the conquest; well may their sons and wives find redress! They will tell me that they were advanced money for the expedition; to this I reply that many go who do not receive payment in advance, and those who do receive it, do not receive much from the commander, who carries no more than his estate, and this one and that one use it up in a brief time, later serving in the expedition for another two or three years, where their flesh is torn. What payment is made to them that may equal or compensate for such a perpetual obligation?

It is bad Christianity, [typical] of men of poor conscience, unless it be that they are to settle a second town, whereby those left without luck

Risks run by an inconsiderate commander

29
Basilica of Our Lady of Chiquinquirá, patroness of Colombia.
Photo by Kris Lane

in the first may be employed in the second. But as it is not like this, the commander who acts thusly runs all of these risks: The first, that of the conscience, for I do not know what will satisfy him, unless it is the weight of money. The second, the bad name and credit he receives, for those who leave so offended are forced to complain about him with such clear reason; and if someday he should need to gather other people, he will find very few who will follow him, fearful of being harmed (having discreetly learned from the mistakes of others). The third, if, after these people have left with or without license, there is an uprising in the land, the risk he runs is great, because those who must make war are those who are missing, as they are the working people; the Guzmán serves only to guard the town, and for the most part they are not foot soldiers, nor persons accustomed to work, and if there are any, they are but a few, and these few should be highly esteemed. The fourth risk, run by whomever would follow this path of settling his town with nothing but Guzmanes and clearing it of the working soldiers, is that he loses obedient soldiers and gains powerful enemies who, in a thousand various ways, finally destroy their governor or commander. And there are many who have suffered from this deed, because of having honored and fed these Guzmanes. I do not condemn this, but with the above-mentioned considerations [recommend] honoring and feeding the humble.

Romulus settled Rome with humble people, and conserved it with them, and made of them the most valiant men in the world at that time.[9]

Romulus took pride in humble people

As a remedy for all these obstacles and to save them from all these injuries, I say that the commander, not having a second town, should feed everyone and divide what the land offers among everyone, to some more and to others less, according to their qualities and merits. And if he who feels this is meager wishes to leave and carry on with another neighbor, he should do so, for in this manner the commander will not burden his conscience, and he who leaves will do so with no true complaint, therefore satisfying him by giving him what there is.

Good remedy for rewarding in the conquest

By this path are the inhabitants sufficiently subjected, and the town sustained, with a good selection of people staying on. And he who wishes to leave with the agreement he has made with his neighbor does so with some remedy and not desperate, nor does he discredit the commander.

With this consideration and account will he make his judicial report, in which, after the general record is made, he will name the boundaries (expanding them) and his provinces, caciques, and native lords, declaring that if one day more should appear within the boundaries and limits, they will be newly appointed to the persons most deserving. And then he will begin his report by chapters, first (before all other things) placing the town, or cacique of the highest consideration and substance in the land, under the royal crown, charging the royal officials with its administration; and if there are none, he will name an administrator for them. This is understood according to what the land requires.

Warning

And then the commander will take for himself from among the comforts remaining. Next will come the magistrates and most worthy people, some receiving more and others less, according to his choosing, noting beforehand to divide the land in two parts, first and second. The first is included in a circle whose border is six leagues from the town, and the second is from there and beyond until the outer limit.

Notice

Warning He is advised that all the householders should fit in the first part, and within the second as well, for the town must be sustained by the first, and all the inhabitants must be sustained by the second. There is so much to guard and traverse in squads that not even one or two may do it in new territory, for the Indians will simply eat them; so for this, the citizens of each province must patrol together without risk, and thus all run risks and labor together, for more security.

The inhabitant observes the fief.—Doctrine is owed to the Indian.—The Indian owes tribute according to vassalage and administration.—The Indians are owed doctrine.—Example of what happened to the first conquerors The commander will make the [encomienda] appointments for three generations or for two, according to the royal decrees, obligating the citizens to keep their arms and horses and harquebuses, or whatever is most appropriate for the land, and to keep their houses inhabited. And whoever should leave for some time for just causes should leave a squire in his name. They are to treat the Indians well, neither burdening nor bothering them, charging their own consciences and thus relieving the Royal Majesty's. And it is their responsibility to provide doctrine for those entrusted to them, managing their affairs like the administrators they are. And in recompense for this and in recognition that they owe the king, the Indians are obligated to see to the tributes and bounties for which they have been assessed. Our commander should make them understand this through interpreters, as well as their obligation in recognition of the royal vassalage and doctrine, which their administrators will give to them, as well as defending them when needed, and curing their illnesses, and instructing them in all good customs and orderly living. The Indians, in turn, will be careful to dress themselves and be farmers and work their fields and crops with care and have their houses occupied and clean and in healthy places, and to sleep above the ground, upon beds elevated by sticks [*barbacoas*], ceasing to sleep on the ground as they normally do. They will be affectionately subjected to the guild of the Holy Mother Church (before all things), so that they may receive the waters of the Holy Baptism, they and their women and children, not permitting any Spaniard to bring them harm, nor take woman or child from them, nor to touch their farmland, houses, or property; for apart from doing an enormous disservice to God and the king by this, it causes deaths, uprisings, and the loss of the town to deaths and injuries; just as what happened to the first settlers whom Columbus left behind in Santo Domingo,[10] and what happens each day in many other places, caused by the poor consideration on the part of the soldiers and little caution on the part of the commanders.

This judicial report should declare, according to the quality of the land, if the Indians from one encomienda may marry Indians from another, to which the children should belong, at what age should they be counted for tribute or be exempt, and if there must be restitution for those Indian women who marry others outside of their encomienda and place of origin.

He will also declare the encomiendas and censuses, making known their existence and [precisely] when the inhabitants were found, be they Indians, native lords, or Spaniards, taking their statements without giving a place for complaints as to whether they were lords from before, by tyranny, or by native lords, or if they belonged to another Indian originating elsewhere when they were found at that time. And these encomiendas or censuses are to be made including waters, fisheries, and mountains, pastures and lands, in the same form that these Indians of the encomienda possessed them, for in this way debates and differences are cut short. The common lands for any livestock that has been or may be introduced in the future will be indicated, and these should be large and wide, so that if the town should grow, there will be enough for everyone.

Warnings

He will create by declaration common watering places and pastures, and will distribute estates and *caballerías* of land,[11] and will grant them in the name of His Majesty and in virtue of his powers, which will be measured, such that there will be decrees in the town council made regarding the areas that estates for large livestock, and also small livestock, will have, and which areas are to be taken for wheat farming, where they will then be obligated to plant, each one in his own, and that they proceed to introduce the livestock suitable to the land, so that they may multiply and the land may be supplied and they do not suffer need.

He will also have the foresight to have the inhabitants begin planting their orchards, and favor them so that they plant the most seeds and legumes possible.

And if they have settled in the rain forest [*montaña*], he will advise whoever opens and cuts and clears the land to do so in a circle of one league, due to the importance of health, so that the air bathes them, and due to the importance of having open ground, and the sooner the better. And when it seems to our commander that the land should be settled, he will take particular care in sending for clerics to divide up the parishes. And our commander will obligate all the encomenderos to build churches in their towns and encomiendas, and supply them with adornments, images, and ornaments; he will assure that they attend to the clerics with stipends and that they take particular care, if possible and the land allows, to settle the Indians in towns [*en república*] and that they not be removed, nor allowed to be taken from their native soil to other lands because of the [health] risk they run. And if there are mines in the land, they will be settled and distributed according to decrees made by the town council for such effect, which will be confirmed, noting that mines must be set aside for the king, giving them to his administrator; and all the miners will be obligated to work them, because of the importance of increasing the royal fifths.[12] And to close this distribution and record, he will send it to the governor or tribunal for confirmation, to the person who gave him license to enter the land, guarding it as secret and not divulging it until the confirmation has been returned. In the meantime, he will place the Indians under the jurisdiction of the inhabitants as he sees suitable, so that each attends to that which he has been obligated, as is necessary to comply with the law.

Note that, although by royal decree commander generals [*caudillos generales*] may take a fourth of the land for themselves, they should not do so, in order to avoid the problems and dissentions which this could engender; and it is true that whoever wishes to embrace much, holds onto little. The highest form of governing is to be generous with deeds for one's own people, spare of words, and not greedy.

The skilled commander does this and, believe me, for all good success this is more valuable to him than powerful armies.

THE FAIR TREATMENT THAT IS OWED TO THE INDIAN

It is good that the newly conquered vassal receives benefit

We have sufficiently addressed the conquests of the Indies and their native inhabitants, so in this chapter we must address the fair treatment owed to them and of what it consists. It is right that we address this, for up to now we have stated only what is important to us; for apart from the fact that in fair justice they are owed charity, natural law obligates us to it. And this obligation should shine all the more in the prince by way of us, his vassals; and the commander and justices must take up this cause in earnest for it concerns them, because the royal conscience is expressed through them. And likewise in his name the newly conquered vassals placed under his dominion and governance ought to take advantage, for the conquered vassal who does not receive benefit for the vassalage that he has agreed to will be like a poorly rooted tree that any wind may uproot. And this is a real danger, for upon seeing the opportunity, they unfurl their pennants, breaking the given peace and forming a confederation with the enemy against us; and when, for some reason, they do not do this, they will be neutral and will follow the victor (as they say, "Long Live the Victor!") because they are such an inconstant people and are more lightly and easily swayed than any other nation.

The French lost Sicily in such a brief time because of this, as well as the state of Milan and the kingdom of Naples, by not having a method to indebt their populations, giving them an interest; whereupon they did not take up arms in their favor, knowing that it was no more important to be under their protection than that of the Spaniard or some other.[13] *Why the French lost Sicily*

The same happened to the dukes of Milan, losing the dominion of Genoa.[14] And the great states that the English had, by not knowing how to earn their trust and govern them in a manner so that they would take an interest. They can be obligated in such a way that it is better for them to live under royal protection and its administrators; when the opportunity should arise to take up arms in our favor and assistance, they do so; and there must exist means with which we can win love and reputation. First, govern them in peace and in justice; and the commander will guard this in such a manner that when they break this and the good faith bestowed, there will be justification for the punishment that must be given to them, making them responsible, substantiating the causes, and providing for their defense; for not only must account of it be made to the king, who may have some means to *The Milanese— The English* spare himself from guilt, but account must be more closely given to God, who is a fair judge.

The commander is moved to punish with justification

Therefore the commander must not be moved by ire or ambition, only by justice and the defense of religion and the conservation of the Christian populace, with which God will aid him. And if the Indian rises up having been given no cause, with few means will he be reduced. And when there is a punishment, may it be more pious than strict, considering the welcome that he gave us in his land, along with other fair considerations.

Caesar always moved others with peace

I know well that they are of such a quality and nature that their conservation requires more rigor than anything. Yet there are times when anything can happen, and it has been seen that one may act [i.e., punish] without reason; but there is always an angel who stops the cut of the sword, so that with this, and treating them well, and doing good deeds for them in which they will be interested, they will be kept in servitude and peace, with which they must always be invited, even though war may be justified. Caesar guarded this well in the Civil War, for the more inflamed it was, he always made offers with peace; and though he desired war, he justified it with this and enflamed the desire for vengeance all the more within his men. These are means with which the enemy is compelled, even though his life is being taken from him.

Nero earned the good will of everyone

Nero, in the beginnings of his empire, earned the goodwill and love of all by understated clemency, such as the day he was to sign a sentence given to one who was condemned to die, saying that he was happy he did not know how to write.

Giving the Indian an interest assures peace

Vassals are compelled and enemies made allies with words. Making the natives interested parties in order to compel them more may be done by many paths, allowing them the husbandry of whatever they have and raise in their own fields and houses (for, as barbarous people, they lose everything), so they may nurture them and benefit from them. Some they shall take to market in town, for which one day of the week will be assigned by law and scheduled, whereupon the whole land may gather voluntarily. From this two fruits are taken: first, the town is favored and supplied; and second, the Indian is given an interest. And it must be communicated to our men, the commander having given orders, with great penalties to the soldier or settler, that neither they nor their Spanish, mulatto, or black servants, are to enter this market, the only exception being female or male Indian servants. This is so that the native may sell and peddle goods with liberty, with only a magistrate present to prevent abuses. For if this is done according to principles, nourishing their interest and gain, all the land will come to each market, because hats, beads, salt, meat, and gold are carried away from there; and later, people will be hired from among these very same native Indians, each one bartering the products of his land, and thus they will go content and better able to pay their tribute.[15]

Methods to compromise the Indians

The Indian is also made interested with gifts from his encomendero: clothing, beads, and salt, which they always need. And if there is livestock on the land, one may give the caciques a few head to raise and some mares to ride, also giving the common Indians hens and pigs to raise.

The Indians are also made interested by having herds of these animals, using largesse with them at first, allowing them to enjoy the cheese and meat, and always providing the caciques with this; and where there are sugar mills, allowing them to enjoy the sweet beer [*guarapo*] made from cane syrup, for there is no birdlime that sticks to them so well. And allow the common Indians and caciques alike to plant sweet cane and the other Spanish legumes in their fields for their own benefit.

They are also made interested by the mining of gold, silver, emeralds, or pearls, the encomendero not fearing that they may hide something, for later they may be caught easily, this being both robbery and ransom; giving a hat is sufficient for its [i.e., the pilfered gold's, etc.] return, or a blanket or shirt, beads, combs, needles, or things to eat or other things of greater or lesser value, with which they are content and secured and serve doubly hard.

They are also made interested when the encomendero sends them off for one or two days or more, and when they return they are given gifts for their women and children and paid with things that they esteem, which are of little value.

They are also made interested by treating them lovingly, and in this, if we should consider which of the two is more interested, we will find that it is the encomendero who, by having them content, has lands, a house, property, authority, and rest.

They are also made interested by not taking their sons or daughters away from them by force, even though it is true that for the conservation of the land it is important to have them among the Spaniards so that they become comfortable and begin to love them and learn the Spanish language. If possible, this should be established not only among the domestic help in the house, but in all the land, and particularly among the caciques. But the taking of children for this purpose should be done with the goodwill of the parents, grateful and cherished, so that they give them away with love; and the orphans, of which there are many among them, are to be carefully taught the Christian doctrine and all the good customs possible, even letting them learn from and relax with the Spanish-speaking servants.

They will make the caciques interested by compelling their subjects to obey and respect them, and punishing them if they do not, for thus they acquire a love for their encomendero.

The caciques will be interested when through good means and offerings those Indians who have run away are allowed to return to their settlements, houses, and crops without allowing other Indians to take them over.

Warning—It is important to fulfill what is promised to the Indian.—Seeing the good treatment given to the vanquished, Nur ad-Din was quickly surrendered to

And the commander is advised that when talking with peaceful Indians he should always speak well of those who remain at large, making them understand that if they should return to their settlements, and also to serve, that they will be well received and will come to no harm; but if they do not come, they will be pursued and their houses and crops will be given to other Indians, this having not yet been done only because they are waiting for them. Many times they come hidden among the peaceful Indians just to "sniff the heart" of the Christians and commander, and if they find it bad, they retreat, and if they find it good, they are reassured and return, for they also tire of walking, fleeing through the forest, dying of hunger and sickness, missing their houses, crops, and fields. And when they come it will be most important to keep the promises made to them, for there is nothing that upsets the conquered Indian more than breaking and not fulfilling the conditions and promises by which they have been subjected to dominion and vassalage. And above all, do not work them too hard, for nothing was so advantageous to Nur ad-Din, King of Damascus, as keeping his word, along with not working the vanquished too hard; and seeing that he kept his promises, they surrendered themselves to him easily.[16]

REWARD FOR THE SETTLERS

Because up to now we have discussed the many labors, risks, and expenses the commanders of this militia endure and have in it, as well as the soldiers who march with it, it would not be outside our purpose to state how much the prince makes use of rewards in order to encourage his conquerors and settlers. And though it is true that princes wish more to be served than advised, although advice is service to them, manifested by purpose and zeal, it should be well received and welcomed, as it always has been with the Catholic Kings of Spain. Therefore, as my zeal is good and from a loyal vassal, known to have always served the Royal Crown, I will say how much is owed to the discoverers and settlers of the Indies, and how they are worthy of great and distinguished favors; for they have acquired for their prince, with the valor of their swords, such famous kingdoms as those that are discovered, conquered, and settled, with such riches, leaving behind their love of their fatherlands in order to provide these services, spending their patrimony and estates, and venturing their lives with innumerable labors.

The reward owed to those who serve well

If these services are rewarded, it is a demonstrable thing that virtue is raised up and valor flourishes, for all desire reputation and comfort. However, if this should be lacking, they procure it by those means they know are valued more by the prince and his governors, for if they are of no value they offend virtue; and the valorous, seeing consideration made of the unworthy, tend to become careless.

If the meritorious are rewarded, virtue is raised up

The remedy for this is to distribute the posts and favors among meritorious persons, because it is a great shame how some of those who govern in those places carry on, for if their aim was only services and they were capable, the thing would go well; for these men serve their

Recompense

prince by the labor of their hands, and the people unworthy of the favors given to them serve with the flattery of their tongues. One deed raises the spirit of the prince and the other corrupts it, which gives rise to murmurings in the Republic.

It is of great importance that the soldier serves gladly

It is most important that the soldiers serve gladly in the expeditions in the Indies, for thus their working strength is doubled and those who see this are encouraged for the same reasons, desirous of gaining honored prizes and being liberated from their labors.

Example of Julius Caesar

Julius Caesar, by being so generous, gained so many victories with his soldiers.[17] Princes are loved because of what they give, and feared because of their power. So, ultimately, they are not followed because of the high status they may have, but rather because they are thought to be generous. All must willingly serve the prince and he must use liberality with all.

Reward of the ancients

The ancients made use of rewards of honor and utility, such as crowns and gold chains, better pay, and promotion from one position to a better one. This is most valuable in increasing valor.

Reward of the Romans

The Romans made use of this with much consideration and justice, for military ranks were given to those who most deserved them.

The soldier is the defense of the kingdom.—The soldier is favored little

The soldier is the one who sustains our peace and honor and life, and is to whom we owe these three things with which they serve our Spain; for if we should lack them, the enemy would quickly enter by a million roads, in every place, having seen where they were lacking, disturbing the peace in which we live, the honor with which we sustain ourselves, and the life we possess by divine permission. And yet it is the soldier who is least favored, honored, and rewarded. And today in those parts [i.e., the Indies], compared with the soldier there is none, I think, so dejected and ashamed. And many of the conquerors and their sons and grandsons are so poor and miserable that it is a pity. And the result of this is there are few who look forward to new conquests and discoveries; they are of no importance to them. How much more than the undeserving are these men owed favors by their governors, and aid to offset costs in the name of the Royal Majesty? After all, they have it in their hands.

If we see so much neglect of the living, what memories will we find of the dead, such as Alexander the Great did with statues for those who died in the battle of Granicus?[18] And as he gave this honor to the dead, it is thought that he rewarded the living as well, honoring them and giving them what they deserved.

Alexander the Great honored his soldiers in life and in death

They gave this same honor in the city of Athens, where they sang praises to those who died in the battle of Marathon.

In Athens they sang praises to the soldiers

Lycurgus never wanted his citizens to practice eloquence, but rather to praise those who valorously died for the fatherland.[19]

Lycurgus was very careful in honoring soldiers

And in Rome they made sepulchers at public expense for those who died in its service and were valorous; the first made was for Valerius Publicola;[20] and titles were given only to those who died fighting. Many of our own die in the conquests of the Indies, at the hands of those barbarians, and if they are caught alive, they are killed with a million kinds of torments; and if they eat human flesh, they are roasted alive.

Rome honored and rewarded its soldiers

It has so happened to some, alive and tied to a pole, that the Indian cuts off their flesh and roasts it, eating it in front of them. Others drown disastrously. Others die of hunger in the deserts and uninhabited places, having no one to give them a tomb, being eaten by vultures or buzzards, and others by sicknesses, many leagues away from Christian settlements where they may have some aid and remedy, left in swamps and jungles without confession.

Indian cruelty

They suffer all of this in service to their prince, as is reasonably done, with the expectation of the reward they deserve. Well, if they escape these dangers, when they return they do so sick, poor, and greatly wounded, one-armed, or ruined. And when he who governs sees this spectacle, he does them no favor, and less to the women and children of those who die there; he does not even remember them.

Great remedy and care are needed to correct this, and the governors, in giving out rewards, if they wish to earn a good name for themselves, must do so in service to God and to the king.

Roman praises to the soldiers   The Romans, once battle was finished, would have their captains and consuls in the presence of the army praise those who had fought most valiantly, rewarding them. Scipio did so when he took Carthage. They also made statues in honor of the living and they gave crowns for the distinguished things that were done. Commanders should be rewarded in this manner if they have done their duty, and they are rightly chosen with consideration and care, as has been said at length.

The Romans always chose robust soldiers   The Romans never entrusted their causes to handsome young men, but rather to the robust and experienced. And so, even when Furius Camillus was hated and banished, he was called upon in time of need and made a dictator.[21] Likewise this must be done with the good commander, calling upon him however distant he may be, to be served by him, having the qualities necessary and having the consideration to reward him, for success is owed to him more than to any other person because of his labor, industry, experience, and expense; whoever risks his life, his honor, his property, and peace well deserves the reward, for he risks everything in serving his prince so that he may be rewarded and honored, and not left to consume himself in this court and die of hunger after the reward. Many have died of this at the end of so many labors and from having abandoned wife and children.

Reward of Scipio   Scipio wished to give the Crown of the Wall to the first to ascend the walls of Carthage.[22] When it was taken, there arose much discord between the soldiers of sea and land, such a dispute, that he was forced to give two, one to Quintus Trebellius, a land soldier, and another to Digitius, a soldier of the sea.

Disagreement over a reward   The same disagreement occurred over another reward between Spanish and Italian soldiers concerning the spoils of Dura.[23]

Virtue is not left unrewarded because it lacks guardians   It is good that those rewards that consist of honor are given in order to encourage the militia, as is customary, along with other prizes; and virtue is not left unrewarded because of a lack of guardians, for many give themselves up to idleness for not having been rewarded, forgetting the foundations of their arms.

And departing from the purpose of this book and from our commander, I charge him to consider four things for the deed he would take in his hands: the ease with which he will prepare it, the quickness with which he should execute it, the benefit which may be acquired by it, and the property and blood which it may cost, always striving, before all other things, for just cause. *Consideration that the commander should make*

A BRIEF DESCRIPTION OF
All The Western Indies With The Hydrography And Geography Of The Sea Coasts, Kingdoms And Particular Provinces

THE INDIES ARE COMPRISED of New Spain, the New Kingdom of Granada, and Peru, with the River Plate and Brazil behind. And close to this province, yet to be conquered, El Dorado, which is a long tract of land, according to the news there is concerning it. New Mexico is a great piece of land as well, which is almost directly north of New Spain. Its exploration would be easy, as it is such a gentle land, having before it many others that run unto the Point of Labrador and the Bacalao Strait,[1] more than a thousand leagues from north to south. Florida is also included, on the coast of New Spain bordering the isle of Havana [Cuba]. And attending to my purpose, I say, that these parts that are inhabited are often more rough than even, and there is much unevenness, and in these parts the roads are bad. However there is also much flatness; therefore there are great swamps and marshes in places.

Lands of the Indians

These lands are mostly filled with forest, which is why it is such a humid land of such powerful rivers, although in New Spain there are not so many nor any so great as those in the New Kingdom [of Granada], Peru, and the plains of Brazil.

In general, all the lands of the Indies are divided and cut into many and various valleys short in length and narrow in width, except one valley that is very large, which runs from the River of Cinnamon and the flanks of the El Dorado range until it flows into the Orellana River, in the Northern Sea, which is more than four hundred leagues in length and two hundred and in some parts more than three hundred in width, and runs from north to south. Another valley also runs from the Marañón, behind the El Dorado range until near Santa Cruz de la Sierra; its course runs only a little less. Another runs from the heights of this land, close to Tucumán, to the River Plate, not so large and in a different direction. There are also the valleys and plains of the coast of Peru and the Southern Sea, as will be addressed later.[2]

Volcanoes In these lands of the Indies, volcanoes rise up in some parts, over the sierras or hills or ranges, reaching and climbing upward, such as the volcano of Puebla de Los Angeles, near [the City of] Mexico. This belches fire and smoke at times by day and at others by night.

Notable things The volcano of Guatemala also belches smoke and ash.[3] This exploded once with a great head of water, because of the blasphemy of a woman (according to the account), and destroyed many houses of the old city. This woman died along with many other people, causing the city to be moved. It has exploded another time since, with ash, which caused much damage.

There are other volcanoes in the province of Nicaragua, such as one in León and another in Masaya; this emits much smoke and fire and it has happened that at night, three leagues away, a letter can be read by its brightness.

There is another volcano in the New Kingdom [of Granada] that is called Cartago.[4] This emits neither fire nor smoke but rather is covered by snow all year, because it is so very high and touches the cold region of the air or is close to it.

A thing not seen before Another volcano is in Quito, which emits fire, smoke, and sulfur.[5] It has exploded and covered the fields (at a great distance, for many days) with ash, in such a manner that the livestock died of hunger. God caused a downpour to come and uncover the grass.

Another is in Arequipa,[6] which exploded once with such a great trembling that it destroyed a large part of the town, and sent much water with it; and as it passed through the town it flooded the fallen houses, causing much damage, and a great quantity of wines, which are much gathered there, were lost. Because of so many volcanoes, there are many tremors of the earth and these tremors affect maritime locations most.

These Indies enjoy three climates: torrid, temperate, and frigid. And each of these climes has its humid places and from one to another, in places, there is but little distance. These climates are not caused in the same way as this zone in Spain; though it is true that it is a temperate zone, there are movements of cold and hot and in some places more than others, according to the elevation from the pole and the degrees and sign in which the sun is found. These movements do not cease from causing sicknesses, for any constitution must counter them. *Climates of the Indies*

In the Indies, those persons who want to live with some precaution live in whatever climate their constitutions demand: these live quite healthy. *In the Indies, man chooses his climate*

These climates are caused by the disposition of the land, being within the confines of the sun [i.e., tropics], for according to this, more or less, are the winds that impede the repercussion of the rays of the sun enjoyed, or they are allowed to freely harm.[7] So then, situated beneath the equinoctial, as are the Indies, whether they be closer to the Arctic or Antarctic, as they are within the tropics, they are forcibly wounded two times per year by the Zenith, and perpendicularly, therefore imposing two winters and two summers per year. Lacking wind, then, at this point, the sun would act with such fire that it would be insufferable, uninhabitable (as the ancients said) due to the poor quality it would engender, particularly when the sun should travel through the thinnest part of the inferior sphere of the heavens, for at that time it would be closer to the inhabitants. *In the Indies there are two summers and two winters*

This disposition of the land is not only inhabitable, but quite agreeable, fruitful, and comfortable, and where whatever things the Orb has today should meet with it, they are accommodated with the climate. This is how these climates are to be understood, I say, according to the aforementioned disposition of the land, which contains deep valleys and high mountain ranges and sierras.

Hot lands These deep valleys are forced to be sheltered from the winds and are not blown upon with any strength, and the rays of the sun enter and are gathered within them, whereby it is a hot land, and the repercussion of these rays defeats the quality of the wind, engendering a heat that heats the land and waters and the very same wind; and if the days were not equal to the nights here, as they are forced to be, this land would be quite ill, greatly so; but as the humidity of the night equals the heat of the day, it tempers in such a manner that, though it is known for the heat, it is not insufferable nor uninhabitable.

Temperate lands The temperate land must be understood thusly: that among these mountain ranges and chains there are other valleys where, as they are higher and do not have great hills that protect them, the winds bathe them well, which causes the land to be temperate by impeding the effects of the sun with more strength, and so neither the cold obligates one to seek fire nor does the heat offend in all the year, because of the defense given by the wind, but instead, coolness is known, and the water is drunk cold as it should be. This land is very healthful and fruitful.

Cold lands Among these temperate ranges, others rise up that are not very high nor close by, where, high within them it is very cold and where there is ice and water too cold to drink. These lands are called páramos or *punas*, and in some it often snows, as they are outside of the tropics; for it is a short distance from these Indies to land that falls outside of them. And so, unless it is a volcano as high, or sierra, such as that of Cartago, which, though it is within the confines [of the tropics], its height provides a place where the snow may run up against it before it converts into water, there are but few other places where it will snow. These páramos or punas are cold lands because of the extensive communication of the winds and closeness to the cold region of the air. They are lands of little utility, even though some valleys within them are inhabited. So, it is the disposition of the land and the communication of the winds within the tropics that are the cause of the equal climates all year; thus winter or summer are recognized only by the rains. In hot lands it rains with more force, as the wind does not impede it, and the drops that fall are very thick by not being scattered by the winds, which [in turn] cause the climes, as has been said, along with other notable things that we will state later.

And so the opportunity may not be lost, I will say that this is caused by the South Wind, for it hinders the course of the rains in more than 450 leagues which run the length of the coast of Peru, which are plains from north to south, and from eight to ten leagues in width in all places. A mountain range runs the same direction in all of which the rain falls all the time; this is called the *cordillera general*.

Lands where it does not rain all year

Because this wind had calmed, it rained once on these plains, in Lima, City of the Kings, so much that, as they were unprepared for such weather and the houses were open, much merchandise from Spain was lost, a thing that had never been seen before nor has happened here since; for this wind is ever present, so dry in its nature that, being continuous, it dries that land and its sands so much that vapors are not permitted to rise, and if some should rise from the rivers that descend from the mountains, the force of the wind does not allow them to rise in this region and takes them off course and consumes them along another path.

Beneath some of these dunes is a whole bedrock of salt, where in some places along the coast ships load it to take to other places, such as Panama. This salt is made and gathered by the two qualities of sea humidity and dryness of the wind. The dryness of this wind prevents trees and any other plant from sprouting in these sands, except in the valleys where waters descend from the mountains, for as they are deep and the wind crosses them and passes over them, the humidity of these rivers provides a place where all seeds yield produce.

Salt works

These sands are so barren of trees that there is not one, and as travelers are forced to travel by night, the land being hot and lacking water, they sleep in those sands at times along their walk; and with the South Wind having swept away the clouds, and there being no species of tree or any other plant that creates shade, and the moon shining so clear and reverberating upon the whiteness of the sand, they drew from it a proverb that says, "May you sleep under the moon of Paita," which is a town in these sands and coast.[8]

Why it is said of the moon of Paita

QUALITIES AND CUSTOMS OF THE INDIANS IN GENERAL

Qualities and customs of the Indians — The Indians who live in hot lands are corpulent, and though dark-skinned, they are of a lighter color than those of temperate and cold lands, and all are lacking beards; and if the hot land is forested, they are lighter-skinned, for the sun does not offend them so much, nor the wind, and the climate aids them with their scant clothing. They live with fortitude and are better looking and of a better condition and more liberal and generous in their dealings, but they are more barbaric than those who live in temperate lands and are not, therefore, so wary.

Notable thing — They have much agriculture, for in the hot climate they more often produce their food; they are generally better warriors, except those of the plains of Peru, who lack such resolve, which may be the South Wind operating upon them, as it does upon the land and cultivation, so lacking in some places that in order to sow his maize (lacking rain, as has been mentioned here), the Indian plants it in the heads of sardines, due to the great quantities of them on that coast, and so in each head they place a grain to plant under the sand, thus growing and taking root with the little moisture therein. The Indians of temperate lands are a cautious and shrewd people, ill looking, miserable; they do not have so much agriculture, nor are so bold in war. They are a people who wear clothing and are clean; but they are all a barbarous people, as they demonstrate in their houses, dress, meals, and odd manner of clothing, something they use but little, unless it is in a temperate land and even there they do not know what a stocking or a shoe is, until, after dealing with us Spaniards, they have been brought to cleanliness, clothing themselves, and covering their flesh with the shirt, the doublet and trousers, stocking and shoe, hat and cape, for in hot lands they always go about naked and still do so in many places.

Indian dress — In the temperate regions they cover themselves with poor blankets made of cotton, which they gather in abundance in hot lands, and they spin and weave, and even today they make their own in some places, wearing these on their shoulders like gypsies and wearing shirts or *patacusmas*, as we would say, a sack dress, having a place for the head and arms to go, and the female Indians go naked, with several blankets wound around the waist which barely cover their shame, although in temperate places they travel about more decently, wearing them down to their feet. In some places in hot, forested lands, they go naked and cover their indecent parts with *viaho*[9] leaves or with river clams, and the headmen among them wear them with gold, but even with these clams they are not covered, for they put them two fingers above, hanging from a few threads from the waist, and the maidens wear nothing. They are friendly, both the men and the women;[10] they wear jewels of gold in their manner in their noses, ears, neck, and lips, and on their wrists and about their waist, for there are smiths for this work.

The Indians paint themselves a color they call *bija* and other black and yellow colors. Some normally tie their member to their body and others stick them into gourds and shells. *The Indians paint themselves*

They are a people who like toys and childish things, such as glass beads, looking glasses, combs, spinning tops, needles, knives, and hats. They use many feathers, which they wear for war or great festivities. They sleep in hanging hammocks or upon cots or on skins thrown on the ground near the fire even in a hot land, sleeping naked. They are a filthy people, as their houses show well, ordinarily dirty in all places, full of fleas and midges, unless the house belongs to a cacique or other principal person, as these are cleaner. They are a people without honor; the most important among them lie whenever they speak and promise. They are very friendly as long as the Spaniard keeps his word, yet they themselves know not how to keep theirs. Adultery among them goes without punishment, and is not a matter of honor, but rather interest; when the husband knows that another is occupying his woman, he becomes angry and until he is satisfied with a payment they take their sides, although in some provinces they reject this when it is noticed and they often kill them with herb venom. They are a people who have four and five or more wives, and those who are Christian have them as well, albeit secretly, unless it is the one had by way of the priest, and for this, nowadays, they are punished. Among these women there is always one who is best loved, whom the rest respect and serve. *Indian habits*

We Spaniards have been bringing them to cleanliness and Christianity, in which some are quite willing and instructed, but up to now, these are few. In general, they are a people who get drunk with maize chicha, *azua*, or *pulque*, which are the customary drinks in the three kingdoms. They chew *hayo* or coca, *yopa*, and tobacco, with which they lose their judgment, and then the Devil speaks to them.[11]

The Indians are sorcerers This occurs most among Indians who are sorcerers, *mohanes*, and *santeros*, representing themselves in a thousand different figures, and in the form in which they appear they make a figure of gold or clay or cotton, which they worship with reverence; and much of this happens these days in secret among the people who are already Christian, for among the idolatrous people it is quite public. These people know many things the Devil has told them, and it is but for their greater harm, as they are mired in the affair and cannot escape.

Sorcery of one mohán I will tell what happened to me concerning this with several Indians called Pijaos, as it serves our purpose, their having caused great massacres and having gone after their punishment myself.[12] After some days spent pursuing and tracking them with my soldiers, I came, one night, within sight of their villages, with an ambush to be given during the dawn watch; and that night their cacique, who was a sorcerer and mohán, having taken *jopa* in order to talk with the Devil, knew that the Christians were to set upon him that night, and warned all of his people, and the village was cleared, leaving it uninhabited, with a few dogs to bark and many fires. They retreated to some great crags close to the village and were armed all night, with such spirit that when we were to come upon the village and be discovered by the dogs, they had prepared an ambush for us so that upon leaving it we would receive harm, which is usually great in all ambushes. And it so happened that while they had their arms at the ready, I arrived as dawn broke, with the difficult labors my people endured all that night, because of a rough and lengthy crag, crawling down along it, not being noticed because of the little noise so that we came to be above the population; and with all this preparation, we would have been noticed had God not used a miracle that night for the punishment of those people. And so it was that at the moment when we wished to descend, there was a moon as bright as if it were midday, and fearing that I would be discovered, I retreated twice; and one of those who was with us had his hands toward heaven and said, "Lord, please cover us with true night, taking this brightness away from us, for without it, it will not be possible to punish those who so offend thee," and as he wished, God heard him, his petition being just; then, within two moments, the sky was covered by great clouds and the moon was hidden and it began to thunder and rain, and seeing this, I attacked the slope and crag with great sureness and prediction of success and so the soldiers went sure of it as well. At the break of dawn I came upon a ravine so thick with giant bamboo that there was no way to break through or pass, and searching out the path in all directions, the day came and the sun was already up when I discovered a passage, and what I imagined to be the cause of losing the opportunity was that of winning it, for if we had come upon the village before, which was to happen later, we would not have found anyone and we would have been discovered, and the aforementioned harm would have befallen me. But as God provided such a good beginning, he had the burden of a good ending; for as the day came and the Indians saw that there was no noise nor rumor of people, making a liar of their mohán and cacique, they all returned to their houses and went to sleep after the labors of the bad night.

At this point I was crossing the bamboo patch and the ravine and coming upon the village, nearing it; and with them defending themselves with a great uproar, we Spaniards (though few) showed ourselves well skilled, along with the friendly Indians whom we took along to help us, being some 150 lancers whom a few days before had suffered the aforesaid deaths at the hands of these Indians [i.e., the Pijaos], and they took more than 100 children and women, who were well fed, except a few who had to be fattened as they were thin, as is the custom among those who eat human flesh. Among these *piezas*[13] was found an Indian named Yaincuma, a lovely girl, whom they had not eaten because of her beauty. From her we were to learn many things, eventually, and the prediction of the mohán, from whence this tale came. And so I say they are great sorcerers, as seen in this case and many others and they have great superstitions. When they must go forth to fight, they cast great spells and are governed by them, going or not going forth to battle.

Their dwellings are often upon hills, unlike those within towns, for living in the heights they communicate with each other using wooden drums and shells, and they use these more in the forests, for if it is

Indian dwellings

savannah, they communicate better with smoke. Others have their dwellings on plains in the mountains, and on shores and islands of great rivers they navigate with canoes. Some live on lake islands, making use of canoes as well.

They are a people who, if they have war with other Indians or Spaniards, are highly vigilant, and any of them who takes up the post of sentinel will be there two days and two nights without being replaced or sleeping, chewing hayo, coca, or yopa.

They are a people who, induced by the Devil, readily hang themselves, out of simple anger or because their women quarrel with them. The women are the ones who work in the fields in many provinces while the men are getting drunk.

Theft is not a crime among them and so they later confess to it without torture. And among some nations they have the custom that the closest relative of him who committed the theft must amend it. Nowadays they cut the hair of the caciques, which is a great dishonor for them. Nephews, not sons, inherit according to their laws. Now inheritance for sons is being introduced. They marry slaves won in war and male Indian slaves are married to sisters and daughters, and so slaves become lords, and there are many of these as it is taken as gallantry and nobility. The majority are idlers, but not in affairs of war. They are obedient to their caciques. They are lascivious, which is why they have so many women. They multiply much in lands where there is an abundance of fish. They lie with daughters, sisters, and mothers. They make much use of herbs that kill and some are given it in drinks and meals and die from it, and among them, neither investigations nor punishments are made for this.

They are great merchants in their dealings, trading some things for others, and for this their markets are well known. And in those places where they eat human flesh, they have their public butcher where it is weighed, such as the Pijaos have for the whole region.

In general, they are great storytellers, talkers, and lovers of ceremony; they worship and sacrifice differently in every province and kingdom and unto the Devil, generally, in all the Indies. But, particularly, some do so to the sun, others to the moon, others to idols, with the mark and image of the demon made of wood or clay, of gold or cotton. Every clan or republic has sanctuaries or tombs (as we have our churches) in which they make their offerings and charities, such as gold, blankets, emeralds, and where possible, bezoar stones, silver, and things of the Spaniards if there are any, beads and other things; they also burn foul-smelling incenses to their idols. They often use many and varied feathers as adornment, such as in Santa Marta and New Spain, and they also wear the skins of tigers. They sacrifice slaves as victims, and in some places, their own people, relatives and children; they go on great fasts. If they cross from a temperate land into a hot land, where the two climates seem to do battle, they make a pile of rocks, sticks, branches, and grass in offering, such that none pass without doing this, as it is a ceremony they do so they do not die, and even in the presence of Spaniards they do this and if it is dismantled or set afire, it greatly angers them.

There are and have been some Indians who have revealed sanctuaries or tombs to some Spaniard and used the wealth from them as gifts or for ire and injustices they may receive from their caciques or women whom they greatly desire, and these guides do not reach the sanctuary, but rather point it out from afar and give signs, for they fear to uncover it, saying that it angers heaven and lightning bolts will strike.

And it happened to me in the New Kingdom of Granada, one clear, moonlit night, an Indian guided me to a sanctuary, trembling, saying that the sanctuary would be angry and lightning would strike from the heavens. I told him that he was a dog of a sorcerer and that this would not happen and he would see, forcibly taking him by the arms. It began to thunder and lightning, the heavens darkening and raining hard with a great storm, and the Indian became so fearful from this that there was no manner of moving him. He told me to go alone, that he would show me the way and the night would then become calm. And being strong, I did this, and it was as the Indian had told me, it cleared and became calm and the moon came out and he believed in his superstition and I reached my sanctuary and found that its marker had been moved, for in that land they have the custom of moving those that are not under the ground, every eight days, so that the Spaniards do not come upon them. Long ago, they used to throw these offerings to the bottom of great lakes, and they still do this for greater assurance.[14] And returning to my Indian, I did not find him where I left him; I found him where we had set forth. I scolded him, for he insisted that

Superstition of an Indian

all he had told me had been true, and although it was, it was not for the causes he said, but rather because of natural weather.

These sanctuaries are guarded by a few elders of a hundred years in age, the santeros, who, even if they are given a million torments, will not declare where and in what place the gold lies.

Indian custom In some provinces, when the Indians die they are often buried with all the gold and jewels they have and they are given some food, for they say they are resurrected in the form they wish to take. In these tombs great fortunes have been found, such as in Zenú and Guazuze [on the Sinú River] and the Darien and great tombs in Peru and in many other places.

In these provinces they are not buried, but rather embalmed in smoke, like the Guanches[15] did long ago in the Canaries and these, embalmed and wrapped in many blankets, are placed in tombs and sanctuaries.

Others are burned and made into powder and are drunk in chicha by the whole clan, and the houses where they die are burned or destroyed. In every kingdom they have a designated land, which they call holy ground or house of the sun, where the most principal among them go when they are very old, to die and be buried in them, taking their riches, as in Sinú atop a great hill which they have there for such effect, which they call the house of the sun (and I believe they still do). Great wealth has been taken from these tombs in Sinú by us Spaniards, and if the warring Indians did not impede it, they would take much more than that already taken.

The women have great ceremonies at childbirth. Some give birth alone in the hills and for nine days they do not cook nor do they eat more than toasted or cooked maize, and in other provinces they fast and do not eat salt during their fast (as we do not eat meat), and there are nations that, if a girl is firstborn, they kill her. They have many other ceremonies that, to not detain myself so, I do not wish to address further; I will only say that they have the custom in giving birth to wash themselves and the newborn in a river, and they birth with such ease that walking along a path, they simply open their legs and give birth and they go to the closest river or ravine to wash. The male Indians have the custom of crouching to urinate, and the females, standing.

They raise their children carrying them on their backs, like the monkeys do, working all day. Others bind them upon boards and at five years they begin to teach them and practice how to carry a load, so that they are ready and accustomed when they are of age. The meals they eat are all very simple, and in war, where they sometimes suffer hunger, they eat many extraordinary roots and wild fruits, which they call *cimarronas*,[16] serpents, lizards, rats, fat worms that are under the ground, monkeys, parrots, all wildfowl, caimans, large ants, and if they have chili pepper or salt, they eat anything even though it may be very bad, but I know of a province where they eat no salt, which is named El Sollo, and if they are forced to eat it, they vomit up their entrails. And because our meals are prepared with salt, if they eat of them not one escapes dying of diarrhea, having experienced this at length with them. Certainly it is a thing of great wonder. *A strange case*

In general, all the Indians eat on the ground even when they are caciques. They are only differentiated by the respect with which they are served, although in their dealings with us in New Spain, Peru, and the New Kingdom, some eat upon tables, but the uncivilized and warlike continue this habit. After dealings with our Spaniards, they eat of all our produce and are great lovers of it and are great drunks with the wine of Castile and great lovers of horseback riding. They are great doctors and herbalists, mostly very old women, and some cure using the vapor from their mouths. They are highly phlegmatic, generally in all of their features, and thus possess little spirit. They make everything they see with their hands, particularly in New Spain, where with such skill they make feather imagery and other things by any artifice.

In general, there are great masters skilled in all things. They are great musicians and craftsmen of trumpets and horns, with which they officiate a mass. *The Indians are ingenious*

Many write and read and some have come to know so much that their studies have been taken from them, for they do everything with their phlegmatic humor. Indeed it is such that with it they can break the most furious colt; and what is more, they calm the bulls and make them work as much or more than oxen, loading their horns with great loads of firewood. *The bulls bear loads upon their horns*

A BRIEF DESCRIPTION OF THE INDIES

This happens in Quito, where groups of them, loaded in this manner, enter every day.

Variety of tongues They have, in general, a great variation in their languages, for, excepting two, which are the Mexicana [Náhuatl] and that of the Inca [Quechua], which occupy some stretch of land, everywhere else the language changes with each town or province. In general they are a people miserable with sickness, left to die in sadness, thus with typhus or side pains, catarrh, pox, and bloody diarrheas, which are the most common sicknesses, when they get it they die in great numbers, and if it is a land where the existence of some pestilence is confirmed, such as in these parts, none will escape, as they are a people of little spirit.

That of which herb venom is made Their arms are the most ordinary, arrow and sling, lance and dart, buckler and club. They use venom on the arrows. This they make by placing into a large bowl or pot all the poisonous vermin and other venoms, principally viper venom; and mixing them all together and covering them, they battle each one therein until they die and are left to rot and placed to cook over a fire in the same bowl, adding the milk of the thorny *ceiba* tree as well as blood from the menstruation of the women. This herb venom is made by the very oldest women, because upon finishing it, they die at once, because of the strength of its poisonous smoke.

In all the Indies this venom has been found only in Santa Marta, and in the New Kingdom of Granada, in Muzo, where it is very fine.[17] Also in the Ariguyes, Panches, Guayles [Gualis], and in the Guazuze and Sinú, which lies on the shoulders of the Province of Antioquia.[18] It is a wonder should anyone wounded by this escape; and there is one of twenty-four hours.

Manner in which the female Indians fight In some places, such as in Carare, the female Indians fight through embrasures in cabins or forts, with blowguns, shooting, in the same manner as a pellet, a thin arrow made of palm, of one span and with a point like an awl; this serves to enervate, and while our men are occupied with fighting the [male] Indians, the females have the opportunity to aim at the face, as they cannot cause damage to the body because of their weapons, and if they hit their marks, when that tip enters the flesh, the arrow shakes and breaks off and what remains inside works with the herb venom. Ten- and twelve-year-old boys also do this.¹⁹

They use their old music in their festivities, and they are very sad-sounding; and when they sing, it is of past wars with other Indians, and with Spaniards; they cry and sometimes sing of their losses and sometimes of their victories. In war they use shells, horns made of gourds, and small drums. And to gather themselves together they use the aforementioned wooden drums, which are heard over a great distance in the mountains but over little distance on [flat] land. They join in many feuding wars [*guerras travadas*] among themselves and these days, in new conquests, it is a wonder not to come upon them, as a result of the tyrannies that well up each day.

Indian music

Before dealings with the Spaniards, they used axes of stone for their crops and to cut trees and other wooden things, and they still use them today wherever they have no dealings with us to take advantage of iron ones. If one Indian kills another, [the death] is compensated for according to [material] interest and in this, as with other offenses, the cacique is the judge and punishes, if such [men] are obeyed, for in some provinces they hardly are.

In some parts, the males have long, braided hair, and in others it is loose, and in some they make a tail, and in others they make a crown like friars and in others it is shaved. These are good warriors. And the Spanish-speaking Indians who serve our Spaniards dress and wear their hair in our style, though some wear their hair in a tail.

Indian habit

Some nations have the custom of killing the daughters when they are born, so they do not multiply, saying that in this manner they will be done with and will not serve the Christians. In general, all are inclined to womanly work, as seen in spinning and other labors they do, and so if the Spaniard wishes to impose upon them, they are taken easily and not unwillingly. They often carry the load of a beast (though not of so great a weight) many leagues and many do this today, even though they have their mares. This is normal among newly conquered people and the strength is on their heads, which is where the load hangs from.

Their manner of counting is with stones or maize-grains or by knots on strings that they have for this purpose, which they call *quipos*, and they do not count higher than twenty and count one [unit of] twenty and more according to the number they have for this.[20]

There are very few poor among them who ask for alms.

The chief Indians have buffoons   In festivals, the men have buffoons for their amusement.

Indian opinion   In many parts the Indians are of the opinion that monkeys and apes are a caste of people who do not wish to talk because they are not made to work. They are given to such barbarity and though they are barbarous in their speaking and language, some of their terms and phrases suggest they are a people of greater understanding [*especulación*].

The Indian has no virtue   I conclude by saying that they are a people with no virtue whatsoever, even when they are not afraid. They are a timid people in every way. The female Indians not only show no love toward the infants they raise, but one is appalled that they have no love for their own children, killing them and suffocating them for petty annoyances. They are a people who sleep very little at night, for they are given to drunken revels or dances or in being by the fire eating their tidbits and chewing their hayo, coca, tobacco, or yopa; there is only light from the flame made by the fire. They love the smoke, which is common, such that no one can bear being inside their houses.

Famous Indians   The most famous Indians in all the Indies are those from Chile, called Araucos [Mapuche]. The next in New Spain, called Guachachiles or Chichimecs, who are now conquered.[21] The third, in the New Kingdom of Granada, called Pijaos. There are others in Santa Marta. Those of Tayrona [in the Sierra Nevada de Santa Marta] have been pacified. Also those of Florida are warlike. There are other provinces famous for this, but the Indians from them are few. In these four or five nations there have been some valorous and remarkable Indians, but very few.

Indian arms   Here I name the most commonly used arms of these bellicose nations. Those of Chile: lances; the Chichimecs or Guachiachiles: arrow; the Pijaos: lance; those of Tayrona: arrow with venom; those of Florida: arrow.

They have priests in some parts, and these were the most principal lords of the land, placing miters on their tiaras and many of these have been found, particularly in New Spain, but not of hammered gold, such as some that were found in one sanctuary in the New Kingdom of Granada, and very large, in the time of Dr. Antonio González, of the Royal Council of the Indies, governor and captain general, reformer and president of that audiencia, who, out of greatness, notably sent them to our king, along with a few breastplates of the same gold, which was very fine, with many idols of various forms inscribed upon them.²² *Indian priests—Miters of hammered gold*

FRUIT TREES FROM OUR SPAIN

The fruit trees in parts of the Indies brought by our Spaniards are: sweet and bitter orange, royal lemon, *ceuti* lemon, sweet and bitter lime, citron, grapefruit, pear, apple, pomegranate, fig, olive, quince, peach. All of these grow in hot lands, except quince and peach, which require temperate land; and though the others grow in temperate land, it is not so well as these two.

Of the peach, I will say that in the New Kingdom of Granada, in the fields of Santa Fe [de Bogotá], which is temperate land, there are trees that do not lack their fruit during the whole year, for on the same tree some are blooming and others budding, and others ripening and others so ripe they fall from the tree, and thus the whole year. Date palms also grow in hot lands. In Canta, ten leagues from Lima [near old Cantamarca], there is a fig tree, half of which withers part of the time, and the other half at other times. Some say this happens according to the variation in climates, that when it is winter in the mountains, the part of the tree that faces them withers, and when it is winter on the plain, the other half withers. *Wondrous production of fruit*

CULTIVATED TREES FROM THE LAND ITSELF

The native trees that are cultivated among the Indians and Spaniards in those lands are: the cacao, this tree grows in hot lands and is quite productive; its fruit is eaten and a good drink is made from it. This [i.e., *Trees of the Indies* the cocoa bean] is the coin of the Indians in New Spain. They have features of a pine kernel with a shell and are of that color, except that they are twice as large and not so round. They grow upon pines, though different from those from here. This merchandise and coin has been and is good trade, from which many Spaniards have grown wealthy.

Hayo or coca is a tree that is not large nor gives fruit; it is very generous, for the leaf is a great trade in Peru and even in the New Kingdom of Granada. In Peru a large number of Spaniards have become wealthy, as with the cacao in New Spain. They strip this tree of its leaves two or three times a year, taking it to trade, and it is the primary sustenance the Indians have, as chewing it they are sustained two and four days if necessary.

Bija or *achiote* is a tree that grows a bud within which there are a few pips covered with a colored flour that resembles henna; they gain benefit from it in such a manner that they make little balls from it, which serve to paint themselves. They also use it in a drink that they call *chocolate*, which the Spaniards use in all the province of Honduras, to give it color.

Maguey is a tree that does not give fruit but is of great use: it is a round shrub close to the ground, with wide leaves a yard and a half in length, with a very hard and sharp thorn at the tip: from the center of these leaves grows its tree, very high and straight and very light and as thick as the thigh of a man, and it gets thinner toward the tip, which is very thin. Before this tree sprout becomes hard, it is cut at the base and its heart is hollowed, from the cavity of which they gather the juice and broth that comes from it, which is not a little, and they make honey from it by cooking it, as well as vinegar and wine that they call *pulcre* [pulque] in New Spain; this drink makes the Indian more drunk than chicha or any other. From these leaves they take fibers like thick hemp, but white, from which they make ropes, headstalls and straps, sandal soles and a million other types of things; and they even make needles from the thorns, cutting and drawing them in such a manner that they come away with their thread and with these they sew their coarse manufactures. They take the wood for their huts from this tree when there is no other wood.

Capulí [*Prunus capuli*] is a large tree, taller than a cherry, that bears fruit very similar to the cherry, but it is sweeter. Guava trees bear a fruit that seemed to smell of bedbugs to our people when they first passed by it: it is a healthy fruit and, cooked, is given to the sick. It is the size of an apple; a preserve is made of it, which, in appearance and quality, is similar to the flesh of the quince and is made in large quantities. Though wild, they cultivate other fruits in the field and forest, such as avocados and sweetsops, papayas, *pitahayas*, *pejivalles*, white and black *zapotes*, *chicozapotes*, prickly pears, *mamey sapotes*, and pineapples. The tree of these pineapples is a squat bush, almost like the maguey, but smaller. This fruit is flavorful but unhealthy.

There are other fruits, such as the plums from Nicaragua [red *mombin*, or Spanish plum] and plantains, whose tree is ostentatious and does not bear fruit more than once.

There are *guanábanas* and *guamás*; the fruit from these trees is flavorful, but unhealthy; most of them are from hot lands and the rest from temperate lands, which I will not detain myself to detail. I will only say that there is a *cañafístola* tree [American drumstick, or native *sen*] whose fruit and purpose everyone knows; it grows in hot lands.[23]

FRUIT TREES GROWN IN THE MOUNTAINS WITH NO CULTIVATION

The uncultivated fruit-bearing trees of the mountains are beechnut, medlar, carob, *tamaca* palm, walnut, almond, *guaimaro* [cow tree], *caimito*, hazelnut, and cacao, and minche and cinnamon trees, such as there are in Quijós,[24] which are different from those of China and the East Indies. But the cinnamon suits and is reasonable and is not shelled, but there is a bell within the blossom and that is the cinnamon. There are also royal palms, which are of great utility if one knows how to make use of them, as in the East Indies. These palms have a very thick and flavorful heart, but it is difficult to harvest and not healthy; after it ripens, its fruit is eaten, but there is little flesh on the pit. It is yellow, and the Indians make a wine of it, placed in the sun a few days.[25] In Portuguese India and in China, a great quantity of oil is made from the stone of this fruit, which is good to eat. They also bore holes in the tree so that the sap flows out of them, of which they make a wine that is little different from that of Castile. I drank a little where the ships coming from the Philippines drop anchor [i.e., in Acapulco], and they fooled me with it, giving it to me as Spanish wine. And in parts of the Indies much of it could be used, for in some provinces there are a great number of these palms, such as those in the New Kingdom [of Granada]. Each of these palms bears a great quantity of its fruit in one great bunch.

There are other palms that are not thorny, that grow a white resin over their bark which, melted and mixed into a bit of wax, is made into candles. There are many of these in the New Kingdom. The palm of Pijivalle or Chontaduro is very useful, as its fruit is great sustenance to the Indian, eating it cooked, and it is very healthy and abundant. There is also a tree that yields a tallow in great quantity; there is no lamb tallow so delightful and it is useful for many things.

There are some trees in the city of Simancas, on the river Iscancé, a land that I conquered and settled on the twenty-sixth of June in the year [15]93,[26] that bear bunches weighing a half arroba and more each, which they call *camairón* grapes; each grain of them is like the large purple grapes of these parts. It is a very delicate fruit, flavorful and healthy, but has a thicker skin. This tree is from hot lands, like those mentioned above. This city lies at two degrees north latitude. It is quite rich in gold mines.

There is also the white mulberry, which is good for silk culture, as is done in New Spain.

WILD TREES WITH NO FRUIT

The cedar is a very large tree and very thick; it is a fragrant wood. Canoes for the rivers are made from it, which are of one piece; they hollow it in such a manner that, if it is large, thirty men fit inside. Other works of carpentry are made of this wood.

There is another tree they call yellow Guayacán.[27] It is this that they call strong wood [*palo fuerte*] for buboes, and it serves for that benefit and for other things.

The black Guayacán is another tree that does not serve for this, yet it is the strongest wood of all in those places, for under the ground it lasts many years. A piece of it has been found between the earth and the bedrock while searching for emeralds in very deep mines, and it was found to be so strong they could only judge that it had been there since the Flood. It is such a strong wood that axes break cutting it. Shelves for churches and homes are made from it.

There are other trees such as *Caracuries* [caracolis, *Anacardium exelsum*] and ceibas. Canoes are made of these as well, though they are not as good as those of cedar, for they are weathered by the water.

There is another type of ceiba that is thorny; these contain the milk with which the venomous herb is dissolved, and with it they make the twenty-four-hour venom. One can fish with this milk, when there is no bait for fishing, by throwing it into the river, the fish become drunk with it and flee downstream and into a cane trap or rack made for the purpose, and there they are caught.[28] This happens in medium-sized rivers.

Manzanillo[29] is a tree whose fruit is similar to miniature apples in these places. A mild venom for arrows is made from this fruit along the great River of Magdalena, and it is a wonder that none have died from it; rather the bodies swell like wineskins, but it goes away in a short while. From this, a soldier of mine whom they wounded on one occasion on this river, though he was very bellicose, was left as bewildered as he was at his birth. He who might sleep beneath this tree will take on a very bad disposition, even from being in its shade as well.

There are other trees they call Arumo or balsa wood; from these they make rafts for the rivers.

Jopa [or yopa] is a wood that bears seed pods like peas and the grains within are similar but smaller. The Indians take this crushed in the mouth in order to speak with the devil in some parts (as we have said).

Guacimo [*Guazuma Ulmifolia*] is a wood of no use and if it has any, it is little.

Guadua [*Guadua angustifolia*, a giant bamboo] is a hollow and very thick cane, that goes to the sky, the tube of which is half a yard long between knots, more or less, and some are as thick at the root as the thigh of a man, and they grow thinner along their length toward the tip: it is useful for many things, primarily for the framing of huts or houses, for Indians as well as Spaniards, in hot lands, which is where it grows. In some places the Indians make water jugs from these guaduas. Soldiers also take advantage of them to mitigate their great thirst, cutting them where they are found in water.

Brasil [*Caesalpinia echinata*] is a wood that everyone knows and knows how it is used.[30] In these humid and hot mountains where these woods grow, there is a great tree which, the natives have assured me, grows from the manure of a very small bird; this is not difficult to believe, for this bird could eat some seed which, in passing it, produces this tree; as we see with the thorns that the livestock spread so much in some of those places, such as goats, by passing its seed, and we also see this in the *guayabas* that the birds eat and scatter in the forests, which is the cause of there being so much of it growing wild on the Windward Islands.

In this forest a type of wood rots, which, in rotting, illuminates a path so that one may follow it by night.

There is also a wild cañafístola tree, more purgative than the other, if one wishes to make use of it.

The sarsaparilla [*Smilax febrifuga*] is a three-cornered thin reed, with a great stock of roots under the ground, which everyone knows of and knows what it is for.[31] It grows in hot and humid lands.

The oak is a tree very similar to those of Spain. This grows in lands colder than temperate; it is useful for wood for houses and carpentry.

Borrachera [*Alternanthera lahmannii*] is a medium-sized tree, from temperate lands, of no use; its seed, powdered and served in a drink, causes such drunkenness that he that drinks it is left for dead for a long time.

There is a reed in the province of Quito that saves the sugar mills the cost of lighting with tallow or oil, for placed like torches, it illuminates whatever is necessary.

There is another reed used to catch fish, like the milk of the Ceiba, but more perfectly, and so more of it is used. It is called *barbasco*, and it is often planted and used for this effect. It must be beaten upon rocks on the shore of the water, so that its juice goes downstream, infecting everywhere.

Notable quality of one reed I will speak of the quality of another reed, which is a notable thing; it is in the rivers of Iscancé and the flats of the Marañón; taking two reeds between four people, from shore to shore in rivulets or ravines and separated by the distance of a harquebus shot, more or less, according to the disposition of the river, one pair approaches the other, dragging the reeds along the surface of the water, the fish are gathered together into the middle between both reeds, into a space of three or four yards, and the Indians shoot them with arrows, which they know how to do marvelously, and other Indians are below catching the soaked and dead fish.

There is a tree in certain mountains of the New Kingdom, in whose roots (over time) a stone comes to be included, making it appear that the root is converted into stone.

AROMATIC TREES

The dragon tree [*Dracaena draco*] is a tree from which dragon's blood is taken for the making of toothpicks.

White copal is another tree that produces a resin whose odor is very similar to incense; this is used for many things.

There is another tree that has black resin, with the same odor, but more brown and sticky and more useful than the white.

Caraña [*Proteum carana*] is another tree that gives a foul-smelling, but useful, turpentine.

Tacamahaca [*Proteum heptaphyllum*] is another tree whose gum does not smell good, but it is useful.

Palo Santo[32] is a tree whose wood and resin have a strong smell and is useful.

Black balsam is a tree that gives its liquor in good quantity; it smells good, and is very useful.

White balsam is another tree whose resin is reddish and clear and hard. This is good for wounds and incenses, though the other smells better.

There are also those same black pines of Spain, which give their turpentine like those here.

Molle [*Schinus molle*, pepper tree] is a tree that does not bear fruit and is fragrant and useful. All these trees grow in hot and humid lands and a few in the temperate, except the pine, which thrives in the temperate and cold lands.

In the cold lands there are *cardones*[33] that produce a very white turpentine, similar to the streaked [variety] and more useful. And in this cold land there are many other trees, of no use but for fire and houses, and implements for farmers. Nature covered these with great vines, appearing to do them the courtesy for the cold. In these three climates, hot, temperate, and cold, no tree grows that does not produce according to the climate and its nature.

There are other trees in hot lands from which the Indians bring smoked and dried sticks for starting fire, as we do with flint, though by a different method.

VERMIN

In these mountains and forests, because of their ruggedness as well as being a hot land, there are more snakes and other venomous vermin than in temperate and cold lands, as we will state here.

Winged Serpent (Sierpe) Of the winged serpents that have so much renown, only a few have been seen in those parts (I have had news of only one). They say that a mestizo or a creole in the district of Quito killed one in a forest with a harquebus, a monstrous and frightful thing, with a large body and with its fins and ears. They say the head was taken to Quito.

Monstrous snakes Boba[34] snakes, as they are called, are in the plains of El Dorado (more than in other places); each like a great beam. They do no evil and it has happened that while soldiers have been marching through scrublands, these have lain stretched among the grasses, and the soldiers, thinking that they were trees have sat upon them, and upon feeling the load, the snake began to move; and then, realizing what it was, they got up and killed it. These sustain themselves by hunting deer and pig, putting themselves on their paths. The natives say that they also enchant the animals with their breath. They can be found in the dense mountain forest, but not so large. They breed in hot lands: they are also in temperate lands, but are quite small.

Occurrence on the Isle of Cuba In the year seventy-eight [1578], in Santiago de Cuba, there happened an earthquake, and these snakes, fleeing from the forests, came to the town in such quantities that there was a procession through the streets that lasted until ten o'clock at night. We often came across them in the middle of the streets, which, by being of the boba type, did not cause an uproar among the people.

In cold mountain lands, there is a type of very small viper, yet as the land is so impassable they rarely cause harm.

In hot lands, in the forest as well as the savannah, there are snakes they call *cascabel*, for at the tip of their tail they have a hollow that sounds like a rattle when they move. These cause much harm, for they live where people pass, and the Indians are in the most danger by constantly being there and going unshod. One bitten often dies within twenty-four hours. *Rattlesnakes*

In mountainous jungle lands in some places there is a beast like a small lizard they call *tiros* [i.e., shots, or leaps], which are in the branches of trees, and if one should happen to pass by, they leap onto him.[35] This is the cruelest bite and that which takes life quickest, although it is true they are few, for God wanted it thus, because of their great danger. These are in the mountains of Muzo. *Notable vermin*

In lowland jungles and hot lands (in places), there are some serpents of four or five yards in length, and I have measured, for a soldier of mine killed one, thick as the thigh of a man in the middle and from there growing thinner toward the tail and head in proportion.[36] Their head is flat and large and shaped like a clog; they have two rows of teeth above and below. These snakes, if they catch an Indian sleeping (it has never been seen with Spaniards), they wind themselves around him, and squeezing him and spitting a milk upon him from their mouths, they kill him in a short time, for the natives say that they do no evil with their teeth. They do the same when some pass close by and they are unable to capture them, spraying this milk, but some escape with the treatment and cure. An Indian showed that in order to kill these snakes it is necessary to catch them sleeping just as they caught the aforesaid Indian. *Strange serpent*

In this hot land there are many scorpions, but they are of no danger though they sting and cause fevers. There are venomous wasps, and ants that cause fevers with their sting; these are reddish.

In temperate lands there are chameleons in some parts. This creature is simple and clumsy. In all hot lands there are many mosquitoes, and *Chameleons* the towns that abut sea coasts and banks of rivers and marshes and forests have even more of them.

Notable thing In hot lands there is a type of worm [either *Dermatobia hominis* or *Cordylobia hominivorax*] so small that they burrow into the flesh without one noticing; here they grow into a large and hairy worm. These greatly disturb; the remedy is to place a patch with unguent or caraña resin over them, with which they suffocate; and with the lack of respiration they then die and are pushed out of the flesh by squeezing. The land where these live is bad and of poor quality.

Cocuyos give much light In hot lands there live some beetles that give light as they fly by night. These are called *cocuyos*, and with one in the hand a letter may be read or written. These are often ground up in order to jest with someone who does not know of them, for spreading this upon the face, and clothed and in the dark of night, one resembles a demon from the gleams and glimmers it makes. Many japes have been done to newcomers with this.

DOMESTIC ANIMALS FROM SPAIN

The first Spaniards who traveled to the Indies began to take some domestic animals, and as they spread out, they have generally multiplied throughout all the land.

Horses Horses, which were the most noble animal and of most use, God wished to greatly multiply, so much so that there is no Spaniard who is unable to breed them and even the Indians [do so], generally in the settled lands. And there is a large quantity of wild horses between Tucumán and the River Plate, but not so many as on the Windward Islands, for there are many there. This animal is used more for service than they are here [in Spain], for the pack trains primarily use horses because those with mules serve little for loads unless it is on firm ground.[37] There are excellent parade horses and the stables are well established. The finest are Mexican but in general they are all good, for apart from being light and marvelously fast, they rein well and respond to punishment, without bad habits like those from here, and they have better and stronger skulls. They have but one fault, that they are not high-steppers, and running well comes from this; but as they are low-steppers they charge better and are lighter, and a horse is not old at fourteen years.

There is also much raising of *burros* and asses, though they are not useful, for they are not used in labor. They are only used for the breeding of pack mules. *Donkeys*

There is a great quantity of mules because of the great attention paid to their raising and husbandry. There are many of them in good colors and sure-footed. *Mules*

The largest part there is bovine livestock, and this may well be seen by the hides that each fleet brings back to Spain, and more must be used there, and much more is lost as they are unable to make use of it all. And so that it may be better known, there are valleys upon valleys that have a hundred thousand head of them, feral and domestic. In hot lands where they are best raised, it is no great thing for a cattleman to have thirty and fifty thousand head, more or less, branded and herded, as well as the land they occupy. In New Spain, there are generally more than in the other kingdoms. In temperate lands where they do not live so well, the number is less, but they are useful because of cheese making. The cheeses are the same size and color as those of Flanders and even better tasting. These cattle are most profitable when the young bulls are removed. This livestock is also raised in the valleys in cold lands. When they are slaughtered, where they make use of the hides to send back here, the meat is wasted. This livestock, in those lands where there are good saltpeter deposits, produce better. *Cattle*

I will speak about a bull that was in Cartago [modern Pereira, Colombia], as we have time, with but one horn in the center of his forehead, of ordinary size. *A strange bull*

Sheep live poorly in hot lands, and quite well in temperate ones, and better still if it is a barren land with saltpeter deposits. This animal is useful for meat and lamb, which is such good eating, and for the wool for textiles, as very good black, gray, and mixed cloth is made from it;

also heavy fabrics, light fabrics, sackcloth, blankets, and many other things; and the Indians make quantities of blankets which they use for carrying and other uses. The cloth is treated with oil from roots, as there are many, or with an oil they call *gordana*, from the castration of bullocks.

Strange monster And as we are addressing these animals, I will tell of two monstrous ones: one was a goat with one foreleg and two hind legs, which was raised very large in the New Kingdom of Granada, in [the town of] Our Lady of Chiquinquirá.

The other monster, in the same kingdom, on a farm, a lamb was born with the hind parts of a lamb, with its wool and other parts, and the front half with the features and face of a person and with smooth skin. This died later, and the best that those of us who knew about it could judge, is that an Indian shepherd was doing the unspeakable.

Goats There are goats that live in hot and temperate lands; they are useful for two things, for eating the kids and for the cordovan hides they make, which are many in those places. The meat is not eaten but given to the dogs or some miserable Indians.

Porcine livestock There are a great many pigs and these live in all climates, and best in the cold, for that is where the best meat is produced, though it is not so fat, and where a quantity of fine hams are made; and in the other climates this cannot be done. However, the skilled fatten them in hot lands and slaughter them in the cold, which is the best advantage, for it cures better; and the lard, which is much, is used in that land for everything and at all times, as we use [olive] oil here (for what we eat), as little goes there and it is expensive. This animal often escapes and becomes feral in the hills and swamps.

Dogs In all climates there are quantities of helper dogs: greyhounds, gundogs, bloodhounds, and little yapping mongrels. None of these animals has been seen rabid in those parts because of the constant abundance of water.

DOMESTIC AND WILD ANIMALS OF THE INDIES

I will tell of the animals of the land, domestic and wild, such as the ram of Peru [llama], which is an animal of great advantage for pack trains and transportation of goods and merchandise from one place to another. Great wealth has come to us from these animals and they are of little expense. They have features similar to a camel, except that they do not have that hump, nor are they as large, about half, and for the most part they are white and some are dark; their wool, which is long and abundant [now referring to alpacas], is useful, for with it the Indians produce a garment which has a luster like a burnoose from Barbary, but heavier; and they make many things from it. *Sheep of Peru*

Guanacos and vicuñas are very similar to the animal mentioned. They are wild and untamed. Many are hunted and killed in collective traps, called *chacos*, which the Indians often make in certain valleys, and then all those hunted die.

Stones are found inside these vicuñas that are called bezoar or vicuña stones. They are small, black, or toast-colored, somewhat golden; they are not as good as bezoar stones from deer. These animals are found only in Peru. *Vicuña stones*

In general, in all of the Indies there are *venados*, which here we call deer, and in all climates, in barren lands, plains, in the forest and savannah, there is only a difference between those of hot lands from those of cold and temperate, for those of hot land are reddish and small and their horns are thorny like the goat horn, and those of temperate and cold lands are dark and large with large antlers.

In the deer that die in temperate lands and that have enjoyed the hot lands at times, the finest bezoar stones are found, as Monardes[38] says; the good ones are olive-colored, and those of this color that are found are few, but large. And it is said that they form because the deer are bitten by snakes from hot lands and they eat an herb with which they resist that venom and the stone hardens. As to their being bitten, this I recognize; but as to their eating the herb I am of a different opinion for many reasons. The first, because in all the time that the Indians have *Bezoar stones* inhabited their native lands, the herb would have been discovered in some way, and also because they would have been found in the deer from hot lands that do not reach the cold, which, if they are bitten, die without remedy. And if some from hot lands have had them, they are those that inhabit those places and enjoy the cold climate when they wish and lack such bites.

And so stating my opinion, I say that the dark-colored, as well as the reddish deer that are bitten in hot lands, some having a tendency to flee and others guided by their natural instinct, enter the coldest water they can find (which is extreme) and do not come out of it until the heat of the venom is placated and not allowed to pass to the brain or heart, rather staying in the stomach where it is collected. And that stone condenses and hardens with the cold, composing itself upon the herb in the belly or another thing it manages to take hold of. In other words, that is why the herb they eat as a remedy for the venom is a basis for this. And for the purpose of argument and proof, one needs only to see that a deer, chased by dogs, with that heat, always searches for and stops at water, where its nature and quality carry it, thus having no other choice.

False bezoar stones   These stones are very fine and the Indians often make similar ones from the earth, as they look alike, and there are many deceptions with them.

Deer with three racks of antlers   And as it serves our purpose, I will tell of one deer, killed in the New Kingdom of Granada, with three racks of antlers.

A white one   Another was killed that was all as white as paper; these were two things never seen before.

There are lions that live in all climates. These are dark-colored, thick haired and small; there are no common lions; they are not savage if not attacked; they leap into trees upon sensing dogs. They often cause damage to livestock.

There are tigers[39] that live in hot lands. This animal is quite harmful; they are savage and kill Indians, whose flesh they enjoy, and by night, in the mountains, they have taken an Indian while he was sleeping between two Spaniards and carried him away. Wherever they are, the remedy the natives have for this is to make great fires and carry firebrands; and if they walk at night, they carry the firebrand in their hands, as they are naturally afraid of this.

It is a strong animal and long in the body and colored with brown, white, and black spots; they cause much harm to cows and calves, for if they feed upon them once, they will eat no other thing.

Quality of tigers

There are very large bears living in hot and cold lands; they are black and are not harmful.

Quality of bears

There are other ant-eating bears, long and dark; these live in hot lands and cause no harm. They feed by finding an anthill and stick out their entire tongue, covering it with ants, swallowing them as they are gathered, and in this way they feed.

There are some wolves, but in few places; they often cause harm to livestock. They live in temperate lands.

There is a great quantity of foxes in temperate, cold, and hot lands, but they do not cause the harm they cause here [in Spain].

In hot lands there is a type of pig they call *baquiras* [white-lipped peccaries], with their umbilicus on their spine. These live in the lowland jungles. It is very good meat; they are quite savage. The dogs that hunt and pursue them are all wounded and many die from their gorings, and their breath or stench clouds the eyes of all the dogs. It is a pleasure to kill these baquiras, for they travel in herds; upon sensing the hunter, they then close upon him, and he climbs atop a fallen branch or tree trunk or large rock, which, if half a yard above them, is sufficient protection; they surround it and he, with a lance or goad, which there they call a needle or *dable*, does nothing but spear them and thus kills many. They also kill them with arrows, and if one or two are caught separately, the dogs kill them. They are of such a quality that even though they may surround the hunter, being of the stated size renders them incapable of offending him. They are the size of a year-old suckling here and do not grow larger. They bristle like a porcupine and the females are stout like a boar and of the same color.

Constellation of pigs

In hot lands there are many tapirs whose hides are wasted, as there are none who know how to tan them. The Indians make bucklers from them; their meat is quite sweet, like that of buffalo, and they are like-

Tapirs

wise inclined to water. They are the size of half a mule and without a tail; they are dark and black; their ears are distinct and the snout is like that of a pig; their hooves are cloven like those of a cow, and the nail from the left leg is said to be good for the heart.[40]

Griffins I have not noticed that there are any, though long ago in the lands of Venezuela I was assured that one was followed by a man on horseback who was hunting, who was able to see what it was; and being close by, it charged him, and when he saw this he fled with his horse with the griffin in pursuit, half running and half flying, until coming to a river where the man jumped in, swimming with his horse, and the griffin stopped on the bank. And in relating this case he described the typical features of a griffin.

Cows of New Mexico In New Mexico they say there is a type of very small cow, with tiny horns, native to the land.

Notable things In hot lands there live some mountain cats, the snout long like a pig, the size of a large and tame cat, called *zazapi* in certain provinces[41]; and in the middle of its stomach it has a sack where its young are raised; usually from four to six are born, and each one has a little tube in its mouth through which they feed. They have this sack near the umbilicus and it is closed and with the young inside; they do not come out to be seen while they are nursing. This is a notable thing and to be considered.

Smartly dressed creature In hot and temperate lands there is a creature they call armadillo, which looks elegantly dressed; its entire body is covered with shells, like the armor on a French horse; they are good to eat. *Guadatinajas* live in hot lands and have good meat.[42] This animal enjoys the water and the land. There are also many nutrias in all climates.

Martens Squirrels and martens live in the bracken in hot and temperate lands. There is a lot of rabbit and in some parts, hares.

Quality of monkeys In all the hot, lowland forests there is a great quantity of monkeys, large, bearded, and otherwise, which are small, with different bodies and colors, which they call *micos*. This animal is hard to kill, for though they are shot through with a harquebus they do not fall. I have seen them pull out all their entrails through the wound in their belly and throw them down in pieces and not die in that hour, until they have completely gone cold. At other times they often pick leaves from trees and chew them and place them into the wound; they have this instinct, and though they die, they remain clutching the tree with their tails. In order to descend from the trees and drink from a river, they often make a bridge, linking themselves to one another so that the females and their young may lower themselves, for from birth they clutch their backs until they are older. They go up and down this bridge until all have drunk, adding and subtracting themselves from the bridge.

There is a creature in hot lands they call a *Perico ligero*,[43] the clumsiest thing there is in the world, as large as a large cat. This moves in the trees and to walk the length of a branch takes it an hour: it has a face almost like a person; it gives screams and babbles by night like a baby. This animal has a bad heart and therefore its nails are good for that illness, because they make use of them when they suffer from it, and it is always found wounded and marked on the side of the heart from striking there with its nail. There is much experience with this; they are very resistant to dying.

Notable animal

RIVERS, SPRINGS, AND LAKES

The most famous rivers of those parts of the Indies are four: they are thus because of the disposition of the land, which provides a place so that they have a long journey and so in such a long stretch, a myriad of them gather, almost as large, and thus they come to be so powerful and famous. There are many in the Indies, but none compare to these. I will state which they are: the great river Magdalena, the river of the Amazons, the river Marañón, and the river of La Plata. The Magdalena is born in the Almaguer range and páramo [of New Granada], on the slopes of the Neiva valley. It runs three hundred leagues, and flows into the Northern Sea between Cartagena and Santa Marta; its mouth is not a league long, as it gathers together and enters deep water.

Famous rivers

The Amazon is born in the central range of the New Kingdom [of

Granada], behind Santa Fe [de Bogotá]; it runs three hundred leagues, making great curves. It flows into the Northern Sea between Cumaná and the coast of Brazil; its mouth measures thirty leagues.

The Marañón is born behind Cuzco; it runs seven hundred leagues and more; it empties into the Northern Sea close to the settlements of Brazil; its mouth measures fifteen leagues. This is the most powerful and famous river.[44]

The Plata [or Plate] is born in a sierra behind Tucumán; it runs more than two hundred leagues. It empties into the Northern Sea between the Magellan Strait and Brazil; its mouth measures more than twenty leagues.

Famous lakes There are many very famous lakes in those parts, and I will say which are among the most important: the Lake of Mexico, that of Granada, that of Maracaibo. That of Mexico is the most distinguished because so many people inhabit it and it is so large; we may say that the city of Mexico and its outskirts are founded upon it; primarily they go to this city by water, and canoes may enter channels that pass along all the streets. Most trade is done this way, and they unload in the middle of the square. And along all the streets that have these channels there are bridges so the people may cross.

Notable occurrence And because this city is founded upon water, it so happened that the monastery of our lord St. Dominic, which is in the center of this city, and whose entire stonework structure is sumptuous and large, sunk straight down on all sides, with not a crack, in such a manner that a stone course upon the outside of the church that had been out of reach to a man upon horseback sank until it set upon the surface of the ground. This lake, though fed by good fresh waters, is partly brackish; many small fish live there. Its circumference measures twenty-five leagues. There is no known drainage, because beneath a very high sierra it drains without being seen and flows for ten or fifteen leagues and enters the Northern Sea. All the laborers enter this city of Mexico by canoes and stone causeways, as the depth of the lake is marked with buoys on one side, and they make these causeways with their canals along the sandbanks. Upon this lake dwell a great number of Indians; they make their stockades and fill them with earth, until a great mound rises from the dampness of the water, and they form and build their houses atop. They also make their crops from maize and other seeds by bringing cut grasses from solid ground in their canoes, throwing them in the water at a height of a stature and a half, and forming a ridge that rises half a yard above the water, three or four yards in width. And the Indians go between the ridges, which they make many of in a field, in canoes, weeding and nurturing, something never before seen in the world.[45]

There are two other lakes, which are those of Granada and Maracaibo. That of Granada [Lake Nicaragua] flows into the Northern Sea between Honduras and Veragua. It measures more than sixty leagues in length. Many good fish live there. Many ships and boats load and unload their trade there.

That of Maracaibo runs more than forty leagues and empties into the Northern Sea between Riohacha and Venezuela. It has much fish. Boats and ships load and unload their trade here. Indians live on the water in this lake, building their houses upon four large, wooden pillars, leaving space below for the passing of waves of water; they fish and pull up drinking water from their houses and enter and leave firm land and their crops with their canoes. And to go up into their houses they have a ladder and they tie the canoes to the pillars.

There are many other lakes in New Spain and in Peru and in the New Kingdom, but none that compare to these.[46]

There are many notable springs, but I will speak of the best known. *Admirable springs* There are tar pits they call *copei*, with which they tar the ships and riggings. One of these is at the tip of Santa Elena, on the coast of Peru, Southern Sea, and it flows copiously here for all that is needed for the ships and boats of Panama, for which they carry many jugs.[47]

Also in the Neiva valley, in the New Kingdom of Granada, there is a low ridge that lengthens the valley; here there are mineral seeps wherever one looks, but they are of no use other than for the Indians to spread upon their faces, mixed with turpentine.

There are springs and pools in many places, one hot and another cold, and they issue so closely together that the hot is tempered by the cold, for it is great. They bathe in these, where two springs flow together, as in Cajamarca, where the Inca took his baths and was captured.

They are also in New Spain and in Nicaragua and in the New Kingdom of Granada. They often take these baths for pains and paralysis, and once taken, they sweat in beds that are in those baths for that purpose.

There are also springs of fresh and salt water close together, and from the brine they make salt, especially from those in the Kingdom [of New Granada].

There is a freshwater river close to Cartago, in the main course of which there springs a source of salt water, and the natives retrieve it with a pump and make salt from it by cooking it.[48]

Strange sort of spring   In one *repartimiento* [encomienda district] in Muzo there is a spring whose water, taken from its source and placed in the sun, turns into a sort of ink, with which one may write quite well. The natives dye their cloth with it.

Notable thing   There is a spring in Granada, Nicaragua, on a cattle farm near Jaramillo, that, if any livestock should go to drink from it and put anything in it that the water may move, it sucks it in and drowns it and leaves nothing but bare bones.

There are other springs and pools where no wood may grow, for later it is drowned.

Strange spring   There is one spring in New Spain, in the Mixteca Alta, in which if any wood is there for a time, it comes to be converted or changed into stone. As I understand it, the water sets as it is absorbed by the wood.

There are other springs that come out so hot and boiling that one may cook a leg of goat in it. One cannot bear to place his hand in it. And so as not to tire, I will not tell more things. But I will finish with a spring in Huancavelica [Peru], close to the quicksilver mines, from which the water is taken from its source and poured into a hollow made in the ground; in a short while it hardens as if it were a transparent and solid stone.

Also, a great river discharges into the Southern Sea, on the Isle of Puná, which passes by Guayaquil and takes its name [today called the Guayas River], whose water takes on the virtue of the great quantity of sarsaparilla roots it passes through, such that people with buboes and pains [i.e., syphilis], by merely drinking it, are free from their sicknesses in a few days, and therefore many go to drink it from far away and stay there a month, more or less, in Guayaquil, drinking the water just as the river carries it, with a regimen of eating without excess.

FISH IN RIVERS AND SOME FROM THE SEA

None of the most common fish live in the rivers in cold lands, and few live in temperate lands, and these are without scales, but flavorsome. In hot lands there are many good ones, served fresh, salted and sun-dried and roasted on a barbecue. They are large catfish, *sardinetas* [*Pellona harroweri*], *boquechicos* [*Prochilodus reticulatus*], golden shad, monkfish, bonefish, *doncellas* [*Hemanthias peruanus*], *viejas* [*Bodianus eclancheri*], *roncadores* [*Genyonemus lineatus*], sardines, and rays: this last is a bad fish that causes great harm to whomever it wounds, an intense pain. These have a menstrual period like a woman, and because of this are they so poisonous. There are crabs and large prawns; this is good food. There are numerous tortoises in the large rivers; they grow on the sandy beaches laying two hundred eggs at a time under the sand, and there they are left. They are good to eat, as they do not have a hard shell like hen eggs; there they incubate and the young tortoises hatch.

Quality of fish

There are iguanas of both land and water, which is why they have been considered fish. This is quite healthy and tasty food. Their appearance is that of a lizard, but larger; they have a crest of spines that rises up and grows from head to tail. It is a very ugly thing.

Iguanas are edible

In these kingdoms there are manatees, which have the appearance of a very fat pig and the hide of a catfish and their meat is exactly like salt pork. It has a property of revealing buboes on those who have them hidden, as eating of it stirs them up and enlivens the pain. It is a fish that comes out of the water to graze on the land.[49] Much lamp oil is made of it.

Manatees

In quaking bogs on the plains of El Dorado [the Llanos of eastern Colombia and Venezuela], while searching for water and digging wells,

Fish under the ground

soldiers discovered pools of water where the fish agitated the water so much that it appeared to be boiling, and they were caught in large quantities. This occurred on an expedition led by don Gonzalo Jiménez de Quesada.[50] What he presumed from this was that under the ground ran a large river full of fish, and so many gathered there because of the [sudden] clarity. On these plains all the rivers have a great number of fish, and it would be well noted that when a fishery is to be made of them for this purpose, as they come downstream from the kingdom, if three or four hundred arrobas are not taken, the fishery is not worth the effort.

Unknown fish On these plains, in a river said to be from Iscancé [near Almaguer, Colombia], which is very large and flows into the Marañón, there is a fish that follows the canoes bellowing. The natives say they are waterdogs.[51]

The remora [suckerfish] In a river that flows into this one, called the Verde, there is another fish that sticks itself to the canoe, which no strength of arms or river current may remove. This occurred to a canoe of my soldiers, having dispatched it for a certain duty, and nothing they could do was of use until the Indians began to clean the canoe with sticks from under the water, as they must know something of this. When I found out I judged it to be the remora fish, which had to be here somewhere, as the ancients tell of it.

Trembling fish On these plains [i.e., the Llanos] there is a fish they call the trembler, which, as it takes hold of the fishhook, causes the one who fishes it to tremble like a leaf, and when it is taken upon the land, it does the same when touched with a pole, until it dies; a notable quality.[52] There are numerous of these trembling fish in all the rivers of the Llanos.

Now, since I have spoken of some notable fish of the rivers, I will tell of those from the sea, the northern [Atlantic] and southern [Pacific] coasts. There are many that are ordinarily eaten, but not so many as on the coast of Spain. On these seacoasts, in estuaries, marshes, and large rivers, there are many caimans, which are called crocodiles on the River Nile. They are also found in the rivers many leagues inland, as it is hot land, and in marshes and lakes. If it is man-eating, it is a bad fish, as it eats many people and domestic animals. They love dogs more than any other meat. They do not hunt in the depths but rather along the shore, where their feet may reach the bottom; nor do they eat under the water, but after they have drowned their prey, they eat it on the shore.

In some places the Indians are so skilled as to seek them out beneath the water, dragging the depths with a looped rope or other invention; they then pull it onto the land with a cord or line where they kill it. This is a lizard that they hang in the churches,[53] which naturally has a friend, a small bird, which, when the caiman is in the sun with its mouth opened for the purpose, uses its beak to clean and take the fish and meat from between its teeth that remain after it eats. With this, it is then ready to feed again. They give birth in the same fashion as the tortoises, on the beaches of the sea as well as of rivers. Their flesh smells of musk. Dewlaps of musk are taken from beneath their arms and used, but it smells so much that it causes headaches. The Indians eat it.

Quality of caimans

On the coast of Peru, dogfish and tuna are caught, not as good as here, but acceptable.

On this [Pacific] coast there are a great number of sea lions,[54] and they are nowhere else. I think it is because of the quality of water, which is so cold that if one should go in to swim or manage to fall in, he would be cut through by the cold and would drown. The quality of this animal or fish is very cold; and regarding this, its hide, made into belts, is good for kidney sickness. It is quite clumsy; its feet and arms are so small that it drags itself upon the ground. It has very long whiskers, which look like quills from a porcupine. It comes onto the land by day and night and a great number gather on the islets near the shore of the coast and they bellow like calves, such that they seem like a herd of cows. The Indians kill them with clubs, striking them on their snouts as they turn to bite, and with any blow there they then fall. A great quantity of oil is made from this, which is used on the binnacles of ships; it is quite foul smelling.

Sea lions

There are a great number of sardines on this coast, with which all the Indians sustain themselves. There are other fish, but few. There are numbers of small whales; these do not go above [the latitude of] Túmbes [Peru], where the South Wind reigns, neither do the caimans, because of the cold of the water. There are tuna and dolphin. There is also great pearl fishing along the [Atlantic] coasts of Riohacha, Venezuela, and Margarita, where large beds of oysters breed. There was also much of this in Cumaná and Panama, though now there is not such abundance.

DOMESTIC AND WILD BIRDS

Generally, in all the Indies there are a great number of [domestic] hens like those here, and they are very common. There are turkeys, which are called cocks of Nicaragua there, and dewlap cocks, which is a good food. These hens are very cheap. They are found domesticated and feral, such as the many between Veracruz and Mexico City and in other parts of New Spain. There are partridge, though different, and quail, wood pigeons, and turtledoves like those here.

Ostrich There are ostrich [actually *Rhea Americana*, a cousin] between Tucumán and the River Plate; they do not carry such fine plumage as those of Barbary. This bird is caught by putting them into pens from horseback, for they cannot be caught any other way, as they run much faster than a horse, and half run, half fly, and are helped by two nails they have, one on each wingtip; and as they are so long in the shanks, there is no creature like them. Chased into these pens, they gather into a bunch, putting their heads in the ground, appearing not to see or as a signal that they surrender, allowing themselves to be tied.

Pelicans There are pelicans on the coast of the Northern Sea. These are very large birds whose jowls can hold an entire water jug. The skin from these jowls is good and appropriate for pain from cold.

Macaws There are *guacamaya* parrots of different colors. This bird is very ugly, but very useful to the Indian because of the plumage they take from it, plucking them, and for this reason they have them tamed. And there are no dogs that guard a house better than them, for they always have these parrots above the houses, and in sensing people afar, they raise their voices such that those who live in the village are forcibly warned of their approach. And whoever is approaching, upon hearing this, knows that he has already been discovered.

There are small she-parrots [*catalinicas*] and parakeets; all these birds live in hot lands.

There are turkey buzzards or vultures, which are like crows, but larger; and though it is a vile and filthy bird, it is useful, for it cleans the fields and settlements of all the filth of dead flesh.

There is a bird called the *guaraguao*, similar to a sparrow hawk, but larger. These prey on chickens in place of kites.

There are dark turkeys and other small ones called *guacharacas*, for they cry out much. These are called pheasants in some parts, but their meat is not similar, as it is tough and bad.

There are guan (*paujies*), which is a very large black bird and good food; it is quite elegant, having a ridge of black feathers upon its head. Taken young, these are domestic and wander about the house. There is another caste of these that has a blue stone of its own flesh upon its forehead, looking like a sapphire.[55] All these birds live in hot lands and some in the mountains in temperate lands.

In Peru there is a small bird, called the *martinete*, from which they take its valued feathers. In these parts they are numerous.

There are dark and white herons, from which they take so many fine feathers.

There are falcons, peregrine falcons, and sparrow hawks, which they use for hunting in Peru to flush out the heron, the dove, the partridge, the owl, and other birds.

There are dark eagles, but there are none golden. These are of no use. There are vultures almost as large as ostrich. In the lakes and swamps there is a great variety of birds. I will tell of an especially elegant one, which is called the flamingo; it is very long in the shanks, more than the crane, very white and reddish; it has a beak like a duck.

There is also a great number of small and large ducks. I will tell of the manner they use in some places of hunting them, which is a laughable thing, particularly in the lakes and places they inhabit.

They throw in a number of calabashes and as the wind takes them from one part of the water to another, the ducks are made to reassure themselves and lose their fear. And after eight days have passed, more or less, the hunter enters the water naked, with a calabash upon his head, with two eye holes, and with a sack in his hand, adjusting himself with the water at his head and moving little by little among the ducks, which are

Extraordinary method of duck hunting

completely unaware of the secret that moves within the calabash. And as they are swimming and their feet are long, the hunter goes grabbing them by their feet, and pulling them under the water and putting them into the sack. And the other ducks are not alarmed at all, for they are used to ducking. And once the sack is full, the hunter leaves, and if he wishes he returns for more. It is a very pleasurable hunt to watch, without getting one's feet wet, for those on foot and hungry.

We will mention two notable birds on the plains of the Iscancé River, which I have already named.

There is a bird the size of a hen and flavorful to eat, with all the meat full of spines, as if it were a bony fish.

I have seen another bird in the rugged lowlands of the great Magdalena River, brightly colored, though of medium size, which has a tongue like a feather, an admirable thing, as if we were to take the feather of a hen and trim it somewhat on the sides. The central nerve is white, like the feather, but it is soft.

SEEDS FROM SPAIN AND THE INDIES AND OTHER USEFUL THINGS

In temperate lands white, golden, and tufted wheat is gathered, and this in some quantity. With the bread wheat, a very white bread is made; none better is eaten in these parts [i.e., Spain]. There are two harvests per year, and where it is irrigated they may sow every month, sowing one month after another, waiting for the necessary weather. This is understood in temperate lands and those within the tropics, which confine the sun. In new, well-nurtured lands a *fanega* [of seed] yields forty or fifty [at harvest]; and in worked lands, from twenty to twenty-five; and if seed were brought from Spain for sowing, it would yield a hundred or more, as was seen in what occurred in the beginning [i.e., just after conquest], for it appears that the seed from here has great strength. Barley yields much and of high quality in temperate lands, as well as in those that are not so temperate.

Grape vines yield well and much wine is produced, such as in Ica and Arequipa. This plant requires lands hotter than temperate, for it yields poorly in temperate lands. Melons grow many and good, and in a valley near Ica they are pruned in order to give fruit, and [the vines] often last six and seven years without replanting.

There are chickpeas and lentils, beans of all types and a number of root vegetables, so much so that the wheat fields are swollen with them. In many parts the weeding is done by them. Artichokes, carrots, and Scotch thistles grow. These are pruned in Lima so that they again bear fruit. There are cabbages, lettuce, radishes, onions, garlic, and mustard. Flax grows well. All of these grow in temperate lands and some grow in hot lands.

The land also yields sugarcane, for which there are a great number of very productive and wealthy sugar mills, not only because of the sugar, but also confections, preserves, and syrup that are used so much.

The seed of the Indies is a grain they call *maíz*. This is common sustenance for all, as both the Indian and the Spaniard eat of it, wherever bread or hardtack cannot be found. They eat it toasted and cooked in the grain or made into cakes, or *arepas*, using its flour, or boiled into rolls, wrapped in the leaf of the maize itself. They make a wine of this maize which most drink, called chicha or azua. They feed the horses with this grain instead of barley, and fatten the porcine livestock; and it is of many other uses to the republic.

They also make cassava bread in some parts, which is a bread they make of a thick root they plant and use called *yuca brava*. If this is eaten raw, a person will die from it; but shredded and squeezed and dried, and its flour made into a cake and cooked over a fire, it is good. And if an animal should drink the juice squeezed from it, it will die from it; but cooked, it will fatten. And so it is added to hot pepper sauces and *locro*, which is a stew they make there, as it has a flavorful broth. There is another, sweet yuca, which is eaten raw, baked, and cooked, and is good. These two roots are found in hot lands.

There are also a great number of yams and truffles in all the mountain ranges of Peru and the New Kingdom, which they call *papas* [referring to several potato varieties]. It is of great sustenance for the Indian, growing in temperate and cold lands. With this in their food, they use much *ají*, which here they call [chili] peppers, which is gathered in high quantity in all climates and places.

In hot lands they gather much cotton, which the Indians use to make their clothes and for many things. And our people use it much, for they make large quantities of linens and many fabrics for ordinary cloth, weaving it, and cottons for doublets for country folk and poor women. From this linen they make hand towels, sheets, trousers, stockings, and shirts for field workers and expeditions. They also use thick and thin *pita* [sisal] thread, which is so useful for labors and curiosities, loose as well as twisted. This is taken from leaves in bushes, like those of the maguey, except that they are longer, thinner and narrower. This pita is not cultivated but grows in rugged hot country.

Indigo is also used, made from two types of herbs, similar to the clover, drying, soaking, and pulverizing, and mixing it in water, then straining it from that water and adding pepper teasels or leaves. They let the substance taken from the indigo leaf settle, and taking the water they make their little loaves, as they do in Nicaragua. Some Indians utilize this indigo, as it is beneficial in sisal production.

Cochineal is also used and is quite rich. This is an insect that is caught on the leaf of the prickly pear, which is similar to the cactus. This is caught in New Spain.

Great quantities of honey are also used, such as in Campeche, in Nicaragua, and a quantity of wax.[56] The honey of Campeche is white and quite good, and that of Nicaragua is somewhat reddish and toasted. Some of the bees that produce this live in the ground among shrubs and under the ground; others live in hollow trees. Some are yellow and hairy and somewhat large, as large as those we have in these parts of Spain. There is another type that is dark and smaller. This honey is the worst. In these two places mentioned, there is a great business in it and it is the produce of the land. It is gathered in hot lands. There is some in the New Kingdom of Granada as well, in hot lands, but little, as it serves only for medicines. And there it is of black wax, whereas in these two places it is yellow.

In all places in the Indies, salt is made, cooking the brine from springs and pools. It is also made from salt pans on the seacoast, and there are also salt mines in some parts, and particularly on the plains of Peru, where from beneath the sands, along the sea shore, they dig up mountains of it, white as snow, and load ships going to the Main [i.e., Panama]. On these plains they collect an herb from whose ashes soap is made, with fat from the castration of bullocks; and the ash of the guacimo tree is used.

And finishing the purpose of this chapter, I state that all the seeds of Spain will grow in those parts, according to the climates of the land.

METALS AND STONES OF ESTEEM

Gold is found in almost all the Indies, in hot lands or savanna or mountain, but most commonly it is found in jungles, and if some is found in temperate lands, it is little; and if in cold lands, it was put there accidentally, having no seam or vein, as if by the Great Flood. Therefore, it has been seen in cold lands in the high plateaus of Pamplona and other parts, spilling upon the surface of the earth, and some upon the hardpan, as the miners call it, and later it ends. It is also found in hot lands in rivers and ravines, brought down with the great floods from their source. This is grain gold, found in the confluences that the water makes, and they wash it at one confluence today and tomorrow in another. It is also found on the plains of the savanna or jungle near powerful rivers where the Flood or great spates spilled it. Here it is sought with test pits and making waist-deep pools, according to the gravel and rocks.

It is also found on the barren fields on hills in hot lands, where the Flood mixed it up and piled it with the land. There are also seams [*criaderos*], which are reddish expanses of earth, which if they are followed along their branches, a good wage is had. This gold is fine, curled, and what they call "flyaway" [*volador*]. Here they use *tambires* in order to wash the gold better, which are reservoirs of water, where there is any, which they empty when they want.

It is also found in mines in solid veins, melted and introduced into the very bedrock, with its guardian minerals, which must be crushed in order to wash and take the gold. In these veins great wealth is often found. Whoever should pursue gold mining will never be lost, as it provides wages and is of little expense.

Silver is of great cost because of the large devices needed to refine it, with a million expenses of quicksilver and other things. The earnings are not so regular as with gold, and there have been very powerful men who have lost from mining it, as when a hundredweight [of ore] yields only twelve ounces or less [of silver], there is barely enough for the cost of the quicksilver. Merchants and other traders grow wealthy from this silver metal, which is found in cold lands. And if there is any in hot or temperate lands, it is little and cannot be followed far, for though it may be rich, it ends quickly, as no more than a few promising signs or pieces are found on the surface of the land. And in cold parts, such as Potosí and others, the veins run very deep and provide wealth to those who mine them.

Emeralds have been found in hot lands, such as those of Portoviejo [Ecuador] and Somondoco and Muzo, which are those that are used today in all of the Indies and even, I believe, the entire world. These other two places [first] mentioned are not worked, as the emeralds there are so few, but those they have found have been of the intensely colored sort [*subida laya*]. And the Itoco Hill in Muzo is renowned, where they dig and gather up to the present day, and all the emerald mines are found here. They strip away from these mines [surface] stones and earth using reservoirs [*tambires*]. They [i.e., emeralds] are sometimes found in the veins gathered and joined. And it may happen that one crew may work all year and not find a glimmer; and other times [the mine] paints right away, yielding great wealth.

Mines of lead are found in hot lands. There are many of these and a great amount is taken.

There are iron mines in some parts of temperate and cold lands; it is of no benefit.

There is much copper in hot lands and in parts of temperate lands, but of little use.

There is much quartz crystal in parts of hot lands, and there are mines for it. The beryls Pliny speaks of are found in forests and very cold lands, such as those above Muzo, and though he attributes many qualities to them, I notice none.

There is turquoise and it is found in hot lands.

Property of amethyst There are amethysts in temperate lands. This is a very advantageous stone, apart from being pleasing to the eye, and no soldier in those parts would go about without one, as they are of so little cost. This is used for any snakebite, such that by opening the bite of the patient and bandaging the stone upon it, it is a marvelous and sure thing, helping any other remedial potion, so that the venom does not work and has no effect.

Garnets have been found, but few, and those in temperate lands.

Much quicksilver has been found in cold lands, such as in the mines of Huancavelica [Peru]. This has produced great wealth. The Indian calls this scum of silver.

30
How emeralds form
and are mined,
ca. 1586.
Courtesy Pierpont
Morgan Library

There are many sulfur mines, an extraordinary thing. There are also those of alum. There are some mines of lodestone, and particularly in the Neiva valley, in the New Kingdom [of Granada]. They are found there loose on some mountains, and it is presumed that on the high mountain chain from which these mountains descend there are well-established mines.

This lodestone is close to the equinoctial. They are also in other parts of Peru and New Spain.

Lightning commonly strikes all these mineral-bearing places, especially in hot lands, but it even occurs in some parts of temperate lands.

In the land of Mexico there is a mined stone, transparent and tawny [i.e., obsidian], from which the Indians make knives with great ease for anyone to shave their hair and beard, as if they were knives from Tolosa [Spain]. They cannot be used more than once for they lose their edge. The Indians sell them cheaply, and though it is such an ordinary stone, it may be considered a notable and marvelous thing.

HYDROGRAPHY
OF THE COASTS AND
Seas Of The Indies

THE TWO COASTS AND SEAS of the Indies make a strait of land between Nombre de Dios and Panama, in all 18 leagues crossing from one sea to the other. And to better order these coasts it has seemed to me best to start with this port of Nombre de Dios, following first the coast of New Spain to Florida, and then that coast to the Magellan Strait, and from there following all the coast of the Southern Sea. And though it is true they could be encircled at one time, I do not do this, in order that anyone from these parts who should consider them may better understand them, and so I will follow this style.

Stretch of land from Nombre de Dios to Panama, 18 leagues

Nombre de Dios is at 10 degrees north latitude. The port was not good and the village unhealthy, this and other respects being the reasons for moving to Portobelo, in which, for its defense, there is a beautiful fort. In this port the fleets and navies unload all that is destined for Peru, having made port first at Cartagena.

From this port to the mouth of Lake Nicaragua, which is at the same northern latitude, the coast runs east and west 90 leagues.

Portobelo, 10 degrees

From this estuary to the cape of Gracias a Dios, which is at 15 degrees north latitude, it runs south by west. There are 70 leagues.

Cape Gracias a Dios, 15 degrees

Cape of Camarones, 54 leagues	From this cape to that of Camarones, which is at 16 degrees north latitude, it runs southwest by south, with a distance of 54 leagues.
Port Higuera, 16 degrees	From this cape to the port of Higuera, which is at 16 degrees north latitude—which is the coast of Honduras and the same latitude—[the coast] runs east–west and there are 110 leagues.
Isles of Women, 20 degrees and a half	From this port to the Islas de Mujeres, which are at 20 degrees and a half north latitude, it runs northeast–southwest and there are 110 leagues.
Yucatán, 20 degrees and a half	From these isles, along the coast of Yucatán, it runs east–west, but for one part at its cape, which runs east by south, and there are 90 leagues along this whole coast, at the same north latitude.
Grijalva Bay, 18 degrees	From the cape of this coast to the Bay of Grijalva, which is at 18 degrees north latitude, it runs north by east, and there are 50 leagues.
Veracruz, 20 degrees	From this bay to Veracruz, which is at 20 degrees north latitude, the coast runs east–west, and there are 90 leagues. This is the principal port of New Spain and the first settled in the Indies, and where the fleets and navies coming from Spain to that kingdom arrive to unload, even though they anchor in San Juan de Ulúa, five leagues distant, which is an islet well protected from the North Wind, which is such that many ships have been lost with it, running aground. Since in this place there is no safer port, they run this risk. There is a fort there to guard the fleets. This town is very unhealthy, where many newcomers die, as much and more than in Nombre de Dios, though it is true that the majority of the people who die are common and poor, coming ashore with so little; but those with means resist the ill quality [of the port].
Fishermen's River, 29 degrees	From the port of Veracruz to the Pescadores River, which is at 29 degrees north latitude, the coast runs north by west, the sea making several inlets. The distance is 180 leagues.
Bay of San José, 29 degrees	From this river of Fishermen to the Bay of San José, which is at 29 degrees north latitude, the coast runs east by south, with a distance of 240 leagues.

From this bay to Cabeza de los Mártires, which is at 25 degrees north latitude, the coast runs southeast by south, with a distance of 90 leagues.

Martyrhead, 25 degrees

From Cabeza de los Mártires to the mouth of the Bahama Channel, which is at 28 degrees and a half north latitude, the coast runs north–south. From here to the Cape of Labrador, the coast is unknown, as it remains unconquered. And returning to Nombre de Dios in order to follow the coast to the Magellan Strait, with the most precise course possible, I state that from this port to that of Cartagena, the coast runs northwest by north until the inlet of Urabá, and from there to Cartagena, what remains runs southwest by south, with a distance of eight leagues along the whole coast.

Bahama Channel, 28 degrees and a half

In this port of Cartagena, which is at 10 degrees and a half north latitude, the fleets and navies loading for the Main and Peru drop anchor first, from which, after having refreshed themselves and unloaded there what they needed for the New Kingdom of Granada, pass those who have not unloaded at the port of Nombre de Dios or Portobelo. After unloading and taking on passengers, silver, and gold they return to Cartagena, where they gather with those who remained there and together they leave for Havana, then making the journey here to Spain, accompanied by the fleet from New Spain, and to the mouth of the Bahama Channel, navigating the remainder. This port of Cartagena is very safe for the ships, and the town and land are very healthy for all types of peoples and there is much business and great wealth. Here there are several forts and more are being built at the present.

Cartagena, 10 degrees and a half

From this port to the Gulf of Venezuela, which is at 11 degrees north latitude, the coast runs east–west, with a distance of 180 leagues, some points extending into the sea.

Gulf of Venezuela, at 11 degrees

From the Gulf of Venezuela to the Cape of Tres Puntas, which is at 10 degrees north latitude, the coast runs east–west, with a distance of a hundred and fifty leagues. And crossing the gulf of Paria from point to point, it runs north–northwest, with a distance of 40 leagues.

Cape of Three Points, 10 degrees

From this point in the gulf of Paria to the Dulce [Orinoco] River,

Sweet River, 6 degrees

which is at 6 degrees north latitude, the coast runs south by east a distance of 30 leagues.

Smoke River, 6 degrees and a half From the Duze [Dulce] River to the Humos River, which is at 5 degrees and a half north latitude, the coast runs east–west, with a distance of 320 leagues.

Orellana River, longitude 30 From this river to the Orellana, which is precisely below the equinoctial, and at 30 degrees of longitude from the bridge of the Canaries,[1] the coast runs, except for the inlet it makes, southeast by east, with a distance of 60 leagues.

To this river, all the latitudes given from Cartagena to Veracruz and from Veracruz to the Bahama Channel and returning from Cartagena to the Orellana River are on the northern side. And from this river, those given, to the Magellan Strait and entering the coast of Peru to Portoviejo, will be on the southern side.

Marañón River, one degree and a half From this Orellana River to the Marañón River, which is at one degree south latitude, the coast runs almost east–west, with a distance of 90 leagues.

Smoke Point, 2 degrees and a half From this river to the beginning of Humos Point, which is at two degrees and a half south latitude, it runs east–west, with a distance of 170 leagues.

Cape of St. Augustine, 8 degrees and a half From this point to the Cape of San Agustín, which is at 8 degrees and a half south latitude, the coast runs north–northwest, with a distance of 100 leagues.

From this cape to the Magellan Strait, taken all together, the coast runs northeast–southwest, though in some parts it runs along different courses, such as from the Cape of San Agustín to the Bay of Todos Santos, which is at 12 degrees and a half, the coast runs northeast–southwest, with a distance of 100 leagues.

Shoals of Eye-openers, 17 degrees and a half From this bay to the shoals of Abreojos, which is at 17 degrees and a half south latitude, the coast runs north–south, with a distance of 90 leagues.

From these shoals to Cape Frío, which is at 23 degrees and a half south latitude, the coast runs northeast–southwest, with a distance of 95 leagues.

Cold Cape, 23 degrees and a half

From this cape to the bay of San Vicente, which is at 23 degrees south latitude, the coasts run east–west, with a distance of 110 leagues.

Bay of St. Vincent, 23 degrees

From this bay to the La Plata River, which is at 35 degrees south latitude, the coast runs northeast–southwest, with a distance of 200 leagues. In this port and river of La Plata there is a fort for its defense.

River Plate, 35 degrees

From this river of La Plata to the Magellan Strait, at the end of the Northern Sea, 52 degrees south latitude, the coast runs northeast–southwest and the farthest latitude this strait reaches is 54 degrees, and it empties into the Southern Sea [Pacific Ocean] at 53 degrees. This strait is a little more than 100 leagues long and ten leagues at the widest, and five at its narrowest and the coast, taken together, runs almost east–west.

Strait of Magellan, 52 degrees—54 degrees—53 degrees

From this strait to Portoviejo [Ecuador], in the Southern Sea and on the coast of Peru, it all runs north–south, taken together, except for an inlet between Chile and Arica, and another between the Isle of Lobos and Portoviejo. But to be clear, the meridian that cuts through Portoviejo crosses in the middle of the strait. And so it runs from this strait to Lima's Callao, the principal port of Peru, where they unload the clothing that goes there from Spain, taking the mentioned course, which is at 12 degrees south latitude, with a distance of 900 leagues.

From this port to Portoviejo, which is at almost 1 degree south latitude, it runs the same course, with a distance of 250 leagues.

Portoviejo, 1 degree

From this port, crossing all the land to the cape of San Agustín, which is from sea to sea, at the widest point the distance may be almost 900 leagues.

From Portoviejo to [the River] Pirú,[2] which is at 2 degrees north latitude, to the northern part and side, the coast runs almost east–west, with a distance of 100 leagues.

Pirú River, 2 degrees

Bay of San Miguel, 7 degrees	From this port to the Bay of San Miguel, which is at seven degrees north latitude, the coast runs south by east, with a distance of 80 leagues.
Panama City, 9 degrees	From this bay to the Main, and the port of Panama, which is at 9 degrees north latitude, the coast runs southeast by east, with a distance of 50 leagues. With this, all the coast of Peru has been run, from the Magellan Strait, from one side of the equinoctial to the other, [but] leaving aside and not addressing many well-known ports all along this coast, since the main route to Lima's Callao and Portoviejo is all one.
Chamé, 7 degrees	From this port of Panama City to the point of Chamé, which is at 7 degrees north latitude, the coast runs Southwest by South, with a distance of 35 leagues.
Higueras, 7 degrees	From this point to Higueras, which is at 7 degrees north latitude, the coast runs east by south, with a distance of 40 leagues.
Brica, 7 degrees	From Higueras to the point of Brica, crossing the small gulf, which is at 7 degrees north latitude, it runs the same course, with a distance of 40 leagues.
Crag Cape, 13 degrees	From this point of Brica to the Cape of Farallón, crossing its small gulf, it runs the same course, and is at 13 degrees north latitude and with a distance of 50 leagues.
Tehuantepec, 16 degrees and a half	From this Farallón to the inlet of Tehuantepec, which is at 16 degrees and a half north latitude, the coast runs northeast–southwest, with a distance of 190 leagues.
Acapulco, 20 degrees	From this inlet to the port of Acapulco, which is at 20 degrees north latitude, the coast runs west by north, except some points of little consideration that jut into the sea; there is a distance of 220 leagues.
California, 23 degrees	From this port of Acapulco to the tip of the Californias, which are at 23 degrees north latitude, the coast runs east–northwest, with a distance of 190 leagues.

From this point to that of Quivira, which is at 40 degrees north latitude, *Quivira, 40 degrees*
the coast runs northwest by west, with a distance of 330 leagues.

This completes the mariner's rutter [*derrotero*] of both coasts and seas, for though the [Atlantic] coast runs to the Bacallao Strait and Cape of Labrador, until now that course has not been described.[3]

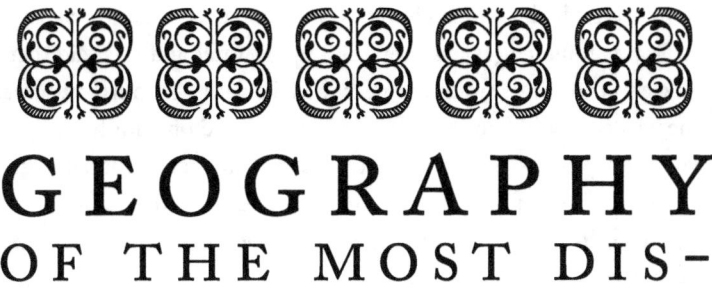

GEOGRAPHY
OF THE MOST DIS-
tinguished Kingdoms And Provinces
Of The Indies

Now that we have drawn the course of the coasts, with their distances and latitudes, it is well that we should make that of the kingdoms, with the distance there may be from one to another, inserting some particular provinces.

And beginning, I say that the city of Mexico, which is at 19 degrees north latitude, was the first city and capital of a kingdom settled in these Western Indies. It was settled by an Extremaduran gentleman, Hernando Cortés, the Marquis of Valle. There the royal audiencia has always resided, along with the viceroy of all the kingdom of New Spain.

Mexico, 19 degrees

There is a royal treasury office. It has the metropolitan archbishop to the other bishops therein. This city is the largest of the Indies, more colorful and opulent. It is a temperate land, healthy and quite prosperous, abundant and affluent and with much trade, and within its jurisdiction, many silver mines are worked, with which many of our Spaniards have grown wealthy. In its districts as well as within the city there are powerful men of great and established fortunes.

There are many gentlemen and nobles and ladies of great importance, and the criollas in particular are quite beautiful.

The site of this city is very flat and the houses are quite spacious and the housing blocks, parish churches, and monasteries are very sumptuous. It is founded (as has been said) upon water and it is said there is a secret [opening] around or near the lake with which Moctezuma, if he wished, could flood the city, a secret reserved only for him. There are many opinions as to how many citizens and settlers inhabit this city and its surroundings; there may be 50,000, with around 7,000 Spaniards. In this district there are some governorships subordinated to the viceroy.

From this city of Mexico to Veracruz, port of the Northern Sea [Atlantic], there are 70 leagues, and the course runs almost southeast–northwest, a road well populated and supplied.

From this city to the port of Acapulco, Southern Sea [Pacific], where the ships coming from the Philippines drop anchor, there are 85 leagues distance, all populated and the course runs northwest–southwest.[1]

Guadalajara, 21 degrees Eighty leagues distant lies the city of Guadalajara, province of Jalisco, which is at 21 degrees north latitude, the course running southeast–northwest. In this city resides the royal audiencia of Jalisco [New Galicia], and the president of this governs as subordinate to the viceroy. There is a royal exchequer and in its district there are governorships subordinate to the royal audiencia. There is a bishopric.

Almost 140 leagues distant lies the Northern Sea, southeast–northwest, and the Southern Sea lies 70 leagues distant, east–west. This city is in healthy land, temperate and abundant. It is not a trade city, but in its district some silver mines are worked. From this city to New Mexico, a land yet to be conquered,[2] there are almost 400 leagues north–south, along a deserted road. The people seeking it generally pass through or around this city [Guadalajara], searching for the best and most passable trails; and the straight road passes through Zacatecas.

Guatemala, 14 degrees and a half Two hundred fifty to 300 leagues distant from the city of Mexico lies that of Guatemala, direction almost southeast–northwest; it is at 14 degrees and a half north latitude. The entire road is inhabited and supplied.

There is a royal audiencia in this city, which they call Honduras,[3] and the president is governor and field marshal, and the governorships he has in his district are subordinate to the royal audiencia. There is a royal exchequer and a bishopric and the city is medium-sized and with little trade, but quite abundant in supplies, healthy and temperate, and silver mines are worked in its jurisdiction.

This city has the Northern and the Southern Seas, almost north to south, at the same distance of thirty leagues. That of the north on one side is northeast–southwest and on the other, north–south, for between these two courses the land makes a promontory into the sea.

From this city of Guatemala to that of Panama there are almost 300 leagues, northwest–southeast, part of the road populated and part of it occupied by warring Indians, except by sea.

Panama, 9 degrees

This city is at 9 degrees, as has been said; it has a royal audiencia, and the president is governor and field marshal. There is a royal exchequer, and the government of [the district of] Veragua is subordinate to the royal audiencia.

It is a bishopric. This city is small, unhealthy, and in a hot land not bathed by the North Wind, which is impeded by the Capira Range, which runs east–west. It is a port of the Southern or (as the sailors say) Dream Sea, as it is so gentle and without danger. Provisions are expensive, as they are mostly brought from other parts, though there is a supply of meats. It is a city of much trade and quite wealthy; most or almost all of the inhabitants are merchants. There are gold mines, from which much is taken, such as in Veragua and other parts nearby. There is also pearl fishing in several nearby islets.

From this city to that of Santa Fe de Bogotá, in the New Kingdom of Granada, and its capital, which is at 4 degrees north latitude, there is no road by land because of the warring Indians and great mountains and forest, and so it is sailed and walked, part by sea and part by land. On the southern side one sails to the port of Buenaventura and goes from there by land, a distance of 250 leagues, and on the northern side, by way of Nombre de Dios or Portobelo. Those 18 leagues of coastland are sailed to Cartagena, and from there [one travels by canoe] up the great Magdalena River; by this route there are 300 leagues. These two cities are in a straight line southeast–northwest.

Santa Fe, 4 degrees   This city of Santa Fe [de Bogotá] is the capital of all the New Kingdom of Granada, which was the third kingdom settled in the Indies. It was settled by don Gonzalo Jiménez de Quesada, a gentleman from Granada.

In this city resides the royal audiencia and the president is the governor and field marshal. There are many governorships subordinate to the royal audiencia, and it has a royal exchequer.

It is a metropolitan archbishopric to the other bishoprics. This city is in temperate country, as is most of its district. It is a very healthy land, pleasant, well supplied, and all the food is easy to come by.

There is little trade, although some have reasonable fortunes. As it was the last kingdom settled, none are as established as in New Spain and Peru. In it there are silver mines now being worked that promise wealth. There are many emerald mines; I believe none other like them are worked in the world, and they are wealthy. They are in the city of Muzo, capital of the governorship of that province.

In this kingdom many gold mines are worked, and most of the gold they bring to our Spain is from here.

The city [of Santa Fe] is medium in size, and there are opinions that it has 2,000 Spanish inhabitants, not including some Indians who inhabit the outskirts. There are reasonable houses, parish churches, and monasteries. Noble people inhabit it, and there are very great and distinguished captains and soldiers inside of it as well as in its area, since they regularly exercise their arms against enemies. The site of this city is completely flat.

Cartagena, government of its district, lies 200 leagues distant from this city, almost to the north, traveling by the Magdalena River, whose greater part is uninhabited, and along whose course goods from Spain are carried. To the northeast there is another path 200 leagues long to Venezuela, completely inhabited, going along the coast of the Northern Sea.

San Francisco de Quito runs southward a distance of 200 leagues, and it is at one degree south latitude, leaving Popayán halfway along the road, a good stretch of land, supplied and rich in many gold mines, and half of this government is subordinate to the Audiencia of Santa Fe and the other half to that of Quito. It [i.e., the Governorship of Popayán] is a bishopric and has a royal post.

This city of Quito has a royal audiencia and the president governs subordinate to the viceroy of Peru. It has a royal exchequer and is a bishopric. It is temperate land, healthy and abundant with all basic necessities, pleasant and affluent and with some trade. There are gold mines in its district, and they are worked. It lies 400 leagues from the Northern Sea, as there are to Cartagena, north to south, and to the Southern Sea it is 100 [leagues], to the southwest.

From this city to the City of the Kings, or Lima, which is at 12 degrees south latitude, there are 300 leagues, by the mountain road as well as by the plains, the entire road populated. *Lima, 12 degrees*

This City of the Kings, or Lima, is the capital of Peru, the second kingdom settled in the Indies, by Francisco Pizarro, Extremaduran gentleman.

In this city reside the royal audiencia and viceroy. There is a royal exchequer, and it is a metropolitan archbishopric to the other bishoprics it has. It is a large city and there are opinions that it has around 6,000 inhabitants, and though it has this number of Spaniards as well as the Indians who inhabit its outskirts, there are times when, for the most part, it does not show the bustle of the people. It is a hot land, but quite healthy because of the steadiness of the South Wind, which is the reason it does not rain there nor upon the plains except for a *garrúa* [i.e., misty fog], as they call it, that is so subtle that it offends nothing. This city and all its kingdom are quite abundant and pleasant and with much trade and great wealth, as everyone knows.

Great, illustrious, and very rich gentlemen inhabit this kingdom and city. In general, they are a valorous and brave people and the criollo ladies are very courteous and graceful and well instructed in song and music and quite discreet.

And finally, all the criollos of all three kingdoms have brave minds [*gallardos entendimientos*] and are great horsemen, and if they were employed to exercise letters and arms, they would be distinguished men.

From this city to the Southern Sea, which is a distance of two leagues, the road runs almost east–west and to that of Quito, north to south. The road is populated, with a distance of 300 leagues.

This city of La Plata is at 19 degrees south latitude, and in it resides the royal audiencia of Las Charcas and the president has his government *Las Charcas, 19 degrees* subordinate to the viceroy; it is a bishopric. This city is in a temperate and well-supplied land; it is healthy and has trade.

Potosí, 20 degrees   Eighteen leagues away are the mines of Potosí, at 20 degrees south latitude, of whose wealth all have heard. There is a royal post; it is a *corregimiento*[4] and it is a land of much trade.

Chile, 33 degrees   From the city of La Plata to Santiago de Chile, which is at 33 degrees south latitude, there is a distance of 300 leagues, more or less; it runs almost north to south. There are some uninhabited places along the road.

This province of Chile is a government subordinate to the viceroy and Audiencia of Las Charcas. There is a royal exchequer and it is a bishopric. It is a land of little trade but wealthy. It is somewhat cold, as it is outside of the tropic and thus, due to its latitude from the pole, and also due to the degrees in which the sun is found, there are movements of cold and heat. It is supplied with much agriculture. There are gold mines and they are worked in hot valleys.

Tucumán, 26 degrees   From this city of Las Charcas or Plata to San Miguel de Tucumán, which is at 26 degrees south latitude, there is a distance of more than 300 leagues. It is entirely uninhabited; the road runs almost northwest–southeast.

This province of Tucumán is a governorship subordinate to the Audiencia of Las Charcas. It is a bishopric and a land of little trade, but prosperous and well supplied, somewhat temperate, and its denizens gain their fortunes from the products of the land.

Buenos Aires   From here to Buenos Aires, on the River Plate, there is a distance of more than 200 leagues. It is entirely uninhabited; it runs southeast–northwest.

This government of the La Plata River is subordinate to the Audiencia of Las Charcas. It is a bishopric and a somewhat hot land, although it lies outside of the Tropic of Capricorn, it is not healthy in parts. It is well supplied.

Pernambuco, 8 degrees   From this river and Buenos Aires to Pernambuco,[5] province of Brazil, which is at 8 degrees south latitude, there are 600 leagues, a little more or less, by sea and by coast, for until now there is no open road. It runs the same course described in the Hydrography.

This governorship of Brazil has a royal audiencia;[6] it is a bishopric. It is a hot land and unhealthy in some parts, and in others temperate and healthy. It is well supplied and prosperous. These settlements are Portuguese.

Between this land and the central mountains of the New Kingdom of Granada and Peru, outside Pasto, El Dorado falls along a ridge of mountains that rises in the middle of this land and its plains, between the Marañón and Cinnamon Rivers, well nigh to the equinoctial, on the southern part, less than one degree. This ridge runs northeast–southwest, according to the most precise accounts. It is three hundred leagues distant from Brazil, and from the central mountains of the New Kingdom [of Granada], a hundred leagues. And the existence of this Dorado and its great wealth is a certain thing, for its fame is extended so widely to all parts. [The search for El Dorado] has cost a great number of lives and fortunes, for lack of true knowledge of it and its road. I could well give a long account of it and clarify things, but, as this is not my aim here, I leave it for now, and may God allow whom He wishes to discover it, giving him the valor and knowledge so that he may conquer and settle it in His service and the service of the king our lord.

Mido el Cielo veloz, la firme Tierra.

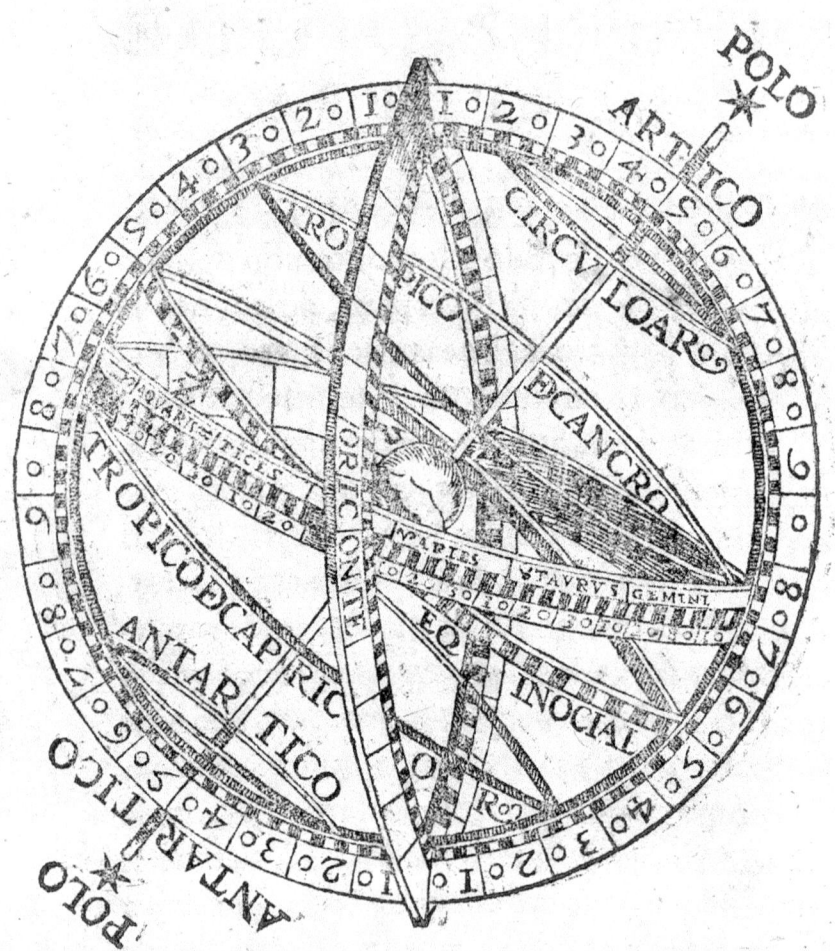

31 *Armillary sphere. John Carter Brown Library*

COMPENDIUM
OF THE SPHERE

THE SPHERE IS A ROUND BODY contained beneath a surface, from whose center equal lines extend to make up its circumference. This sphere is divided in two parts, celestial and elemental, of which the universal machine of the world is composed. The elemental are the four simple elements, or bodies: earth, water, air, and fire, of which all living things are composed. The water and earth make a round globe, around which the air circulates, divided in three parts, the inferior, middle, and supreme regions. The inferior, which we enjoy, is tempered by the repercussion of the rays of the sun. The middle is cold, where water as sleet and hailstone is engendered. The third is hot from the closeness of the sphere to fire, which is pure, not mixing with other elements. And the celestial part is divided into eleven contiguous heavens, like the layers of an onion skin; they do not share elemental matter but are made of the fifth essence, which is the same as saying the fifth element. And each of these heavens is moved by an intelligence that is an angel. They have no color, but though we see them as blue, it is because of the distance.

The eleventh heaven does not move, as it is the most perfect, the fundament, dwelling and tabernacle of the Most Holy Trinity. This is called Paradise, heaven of brilliance, for God and his chosen.

The tenth heaven, which is called the first motor, makes its movement from the east to the west and makes one turn in twenty-four hours, dragging along behind it the other inferior heavens, causing them to turn in kind.

The ninth heaven, called crystalline, is that of which David spoke: "The waters in the heavens worship the Lord." This has two movements, one caused by its abduction by the tenth sphere, like the others, and another, its own, retrogressing from west to east, against the force of the first motor, so little by little that this one turn will take 49,000 years.

The eighth heaven, where are found the stars we see, except the seven planets, is called the starry heaven and also firmament, because the stars are fixed there, like knots on a plank. It has three different movements. One is from east to west in twenty-four hours carried by the first motor. The other is that which the ninth heaven communicates to it from west to east, which takes 49,000 years. The third is its own nature, called trepidation, or accession and recession, which takes 7,000 years to occur, the northern part turning once around a point over 3,500 years, and in the southern part over the other 3,500 years.

The seventh heaven is that of Saturn. It has two movements, that of the tenth sphere, in twenty-four hours, and its own, retrogressing from one turn in thirty years.

The sixth heaven, which is that of Jupiter, has another two movements: those of the tenth sphere, of twenty-four hours, and its own, which takes twelve years to turn once from west to east.

The fifth heaven, which is that of Mars, has the same movements: that of the tenth heaven, in twenty-four hours, and its own, from west to east, which takes two years.

The fourth heaven is that of the sun, which takes 365 days and eleven minutes short of six hours to make its own movement from west to east (an hour being sixty minutes). This is exactly one year. With these six [remaining] hours, every four years the Church makes a natural day of twenty-four hours, which is inserted at the end of the twenty-fourth [*sic*] of February, which used to be the last month of the year. The fourth year is leap year and the Church says on the twenty-fourth of February, *sexto calendas Martii*, and the same on the twenty-fifth, and eleven minutes less, as has been said, have caused the reformation of the ten days that were taken away.[1]

The third heaven is that of Venus, making its own movement against the force of the first motor; and it takes almost the same time as the Sun to make its turn.

The second heaven is that of Mercury, making its movement in the same time as Venus.

The first heaven, which is that of the moon, makes its own movement in twenty-six days and eight hours, returning to the point where it began, though the sun is not found there, because on these days it falls almost a sign behind, which is thirty degrees, and the moon takes time to catch up, in order to put itself in conjunction, which is said to be from twenty-seven days and eight hours to twenty-nine-and-a-half days.

The heavens are adjacent to each other, as has been said, in such a manner that between one and another there is no distance. In thickness there are, as with the earth, 3,250 miles from its center to the surface.[2] The stars show us the heavens move circularly, as we see them rise from the horizon and we see them rising little by little with the same uniformity until they come to the middle of the heavens and pass to the west, and in any part they have the same distance from us, which demonstrates to us the roundness of the heavens, for if this were not so, they would be seen larger at some times. The same for the sun and the moon, and if the sun appears larger to us upon rising, it is not, but rather the vapors that are over the earth come between the sun and us and, as they are diaphanous, they divide the visual rays, with which seeing things in their nature is lost and they are perceived to be larger, as a coin thrown into water. That the earth is round is clear, for moving ourselves from one province to another, we lose sight of the stars we always saw in the other province. And upon water the stars behave in the same fashion; and we also see that the landmarks that we leave upon the coasts are lost from sight as we begin to sail.

That this globe of earth and water is at the center and middle of the universe is known, as we see the greatness of the stars is the same in the Orient, as above us, as in the Occident. And if this globe is sustained in the air, it is because all that has weight seeks its center, and the center of the firmament is one point. As the earth is so heavy, it seeks its center and is sustained in it.

The hinges where the sphere makes its movement are two imagined points, as will be the other points and circles. These two points are called the poles of the world, different from the poles of the Zodiac. It must be noted that the star commonly called North is not, for it lies three and a half degrees distant from this fixed point or Arctic pole. And the same from the Antarctic pole. The closest star to this pole that may be seen lies 30 degrees distant; and the line that may be imagined to pass through the center of the world, from one pole to the other, is called the axis of the world.

The poles of the zodiac lie 23 degrees and a half distant from the poles of the world; upon them moves the axis of the zodiac.

Zenith is a point that corresponds truly or perpendicularly to each over his head, from the heavens to wherever they are found.

Nadir is another point corresponding to the zenith, as if it were to pass through the head and body of a man and the earth to the inferior hemisphere to our antipodes, passing through the center of the earth, where zenith and nadir may be named by those of the Orient, and each of these points will have ninety degrees at their horizon, of the 360 in which the astrologers divide the sphere.

There are ten circles of the sphere, the major six and the minor four. That which cuts into two equal parts is called major circle and unequal parts is minor.

The first of the major circles is the equinoctial line, in which the sun enters two times a year, and so the day is equal to the night and for this reason it is called equinoctial and it lies equidistant from the poles of the world.

The equinoctial is cut on one side by a wide band called zodiac, in two equal parts: one half declines toward one pole and the other half to the other, called zodiac, which means "life," as the twelve signs and seven planets move within it, which are the governors of the world. From them are taken the names of the days of the week. The first is Sunday, because of the sun; the rest declare themselves. The life of all inferior things is below this. This band is adorned with twelve figures, which are the twelve signs. Their names are: Aries, Taurus, Gemini, Cancer, Leo, Virgo, Libra, Scorpio, Sagittarius, Capricorn, Aquarius, and Pisces. Six decline toward one pole and the other six to the other. Each sign has 30 degrees of longitude, which make 160 [*sic*] of a circle. Each makes its movement over poles different from those of the world [*universo*], as has been said.

Through the middle of the zodiac a line called the ecliptic is imagined, for in it the eclipses of the sun and moon are caused; the zodiac is cut into equal parts, which are the twelve degrees, fitting six in each part.

There are two other major circles, called *coluros*,[3] which are imagined to pass through the poles of the world, one passes through the equinoctial, cutting the first degrees of Aries and Libra, called the coluro of the equinoxes. The other cuts the poles of the zodiac and the first degrees of Cancer and Capricorn, called coluro of the solstices, understood to make the closest approximation to the Sun and farthest from the equinoctial. These two coluros cut the sphere in four equal parts, and the four seasons of the year are within them.

The meridian is a major circle that each person imagines and is drawn wherever one may be, from one pole to the other, under which all who find themselves on it will have the same midday and midnight hour.

The horizon is a circle and is what the sight is able to measure and discover, cutting off the lower part of the earth, and so it is called the terminator of view, and what remains above is the superior hemisphere and what is below, the inferior. Those who live below the equinoctial have the horizon and sphere precisely straight; and the rest, oblique.

The sun most nears the northern part, moving along its ecliptic, and moving one degree each day until the first of Cancer, on June 22. When it reaches this, it describes a circle we imagine from the east to west. This is the Tropic of Cancer. And where it moves most to the south it describes another circle, which is called the Tropic of Capricorn. The sun moves between these two tropics all year, not traveling outside of them, making 182 turns which are the so-called spirals, which are like those made by a string wrapped around a top. These are minor circles.

The poles of the world lie 23½ degrees distant from those of the Zodiac, as we have stated, and, full of the impulsive movement of the tenth sphere, describe two more minor circles. These take the names of the two poles, and so one circle is called Polar Arctic, and the other circle, Polar Antarctic.

With these four circles the sphere is divided into five zones, all inhabited, though the ancients believed otherwise.

All the other circles, which are those that divide the sphere into equal parts, have 360 degrees together; and however small the circle may be, it will have the same [number], but the degrees will be smaller when the circles are smaller. Each degree is divided into sixty minutes and each minute in sixty seconds and diminishing in this manner to tenths.

Those who dwell opposite our feet are called antipodes,[4] imagining a line that passes from one to the other through the center of the world, in such a manner, that my nadir is his zenith and his nadir is my zenith, and when it is summer for him it is winter for me, and to the contrary, when I am in summer he is in winter, and when I have the longest day of the year, he has the shortest, and when it is day for me, it is night for him.

The *periecos* [or *piriecos*, as spelled in book 1] are those who are on my same parallel and at the same distance from the same pole. I am in the same hemisphere, only he is on the opposite side, and we correspond in having winter, summer, spring, and autumn at the same time, and the days wax and wane equally; we are only different in that when they are at midnight, I am at midday.

Antecos are those who dwell on the same meridian on my side and lie at equal degrees latitude distant from their pole as I do from mine and we have midday and midnight at the same time.

The *pericios* [or *piriseos*] are those who dwell under the poles, where half of the year it is completely day and the other half year it is night and the sun makes shade all around them at all times, like a millwheel.

Anfiscios [or *anfiseos*] are those who dwell beneath the equinoctial, whose shadows fall to four directions, east, west, north, and south, over the course of one year.

DECLARATION OF THE PROPER NAMES OF THIS BOOK

A

AMAHAGUA, is tree bark that, when crushed, is used as hemp.
AMBIRE, is an antivenin the Indians make in Santa Marta.
ARCABUCO, is dense and impenetrable woodland.

B

BALSAR, is a thick bracken.
BALSAS, is a sheaf of poles gathered and tied together, on which a river is crossed.
BAQUIANO, is the skilled people of a land.
BARBACOA, is a bed of posts made for sleeping.
BEJUCO, is a vine that hangs from the trees, which is used for many things.
BENCENUCO, is a small tree which is a proven antivenin.
BIHAO, is a very large leaf, larger than that of burdock, quite useful.

C

CABUYAS, are ropes.
CACAO, is a fruit used as money and also eaten.
COCA or HAYO, is a tree leaf which the Indian chews.
CACONA, is what the Indian steals in mines of gold, emeralds, pearl fisheries.

CAIMANES, are the lizards that hang in the churches.

CANOAS, is a river boat, except that it is made of one trunk of wood and is longer.

CARACURI, is a ring of gold that the Indians hang from their noses for show.

CATHABRE, is a basket, or similar thing.

CEMBE [cumbi], is a cloth of wool of the sheep of Peru.

CHAGUALA, is a round jewel of gold like a paten, which the Indians hang from their necks.

CHAPETÓN OR CACHUPÍN, is a man who is new to the land.

CHICHA, is a wine made from maize.

CHINA, is an Indian maid of service.

CHONTARURO, is a palm that bears a fruit of great sustenance for the Indian.

COCUYO, is a beetle that gives light by night.

CORDONCILLO, is a tree blossom that is antivenin.

CRIOLLO, is the person who is a son or daughter of Spanish parents, born in the Indies.

F

FOTUTOS, is a musical instrument the Indians use in war.

G

GACHA, is a clay vessel like a half-size jug.

GANDIL [gandul], is a corpulent Indian.

GUARAPO, is a drink made from the syrup of sweet cane.

GUAZAVARA, is to battle.

H

HAMACA, is a cloth of cotton, or made of netting, which is hung for sleeping.

I

IAGUA [jagua], is a wild fruit whose juice the Indians use to paint themselves.

M

MACANA, is a weapon almost like a two-handed sword, made of palm.
MAÍZ, is grain of the Indies.
MAZATO, is a sour dough of maize that is drunk dissolved in water.
MESTIZO, is the son of a Spaniard and an Indian.
MOTO, is cooked maize.

N

NIGUAS, is a type of flea that burrows into the flesh of the feet, and grows larger than a lentil; until it is removed it is fastidious.

P

PAMPANILLA, are clothes the Indians use.
PAPAS, is a type of truffle that is gathered and eaten.
PATACUSMA, is an Indian garment.
PULCRE [pulque], is a drink the Indians in New Spain use.

T

TOTUMA, is like a washbasin, and is made of a type of gourd.
TROCHA, is when one leaves branches in a thick forest to show the path.

V

VIJA, is a color like henna, with which the Indians paint themselves.

Y

YOPA, is a seed the Indian chews to speak to the Devil.

YUCA, is a root that is planted, from which is made a bread called *cazabe*.

Z

ZABANA, is flatland with no mountains.

ZIMARRÓN [cimarrón], is all things fled and retreated.

APPENDIX ONE
A POSTHUMOUS REPORT ON BERNARDO DE VARGAS MACHUCA'S SERVICES, CA. 1622

SERVICES

of the Captain don Alvaro Félix de Vargas Moxica, and of the Governor don Bernardo de Vargas Machuca his father, and of the Captain Juan de Vargas his grandfather.

By certifications, titles, and proofs be it known that the aforesaid don Alvaro Félix de Vargas has served his Majesty for thirteen years, six in the city of Portobelo, his father don Bernardo de Vargas serving as chief magistrate and commissioner of its fortifications, and another six on Margarita Island as governor and captain general, finding himself continuously at his side on all the opportunities offered to him for the Royal Service.[1]

Likewise, may it be known that the aforesaid don Alvaro served three years as captain in the castle of San Bernardo, of the aforesaid island, and assisted in its construction.

And be it known that, by appointment of the town council of that island, he served the post of keeper of arms and munitions [*tenedor de las armas*], which his Majesty has on that island for its guarding and defense.

And be it known that in the year [1]617 he served in the company of Captain don Juan de Vega Bazán, [on his] journey to New Spain, giving very high account of all that was charged of him, as is evident in the reports referred to.

Likewise may it be known that the Governor don Bernardo de Vargas, his father, served in all the wars of Granada and in Italy, and in the fleets in defense of the Indies, with satisfaction. And that afterward he transferred to the New Kingdom of Granada where, as Conqueror, he continued for twenty-two years, until 1602, on occasions and enterprises of great importance that were commended to him, being a notable and a man of service, by the president and audiencia, as well as by other governors in provinces of that kingdom. May it be especially known that he served as field marshal on the Carare expedition, done to punish the Indians occupying the great Magdalena River and committing many murders and robberies. And afterward he was charged with the enterprise of the same Carare Indians, under his leadership as commander general, and defeated the brigands and calmed the land, punishing them greatly. And afterward he was charged to defeat the banditry of the Muzo and Colima Indians; and he defeated their captain and ordered him hanged, and reduced the rest. And in the year [fifteen] ninety, by provision of the royal audiencia of Santa Fe, he rescued the city of Altagracia that was surrounded by the Pijao Indians, whom he defeated, and brought the cacique to justice and calmed the uprising and left that city becalmed, having assisted as chief justice and captain. And in the year [fifteen] ninety-two, he accomplished the rescue of Medina de las Torres, which was surrounded by the Breco Indians and in great hardship; and he saved [the city] and left it in peace. And that same year he rebuilt the city of Santiago de Atalaya in a better place, and with men at arms [*gente de guerra*], defeated the rebelling Indians who had murdered Captain Pedro Daza, their conqueror and settler, with other Spaniards in his company, and punished the guilty, and with this he calmed the land. And in the year [fifteen] ninety-three he took a place with the Governor Bernardino de Moxica, uncle to the aforementioned Alvaro, for the settling and conquest of the provinces of the Pijaos, and he went to them and had many encounters and battles against them, and he defeated them many times as lieutenant general of the expedition. And in the same year he crossed the *Cordillera General* with men of war in order to raise and conquer the Provinces of the Andaquíes, where he founded the city of Simancas as captain general, and distributed the land and Indians among the soldiers and arrested the tyrant Captain Palomino, principal leader of the uprising of Quito, regarding sales taxes, and brought him to justice. And by commission of the president of the New Kingdom, in the year [fifteen] ninety-five he went to Timaná, sixty leagues from where he was and at his expense, to sell the positions of the town council, which he did to great satisfaction and growth of the Royal Treasury, and quite good effects came of those services. And this audiencia states the opinion that he was not remunerated, and that he deserved to be, and that he should have been done the favor.

Be it known that afterward, in the year of 1602, he was given the title of Chief Magistrate of San Felipe de Portobelo, and Commissioner of its fortifications and Residing Magistrate, and attended to all the things these posts obligated him to, having well disciplined the men of war. And he was the first officer [*Cabo*] of two companies and built three castles and, in a warning he received that the enemy was approaching that land, he entrenched and put the city on its defense at his expense, taking great pains to do so, as is entirely known by the certifications of the presidents and town councils. And the general of the fleet of the Carrera [de Indias] certifies that he always attended to his duty with great punctuality and that his final audit was freely given. And for having given good account, he was promoted to governor and captain general of Margarita Island and Residing Magistrate.

And being given the governorship of Margarita, it appears in a letter by three English captains that, respecting his person and the good preparation of the island, they did not dare to attack it, but rather sent him soldiers that they had captured, along with a royal official from a vessel they had taken, that was going to rescue a group of blacks who had been lost among the Windward Islands.

And it appears by certification of the town council of Margarita that the city has been distinguished with buildings that he made for its adornment, order, and benefit, at his own expense and credit, for which he was left owing three thousand ducats for not having enough to pay: as it appears in testimonies that the republic is found quite grateful for the common good of having brought a source of water from a great distance, and made a bridge over the river, butcher shops and fisheries, and a slaughterhouse; the town council building, a prison, offices for scribes, the courtroom [*audiencia*], a millstone, a water fountain beyond the walls for the livestock; having strengthened the gates and walls of the city and [built a] battery and a roof for a market; and clocks, and an enclosed avenue for the people on horseback to exercise for times of war, and a shrine [*Humilladero*] and hospital and much of the principal church. And be it known through testimonies that he founded two churches in the field in order to indoctrinate the native Indians and administer the Holy Sacraments to them, at no cost to the royal treasury. And be it known that he set up a granary with three hundred *fanegas* of maize to relieve the poor.

And be it likewise known that he finished enclosing the Fort of Pampatar, which is in the principal port of the island, at his own expense, as there was not enough money in the royal treasury for it, and the enemy was in sight.

Be it known, by certifications and the royal commission made for it, that he took accounts of the royal officials of the aforesaid island, with no remuneration whatsoever; these he took with great increase to the royal treasury.

Likewise be it known, and it appears in reports and certifications of the city and his successor, that he rebuilt the castle of San Bernardo at his expense, for a knight of the city, for its guarding and defense, giving it a chapel and ornamentation for the divine cult, and part of the artillery and two slaves, a drummer and a builder, for its conservation.

And it appears that, according to assessment of the masters, his expenditures exceeded twenty thousand ducats. And afterward, by certification he appears to have enlarged the building with new expenses, personally overseeing the completion of that castle, after more than ten months of his governance. And the city entreated that he be rewarded because of the many and great benefits received and services rendered, and gave him power for all his causes.

By certification of the city of Santa Fe, may the many services he has done in that kingdom be known, for which it is quite grateful, entreating his reward and that he personally see to the government of that kingdom, because of their satisfaction, in affairs of peace as well as war; and he is known to have written books on the military arts, with which he has given instruction to the militia of the Indies.

Don Bernardo died in [the service of] this court, having been named governor of the provinces of Antioquia. And be it known that by having spent his estate in the service of his Majesty and for just causes, and having died very poor, the council ordered to give to the aforesaid don Alvaro, his son, one hundred ducats for his burial.

And Captain Juan de Vargas, his grandfather, served his Majesty sixty-four years, and the most serene Empress Queen of Hungary for a long time, in things of quality and importance, and on the expedition he made to Germany, where he married doña Agueda de Soto, servant of his Majesty, upon whose orders he and his wife returned to Spain, accompanying doña Teresa de Vargas, his sister, who had also served his Majesty in the expedition as matron, to raise the most serene Prince don Fernando and, having returned, he was given the honor of a commission of captain, and raised people [of war] in the city of Córdoba, with which he served in the entire war of Granada and in that of Portugal.

And he likewise served thirty-four years as paymaster of the Royal Archives of Simancas; and simultaneously as lieutenant to the major of the aforementioned fortress; where he was in charge of, by order of his Majesty, the six-year imprisonment of don Juan de Granada y Mendoza, without guards and at his expense, lacking many other things needed for that order, and having been given no reward whatsoever for those services.

APPENDIX TWO

SELECTIONS FROM
THE DEFENSE OF WESTERN CONQUESTS,
CA. 1603

The following is a brief selection from Bernardo de Vargas Machuca's *Defense of Western Conquests* (also known as the *Apologetic Discourses*), a manuscript he rewrote while serving as governor of Margarita Island in 1612. He says in a portion of his advice to the reader not included below that he had initially written this proposed book (about 100 printed pages' worth in all) while serving in Portobelo, on the Caribbean coast of Panama, but that his original manuscript was stolen while on its way to a publisher in Lima. Unfortunately for the author, permission to print the 1612 rewrite was denied repeatedly in Spain, and the manuscript remained unpublished until 1879, when it appeared in a larger collection of miscellaneous colonial writings.[1]

Bartolomé de Las Casas's *Brevísima relación de la destrucción de las Indias* (often translated as *A Brief Account of the Destruction of the Indies*), on the other hand, circulated not only in Spanish but also in several other European languages by the end of the sixteenth century. Although this was hardly its author's purpose, the *Brevísima relación* served very well as propaganda against the expansive empire of Catholic Spain, particularly in England and the Low Countries, but also in Protestant regions of France and Germany (Vargas Machuca refers vaguely to "Huguenot" versions of the text). The militiaman from Simancas was not alone in his distaste for Las Casas's writings, but up to his time few had been willing to challenge the famed "Protector of the Indians" head-on. As some scholars have noted, Vargas Machuca was in fact in the vanguard of a Spanish backlash against Las Casas that lasted into the nineteenth century.² In reading Vargas Machuca's shrill *Defense of Western Conquests*, however, it is difficult to say if anyone would have been convinced by his arguments. Not only did he lack eloquence, as he himself admits below, but his blanket statements about "Indians" are every bit as overdrawn as Las Casas's claims about Spanish conquistadors and encomenderos. What purports to be an impartial defense of Spanish American imperialism, then, soon devolves into an emotional diatribe against Native Americans that all but prefigures modern racist rants.

APOLOGETIC DISCOURSES

against the treatise written by don Fray Bartolomé de las Casas, Bishop of Chiapa[s], in the year 1552, entitled Destruction of the Indies, *condemning their conquest and opposing the defense of it.*

TO THE READER

Self-defense being, such as it is, a natural thing, I have not been able to avoid defending my own honor and that common to our nation, which with pious countenance and appearances the learned Bishop of Chiapa[s], don Fray Bartolomé de las Casas (or Cassaos), attempted to tarnish in the discourse he wrote in the year [15]52, with that contemptible title *The Destruction of the Indies*, in which he tried to depict as cruelties the legal punishments in all the West, which the conquerors executed (and presently carry out) in the Indies for heinous crimes that were (and are) committed every day. And [this treatise] has had such an effect on the Huguenots, conforming to their ancient malice and scorning the great Christianity of Spain, that they have published tracts that describe the Indies with various forms of cruelties, citing the Bishop of Chiapa[s] with chapters from his treatise, some of which he truly wrote and some that they invented, and beyond these, words written against good opinion, clemency, and Christian piety. . . .

FIRST DISCOURSE AND DEFENSE
in favor of the conquest of the isle of Hispaniola.

The Devil's malice ordinarily seeks to take away reason from humans so that they are converted into brute animals, and it is in this way that he has possessed these Indians for such a long time. This is easily seen in what the very same bishop of Chiapa[s] writes in his *Treatise on the Isle of Hispaniola*, upon which they imagined Spaniards to be children of the sun, and when discovered that they were not, they fled into the jungles where they ended up as barbarians; and I confess this is true. In addition to this, he says that the cruelties done to them by the Spaniards were innumerable, charging [the Spaniards] first with eating the provisions of the fugitives, and obligating the rest to give them their usual rations, and likewise, in the rebellions, of causing great harm, killing a hundred for each one of ours killed by them, so that in time most if not all of them came to a miserable end. He also tells of five powerful kingdoms on the isle of Hispaniola, omitting the innumerable and inferior others. He says more: that the Spaniards used dogs in order to finish them off, fattening [the dogs] on them and cruelly tearing them apart. He says more: that they took advantage of the women of the [cacique] lords, dishonoring and offending them, which caused the Indians to abhor them and to go and die in the jungles and forests due to their sense of honor. Of all the things referred to here, some may be conceded, but everything else is denied. We will demonstrate this by giving sufficient reasons, on particular points and in general, so that everything that follows is correct, having founded this defense on principle.

As for the Indians' imagining that the Spaniards were children of the sun and that man and horse are one, this has generally been true, at first sight, in all of the Indies, and remains so in the new conquests. From this, one may well understand their barbarity, as they neither made nor make discourse about, nor consider the division of the two bodies. And if they were seen as humble, submissive, obedient, and servile, it is because of this imagination and apprehension they had, as well as the fear caused by the furious horses and frightening thundering of the harquebuses, appearing as cruel lightning bolts from the heavens. But in time, discovering the truth and realizing that [the Spaniards] were mortal men, subject to die as they were, they lost all respect, along with that first obedience, gathering the courage to take up arms against our men and forging in their malice diverse betrayals, putting into execution as many as they could; and those that had no effect were because they were discovered and punished in time, discovering their evil intentions. But those acts that have succeeded have caused inhumane cruelties: setting Spanish towns afire, first burning the churches and the sacred Sacrament within; making martyrs of the religious with many and varied torments and deaths, eating them grilled and cooked; bringing many men and women whose eyes were torn out to dance in their drunken revelries and gatherings on leashes they attach through a hole pierced under the lower jaw.[3] Some of these they fatten in order to eat, and others guard their crops from the parrots, shouting all day from atop high structures made of four poles and suffering this cruel torment until they die. Others are burned and made into ash in order to drink in chicha, which is a wine they make. They make war flutes of [human] bones and eat on plates made of the crowns of skulls, triumphant. In effect, at every turn they are the most cruel people in the world, as brutish as they are cruel, and it is my opinion (and that of many who have dealt with them) that in order to paint a perfect picture of cruelty one must but paint a portrait of an Indian.

As for their trade and communication, it is true that they do not tell the truth, nor have ever known how to keep faith, nor word, nor promise with those who have trusted them. One is forced to believe they are a people with neither honor nor esteem, and this truth is verified in knowing for certain that they sell wife, daughter, and sister to any Spaniard to make use of lasciviously. One may infer that they are a people with no reason, depraved and without honor. Without this, virtue cannot be sustained, for a sense of shame is its most important foundation. Honor is a dignity acquired with virtue, such that this is the mother of honor and forms a substantial part of its very definition, for virtue is what creates all that is good. As all of their acts are evil, it follows that they have no honor, and whoever should lack this lacks virtue as well, and for peoples who lack both, one wonders who they might be. I know not why I tire myself with presenting the material further, as we know that they eat their own children and vassals. And so that their barbarity may be seen, I can say that they disobey and break the laws of nature itself, which normally inclines one to the conservation of man and to desire a long life and flee from death; they, voluntarily and for slight causes, hang themselves. One may believe that a people who do this are without faith and without God, and I say this not only of the true Creator, but even of the pagan, for if they had any faith, it would be recognized, for man is a royal possession and property of this same God, to whom injury is done when one takes his [own] life, as the slave would do to his master, killing himself against his [master's] will.

Not only that, they are even more brutish than irrational animals, for we see that [the animals] procure to feed and preserve their species and there is none that do not love and care for their children, placing their lives in danger so that they may live. Yet these indomitable savages go against the universal law of nature, wishing to destroy themselves, for they do not make their descendants heed [Christian] doctrine and serve the Spaniards. The females are drowned at birth, and this has sometimes been observed in the provinces of the Panches and Colimas[4] and in many others. Finally, though they may have been baptized, most of them are idol worshippers and speak with the Devil, and according to their inclination it may be understood that they will die as they have lived. [They do] all this and many other things of no lesser gravity of which I will not speak so as to not tire nor be thought of more as one impassioned rather than a true author.

And the bishop [Las Casas] kept silent about this because his primary intention was to lend credence to them [i.e., the Indians], blaming the Spaniard for cruelty and tyranny; and to the legal punishments which we are addressing here he gave the unjust name of cruelties, without considering nor admitting the preceding causes nor the motive of the Spaniards; for many things that are not clearly seen nor well understood from the beginning are poorly judged. And what happened to a cleric of one of those provinces confirms this: Wanting his parishioners to learn and love the evangelical doctrine and observe it with Christian zeal, he brought the cruel sorrows of purgatory to their minds in a sermon. And after extolling what he could, he said that he would show them to whomever wished to see. At this point two curious, or rather garrulous, Indians asked the priest to show them and so the good cleric tied them to a pole that was set in the ground for a pillory or gibbet, and made a circle of firewood around them, two paces away. It must have been well made, because of the effect, for he set it afire all around with the spirit and intention that when it became too hot he would tear the wood from the circle and untie them. He did this but was unable to undo it, for when he tried to save them it was too late, or he was prevented, or the Devil stoked the fire so that the Indians died. The archbishop of this place, knowing the case, sent for the prisoner and pardoned him for his simplicity, knowing that it had not been done with malice, but with pure innocence. After having taken the measures required by the case, [the priest] returned to his rural parish and priesthood with a just punishment. This well-known occurrence was no cruelty, as it clearly would have been passed [without being judged as such] before a learned and Christian tribunal. But who would doubt that whoever might be told of this deed—that a priest tied two Indians up and surrounded them with firewood and lit them on fire and burned them—would say that it was a great cruelty? However, telling it with its circumstances he would not say so, but would instead recognize its simplicity.

He charges that the Spaniards ate the provisions of the Indians and forced them to sustain the Spanish republic, and out of fear of not being able to do so [the Indians] fled to the jungles and forests where great numbers of them died. This offense is satisfied by natural law, for in times of necessity and gravity such as that which our men suffered then, goods are common and are to be made use of as if they were one's own, for there was no quick rescue that they could hope for, nor anywhere to buy [provisions], nor could the provisions they had taken when they set sail from Spain be expected to last so long and assuage their hunger on land, and so it was necessary to sustain themselves and make the Indians bring them supplies. But because it was in so strange a place and so mysterious and unknown to them, it was just and necessary to have compelled them to it [i.e., to steal the Indians' food supplies], for man defeats all things but hunger. Yet [the Indians] are of such quality and nature that so as not to work they place themselves in danger of losing their lives to hunger, eating only fruits and wild roots—how much more to double their labors in their plantings in order to sustain their guests? And it is believed that the Spaniards, while they wished to work with their hands, understood neither the art nor the season of the land, and so it was justified to force [the Indians] to enlarge their fields; and they [must] do so to this day—although [the Indians] may be better Christians and friends—for if the encomendero in charge of the administration of a town does not do this or does not mete out justice, neither the republic of the Spaniards nor that of the Indians could be sustained as it is.

I would like to know what blame the Spaniard and justice should have if these idlers rebel every day, hiding in the jungles, eating and surviving on wild fruits and roots as mentioned. They are of such a condition that when they rebel and become fugitives, they burn their own houses and cut down the crops and fruit trees that they have in their fields, determined to die in the wild and prevent the Spaniard from making use of them [i.e., their crops and houses]. And it is true that if they move from one climate [zone] to another, however short the distance may be in those parts [i.e., the American tropics], even two or four leagues, they later fall ill and die miserably; and the reason is that in hot lands and sea coasts the Indians have wasted away. First, because of the poor disposition and sickness of the land itself, and second, because they trust that since it is hot land they can sleep wherever they want without lacking water and a palm heart, though sweet and tasty, will sicken. And also because in these places their dwellings are dispersed; this does not happen in cold lands as they are congregated in groups where they may recover; and they do not dare abandon their houses, not only because of this, but so that others do not occupy them, fearing the cold. And since [these] lands are cold they are lacking in wild food, and the Indians are better workers; and so they have survived and prospered there in such a manner that we will prove that there are even more of them today than when the Spaniards entered, as we will later give evident reasons.[5] It is true that some have survived in hot lands, but since they work so little they too are wasting away, and [in truth] this is a general rule in hot lands, made worse by the illnesses that overtake them.

He [Las Casas] also charges that the Spaniards take wives and daughters away from the caciques, taking advantage of them and making use of their manual labor. To this I respond with a well-known truth, that the Indians' customs in matrimony were always [nothing more than] a tacit agreement and conformity of wills, without any further ceremony, using this liberty to have up to twenty or thirty wives, and among them there are often a sister, a cousin, or a daughter, and all are used, even the mother. All the women serve and respect the one who is most loved and each night [the caciques] choose with whom they will sleep. Well, considering thirty women married to only one man, and that among them there is only one who is desired while the rest are scorned, it is no surprise that they lay eyes upon the Spaniards, and freely solicit and provoke them. Therefore, it is not such a guilty crime that an incited man has his way with a woman; likewise it is different for a man to receive a woman in his house than go to take her from hers; and if the priest or Spanish encomendero takes one into the service of his house, it is no great offense, as the cacique has so many to serve him, he will not miss one. This, however, rarely happens, and if the cacique is married according to our religion, it is a sure and true thing that there is no encomendero or soldier who would have knowingly taken his wife.

But if this cacique or other Indian has another dozen women more than the one given by the hand of the priest, and among them the sister, daughter, or cousin, with whom he sleeps with no respect for God or the legitimate one, it would be meritorious to take her and separate her from him. But there is the problem that there are many encomenderos who ignore this and take no such action so as to not offend their caciques, and I know of some who are worthy of great punishment for ignoring this, as those who permit it are as guilty as the one who commits the act. Saying that they take their children, I wish to confess this, although this also rarely happens; one should first blame the encomenderos, for they generally do this with little care. Yet they should be permitted to do it, as a million benefits would come of it. First, [the children] would be well indoctrinated in the house of the Spaniard, in our holy faith as well as in all the other customs; second, they are well dressed and cared for; and third, they learn the Spanish language and become accustomed to the Spaniards in such a way that they themselves call their parents and family savages. Because of these servants and children Spaniards have discovered great uprisings planned by the Indians and have avoided them in time, so that they could not succeed. Likewise, if the son of the cacique and lord inherits [anything], he leaves the house of the encomendero with great respect and courtesy, and it is a certain thing that they govern their people better, making them friendly to the Spaniards, showing how much they are indebted to them, and I have heard it from them myself on occasion, and few who have been in the Indies can deny that if the Spaniards had not gone to that land, all would be condemned as idol worshippers and savages; and apart from this they would know nothing of civility [*política*], such as riding a horse or being well-dressed, nor would they have such good and abundant provisions, nor the arts of song and music, reading and writing and knowing how to wield a sword, nor would they know how to paint so curiously, nor work silver and gold, nor the other arts and trades, or any of the other educated and urbane customs; this is addressed often among Indians who attain some sort of thankfulness and nobility, for good works are tied to noble hearts, and as Saint Augustine says, thankfulness must be as great as the benefit received. Such is the harm the Spaniards cause when they take the [Indians'] children into their service, as the bishop of Chiapa[s] exaggerates. If it is a girl, when her parents ask to marry her off, the encomendero is pleased, because the [good] treatment and Christian communication, and the good manners and exercises she carries with her, having learned them from her master, are thereby extended.

Likewise, he [Las Casas] charges that they mistreat the Indians, punishing them, and this I do concede to him, but [they do] not [do it] with the intent he claims. He refers to it as harsh cruelty where it is none other than brotherly punishment and correction, and this is not a general thing done by all Spaniards, but rather only by the administrator, their encomendero, who is responsible for them. And if this is guilt, then the friars and rural parish priests fall into it as well. After all, they and their agents punish [the Indians] for [not] observing doctrine with zeal,[6] their strictness being required due to their evil inclination. And the cause of their punishment is for running away despite being Christians, failing to attend services during holidays. And [they are punished] because they do not send their children to services morning and afternoon during the week, as is customary, taking them away instead so they do not attend. And once it so happened that a priest had been teaching doctrine for two years when he happened upon Indian boys and girls who had been hidden away all that time. At other times they are punished because of complaints by their caciques that they are disobedient, and [for some reason the caciques] do not dare punish them. Others [are punished by the priests] for mistreating their mothers and daughters, lying down with them, and also for things no less blameworthy, such that finally their poor behavior and lack of Christianity require severity. Well, if the missionary priests, so pious, are permitted to punish them, why are their encomenderos and administrators charged and blamed for the same causes and others equally just for having laid hands on them? After all, they are responsible for them and are obligated to punish whatever crimes are brought to their attention, [particularly] if they are unable to pursue justice because it is far away and remote, and thereby avoid other crimes, great or small, upon which the good government and order of their town depend. And so it is not so great a thing if sometimes, moved to anger, incited by the liberties and depraved things that are committed in their presence, [the encomenderos] give them a few slaps on the wrist. And it is a thing of no importance, for in Spain this is often done with house servants. And [in the Indies such punishments] are administered only by the encomendero, no one else daring to do so, nor the Indians consenting to it, for they know well how to exaggerate their complaint to the justice [system], as we have seen;

and we know that if they receive a blow from anyone, they strike others, punching them in the nose so that the blood runs. They spread it over their face, shirt, and garments, and in this state they go before a judge, making a great fuss and a thousand gestures, for they are extremely inventive. And the Spaniard, in order to not be troubled with the justice sought in this manner by the Indian, agrees with him, paying him in gold or blankets, as that is their manner of clothing, for the Indian wants nothing more than to satisfy his greed. His accusation is not made in order to punish the Spaniard whom he accuses of the offense, but rather he aspires only for the pay. They would sell their daughters and wives out of greed for money or clothing or another thing of value, and this goes well with what the bishop says, that they are not greedy. But they are so much so that before God I say it once happened to me that, while walking through a peaceful [i.e., conquered] land, I arrived at a crossroads not knowing which way to go. Asking a nearby Indian which path to take, he responded, "Pay me." And I am quite certain that there are few Spaniards who have wandered these parts to whom the same has not occurred. Well, I wonder if there is any human greed in the world so great that they even wish to sell benevolence, something no other nation does, rather being moved to compassion for the one who does not know and asks and responding graciously and showing him the way. In such a situation, it seems to me that if this were to happen to an honorable Spaniard who does not know the way he is to take, it would be correct if he, being somewhat phlegmatic, were to pay for his guidance and statements; but being choleric, to charge at him with his horse and run him down and force him to tell him regardless, and so that he does not lie or lead him astray, to grab him and make him serve as a guide until they should happen upon someone who can assure that he is going in the right direction.

Concerning their possessions and food, if a Spaniard arrives in need and without money and asks for some necessary thing, I know well that they will not give anything voluntarily without pay regardless of how necessary it is, unless the Spaniard is not already determined to take it away by force, at which time they are silent and let him carry it off; and concerning this there is no one in the Indies who would not confess all of this to be true. And they are commonly referred to as being a cunning people for these and worse things. It is taken for certain that the Devil has ordered them to commit these bad deeds and worse customs. Lacking good communication with the Spaniard, they will not follow our holy faith correctly, and they have made promises to [the Devil] and follow his orders, as they often talk with him. The Devil is so perverse that he may neither do good nor speak nor imagine good, and we suppose that he must always deceive us into being pleased with his actions. And so we see that the Indian will not forget the evil done to him unless it is because of one of two things: either fear of the person who does it, or greed, and when it is greed and not fear, they have an infinity of lies. And so that one may see what they are, I will tell of a thing that happened in the city of Trinidad, in the province of the Muzos in the New Kingdom of Granada as proof. And it so happened, while [I served as] governor in that place and province, that a newly arrived gentleman who still lives there named Juan Juárez de Zepeda, son of Alonso Ruiz Lanchero, an encomendero and conqueror of that province and city, apparently struck or kicked an Indian twice, and nothing more according to the evidence in the case. The Indian, having taken the bit in the teeth, was so troubled that he had three or four family members carry him to the house of the governor, feigning his death. [The effect] was so extreme that the governor was greatly alarmed and took both ordinary and extraordinary actions to revive his Indian, but was unable, the body appearing pale, the eyes turned back, the limbs dislocated and the arms and legs in such a state that they remained in whatever position they were placed, all of which so confused the governor that he resolved to arrest the encomendero and his son, the aggressor. Once captured, he began proceedings against them with great rigor, and looking further into the case, had a doctor summoned who, upon carefully examining [the Indian], found his pulse to be normal.

Having been assured that he was not dead, the governor made use of just the right stratagem, discovering the trickery and lie, and the first thing was to give him a speech, offering that if he were to regain consciousness, he would order the encomendero to give him and his wife a gift of clothing of some importance. And sending for some food, wine, and a bowl of seasoned broth, he poured it into his mouth but [the Indian] remained still and drooled like a dead person. Seeing that his efforts were in vain, he used his first idea, which was to set a handful of straw on fire and bring it close to the Indian who, when he felt it gave a shriek, stood up and began to flee, and it was not so light as to not reach his body. The indignant governor justly tied him up and cut off his hair, along with his accomplices, and they accused [the Indian] and testified that he had killed the foreman of the encomendero with a club. The doctor, upon examining [the foreman], found no signs of life.

This same governor was told of Indians who had been killed in punishment by their administrators in different places, and that they were buried and they swore to it and showed the place; and when he sent constables and scribes with them they found no one, even when they dug up the earth, and they later were found to have fled and the "buried" were fugitives. Once this trickery was verified, he punished the informers and false witnesses, but even in serving them justice he was unable to avoid similar testimonies and lies. Finally, in this manner he discovered and brought the truth to light, avoiding a million treacheries, appearances, and deceptions which, as Saint Augustine says, "Malice and evil cannot blossom long; just as lies and feints soon return to their natural states." The same occurred several times to Dr. Salazar, the oldest-serving president of the royal audiencia of that kingdom [of New Granada], dead Indians being brought into his presence because of abuses by Spanish soldiers, and being revived, a brave custom of theirs.

The truth, naked of all deception or lies, was never observed in this people, and they will continue to be this way as long as they follow the Devil with their idolatries and sacrifices, hanging and killing themselves by the moment for him. Another notable thing which furthers our purpose occurred to this same governor, having been advised by the royal audiencia of Santa Fe that a judge named Dr. Francisco Guillén was coming to visit the land and punish the excesses that had been committed against the Indians, fulfilling royal will and letters patent. He noticed a house in the city that seemed to him a comfortable place to stay, and in order to provide the best and most spacious hospitality, its owner, named Marmolejo, took his entire family to a nearby Indian village where he was encomendero, leaving a room in the kitchen to an Indian servant girl so that she would keep the house and cook for the new guest. It so happened that when the judge and visitor was moving into the house, the girl hanged herself in her room; and when they went looking for her to put the kitchen in order, they found her already dead and hanging from a beam. The visitor was so upset by this scandal that he thought he would lose his judgment [*juicio*], considering that he was to punish apparent excesses caused by the encomenderos and here he saw with his very eyes just how such a spectacle occurred. He quickly sent for the governor and, once he arrived, ordered him to pursue the case and do it justice. The governor answered that he would do it with great care, but that being such a great scholar, he begged to know against whom he should bring his case, if it was to be against the master who left her to guard the house and provide hospitality to him, or against [the judge himself] who received it, or against the Indian girl who hung herself so as not to welcome new people, or against the conqueror or settler of the city. The judge and visitor was left so confused by all this that the case is unresolved to this day, and I doubt that the bishop [i.e., Las Casas] could resolve it (even though he would record it as a cruelty). And who would not judge it so, if it was written simply that this Indian girl hung herself in the house of her Spanish encomendero, without telling the case as it happened, as all the cruelties he claims and tells of are written in his treatise, not telling of the circumstances and reasons behind them?

This case opened the eyes of the judge, though still a greenhorn in the land, to consider all those he had the opportunity to punish, or how closely examining things he found very little blame on the part of the Spaniards, or on the part of the governor who was a great gentleman and Christian, experienced and skilled in the land, as an example of the many deceptions and cunning that the Indians had wished to use with him as with all who govern the Indies. And if I do not present them as evidence in this matter, knowing the ruses, tricks, wiles, lies, and deceptions of the Indians, there is no one who will treat them as credible arguments, and I trust God that those who should finish reading this proof will find that the deception of the Bishop [of Chiapas] is clear.

NOTES

PREFACE

1. Ferguson and Whitehead, *War in the Tribal Zone*.

INTRODUCTORY STUDY

1. On the difficulties at court faced by even such an accomplished dissimulator as Cortés, see J. H. Elliott's introduction to Pagden, *Hernán Cortés*, xi–xxxvii.
2. The most comprehensive study is Anglo, *The Martial Arts of Renaissance Europe*.
3. See Leonard, *Books of the Brave*, esp. chap. 6.
4. Ibid.
5. On Philip's changing fortunes and their consequences for military volunteers such as Vargas Machuca, see Parker, *The Grand Strategy of Philip II*.
6. Solórzano Pereira, *Política Indiana*. The best study of Solórzano in English is Muldoon, *The Americas in the Spanish World Order*. On Vargas Machuca's beasts, see Asúa and French, *A New World of Animals*, 39–42.
7. On the early modern indiano predicament in particular, see Simerka, *Discourses of Empire*. On soldiers' tales in Vargas Machuca's era, see Puddu, *El soldado gentilhombre*.
8. The term is borrowed from Jeremy Adelman, ed., *Colonial Legacies: The Problem of Persistence in Latin American History* (New York: Routledge, 1999), although paramilitary violence is not one of the "persistent problems" cited by contributors.
9. Credit goes to María Luisa Martínez de Salinas for pointing out this section's epigraph in her biography of Vargas Machuca, *Castilla ante el Nuevo Mundo*.
10. Cervantes, *Exemplary Stories*, 147–80.
11. Garcilaso de la Vega, El Inca, *The Royal Commentaries of the Incas and General*

History of Peru. On the plight of Peruvians in sixteenth-century Spain as a general phenomenon, see Merino Hernando, *Historia de los inmigrantes peruanos en España.*

12 The entire text, held by the Royal Library of Denmark, is available online at www.kb.dk/elib/mss/poma/. The definitive critical study is Rolena Adorno's *Guaman Poma.*

13 As Rafael Varón Gabai has shown, the Pizarro legacy was more complex than usually believed. See his *Francisco Pizarro and His Brothers.* Discussion of the Pizarros as *peruleros* is on 5–7.

14 On American sales of Alemán ca. 1600, see Leonard, *Books of the Brave,* chap. 17, "The *Pícaro* Follows the Conquistador." For a class-minded reading of the genre, see Sánchez, *An Early Bourgeois Literature in Golden Age Spain.*

15 A superb overview is Henry Kamen's *Empire.* Kamen quotes Vargas Machuca several times, mostly in reference to the plight of unrequited conquistadors and soldiers.

16 On this and the related pattern of "conquistador" intermarriage with indigenous elites, see Socolow, *The Women of Colonial Latin America,* esp. chaps. 4 and 5; and Burkett, "Indian Women and White Society," 101–28. A revealing case study from just before Vargas Machuca's time is Noble David Cook and Alexandra Parma Cook's *Good Faith and Truthful Ignorance.*

17 In one of his many petitions for crown aid, Vargas Machuca admitted in 1595 of having spent his two wives' dowries to the tune of 30,000 ducats! See Archivo General de Indias (hereafter AGI), Patronato 164, ramo 1:2.

18 In his classic study of the conquerors of Peru, James Lockhart emphasized the utter lack of military experience that marked participants. Most successful conquistadors were not *soldados* (*The Men of Cajamarca,* 17–22). Matthew Restall describes how this changed in the later sixteenth century in his superb critical study *Seven Myths of the Spanish Conquest,* 28–33.

19 For recent reinterpretations of this phenomenon in Mexico, where it was first described, see Schroeder, *Native Resistance and the Pax Colonial in New Spain.*

20 For models and examples of these processes, see Ferguson and Whitehead, eds., *War in the Tribal Zone.* See also Schwartz and Salomon, "New Peoples and New Kinds of People: Adaptation, Readjustment, and Ethnogenesis in South American Indigenous Societies (Colonial Era)," in *The Cambridge History of the Native Peoples of the Americas,* 3:443–501.

21 See Robert Padden's 1957 article, "Cultural Adaptation and Militant Autonomy among the Araucanians of Chile," 71–91; and Jones, "Warfare, Reorganization, and Readaptation at the Margins of Spanish Rule," 138–87.

22 See Toribio Medina, ed., *Colección de documentos inéditos para la historia de Chile,* 5:119–32.

23 On Spanish attempts to dislodge the Esmeraldas maroons, see Lane, *Quito 1599,* chaps. 1 and 6.

24 Archivo General de la Nación, Bogotá, Colombia (hereafter AGNC), Historia Civil 1, fols. 83–130.
25 Detailed studies of this institution in colonial Colombia include Ruiz Rivera, *Encomienda y mita en Nueva Granada*, and Padilla, López, and González, *La encomienda en Popayán*. On the origins of the institution, see Haring, *Spanish Empire in America*, chap. 1.
26 For a detailed examination of the Spanish participants, including commoners, see Avellaneda, *The Conquerors of the New Kingdom of Granada*.
27 The best study of population decline in the central highlands is Francis, "Población, enfermedad y cambio demográfico." On the nature of indigenous polities in this region upon Spanish arrival, see, for example, Tovar Pinzón, *No hay caciques ni señores*, and for early Colombia more generally, see Villamarín and Villamarín, "Chiefdoms."
28 On this controversial matter, see Caillavet, "Antropofagia y frontera: El caso de los Andes septentrionales," in *Frontera y poblamiento*, 57–109, and Herman Trimborn's classic study, *Señorío y barbarie en el Valle del Cauca*.
29 On gold, see the classic study by Robert C. West, *Colonial Placer Mining in Colombia*.
30 Similar legends of the "Great Moxo," "Paititi," and "Candire" survived, however, in eastern Bolivia and Paraguay.
31 On these competing El Dorado expeditions, see Neil L. Whitehead's richly annotated edition of *The Discoverie of the Large, Rich, and Bewtiful Empyre of Guiana by Sir Walter Ralegh*, especially 39–45. On the El Dorado legend generally, see Hemming, *The Search for Eldorado* and Magasich-Airola and de Beer, *America Magica*.
32 The best examination of Pacific Coast struggles is C. Williams, *Between Resistance and Adaptation*.
33 Otero D'Acosta, "Biográfica disertación sobre el capitán don Bernardo de Vargas Machuca." This was an expanded version of an earlier biographical study published in Bogotá in 1927.
34 Ibid., 49.
35 Macleod, "Self-promotion"; and Restall, *Seven Myths of the Spanish Conquest*, 12–14.
36 Martínez de Salinas, *Castilla ante el Nuevo Mundo*, 12. The well-known Mexican bullfight historian Benjamín Flores Hernández has followed the openly celebratory tone of Otero D'Acosta in his several articles on Vargas Machuca's life and achievements. See, for example, his "Bernardo de Vargas Machuca y el Caribe." Flores Hernández's unpublished 1987 Universidad Autónoma de Méjico (UNAM) PhD dissertation, like Martínez de Salinas's, was a full-length biography.
37 See *Milicia y descripción de las Indias*, ed. Domingo and López-Rios Fernández, and *Milicia y descripción de las Indias, Escrita por el Capitan D. Bernardo de Vargas Machuca*, ed. Langeback. The Japanese edition is part of a series of

translations of sixteenth-century Spanish texts called "Challenge of the New World."

38 Archivo Histórico de Protocolos de Madrid (hereafter AHPM), Signatura 3029, fols. 490–524.

39 This is what Vargas Machuca later claimed in his many merit reports, but Martínez de Salinas notes that his license to leave Spain lists him as a *criado*, or squire, in the service of Mexican audiencia judge Antonio Maldonado (*Castilla ante el nuevo mundo*, 34). The license is in AGI Contratación 5538, Libro 1, fols. 123v–124 (Martínez de Salinas mistakenly gives folios as 119v–120, perhaps based on an older marking system).

40 Many of Ortega's letters detailing this war are available in Jopling, *Indios y negros en Panamá en los siglos XVI y XVII*, 357–409, but I could find no mention of anyone named Vargas Machuca (a list of participants in the Bayano War is on 365–66).

41 On the Chiriguano frontier in this period, see Renard Casevitz and Saignes, "Los piedemontes orientales de los Andes centrales y meridionales: Desde los Patagua hasta los Chiriguano," 167–79.

42 AGI Patronato 164, ramo 1, no. 3.

43 AGI Patronato 253, ramo 1. The document is reproduced in facsimile in González García, *Discovering the Americas*, 206.

44 AGNC Historia Civil 12, fols. 718–36 (1595); 22, fols. 887–972 (1590). In his 1590 petition, Vargas Machuca says he came to New Granada "a buscar algo en que ocuparme" (looking for something in which to occupy myself), fol. 889.

45 His father-in-law was Rodrigo López Cerón. Grandfather Lázaro López de Salazar had come to New Granada with Jerónimo Lebrón in the late 1530s. J. Michael Francis notes that in 1600 the village of Motavita had a tributary population of 144 male heads of household who owed annual rents of 560 pesos in thirteen-karat gold. See Francis, "Población, enfermedad y cambio demográfico, 1537–1636," 82.

46 "So-called" because as in so many parts of the Americas, the Carares appear to have been a neotribe, or at least in part an ethnic product of the contact zone. Many Carares were likely refugees from other regions, along with some captives and their descendants. Toward the end of the colonial period some men said to be Carares were described as Afro-indigenous or mulatto.

47 AGNC Historia Civil 22, fols. 887–972.

48 For a thorough description of this punishing labor system in Vargas Machuca's day, see Gomez, *L'envers de l'Eldorado*.

49 AGNC Historia Civil, 22, fol. 937: "a la ligera y sin comyda."

50 AGNC Historia Civil 22, fols. 938v–942v: "caneyes . . . en donde los dichos yndios se dexaron quemar antes de rendirse," "con un tiçon les pego fuego."

51 Tovar Pinzón, *Relaciones y Visitas a los Andes (Siglo XVI)*, 3:446: "Al salir en las primeras sierras topó un canei que es casa de yndios, defendiéronsele los que en ella estaban prendió catorze o quinze y estos no salteaban ni llegaban al Rio grande ni tenín prenda en Hespañoles, ahorcó a dos mugeres, una cria-

tura de teta la pusieron en un cataure que es lo mismo que sestillo, cubierto de palmicha para que allí los padres a los gritos acudiesen y la criasen y un soldado llamado Carnero que el Audiencia echó a galeras este año de seiscientos y uno llegó con la cuerda encendida y le puso fuego." On the matter of the Moses-like incident with the child in the rushes, see the next incident; this was apparently a distortion of the story of the drowning later recalled by Vargas Machuca.

52 AGNC Historia Civil 17:7 (1559). The sentence is described on fol. 784. In this case, a man identified only as Rodríguez Juárez of the mining town of Pamplona, near modern Bucaramanga, was charged with burning indigenous people in their huts, feeding others to dogs; forcing his men to rape indigenous women, especially virgin girls; impaling indigenous men and leaving them to die; and other such atrocities. His rage was said to have been provoked in 1557 when he discovered that the Indians of his encomiendas of Batagua and Catagua were not panning gold in the desired quantities (fol. 698v). He escaped from jail in Bogotá as crown magistrates heard the bishop's appeal for clemency.

53 Although at the outset Vargas Machuca calls his response to Las Casas *Defensa de las conquistas occidentales*, the work was published in 1879 under the title *Apologías y discursos de las Conquistas Occidentales*, in Sancho Rayón and Zabalburu, *Colección de documentos inéditos para la historia de España*, 71:245–46. See appendix 2.

54 Ibid., 247.

55 Ibid. This incident is mentioned by Lewis Hanke in an extended review of Ramón Menéndez Pidal's monumental 1963 biography, *El Padre Las Casas: Su doble personalidad*. Hanke takes issue with Menéndez Pidal, who in criticizing Las Casas suggests he would have condemned Vargas Machuca to hell. See "More Heat and Some Light." Hanke mentions the *Defense of Western Conquests* again in "The Meaning Today of the Las Casas Treatises Published in 1552," 100.

56 See part 7, chap. 53 of Simón, *Noticias historiales de las conquistas de Tierra Firme en las Indias Occidentales*, 4:384. A fortress was built on Carare Island about the time Simón was writing, but this was not where Vargas Machuca had set fire to the village.

57 AHPM Sig. 3029, fol. 502bis. Son Alvaro Félix de Vargas seemed not to have any details on these mines, although they were presumably located near Muzo. The will states: "He declared that the said don Bernardo, his father, left some emerald mines, and demanded they be accounted for by the person or persons who have been in charge of them so that the part pertaining to his said father be established and payment made." It is unlikely the claims could have been recovered, since under Spanish law mines not worked within a year of being staked were forfeited.

58 Vargas Machuca filed a posthumous will for his first wife, María Cerón, in Bogotá on April 6, 1591, AGNC Notarías 2:10, fols. 352–53. She was buried in Franciscan habit in the chapel of Our Lady of Chiquinquirá, near which she

owned a sizeable *estancia*, or country estate, but the will stipulates that her remains be moved to a new church already planned to commemorate this, Colombia's most important marian apparition. One hundred masses were said for her soul. Her heirs were her three small children ("de poca edad"), but Vargas Machuca was of course named administrator. Within a month of filing his wife's will, he sold her estate, which included a wheat farm, herb garden, corral, cattle, sheep, mares, and mules, plus shared pasture rights, for 1,500 pesos of taxed and stamped twenty-karat gold. The place was also said to produce truffles (*turmas*), probably a reference to potatoes. The buyer was a family friend, Andrés Sánchez Carrión. AGNC Notarías 2:7 (unclear foliation). There are probably more such filings in the regional Archive of Boyacá in Tunja, which I have sampled only briefly for the 1580s.

59 See Lane, *Quito 1599*, chap. 3.
60 These campaigns are briefly elaborated by Martínez de Salinas in *Castilla ante el Nuevo Mundo*, but the sources are the same service reports mentioned above, housed in Seville and Bogotá.
61 On these events in Quito, and for a thorough discussion of the problem of restless soldiers in the northern Andes, see Lavallé, *Quito et la crise de l'Alcabala*. The strange case of Polo Palomino, who narrowly escaped the noose, is discussed on 174.
62 Restrepo, "A Place to Live, a Place to Think, and a Place to Die."
63 Friede, *Los Andakí*.
64 Park's attack is described in AGI Panamá 45:12 (February 15, 1601). On the duties of *alcaldes mayores* and other officials, see Haring, *The Spanish Empire in America*, chap. 8.
65 On this process, see Ward, *Imperial Panama*, chap. 6.
66 In July 1603 Vargas Machuca complained that after he filed a negative report on his predecessor everyone in the region was "passionately against me," AGI Panamá 45:45 (July 17, 1603).
67 Martínez de Salinas, *Castilla ante el Nuevo Mundo*, 97–101.
68 AGI Santo Domingo 182, ramo 4.
69 AGI Santo Domingo 180, 6:31.
70 Martínez de Salinas, *Castilla ante el Nuevo Mundo*, 162. On disease, see AGI Santo Domingo 182, ramo 5.
71 AGI Santo Domingo 180, 6:32 and 182, ramo 5. The strange case of Francisco Congo is recounted in Santo Domingo 180, 6:45.
72 Vargas Machuca admitted as much in a letter to the Indies Council, saying that "although it is true that on this island of Margarita they have not touched me, nor dared attempt to, they could easily do such a shameful thing tomorrow." AGI Santo Domingo 180, 6:44.
73 AGI Santo Domingo 182, ramo 4 (October 1609).
74 AGI Santo Domingo 182, ramo 5.
75 Again, for details on these bureaucratic procedures see Haring, *Spanish Empire*, chap. 8.

76 His will notes also a house lot on the Santo Domingo Plaza in Asunción, Margarita, and an enslaved African laundress named Maria, both to be sold at auction to cover debts (AHPM Sig. 3029, fol. 499).
77 A number of early works in this vein are examined by Antonio Barrera-Osorio in *Experiencing Nature*.
78 Lupher, *Romans in a New World*.
79 MacCormack, *On the Wings of Time*.
80 See, for example, Hall, *Weapons and Warfare in Renaissance Europe*, and Hale, *War and Society in Renaissance Europe*.
81 See, for example, Malone, *The Skulking Way of War*, and Chet, *Conquering the American Wilderness*.
82 Guevara, *Guerrilla Warfare*. On "Medical Problems," see chap. 3, part 4.
83 See, for example, U.S. Army Field Manual 100-20/Air Force Pamphlet 3-20.
84 Cuesta Domingo and López-Ríos Fernández, "Estudio introductorio," 29–39. For more details on these texts, see Amasuno, *La Materia Médica de Dioscorides en el Lapidario de Alfonso X el sabio*, and Jarcho, "Medicine in Sixteenth-Century New Spain." On European medical arts and their Hippocratic and Galenic foundations, see French, *Medicine Before Science*.
85 *Milicia Indiana* (2003 Valladolid ed.), 30.
86 For a reprint of the 1577 English edition, see Monardes, *Joyfull Newes out of the Newe Founde Worlde*.
87 For an annotated translation of a portion of Hernández's massive corpus accompanied by informative essays, see Varey, *The Mexican Treasury*, and Varey, Chabrán, and Weiner, *Searching for the Secrets of Nature*. On medical regulation in the Spanish colonies from the earliest days to independence, see Lanning, *The Royal Protomedicato*.
88 The scribe's copy of the royal publication license follows a power of attorney to the merchant.
89 Benjamín Flores Hernández studies this text in some detail in "*La jineta indiana* en los textos de Juan Suárez de Peralta y Bernardo de Vargas Machuca." His main point is that Vargas Machuca identified and promoted a specifically "American" style of light cavalry, already highly developed by 1600.
90 Anglo, *The Martial Arts of Renaissance Europe* (the rise and fall of the Spanish masters is treated in most detail on 66–73).
91 On this and other Spanish tilting treatises, see ibid., 229–43. For closer examination of the medieval knightly manual in Spain, see Fallows, *The Chivalric Vision of Alfonso de Cartagena*. In structure if not content, Vargas Machuca's *Milicia Indiana* closely resembles Cartagena's mid-fifteenth-century compendium.
92 AGI Patronato 164, ramo 1:2.
93 A classic, if highly romantic, study of the conquistador gineta is Cunninghame Graham, *The Horses of the Conquest*.
94 There is at least one last item of interest: the author's final comments on horse color and physiognomy sound almost racial, for example: "El caballo hovero

es galán pellejo, pero desbaydo en la travazón del cuerpo, y por la mayor parte flojo, mal sano, y mala boca. El caballo rosillo, cabeza de moro, es recio de boca, y el que acierta es bueno, pero no galán. El caballo zayno en las Indias aprueva bien, y acá mal" (117v).

95 For a venerable and graceful translation, see Díaz del Castillo, *The Conquest of New Spain*.

96 Vargas Machuca even wrote a dedicatory sonnet for the opening of the second part of Castellanos's great work, first published in 1589. See Castellanos, *Elegías de varones ilustres de Indias*, 349. Interestingly, despite Castellanos's carrying of the story of New Granadan conquest to 1592, Vargas Machuca never makes the cut as a "varón ilustre."

97 A likely possibility was Francisco de Encinas's 1551 edition, sold under the title *Las vidas de ilustres y excelentes varones Griegos y Romanos* (published in Strasbourg and Cologne), but Plutarch had been available in Spanish since 1491.

APPROVALS, DEDICATIONS, AND SONNETS

1 Johannes de Sacrobosco, author of *De Sphaera*, ca. 1230 CE.
2 Greco-Roman god of medicine, but also refers to any student of healing arts.
3 In the original, "tanto Cortesano," to play on Cortés's name.

BOOK ONE

1 Vargas Machuca explains these various names for people living at opposite ends of the earth (with variant spellings) in his "Compendium," 234). It was common well before Vargas Machuca's time to assume inhabitants of different parts of the earth's surface were subject to variant astrological forces. See Wey-Gómez, *Tropics of Empire*.

2 *Capacetes*: Spanish helmets with a turned-down brim and an almond-shaped skull; *corazas*: steel body armor for chest and back; *braceletes*: armor for the lower arm; *grevas*: armor for the leg from the knee to the ankle. For an illustrated catalogue, see Calvert, *Spanish Arms and Armour*. Also useful is Hoffmeyer, *Arms and Armour in Spain*, and Peterson, *Arms and Armor in Colonial America*.

3 On these early guns, originally called *hacabuches*, see Lavin, *A History of Spanish Firearms*, 41–47. The *mosquete* of this period was simply a heavier version of the harquebus (47–49). *Coseletes*: light armor consisting of gorget (*gola*), breast and back plates (*peto* and *espaldar*), tasset or cuishe (*escarcela*), vambraces, and visor (*celada*).

4 *Sayos de armas*: battle tunics.

5 *Espadas anchicortas*: short, wide swords.

6 *Cueras de ante*: buffalo hide jackets.

7 On canine conquistadors, see Varner and Varner, *Dogs of the Conquest.*
8 *Yerba de veinticuatro horas*, i.e., poison (not necessarily herbal) that kills in twenty-four hours. For earlier descriptions of indigenous weapons in northern Colombia, see J. Michael Francis's annotated translation of Gonzalo Jiménez de Quesada and other conquistadors in *Invading Columbia*, 73–74.
9 *Vija* or *bija*: body paint; *jagua*: fruit of *jachalí*.
10 A reference to leaves of the *Erythroxylum coca* bush (var. *novogranatense*), a common Andean stimulant.
11 Alonso de Ercilla (1533–94), author of the epic poem of Chile's early Mapuche Wars, *La Araucana*, first published in 1569, was widely read in both Spain and the colonies. The reference is to the warrior chieftain Lautaro.
12 Vargas Machuca here carries on the convention dating to Columbus's time of seeing the Americas as primarily south rather than west of Europe and the Mediterranean. See Wey-Gómez, *Tropics of Empire.*
13 Pre-Columbian missionary visits were a frequent discussion topic in both Spain and its colonies. In the New Granada of Vargas Machuca's time, Jesuits Alonso de Medrano and Francisco de Figueroa mentioned in a 1598 letter that the bones of St. James's llama (!) were thought by some to be located in Muisca country; see Francis, "Descripción del Nuevo Reino de Granada."
14 The reference is apparently to piratical attacks such as those carried out by Vargas Machuca's contemporary and first foe in the Indies, Francis Drake. See Andrews, *The Spanish Caribbean*, and Kelsey, *Francis Drake.*
15 Hospitals for wounded veterans were becoming common in Spanish towns and cities, including Vargas Machuca's hometown of Simancas, about this time. Colonial hospitals rarely served such a specialized purpose.
16 For statistics on treasure flowing out of Spanish America—and especially New Granada—in Vargas Machuca's time, see Sluiter, *The Gold and Silver of Spanish America.*
17 Presumably a reference to late Roman Emperor Theodosius (r. 379–95 CE), who oversaw the shift to Christianity. The Theodosians are mentioned in many ecclesiastical histories, so it is difficult to know precisely where Vargas Machuca read of them. On Theodosian warfare, see S. Williams and Friell, *Theodosius.*
18 Blasphemy was punished by the Inquisition in Vargas Machuca's time. See Villa-Flores, *Dangerous Speech.*
19 For Cortés's version of this encounter, see Pagden, *Hernán Cortés*, 115–27.
20 For definitions of these terms, see the "Declaration," 234–37.
21 Cotton cord for igniting a charge with a matchlock mechanism.
22 From about the time of Columbus, Spanish subjects were ordered to introduce breeding pairs of swine, cattle, and other livestock whenever entering "new" lands. On the effects of this policy, see Crosby, *The Columbian Exchange*, 74–113.
23 In the original, "Villano del Danubio." Vargas Machuca is referring to the popular title of a fictional speech composed by Charles V's Franciscan chap-

lain, Antonio de Guevara, first published in 1528 in *El libro aúreo del emperador Marco Aurelio*. The story, about a German peasant outraged by greedy and cruel Roman conquistadors, circulated in manuscript form by 1524, and was published a second time in 1529 in a collection called *Reloj de príncipes*. Vargas Machuca turns this tale, intended as a metaphor of the archetypal injured American Indian pleading for mercy before the Holy Roman Emperor, entirely on its head. He compares the peasant instead to the injured *indiano*, the unrequited Spanish conquistador as victim. On the early reception of this story, see Lupher, *Romans in a New World*, 50–56.

24 King of Sparta. The story is probably taken from Plutarch's *Lives* (ca. 110 CE). Here and throughout we refer to the two-volume Dryden translation edited by Clayton M. Lehman (New York: Barnes & Noble, 2006); see 2:44–76.

25 Pedro de Valdivia, conquistador of Chile, was said to have died this way at the hands of the Mapuche chieftain Lautaro following the Battle of Tucapel in 1553. An early (ca. 1558) alternative version of this incident is related in Vívar, *Crónica de los reinos de Chile*, 290–91.

26 The term *montaña* was used throughout the Spanish tropics to refer to areas covered by rain or cloud forest.

27 This is a reference to *tungiasis*, or foot infections caused by burrowing chiggers.

28 "Lagartos que cuelgan por las iglesias," presumably a reference to a famous stuffed crocodile (a replica of which can still be seen) that hangs above a patio-covered side door of Seville's cathedral near the famous Giralda tower. This "lizard" was said to have been given to King Alfonso X "the Wise" in the year 1260 by one Kutuz, Mamluk sultan of Cairo, in hopes of winning the hand of the former's daughter, Berenguela. This offering, which also included a giraffe, is noted in the ca. 1350 history of Alfonso's reign. See O'Callaghan, *Chronicle of Alfonso X*, 47. Crocodile amulets and ex-votos date to Egyptian times, and many imaginative variations on the lizard theme joined gargoyles in Gothic and Renaissance architecture to help ward off evil spirits.

29 A reference to Cortés's destruction of ships at Veracruz so that his men would have no choice but to follow him to Mexico. For Cortés's own version of events, see Pagden, *Letters from Mexico*, 52.

30 The Muiscas of Colombia's eastern highlands were often called "moscas," or flies, in early Spanish documents. This was probably a corruption of the Chibcha term *moxca*, which apparently meant "man" or "person." See Langebaek, *Mercados, poblamiento e integración étnica entre los Muiscas*.

31 Vargas Machuca apparently confuses Pompey with Cornelius Sulla (138–78 BCE). See Plutarch's life of Caius Marius (*Lives*, 1:604–41), from which Vargas Machuca probably also drew his next, erroneous example.

32 *Cimbrios*, or "Cimbri," enemies of the Romans mentioned by Plutarch in his life of Caius Marius, although the reference may also be to their alleged ancestors, the Cimmerians, whom Alexander fought. Vargas Machuca appears

to have an alternative version of Alexander's death in mind, too, since Plutarch and most other sources say he died of fever or poisoning.

33 The reference is to the murderous factionalism that grew out of disagreements between Francisco Pizarro and Diego de Almagro. For an early account of this troubled relationship, see Cook and Cook's annotated translation of Pedro de Cieza de León's *Discovery and Conquest of Peru*. Part 1 was originally published in 1553.

34 In the original, "Focideles." The reference is presumably to the so-called Melian Debate; see book 5, chapter 17 of Thucydides, *The Pelopponesian War*, 227–31.

35 Vargas Machuca seems to be continuing his earlier complaints about unworthy governors.

36 The Neapolitan Fernando Francesco de Avalos (1490–1525), Marquis di Pescara, led Charles V's forces against the French under Francis I, securing victory at Pavia, near Milan, against great odds.

37 This is Vargas Machuca's own interpretation of the 1532 capture of the Inca Atawallpa, described even by willing participants as a Spanish ambush. See Cieza de León, *Discovery and Conquest of Peru*, 209–13. For a modern narrative constructed from this and other original sources, see Hemming, *The Conquest of the Incas*, 23–45.

38 The natives of the city-state of Tlaxcalla, near modern Puebla, Mexico, became Cortés's main allies before the arrival of Narváez and his followers. On the role of these and other "friendly Indians," see Restall, *Seven Myths of the Spanish Conquest*, 46–49.

39 On the art of dissimulation leading up to Vargas Machuca's time, see Martin, "Inventing Sincerity, Refashioning Prudence."

BOOK TWO

1 Vargas Machuca probably has in mind the failed 1560 Amazon mission of Pedro de Ursúa and Lope de Aguirre, which included the former's mistress and the latter's daughter. The tale is recounted by Fray Pedro Simón and many others, but for an excellent interpretive account in English, see Minta, *Aguirre*.

2 A reference to the so-called *repúblicas*, or legally separate worlds, of *españoles* and *indios* created in sixteenth-century Spanish America; see Haring, *Spanish Empire in America*, chapters 2 and 3. It may also be worth noting that much of this discussion of Cortés is in the present tense despite his having died some fifty years before Vargas Machuca was writing.

3 Either *Ipomoea jalapa* or *Exogonium purga*, both Mexican cathartic roots. For contemporary references to these and similar remedies, see the introductory study.

4 *Trattinnickia aspera*. The chemical identity of the Buga stone, described below

as a powerful astringent, remains unclear, but was probably a variety of alum. Its origin was presumably near the town of Guadalajara de Buga, along the Cauca River northeast of Cali. It appears in later Peruvian pharmacopeia.

5 As Jarcho notes ("Medicine in Sixteenth-Century New Spain," 440), Acosta described the worst symptoms of altitude sickness, or hypoxia, in his widely read 1590 *Natural and Moral History of the Indies*; see the edition edited by Jane E. Mangan and translated by Frances López-Morillas, 119–21. Most Spaniards in New Granada were not exposed to the extreme altitudes (15,000-feet-plus) typical of travel in Peru and Bolivia, but passes well over 10,000 feet above sea level were common.

6 An almost identical procedure, fishhook and all, is described by Fray Pedro de Aguado in his unpublished but widely circulated manuscript history of New Granada from around 1582. The description is in the midst of a section on the native peoples of the Middle Magdalena region, with whom Vargas Machuca was most familiar. See Aguado, *Recopilación historial*, 2:23–24.

7 Juice of cooked tobacco.

8 Probably *Piper hipsidum Sw.*, described by Vargas Machuca in his brief glossary as "a flower of a bush that serves as antivenin." (The crushed leaf rather than root juice is still prescribed in Ecuador and Peru.)

9 Native peoples living along the margins of the Guali River, which flows into the Magdalena at Honda, long resisted forced labor in gold mines near the town of Mariquita. The "war" in question was in fact the Spanish annihilation of the Gualis that came in response to a 1574 uprising. See Simón, *Noticias historiales de las conquistas de Tierra Firme en las Indias Occidentales*, 4:261–66, and Castellanos, *Elegías de varones ilustres de Indias*, 1382–86.

10 Probably sarsaparilla or *guayacán* (*lignum sanctum*), both popular, if ineffective, syphilis remedies.

11 In its original, *masçato*; a shakelike beverage made from mashed rice, cornmeal, or plantain.

12 Both enslaved and free paramedics and phlebotemists of African or part African descent were common throughout the Spanish colonies by Vargas Machuca's time. Native Americans also practiced both trades soon after conquest and were sometimes individually famous for their skill. See TePaske, "Regulation of Medical Practitioners in the Age of Francisco Hernández," 60.

13 *Yuca brava*, i.e., *Manihot* flour not cleansed of naturally occurring prussic acid.

14 *Albayalde*, or lead acetate; used by the ancient Romans to sweeten wine.

15 Diachylon was a decoction of iris, "oil of mucilage," and litharge. Diapalma was made up of litharge, white vitriol, wax, oil, and young shoots of the palm tree, whence its name.

16 Colonial Catholics relied on a number of these "holy incantations to cure wounds." Pedro de Aguado mentions this in a passage on the conquest of Muzo headed by Luis Lanchero in his *Recopilación historial*, 2:275: "Fueron

todos curados por mano del propio Lanchero, con el beneficio de cierto devoto ensalmo que les decía, y así no murió ninguno" [they were all cured by the hand of Lanchero himself, with the aid of a certain holy incantation he recited for them, and thus not one died].

17 *Mosquete*, a cumbersome sixteenth-century version of the musket. See Lavin, *History of Spanish Firearms*, 48.
18 Vargas Machuca elaborates considerably on these matters in his equestrian manual, *Exercicios de la gineta*, which expanded in the course of three editions between 1600 and 1621.
19 Agave or aloe, respectively.
20 Apparently referring to the seed-pod cotton of the common sea hibiscus.
21 In the original, "*principal conquista*." Vargas Machuca's intention appears ironic, as "principal" means both "first" and "main."
22 The reference is to certain types of chicha that were brewed in buried containers to control temperature.
23 Presumably a reference to the difficulty of herding these small, slow animals when mounted.
24 The conquest of Muzo, New Granada's main emerald region, is described by Fray Pedro Simón in part 7, chapter 19 of his 1625 *Noticias historiales de las conquistas de Tierra Firme en las Indias Occidentales*, 4:190–94. The decisive role of "perros bravos" in Capt. Luis Lanchero's expeditions of 1558 and 1559 is noted on 193. An earlier version of this story is told by Fray Pedro de Aguado in book 12 of his *Recopilación historial*, 2:205–342.
25 Dogs used in such expeditions were often outfitted with steel neck guards and padded cotton body armor. See Varner and Varner, *Dogs of the Conquest*, frontispiece.

BOOK THREE

1 The example is apparently drawn from Plutarch's life of Fabius (*Lives*, 1:266).
2 In the original, "quien te dize la copla, esse te la echa," a variation on the proverb "quien te dice la copla, ese te la hace." *Coplas* are four-line rhymes.
3 Vargas Machuca participated in Berrío's two Eldorado expeditions in the 1580s. These are briefly summarized in Hemming, *The Search for El Dorado*, 151–82. We have found no reference in other works to "comrades" Pérez and Chacón.
4 In colonial times, an *arroba* was roughly 12–14 kilograms, or 25–30 pounds.
5 The incident is noted in *The Alexandrian Wars* (vol. 3 of the *Commentaries*), but Vargas Machuca was more likely to have read of it in Plutarch's life of Caesar (*Lives*, 2:251).
6 The Spanish belief that indigenous Americans took them for gods dates to Columbus's time. The "white god" legend is discussed in detail by Restall in *Seven Myths of the Spanish Conquest*, 112–20; and in Townsend, "Burying the White Gods."

7 Standard war cry invoking St. James the Moor-slayer, patron saint of Spain.
8 In the text, "Calceratidas." The incident in question was the Battle of Agucinae (406 BCE), toward the end of the Peloponnesian War. Vargas Machuca likely drew the exemplum from Plutarch, who describes Callicratidas's noble death in contrast to his predecessor, Lysander (*Lives*, 1:645–46).
9 An obscure quote, possibly taken from a version of Livy's *History of Rome*.
10 The example is most likely drawn from Herodotus's account of Xerxes's 480 BCE attack on Greece. See Herodotus, *The Histories*, 418–21.
11 Known as the "Laughing Philosopher," Democritus of Abdera (ca. 450–370 BCE) was known both for his theory of atoms and for his many clever aphorisms. We have not been able to locate the source of this one, although it may have appeared in a Spanish version of Aristotle's writings.
12 The Battle of Cannae, one of imperial Rome's greatest defeats during the Punic Wars, took place in 216 BCE. The reference is most likely drawn from Plutarch's life of Fabius (*Lives*, 1:271). Here also Plutarch stresses again and again Hannibal's cunning tactics and stratagems.
13 Pedro de Betanzos (d. 1570) was among the first Franciscans active in Central America and a master of Mayan languages. Vargas Machuca apparently learned of him in a sermon or other oral form or from Gerónimo de Mendieta, whose *Historia eclesiástica indiana* was composed in 1596 and widely circulated in manuscript.
14 In the original, "requerido al Indio con la paz," a reference to the so-called *requerimiento*, a speech delivered by law to all native peoples prior to engagement in battle. For a thorough discussion of this conquest tradition, see Seed, *Ceremonies of Possession*, 69–99.
15 Native people of Colombia's Central Cordillera against whom Vargas Machuca fought in the early 1590s. See the introduction.

BOOK FOUR

1 The reference is to the encomienda system, at this time inheritable for two generations, or "vidas." Holders of encomiendas were called *encomenderos* (see introduction).
2 Here and below, Vargas Machuca follows and elaborates on Philip II's 1573 codification of laws regarding town founding in newly conquered areas. See Kinsbruner, *The Colonial Spanish American City*, 23–29.
3 The *Santa Hermandad*, a militia-like rural police in the fifteenth through nineteenth centuries.
4 Apparently referring to the north Andean *páramo*, or barren moorlands above about 3,000 meters.
5 The reference is most likely from Herodotus, *Histories*, 236–39.
6 Known in English as Denis the Farmer, Dom Dinis ruled Portugal from 1279 to 1325.
7 The reference is to the early Ottoman sultan Selim I (1512–20), famous for

absorbing Mamluk Egypt and its vast dominions by 1517 and also expanding Turkish influence well into Safavid Azerbaizhan, with its capital of Tabriz.

8 That is, "worthless nobles." The original reference is to petty nobles who served as common soldiers but with special, unearned rank in the royal armada and other armed units.

9 The reference probably comes from Plutarch's life of Romulus, whose founding of Rome is described in detail (*Lives*, 1:35–38).

10 The reference is to the "lost colony" of La Navidad, destroyed in 1492 or 1493 by the Taínos of Hispaniola.

11 A land allotment of varying size (usually about 42 hectares), given to those who contributed to the conquest or colonization.

12 *Quintos reales*, one-fifth of treasure found or discovered, paid to the king.

13 Vargas Machuca is here running together disparate incidents from the late thirteenth, late fifteenth, and early sixteenth centuries (specifically the Sicilian Vespers and Italian Wars).

14 The reference may be drawn from Machiavelli's *History of Florence*, but this could have been common knowledge given Vargas Machuca's personal experience in Italy.

15 This passage is cited as an example of Spanish promotion of market activity as a tool of conquest by John H. Parry and Robert G. Keith in their edited collection *New Iberian World*, 1:332–34.

16 In the original, "Norandino." The reference, possibly drawn from the contemporary hagiography *Flos Sanctorum*, is to the Turkish *atabeg* Nur ad-Din of Aleppo (1118–74 CE), known for his merciful treatment of Christians captured in his siege of Damascus and elsewhere during the early Crusades.

17 Vargas Machuca is probably drawing from Plutarch's life of Caesar, which mentions his liberality with soldiers several times (*Lives*, 2:228–29).

18 In original "Rusianico." The 334 BCE Battle of Granicus (near Troy) was Alexander's first major victory over the Persians. The reference is probably from Plutarch (*Lives*, 2:163–65).

19 Lycurgus was King of Sparta in the seventh century BCE, and is famous for his strict law codes favoring the military. The reference is probably from Plutarch (*Lives*, 1:77).

20 Publius Valerius Publicola (aka "Poplicola," or "People lover") was one of the Roman Republic's first consuls in the sixth century BCE. The reference is probably from Plutarch's life of Publicola (*Lives*, 1:157).

21 Marcus Furius Camillus, "Second Founder of Rome," was a five-time dictator in the fourth century BCE. The reference is probably from Plutarch's life of Camillus (*Lives*, 1:205).

22 Scipio's siege of Carthage in 146 BCE ended the Punic Wars. The reference may be from Livy, although this event was mentioned by many Renaissance authors, including Machiavelli (e.g., book 7 of his *Art of War*).

23 An obscure reference, possibly to an incident witnessed by Vargas Machuca on the Dora River near Turin in the early 1570s.

A BRIEF DESCRIPTION OF THE INDIES

1 Probably today's Belle Isle Strait, separating Newfoundland from Labrador between 51 and 52 degrees N latitude. The region had been colonized by Basque whalers and fishermen (most of them Spanish subjects) by Vargas Machuca's time.

2 "Southern Sea" refers to the Pacific Ocean. Here, as elsewhere, Vargas Machuca is somewhat confused regarding the Orinoco, Amazon, and Plate basins.

3 Guatemala has numerous volcanoes, but here Vargas Machuca is referring to Agua, which caused a massive mudflow in 1541.

4 Apparently a reference to the Nevado de Tolima, a 5,280-meter (17,000-foot) volcano that towers above modern Pereira, Colombia, original site of Cartago.

5 Could refer to the volcanoes Pichincha, Cotopaxi, or Tungurahua, all of which experienced recorded eruptions in the sixteenth century.

6 Possibly referring to El Misti (5,822 meters/19,000 feet), but nearby Huaynaputina Volcano is known to have erupted in February 1600, just after publication of *Milicia Indiana*, causing even more extensive damage to homes and vineyards. The reference may be to an earlier and less dramatic explosion of this mountain.

7 Here Vargas Machuca offers a geocentric explanation for what is today called the Inter-Tropical Convergence Zone. His interest in altitude reflects the more extensive writings of the Jesuit José de Acosta (noted in the section on mountain sickness in book 2). See Acosta, *Natural and Moral History of the Indies*, book 2, 75–98. Vargas Machuca may well have drawn from Acosta on this and other geographical matters.

8 The town of Paita, on Peru's north coast, was a key naval provisioning port in colonial times.

9 Also *vijaó* (*Heliconia bihai*).

10 "Son amigos asi ellos como ellas": This seemingly out-of-place statement probably refers to nonmarital sexual relations, *amistad* meaning also "concubinage" in sixteenth-century usage.

11 Chicha and azua (Quechua, *aswa*) are varieties of maize beer still drunk in the Andes; pulque, which Vargas Machuca or his typesetter misspells as "pulcre," is the fermented agave sap drunk in Mexico. Coca is of course *Erythroxylum coca*, its raw leaves chewed as a stimulant with the aid of lime solvent. Yopa (or *jopa*) is a North Andean term for a powerful hallucinogen derived from the ground seeds of the acacia shrub *Anadenanthera peregrina*, usually inhaled as snuff (although Vargas Machuca suggests oral intake below). As snuff, smoked leaf, or concentrated juice, *Nicotiana rustica*, a wild variety of South American tobacco, is still used alone and in combination with other hallucinogens among northern forest peoples. See Johannes Wilbert, *Tobacco and Shamanism in South America* (New Haven, Conn.: Yale University Press, 1993).

12 The Pijaos of Colombia's Central Cordillera were "punished" by militiamen

such as Vargas Machuca in a series of wars beginning in the late sixteenth century. Many were sold into slavery as far away as Quito. See the introduction.

13 The Spanish used the term *pieza*, or "piece," to describe captive Africans and Amerindians.

14 The reference is to one variation of the El Dorado legend that led to the draining of various New Granadan lakes in colonial and later times, including Guatavita, near Bogotá. For earlier descriptions of this practice, see Francis, *Invading Columbia*, 106. *Guaquería*, or tomb robbing (from the Quechua *huaca* or *waka*, meaning "sacred place"), is still widely practiced in Colombia.

15 Indigenous peoples of the Canary Islands, conquered in the late fifteenth and early sixteenth centuries.

16 The term *cimarrón/a*, apparently of Caribbean origin, was widely used in the sixteenth century to refer to feral or fugitive people, plants, and animals.

17 The historian Pedro de Aguado describes the Muzos's poison as follows: "This poisonous tar which they put on their arrows contains no juice or other plant matter, but rather only mixtures of snakes, frogs, and other poisonous creatures," *Noticias historiales*, 2:337. Poison-dart frogs were probably the main active ingredient.

18 In the 1580s Vargas Machuca participated in expeditions against the Muzos, who inhabited the rugged lowland emerald mining zone just west of his wife's estate near the highland town of Chiquinquirá. See the introduction. The Ariguyes, Panches, and possibly Guayles were peoples of the Magdalena basin.

19 Descriptions of indigenous women joining in war are quite rare in Spanish accounts and are usually linked to the legendary Amazons. On Vargas Machuca and the Carares, see the introduction.

20 *Quipos* refers to the Quechua *quipu*, one of several Andean record-keeping and possibly writing systems. See Urton, *Code of the Quipu*, and Salomon, *The Cord-Keepers*.

21 This was not entirely true in 1599. See, for example, Naylor and Polzer, *The Presidio and Militia on the Northern Frontier of New Spain*.

22 Dr. Antonio González was president of the Bogotá audiencia in the late 1590s and was promoted to Spain's Indies Council just before *Milicia Indiana* went to press. It was common practice to send portions of indigenous burial goods, which were taxed by the crown at higher rates than mined gold (as much as one-third), to the king.

23 The most-used colonial purgative.

24 A lowland province east of Quito.

25 Vargas Machuca is here describing a number of different palms, including peach palm. Today's royal palm is not apparently one of them.

26 See map 1. This town, which Vargas Machuca named after his home in Spain, was in the Central Cordillera south of Popayán. As noted in the introduction, it did not survive more than a few months. Juan Friede placed it across the Iscancé River, a tributary of the Caquetá, from the modern town of Santa Rosa (just southwest of the archaeological site of San Agustín, where Friede was

excavating and writing at the time). See his *Los Andakí*, map between 16 and 17. Vargas Machuca mentions the Iscancé several times.

27 Lignum vitae, an effusion of which was used to treat syphilis.
28 *Palo Borracho*, or floss silk (thorny ceiba) tree. See also Vargas Machuca's discussion of barbasco.
29 *Hippomane mancinella*, a shoreline shade tree known for its high toxicity.
30 *Pau brasil*, for which the country was named, was commercialized in New Granada only late in colonial times.
31 Sarsaparilla was widely used in Vargas Machuca's day to treat syphilis.
32 "Holy wood," often confused with *guayacán*, or lignum vitae.
33 Species of giant cactus.
34 Literally "silly," a variation on *boa*.
35 Since only the large, desert-dwelling lizards of Mexico are known to be venomous, this is more likely a reference to one of the many Dendrobatid, or arrow/dart-poison frogs native to the northern Andes. They do not attack or bite, but even minimal contact with their skin secretions can be deadly.
36 Vargas Machuca seems to be blending descriptions of boas, bushmasters, and cobras, the last of which are not found in the Americas. The large and highly venomous bushmaster (*Lachesis muta muta*) seems the closest match, although it does not spit, constrict, or prey on sleeping humans.
37 Vargas Machuca's low opinion of mules was not widely shared, especially among creoles. See the introduction for discussion of his treatise on horsemanship.
38 The reference is to Spanish physician Nicolás Monardes, whose *Historia medicinal de las cosas que se traen de nuestras Indias Occidentales* was published in three parts in Seville between 1565 and 1574. It is famous for incorporating many New World items such as tobacco and coca into the Old World apothecary. See the introduction.
39 The reference is to pumas, or jaguars, rather than the smaller neotropical cats.
40 The toelike hoof of the tapir is still used medicinally throughout the Andes. See Gade, "Epilepsy, Magic, and the Tapir in Andean America," in his collected essays, *Nature and Culture in the Andes*, 118–36.
41 Presumably referring to an opossum.
42 Apparently referring to the capybara.
43 Sloth (in Colombia both the two- and three-toed varieties are found).
44 Not unusual for the time, Vargas Machuca treats the Amazon and Marañón as entirely separate rivers, with different mouths.
45 The reference is to *chinampa* building, a mix of aquaculture and agriculture.
46 Vargas Machuca is of course forgetting Lake Titicaca. Lake Maracaibo is in fact a huge estuary.
47 The reference is to the petroleum seeps of Ecuador's Santa Elena Peninsula.
48 Of the many saline springs of Colombia, this one, near modern Pereira, capital

49 of Risaralda Department, is perhaps best documented in the historical and archaeological record.
49 Manatees have been observed grazing on land at the edge of shallow estuaries.
50 Vargas Machuca may have heard survivors speak of this incident, which probably relates to Jiménez de Quesada's 1569 El Dorado expedition.
51 The reference is almost certainly to giant river otters.
52 Probably a reference to the so-called electric eel (*Electrophorus electricus*).
53 See also book 1, figure 24. The bird subsequently noted may in fact be a borrowed description of the Egyptian plover, "toothpick" of the Nile crocodile.
54 In the original, *lobos marinos*, literally "sea wolves" (South American sea lion, *Otaria flavescens*).
55 Possibly referring to the great curassow, or a now-extinct relative.
56 Campeche is in fact located on the west coast of Mexico's Yucatán Peninsula.

HYDROGRAPHY OF THE INDIES

1 In this period, longitude was measured (without much accuracy) starting from the Canary Island of Fierro. Vargas Machuca once again treats the Orellana and Marañón, today's Amazon, as separate rivers, and seems to use Dulce to refer to the Orinoco.
2 There is some confusion as to the location of the original Río Pirú, which attracted the attentions of Francisco Pizarro and others in the Conquest era and gave the whole of Spanish South America its name: Peru. Vargas Machuca gives the approximate latitude of the modern Mira River, which empties into the Pacific near Tumaco, Colombia. For another version, see Cieza de León, *The Discovery and Conquest of Peru*, 48–51.
3 Vargas Machuca is largely incorrect here, as Spaniards had reconnoitered much of northeastern North America's coastline by 1599. Basque whalers, for example, were long active in the northern fisheries, and Spanish Jesuits attempted to found missions in the Chesapeake Bay area around 1570. Translations of relevant documents are in volume 2 of Quinn, *New American World*.

GEOGRAPHY OF THE INDIES

1 Vargas Machuca presumably means north*east*–southwest.
2 Many of the Pueblo peoples of New Mexico were fighting the brutal conquistador Juan de Oñate and his followers at the time *Milicia Indiana* was going to press in 1598. See, for example, the classic study by George P. Hammond, *Don Juan de Oñate and the Founding of New Mexico*, and the more recent biography by Marc Simmons, *The Last Conquistador*. Neither of these books has much to say about Tewa or other indigenous views of all this, however.

3 Vargas Machuca is mistaken, as the capital was in fact old Guatemala City, today's Antigua. Honduras was a sub-district with modest gold and silver mines near Tegucigalpa.
4 A *corregimiento* was essentially a province, overseen by a corregidor.
5 Vargas Machuca (or his typesetter) renders it "Fernanbuco."
6 Vargas Machuca is mistaken on this point, as Brazil's first Spanish-style appeals court, called the *relação*, was not established until 1609.

COMPENDIUM OF THE SPHERE

1 Vargas Machuca is referring to the inauguration of the Gregorian calendar in October 1582.
2 Vargas Machuca is quite close, as the earth's equatorial radius is today calculated as 6,378 km, or 3,444 nautical miles. Spanish cosmographers such as Pedro de Medina (*Arte de Navegar*, 1545) had long since corrected Columbus's mistakes regarding the earth's size.
3 "Maximum circles," from Latin, *coluri*.
4 Literally, "feet opposite," an obsession since at least Aristotle's time. On this and the terms that follow, see also Vargas Machuca's beginning "Exhortation."

APPENDIX ONE

1 This translation is based on a microfilmed copy of the report filed by Vargas Machuca's son, probably published in Madrid upon his father's death in 1622. The original is in Chile's Biblioteca Nacional, Medina Collection, No. HA M192–10.

APPENDIX TWO

1 Our translation is based on the published version, *Apologías y discursos de las Conquistas Occidentales*, in Sancho Rayón and Zabalburu, *Colección de documentos inéditos para la historia de España*.
2 Keen, "The Black Legend Revisited." Vargas Machuca's unpublished defense is mentioned on 704. The only comprehensive examination of this text is Flores Hernández, "'Pelear con el Cid después de muerto.'" We discuss Flores Hernández's essay in detail in our full translation of the *Defense*. Suffice it to say here that as in his other writings on Vargas Machuca, Flores Hernández here takes the classic Hispanidad position of defending the defender.
3 Such treatment of Spanish captives was widely documented among the Carib-speaking peoples of lowland Colombia, including the Muzos and Carares, whom Vargas Machuca fought on several occasions. See, for example, Aguado, *Recopilación historial*, 2:219.
4 Carib-speaking groups who resisted the first conquistadors and preyed upon

their sedentary, highland neighbors, the Muisca. See the introduction and map 1. Charges of infanticide were a frequent refrain among conquistadors.

5 Given what we know of indigenous demographic decline, in New Granada and elsewhere, this is perhaps Vargas Machuca's most preposterous claim. No surviving original conquistador (had there been any) would have agreed. See Francis, "Población, enfermedad y cambio demográfico."

6 Vargas Machuca has a point here; missionary priests were often abusive, both psychologically and physically. See, for example, Clendinnen, *Ambivalent Conquests*, 74–77.

BIBLIOGRAPHY

EDITIONS OF *MILICIA INDIANA*

Milicia y descripción de las Indias, por el Capitan don Bernardo de Vargas Machuca, Cavallero Castellano, natural de la villa de Simancas. Madrid: Pedro Madrigal, 1599.

Milicia y descripción de las Indias, Escrita por el Capitan D. Bernardo de Vargas Machuca. Presentación por Carl Henrik Langebaek. Bogotá: Banco Popular/ Fondo de Promoción de la Cultura, 2003.

Milicia y descripción de las Indias. Edición y estudio por Mariano Cuesta Domingo y Fernando López-Rios Fernández. Valladolid: Universidad de Valladolid, 2003.

Milicia Indiana (does not include the "Description" or "Compendium"). Caracas: Biblioteca Ayacucho, 1994.

Michi no senshi to no takakai. Translated by Aoki Yasuyuki. Tokyo: Iwanami Shoten, 1994.

Milicia y descripción de las Indias. 2 vols. Madrid: Victoriano Suárez, 1892.

OTHER WRITINGS OF VARGAS MACHUCA

Apologías y discursos de las Conquistas Occidentales. In *Colección de documentos inéditos para la historia de España*, edited by José Sancho Rayón y Francisco de Zabalburu. 112 vols. Madrid: Miguel Ginesta, 1849–88, vol. 71 (1879; orig. ca. 1604): 201–309.

Libro de exercicios de la gineta. Madrid: Pedro Madrigal, 1600.

Teoría y exercicios de la gineta. Madrid: Diego Flamenco, 1619. This edition is available in *Tred libros de la jineta de los siglos XVI y XVII*, edited by Sanz Egaña. Madrid: Sociedad de Bibliófilos Españoles, 1951.

Compendio y doctrina nueva de la gineta. Madrid: n.p., 1621.

"Carta de don Bernardo Vargas Machuca a S.M. y discurso sobre la pacificación y allanamiento de los indios de Chile." In *Colección de documentos inéditos para la historia de Chile*, edited by José Toribio Medina. 2nd ser., 6 vols., 5:119–32. Santiago: FHBM, 1961.

REFERENCES

Acosta, José de. *Natural and Moral History of the Indies*, edited by Jane E. Mangan, translated by Frances López-Morillas, with introduction and commentary by Walter Mignolo. Durham, N.C.: Duke University Press, 2002.

Adorno, Rolena. *Guaman Poma: Writing and Resistance in Colonial Peru*. 2nd. ed. Austin: University of Texas Press, 2000.

Aguado, Pedro de. *Recopilación historial*, edited by Juan Friede. 4 vols. Bogotá: ca. 1582; Biblioteca de la Presidencia de Colombia, 1956.

Amasuno, Marcelino. *La Materia Médica de Dioscorides en el Lapidario de Alfonso X el sabio*. Madrid: CSIC, 1987.

Andrews, Kenneth J. *The Spanish Caribbean: Trade and Plunder, 1530–1630*. New Haven, Conn.: Yale University Press, 1978.

Anglo, Sydney. *The Martial Arts of Renaissance Europe*. New Haven, Conn.: Yale University Press, 2000.

Asúa, Miguel de, and Roger French. *A New World of Animals: Early Modern Europeans on the Creatures of Iberian America*. Burlington, Vt.: Ashgate, 2005.

Avellaneda, José Ignacio. *The Conquerors of the New Kingdom of Granada*. Albuquerque: University of New Mexico Press, 1995.

Barrera-Osorio, Antonio. *Experiencing Nature: The Spanish American Empire and the Early Scientific Revolution*. Austin: University of Texas Press, 2006.

Bolaños, Alvaro Félix, and Gustavo Verdesio, eds. *Colonialism Past and Present: Reading and Writing about Colonial Latin America Today*. Stony Brook: SUNY Press, 2002.

Burkett, Elinor. "Indian Women and White Society: The Case of Sixteenth-Century Peru." In *Latin American Women: Historical Perspectives*, edited by Asunción Lavrin, 101–28. Westport, Conn.: Greenwood, 1978.

Caillavet, Chantal, and Ximena Pachón, eds. *Frontera y poblamiento: Estudios de historia y antropología de Colombia y Ecuador*. Bogotá: IFEA/SINCHI/Universidad de los Andes, 1996.

Calvert, Albert F. *Spanish Arms and Armour, Being an Historical and Descriptive Account of the Royal Armoury of Madrid*. London: John Lane, 1907.

Cañizares-Esguerra, Jorge. *Nature, Empire, and Nation: Explorations of the History of Science in the Iberian World*. Stanford, Calif.: Stanford University Press, 2006.

Castellanos, Juan de. *Elegías de varones ilustres de Indias*. Bogotá: Gerardo Rivas Moreno, 1997.

Cervantes Saavedra, Miguel de. *El ingenioso hidalgo don Quijote de la Mancha*. Edited by Tom Lathrop. Newark, Del.: Juan de la Cuesta, 2003.

———. *Exemplary Stories*. Translated by C. A. Jones. New York: Penguin, 1972.

Chet, Guy. *Conquering the American Wilderness: The Triumph of European Warfare in the Colonial Northeast*. Amherst: University of Massachusetts Press, 2003.

Cieza de León, Pedro de. *The Discovery and Conquest of Peru*. Edited and translated by Noble David Cook and Alexandra Parma Cook. Durham, N.C.: Duke University Press, 1998.

Clendinnen, Inga. *Ambivalent Conquests: Maya and Spaniard in Yucatán, 1517–1571*. 2nd ed. New York: Cambridge University Press, 2002.

Colmenares, Germán. *La provincia de Tunja en el Nuevo Reino de Granada: Ensayo de historia social*. Tunja: UPTC, 1984.

Cook, Noble David, and Alexandra Parma Cook. *Good Faith and Truthful Ignorance: A Case of Transatlantic Bigamy*. Durham, N.C.: Duke University Press, 1990.

Crosby, Alfred. *The Columbian Exchange: Biological and Cultural Consequences of 1492*. 2nd ed. Westport, Conn.: Praeger, 2003.

Cuesta Domingo, Mariano, and Fernando López-Ríos Fernández. "Estudio introductorio." In *Milicia y descripción de las Indias*, 29–39. Valladolid: Universidad de Valladolid, 2003.

Cunninghame Graham, R. B. *The Horses of the Conquest*. London: W. Heinemann, 1930.

Díaz del Castillo, Bernal. *The Conquest of New Spain*. Translated by J. M. Cohen. New York: Penguin Classics, 1969.

Fallows, Noel. *The Chivalric Vision of Alfonso de Cartagena: Study and Edition of the "Doctrinal de cavalleros."* Newark, Del.: Juan de la Cuesta, 1995.

Ferguson, R. Brian, and Neil Whitehead, eds. *War in the Tribal Zone: Expanding States and Indigenous Warfare*. Santa Fe, N. Mex.: School of American Research, 1992.

Flores Hernández, Benjamín. "Bernardo de Vargas Machuca y el Caribe." *Revista Mexicana del Caribe* 14 (2002): 81–103.

———. "*La jineta indiana* en los textos de Juan Suárez de Peralta y Bernardo de Vargas Machuca." *Anuario de Estudios Americanos* 54 (1997): 639–64.

———. "Las Apologías y Discursos de las Conquistas Occidentales de Bernardo de Vargas Machuca, en controversia con la *Brevísima Relación de la Destrucción de las Indias* de Fray Bartolomé de Las Casas." *Estudios de Historia Novohispana* 10 (1991): 45–107.

———. "'Pelear con el Cid después de muerto': Las *Apologías y Discursos de las Conquistas Occidentales* de Bernardo de Vargas Machuca, en controversia con la *Brevísima Relación de la Destrucción de las Indias* de Fray Bartolomé de Las Casas." *Estudios de Historia Novohispana* 10 (1991): 45–107.

Francis, J. Michael. *Invading Colombia: Spanish Accounts of the Gonzalo Jiménez de Quesada Expedition of Conquest*. University Park: Pennsylvania State University Press, 2007.

———, ed. "Descripción del Nuevo Reino de Granada." *Anuario colombiano de historia social y de la cultura* 30 (2003): 40–60.

———. "'In the service of God, I order that these temples of idolatrous worship be razed to the ground': Extirpation of Idolatry and the Search for the *Santuario Grande* of Iguaque." In *Colonial Lives: Documents in Latin American History*,

1550–1850, edited by Richard Boyer and Geoffrey Spurling, 39–53. New York: Oxford University Press, 2000.

———. "Población, enfermedad y cambio demográfico, 1537–1636: Demografía histórica de Tunja, una mirada crítica." *Fronteras de la Historia* 7 (2002): 15–95.

French, Roger. *Medicine Before Science: The Business of Medicine from the Middle Ages to the Enlightenment.* New York: Cambridge University Press, 2003.

Friede, Juan. *Los Andakí, 1538–1947: Historia de la aculturación de un tribu selvática.* Mexico City: FCE, 1953.

Gade, Daniel. *Nature and Culture in the Andes.* Madison: University of Wisconsin Press, 1999.

Garcilaso de la Vega, El Inca. *The Royal Commentaries of the Incas and General History of Peru.* Translated by Harold V. Livermore. Foreword by Arnold J. Toynbee. Austin: University of Texas Press, 1966.

Gomez, Thomas. *L'envers de l'Eldorado: Economie coloniale et travail indigène dans la Colombie du XVIème Siècle.* Toulouse: Association des Publications UTM, 1984.

González García, Pedro, ed. *Discovering the Americas: The Archive of the Indies.* New York: Vendome, 1997.

Guevara, Ernesto "Che." *Guerrilla Warfare.* Edited by Brian Loveman and Thomas M. Davies Jr. Wilmington, Del.: 1960; SR Books, 1997.

Hale, J. R. *War and Society in Renaissance Europe, 1450–1620.* Baltimore: Johns Hopkins University Press, 1986.

Hall, Bert S. *Weapons and Warfare in Renaissance Europe: Gunpowder, Technology, and Tactics.* Baltimore: Johns Hopkins University Press, 1997.

Hammond, George P. *Don Juan de Oñate and the Founding of New Mexico.* Santa Fe: New Mexico Historical Society, 1927.

Hanke, Lewis. "The Meaning Today of the Las Casas Treatises Published in 1552." In *Selected Writings of Lewis Hanke on the History of Latin America*, 96–102. Tempe: ASU Center for Latin American Studies, 1979.

———. "More Heat and Some Light on the Spanish Struggle for Justice in the Conquest of America." *Hispanic American Historical Review* 44 (1964): 293–340. Reprinted in *Selected Writings of Lewis Hanke on the History of Latin America*, 26–48. Tempe: ASU Center for Latin American Studies, 1979.

Haring, Clarence. *The Spanish Empire in America.* New York: Harcourt Brace, 1947.

Hemming, John. *The Conquest of the Incas.* New York: Harcourt Brace, 1970.

———. *The Search for Eldorado.* London: Harmondsworth, 1978.

Herodotus. *The Histories.* Translated by Aubrey de Sélincourt. Edited by John Marincola. New York: Penguin, 2003.

Hoffmeyer, Ada Bruhn de. *Arms and Armour in Spain, II: A Short Survey.* Madrid: CSIC, 1982.

Jarcho, Saul. "Medicine in Sixteenth-Century New Spain as Illustrated by the Writings of Bravo, Farfán, and Vargas Machuca." *Bulletin of the History of Medicine* 31 (1957): 425–41.

Jones, Kristine. "Warfare, Reorganization, and Readaptation at the Margins of

Spanish Rule: The Southern Margin (1573–1882)." In *The Cambridge History of the Native Peoples of the Americas*, vol. 3: *South America*, part 2, edited by Stuart B. Schwartz and Frank Salomon, 138–87. New York: Cambridge University Press, 1999.

Jopling, Carol F., ed. *Indios y negros en Panamá en los siglos XVI y XVII: Selecciones de los documentos del Archivo General de Indias*. Antigua, Guatemala: Centro de Investigaciones Regionales de Centroamérica, 1994.

Kamen, Henry. *Empire: How Spain Became a World Power, 1492–1763*. New York: Harper Collins, 2003.

Keen, Benjamin. "The Black Legend Revisited: Assumptions and Realities." *Hispanic American Historical Review* 49 (November 1969): 703–19.

Kelsey, Harry. *Francis Drake: The Queen's Pirate*. New Haven, Conn.: Yale University Press, 1998.

Kinsbruner, Jay. *The Colonial Spanish American City*. Austin: University of Texas Press, 2005.

Lane, Kris. *Quito 1599: City and Colony in Transition*. Albuquerque: University of New Mexico Press, 2002.

———, and Timothy F. Johnson, eds. *The Defense of Western Conquests of Bernardo de Vargas Machuca*. University Park: Pennsylvania State University Press, 2007.

Langebaek, Carl. *Mercados, poblamiento e integración étnica entre los Muiscas*. Bogotá: Banco de la República, 1987.

Lanning, John Tate. *The Royal Protomedicato: The Regulation of the Medical Profession in the Spanish Empire*. Edited by John Jay TePaske. Durham, N.C.: Duke University Press, 1985.

Lavallé, Bernard. *Quito et la crise de l'Alcabala, 1580–1600*. Paris: Centre National de la Recherche Scientifique, 1992.

Lavin, James D. *A History of Spanish Firearms*. London: Herbert Jenkins, 1965.

Leonard, Irving. *Books of the Brave: Being an Account of Books and Men in the Conquest and Settlement of the Sixteenth-Century New World*. 2nd ed., with introduction by Rolena Adorno. Berkeley: University of California Press, 1992.

Lockhart, James. *The Men of Cajamarca: A Social and Biographical Study of the First Conquerors of Peru*. Austin: University of Texas Press, 1972.

Lupher, David. *Romans in a New World: Classical Models in Sixteenth-century Spanish America*. Ann Arbor: University of Michigan Press, 2003.

MacCormack, Sabine. *On the Wings of Time: Rome, the Incas, Spain, and Peru*. Princeton, N.J.: Princeton University Press, 2007.

Macleod, Murdo J. "Self-promotion: The *Relaciones de Méritos y Servicios* and their Historical and Political Interpretation." *Colonial Latin American Historical Review* 7 (1998): 25–42.

Magasich-Airola, Jorge, and Jean-Marc de Beer. *America Magica: When Renaissance Europe Thought It Had Conquered Paradise*, translated by Monica Sandor. London: Anthem Press, 2006.

Malone, Patrick. *The Skulking Way of War: Technology and Tactics among the New England Indians*. New York: Madison Books, 1991.

Martin, John. "Inventing Sincerity, Refashioning Prudence: The Discovery of the Individual in Renaissance Europe." *American Historical Review* 102 (1997): 1309–42.

Martínez de Salinas, María Luisa. *Castilla ante el Nuevo Mundo: La trayectoria indiana del gobernador Bernardo de Vargas Machuca*. Valladolid: Diputación Provincial, 1991.

Merino Hernando, María Asunción. *Historia de los inmigrantes peruanos en España: dinámicas de exclusión en una Europa globalizada*. Madrid: CSIC, 2002.

Minta, Stephen. *Aguirre: The Re-creation of a Sixteenth-Century Journey across South America*. New York: Henry Holt, 1993.

Monardes, Nicholas. *Joyfull Newes out of the Newe Founde Worlde*, vol. 1. Translated by John Frampton, introduction by Stephen Gaselee. New York: AMS, 1967.

Muldoon, James. *The Americas in the Spanish World Order: The Justification for Conquest in the Seventeenth Century*. Philadelphia: University of Pennsylvania Press, 1994.

Naylor, Thomas H., and Charles W. Polzer. *The Presidio and Militia on the Northern Frontier of New Spain, 1570–1700*. Tucson: University of Arizona Press, 1986.

O'Callaghan, Joseph F., ed. *Chronicle of Alfonso X*. Translated by Shelby Thacker and José Escobar. Lexington: University Press of Kentucky, 2002.

Otero D'Acosta, Enrique. "Biográfica disertación sobre el capitán don Bernardo de Vargas Machuca." *Revista de Indias* 12 (1952): 49–79. Originally published in *Boletin de historia y antigüedades* (Bogotá) 16, no. 181 (1927): 37–58.

Padden, Robert C. "Cultural Adaptation and Militant Autonomy among the Araucanians of Chile." Reprinted in *The Indian in Latin American History: Resistance, Resilience, and Acculturation*, rev. ed., edited by John E. Kicza, 71–91. Wilmington, Del.: Scholarly Resources, 2000.

Padilla, Silvia A., María Luisa López, and Adolfo Luis González. *La encomienda en Popayán: Tres estudios*. Seville: EEHA, 1977.

Pagden, Anthony, ed. *Hernán Cortés: Letters from Mexico*. New Haven, Conn.: Yale University Press, 1986.

Parker, Geoffrey, ed. *The Cambridge History of Warfare*. New York: Cambridge University Press, 2005.

Parker, Geoffrey. *The Grand Strategy of Philip II*. New York: Cambridge University Press, 1998.

———. *The Military Revolution: Military Innovation and the Rise of the West, 1500–1800*. New York: Cambridge University Press, 1988.

Parry, John H., and Robert G. Keith, eds. *New Iberian World*. 5 vols. New York: Times Books, 1984.

Peterson, Harold L. *Arms and Armor in Colonial America, 1526–1783*. New York: Bramhall House, 1956.

Plutarch. *Lives* (ca. 110 CE). Edited by Clayton M. Lehman. Translated by John Dryden. New York: Barnes & Noble, 2006.

Puddu, Raffaele. *El soldado gentilhombre*. Barcelona: Argos Vergara, 1986.

Quinn, David B., ed. *New American World: A Documentary History of North America to 1612*. 5 vols. New York: Arno, 1979.

Renard Casevitz, F. M., Thierry Saignes, and Anne Christine Taylor, eds. *Al este de los Andes: Relaciones entre sociedades amazónicas y andinas entre los siglos XV y XVII*. Quito: Abya-yala, 1988.

Restall, Matthew. *Seven Myths of the Spanish Conquest*. New York: Oxford University Press, 2002.

Restrepo, Luis F. "A Place to Live, a Place to Think, and a Place to Die: Sixteenth-Century Frontier Cities, Plazas, and 'Relaciones' in Spanish America." In *Mapping Colonial Spanish America: Places and Commonplaces of Identity, Culture, and Experience*, edited by Santa Arias and Mariselle Meléndez, 275–93. Lewisburg: Bucknell University Press, 2002.

Rodríguez Freile, Juan. *El Carnero*. Caracas: Biblioteca Ayacucho, 1979.

Ruiz Rivera, Julián B. *Encomienda y mita en Nueva Granada*. Seville: EEHA, 1977.

Salomon, Frank. *The Cord-Keepers*. Durham, N.C.: Duke University Press, 2005.

Sánchez, Francisco J. *An Early Bourgeois Literature in Golden Age Spain: Lazarillo de Tormes, Guzmán de Alfarache, and Baltasar Gracián*. Chapel Hill: North Carolina Studies in the Romance Languages and Literatures, no. 277, 2003.

Sancho Rayon, José, and Francisco de Zabalburu, eds. *Colección de documentos inéditos para la historia de España*. 112 vols. Madrid: Miguel Ginesta, 1849–88.

Schroeder, Susan, ed. *Native Resistance and the Pax Colonial in New Spain*. Lincoln: University of Nebraska Press, 1998.

Seed, Patricia. *Ceremonies of Possession: Europe's Conquest of the New World, 1492–1640*. New York: Cambridge University Press, 1995.

Sepúlveda, Juan Ginés de. *Demócrates Segundo o de las justas causas de la guerra contra los indios*. 2d ed. Edited and translated by Ángel Losada. Madrid: CSIC, 1984.

Simerka, Barbara. *Discourses of Empire: Counter-Epic Literature in Early Modern Spain*. University Park: Pennsylvania State University Press, 2003.

Simmons, Marc. *The Last Conquistador: Juan de Oñate and the Settling of the Far Southwest*. Norman: University of Oklahoma Press, 1991.

Simón, Pedro. *Noticias historiales de las conquistas de Tierra Firme en las Indias Occidentales*. 9 vols. 1625. Bogotá: Biblioteca de Autores Colombianos, 1953.

Sluiter, Engel. *The Gold and Silver of Spanish America, c. 1572–1648*. Berkeley, Calif.: Bancroft Library, 1998.

Socolow, Susan Migden. *The Women of Colonial Latin America*. New York: Cambridge University Press, 2000.

Solórzano Pereira, Juan de. *Política Indiana*. 1629. Madrid: n.p., 1648.

TePaske, John Jay. "Regulation of Medical Practitioners in the Age of Francisco Hernández." In *Searching for the Secrets of Nature: The Life and Works of Dr. Francisco Hernández*, ed. Simon Varey, Rafael Chabrán, and Dora B. Weiner. Stanford, Calif.: Stanford University Press, 2000.

Thucydides. *The Peloponnesian War*. Translated and edited by Walter Blanco. New York: Norton, 1998.

Toribio Medina, José, ed. *Colección de documentos inéditos para la historia de Chile*. 2nd ser. 6 vols. Santiago: FHBM, 1961.

Tovar Pinzón, Hermes, ed. *Relaciones y visitas a los Andes, Siglo XVI*. 4 vols. Bogotá: Colcultura/ICANH, 1993–95.

Tovar Pinzón, Hermes. *No hay caciques ni señores*. Barcelona: Sendai, 1988.

Townsend, Camilla. "Burying the White Gods: New Perspectives on the Conquest of Mexico." *American Historical Review* 108 (June 2003): 659–87.

Trimborn, Herman. *Señorío y barbarie en el Valle del Cauca*. Translated by José María Gimeno. Madrid: CSIC, 1949.

Urton, Gary. *Code of the Quipu*. Austin: University of Texas Press, 2004.

Varey, Simon, ed. *The Mexican Treasury: The Writings of Dr. Francisco Hernández*. Translated by Rafael Chabrán, Cynthia L. Chamberlin, and Simon Varey. Stanford, Calif.: Stanford University Press, 2000.

Varey, Simon, Rafael Chabrán, and Dora B. Weiner, eds. *Searching for the Secrets of Nature: The Life and Works of Dr. Francisco Hernández*. Stanford, Calif.: Stanford University Press, 2000.

Varner, John G., and Jeannette Johnson Varner. *Dogs of the Conquest*. Norman: University of Oklahoma Press, 1983.

Varón Gabai, Rafael. *Francisco Pizarro and His Brothers: The Illusion of Power in Sixteenth-Century Peru*. Translated by Javier Flores Espinosa. Norman: University of Oklahoma Press, 1997.

Villa-Flores, Javier. *Dangerous Speech: A Social History of Blasphemy in Colonial Mexico*. Tucson: University of Arizona Press, 2006.

Villamarín, Juan, and Judith Villamarín. "Chiefdoms: The Prevalence and Persistence of 'Señoríos Naturales': 1400 to European Conquest." In *The Cambridge History of the Native Peoples of the Americas*, vol. 3: *South America*, edited by Frank Salomon and Stuart B. Schwartz. New York: Cambridge University Press, 1999.

Vívar, Jerónimo de. *Crónica de los reinos de Chile*. Edited by Ángel Barral Gómez. Madrid: Historia 16, 1988.

Ward, Christopher. *Imperial Panama: Commerce and Conflict in Isthmian America, 1550–1800*. Albuquerque: University of New Mexico Press, 1993.

West, Robert C. *Colonial Placer Mining in Colombia*. Baton Rouge: Louisiana State University Press, 1952.

Wey-Gómez, Nicolás. *The Tropics of Empire: Why Columbus Sailed South to the Indies*. Cambridge, Mass.: MIT Press, 2008.

Whitehead, Neil L., ed. *The Discoverie of the Large, Rich, and Bewtiful Empyre of Guiana by Sir Walter Ralegh*. Norman: University of Oklahoma Press, 1998.

Wilbert, Johannes. *Tobacco and Shamanism in South America*. New Haven, Conn.: Yale University Press, 1993.

Williams, Caroline A. *Between Resistance and Adaptation: Indigenous Peoples and the Colonisation of the Chocó, 1510–1753*. Liverpool: Liverpool University Press, 2005.

Williams, Stephen, and Gerard Friell. *Theodosius: The Empire at Bay*. New Haven, Conn.: Yale University Press, 1995.

INDEX

Acapulco, lii, 184, 218, 222
Aguirre, Lope de, xv, xxxi, liii, 269n1
Alexander the Great, 33, 36, 42, 48, 49, 57, 161, 268n32
Altagracia, xlix, 240
Amazon River, xliii, 197, 269n1, 274n2, 276n44, 277n1. *See also* Marañón River
Ambushes, xii, xxviii, lxi, 7, 19–21, 53, 70, 77, 81, 91, 94–98, 107, 110, 113, 116–24, 132, 172; capture of Atawallpa and, 269n37
Antioquia, Santa Fe de, xxxiii, l, lviii, 77, 178, 242
Antipodes, 9, 12, 17, 34, 232, 234
Araucanians (Mapuche), xxviii, xlii, xlix, 23, 180, 260, 267n11, 268n25
Arequipa, 166, 206
Aristotle, 36, 46, 272n11, 278n4
Armor, lxiii, lxv, 19, 72, 77, 196, 266n2, 271n25

Berrío, Antonio de, xxxiv, xlii, 15, 84, 271n3
Bogotá, Santa Fe de, xxxii–xxxvii, xlii–xliii, xlvi, xlix, lxviii, 1, 41, 181, 198, 223–24, 261, 263–64; El Dorado and, 275n14
Brazil, 24, 165, 198, 226–27, 278n6
Buenos Aires, lii, 226

Cacao (chocolate), 181–83, 235
Cannibalism, xxxii, xlix, 77, 130–31, 152, 161, 173–74, 248
Carares, xliii–xlviii, li, lxiv, 52, 178, 240, 262n46, 263n56, 275n19, 278n3
Caribs, xxix, liii, liv–lv, 278nn3–4
Cartagena de Indias, xxviii, xxix, xl, liv, 197, 213, 215–16, 223–25
Cartago, 166, 168, 191, 200
Cerón, María, xlii–xliii, xlix, 263n58
Cervantes, Miguel de, xv, xvii, xxi, xxiii–xxv, xlii, li, lxxi–lxxii
Chichimecas, 4, 180
Chile, xii, xviii, xxviii, xxxi, xlii, lx, 4, 20, 180, 217, 226, 260n21, 267n11, 268n25
Chiquinquirá, x, xliii, 150, 192, 263n58, 275n18
Coca (Hayo), 21, 43, 172, 174, 180, 182, 235, 267n10, 274n11, 276n38
Columbus, Christopher, 11, 40, 48, 152, 278n2

Cortés, Hernando (Marquis of Valle), xi, xv–xvi, xxi, xxiv, xxxvi–xxxvii, lix–lx, lxx, 6, 15, 34, 40, 48, 59, 126, 221, 267n19; at court, 259n1; conquest of new Spain and, 50–51; destruction of ships by, 268n29; friendly Indians and, 269n38; "tanto Cortesano" and, 266n3

Dogs, lxix, 22, 33, 172, 192, 247, 263n52, 267n7, 271n24; ambushes and, 19, 94, 98, 120, 122–23; eating of, 40; help from, 19, 77–79, 120, 122–23; in night attacks, 113, 115; versus parrots as house guards, 204; wild animals and, 194–95
Drake, Francis, xxxi, xxxix, xl, lii, 267n14
Dress (indigenous), 152, 170–71, 179

El Dorado, xi, xxxii, xxxiv, xlii, 84, 165–66, 188, 201, 227, 261n31, 275n14, 277n50
Emeralds, xviii, xxxi–xxxiii, xliii, xlix, 175, 184, 210–11, 223, 235, 263n57, 271n24, 275n24
Encomiendas, xxxi–xxxii, xlii–xliv, l, liii, 35, 148, 152–54, 200, 263n52, 272n1

Fish, 201–4
Florida, lxiv, 24, 165, 180, 213

Garcilaso de la Vega, El Inca, xxiii, lx
Gold, xxix, xxxi–xxxiii, l, lviii, 20, 215, 252, 261n29, 263n52, 264n58, 275n22: drinking of, 37; gold mines, 184, 223–26, 278n3; implements for, 75; Indians and, 129–30, 157, 171–72, 181, 270n9; Indies wealth in, 27, 209; as offering, 174–76; payment in, 254, 262n45; prospecting for hidden, 144, 148; as reward, 160; rheumatism and, 69; in sonnets, 13–15
Gualis, 63, 77, 178, 270n9
Guayaquil, 200–201
Gunpowder, xvii, lxv, 91, 98, 103, 120–21; failure to ignite, 70–71; making of, 73–75; as medicine, 61, 64; provision of, 35; warnings about, 113–14
Guns. *See* Harquebuses.

Hannibal, 9, 57, 125, 132, 137, 272n12
Harquebuses (matchlock guns), xlvii, 21, 101, 152, 247, 266n3; alerting with, 85; ambushes and, 117–23, 126–28; animal killings with, 188, 197; ceremonial uses of, 139; defense of camp and, 105–9; dogs and, 79; Indian fear of, 77; marching with, 89–91, 94, 96; night attacks and, 113–15; preparation of, 70–73, 95; provision of, 35; river crossings and, 97–99, 101; Spaniards use in Indies, 18–19
Horses, xxviii, xli, lxv, lxviii–lxx, 4, 47, 57, 190–91; ambushes and, 118–19; arms and garments and, 72–73, 105; carrying stores and, 76; color of, 265n94; fear of, 77; feeding of, 207; French and Spanish use of, 18–19; griffins and, 196; horseshoes and, 76; Indian beliefs about, 247; Indian owners, 86, 152, 177, 252; lack of, 40, 47, 90; landscape of expedition and, 70, 90, 95, 104–5, 107; Lima and, 225; in Margarita, 241; night use, 105, 108; ostriches and, 204; porters and, 92; positioning of, 89, 128, 131; provision of, 34; river crossings and, 103; stockade form and, 106

Iscancé River, l, 184, 186, 202, 206, 275n26
Italy (wars and militia), xxxix, xl, lxii, lxiv, 7–8, 14, 20–23, 24, 26, 38, 47, 53, 56–57, 125, 155, 162, 240, 273n9

Jiménez de Quesada, Gonzalo, xxxii, xxxvii, lx, 41, 50, 52, 201–2, 224, 267n8, 277n50
Julius Caesar, 9, 12, 49, 51, 110, 132, 134, 156, 160; Plutarch and, 271n5, 273n17

Las Casas, Bartolomé de, xii, xvi–xviii, xxi–xxii, xxxvi, xxxix, lii, lix–lx, lxvii, lxxi, 245–57, 263n53
Leiva, Villa de, x, xxxiii, 141
Lima, xl–xli, 181, 207, 217–18

Madrid, xxiii, xxv, xxviii, xxxix, xli, li, lviii, lviii, lxvi–lxviii, 1, 2, 6, 262n38, 278n1
Magdalena River, xxxii, xliii, xlv, xlvii, xlix, li, lxiv, 185, 197, 206, 223–24, 240, 270n9
Man–traps, 20, 39, 92, 115
Mapuche. *See* Araucanians
Marañón River, 166, 186, 197–99, 201–2, 216, 227, 276n44, 277n1. *See also* Amazon River
Marcus Cato, 43, 47
Margarita Island, ix, xviii, xxxi, xxxvii, lii–lviii, 204, 239, 241, 245, 264n72, 265n76
Maroons (runaway slaves), xxix, xxxi, xxxiii, xl–xli, xliii, 260n23
Medicines and medical treatments, xii, xix–xx, xxii, lii, lviii, lxiii, lxv–lxvi, lxx, 35, 60–69, 190, 194, 208, 210, 270nn5–8, 270nn10–16; Greco–Roman God of, 266n2; texts on, 265n84
Mexico, xi, xix, xxiii, xxviii, xxxii, lxv, lxvi, lxx, 4, 7, 166, 198, 204, 211, 221–22; Campeche, 277n56; Cortes in, 268n29, 269n38; drinks of, 274n11; native resistance in, 260n19; venomous lizards of, 276n35
Mines and mining, xvi, xviii, xxvi, xxviii, xxix, xxxi, xxxiii, xxxv, 261n29, 263n57, 270n9, 275n18, 278n3; geographical breakdown of, 221–26; Indian interest in, 157; metals and stones found in, 209–12; in Muzo, xliii, xlix; in persuasive epistle, 10; in Peru, xli, lii; royal decrees on, 154; stealing from, 235; trees found in, 184; uprisings in, l, lxiv; of Zacatecas, 4
Monkeys, 40, 108, 123, 177, 180, 196–97
Music (indigenous), 130, 177, 179
Muzo and Muzos, lxiv, 240, 263n57, 270n16, 271n24, 278n3; Carare attacks, xliii–xlv, xlviii–xlix; mines of, 210, 224; pacification of, 77; poison of, 178, 275n17; revenge attack in, 255; springs in, 200; venomous lizards of, 189

New Granada (New Kingdom of Granada), xxv, xxix, xxxi–xxxix, xl–xliv, xlviii–xlix, l, lviii, lxiv, lxvi, lxxi, 4–5, 9, 19, 255, 262n44, 270n5, 275n14, 279n5; conquest of, xix, 50, 266n96; deer in, 194; discovery of, 41, 52; El Dorado and, 227; food stuffs in, 207–8; history of, xxi; Indians in, xii, 177, 180; as part of Indies, 24, 165; mines in, 211, 271n24; missionaries in, 267n13; *pau Brazil* in, 276n30; priests in, 181; river, lakes and springs in, 197, 199–200; Santa Fe, 223–24; trees in, 181–82, 184, 187; unconquered backcountry of, xviii; Vargas Machuca in, xx, 240; venom found in, 178; volcanoes in, 166
New Mexico, xii, xxxi, 24, 165, 196, 277n2
New Spain, xxxiii, xxxix, lxvi, 19, 213–15, 224, 237, 239; animals in, 191, 204; Cortés and, 50–51; Indians in, 177, 180; as part of Indies, 24, 165; insects of, 208; mines of, 4, 211; rivers and springs in, 199–200; trees in, 181–82, 184. *See also* Mexico
Nicaragua, xxvii, 166, 183, 199, 200, 204, 208, 213
Night raids, xii, xxviii, xxviii, 106–16, 132, 172–73

Orinoco River (or Dulce River), xxvii, xxxv, xlii, 215, 274n2, 277n1

Paita, 169, 274n8
Panama, xv, xxviii, xxxi, xxxiii, xxxix, xl–xli, lii, lv, lviii, 169, 199, 204, 208, 213, 218, 223, 245
Pánfilo de Narváez, 34, 48, 51, 269n38
Peace treaties, 133–37
Pearls, xxxii–xxxiii, liv–lv, 148, 157, 204, 223, 235
Peru, xi, xxiii, xxxix, lxvi, 19, 236, 269n37, 277n2; altitude sickness in, 270n5; animals in, 193, 203, 205; conquest of, xix; El Dorado and, xxxii–xxxiv, 227; food stuffs of, 207–8; Indians of, 170, 176–77; as part of Indies, 24, 165–66; lakes and springs in, 199–200; Lima, 225; mines in, xli, lii, 4, 210–11; Pizarro in, 41; ports of, 213, 215–18; rain in, 169; Roman heritage in, lx; trees in, 182
Philip II, xviii, xxiv–xxvi, xxxi, xlix, li, lxii, lxvi, lxxi, 13, 272n2
Philippines, xxv, lxiv, 3, 4, 184, 222
Pijaos, xxxv, xlix, l–li, lxiv, 131, 172–74, 180, 240, 274n12, 275n13
Pizarro, Francisco, xi, xv, xxiii, xxxvii, 41, 49–50, 225, 260n13, 269n33, 277n2
Plato, lxxii, 30, 33
Pliny, lx, lxxii, 47, 210
Poison and poisoning, 20, 185, 193–94, 210, 267n8, 276n29; arrows and, xlvi–xlvii, lxxxi, 180; herb venom, lx, 52, 134, 171, 178–79; Muzo, 77, 275n17; protective clothing, 72; remedies for, 61–64, 66–67; risk of, 39
Poma de Ayala, Felipe Guaman, xxiii, lx
Pompey the Great, lx, 31, 42, 51, 268n31
Portobelo, xv, xvii–xviii, xxix, xxxi, xxxvii, xlvii, lii, lvi, 213, 215, 223, 239, 241, 245
Potosí, xxv, xli, lii, 4, 210, 226
Priests (Catholic), xii, xxi, xxix, xxxvii, xlviii, 4, 30–31, 55, 58–60, 88, 139, 142–43, 171, 181, 249–53; abusive, 279n6

Quipos (quipus), 180, 275n20
Quito, 166, 178, 186, 188

Riohacha, 199, 204
River crossings, xii, 39, 41, 53, 64, 67, 73, 75, 93, 97–103, 112, 120
River Plate (Río de la Plata), 166, 190, 197–98, 204, 217, 226
Roads, 22, 59, 76, 93, 96, 134, 165

Santa Marta, xxviii–xxix, xxxiii, 62, 77, 131, 175, 178, 180, 197, 235
Santiago de Cuba, xxxix, 188
Scipio Africanus, lix, 9, 162, 273n22
Seeds, 206–8
Seville, xxiv–xxv, xxxix, xli, lviii, 18, 39, 138–39, 268n28
Shamanism ("sorcery"), 172–73, 175
Simancas (Colombia), l, 10, 184, 240
Simancas (Spain), xv, xxvi, xxvii, xxxvii, xxxix, xli, xlii, lii, lvi, lxvi, 28, 243, 245
Sinú, 176, 178
Springs, 199–200
Swearing, 30–31, 60, 84
Swords and swordsmanship, xvi, xxii, xxiv, xxxvi–xxxvii, lxi, lxvi, 18–21, 237; ambushes and, 117; carrying of, 70–71; ceremonial uses of, 139; commanders and, 129; *espadas anchicortas*, 266n5; gambling and, 85; marching and, 92, 95–96; provision of, 34; punishment and, 110, 147; river crossings and, 98; in sonnets, 14–15
Syphilis ("buboes"), lxvi, 56, 61, 65, 184, 200–201, 270n10, 276n27

Thucydides, 46, 269n34
Tobacco, liii–liv, lvi, lxvi, lxx, 61–65, 67–69, 172, 180, 270n7, 274n11, 276n38
Town-founding, xii, xxxvii, l, 137–45, 148–56, 272n2, 275n26

Trees, 181–88

Tucumán, xli–xlii, 166, 190, 198, 204, 226

Tunja, xxxii–xxxvi, xli–xlii, lxviii, 9, 10

Vargas Moxica, Alvaro Félix de, xxxvii, 239

Venezuela, xxxiii, 196, 199, 201, 204, 215, 224

Veracruz, xxxix, lii, 204, 214, 216, 222, 268n29

Weapons (indigenous), 19–20, 70–71, 78, 130, 142, 178, 237, 267n8

Women, xxv, xxix, xlviii, 57, 157, 161, 171, 173–74, 247, 251–52, 260; childbirth and childcare, 176–77, 180; fighting and, 178; marriage and, 153; rape of indigenous, 263n52; in war, 275n19

Zacatecas, 4, 222

Zaragoza (Colombia), xxix, xxxiii

KRIS LANE is professor of History at the College of William and Mary. He is the author of *Quito, 1599: City and Colony in Transition* and *Pillaging the Empire: Piracy in the Americas, 1500–1750*.

TIMOTHY F. JOHNSON is an associate instructor at the University of California, Davis where he is pursuing a MA in Hispanic literature.

Library of Congress Cataloging-in-Publication Data

Vargas Machuca, Bernardo de, 1557–1622.

Milicia y descripción de las Indias. English] The Indian militia and description of the Indies : an English translation of the original Spanish edition published in Madrid, 1599 / Bernardo de Vargas Machuca ; edited by Kris Lane ; translated by Timothy Johnson.

p. cm. — (The cultures and practice of violence series)
Originally published with title: Milicia y descripción de las Indias.
Includes bibliographical references and index.

ISBN 978-0-8223-4297-7 (cloth : alk. paper) —
ISBN 978-0-8223-4314-1 (pbk. : alk. paper)

1. America—Early accounts to 1600.
2. Indians of the West Indies—Early works to 1800.
3. Indians of South America—Early works to 1800.
4. Military art and science—America—Early works to 1800.
5. Guerrilla warfare—America—Early works to 1800.
6. Colombia—Description and travel—Early works to 1800.
7. Venezuela—Description and travel—Early works to 1800.
8. West Indies—Description and travel—Early works to 1800.
I. Lane, Kris E., 1967–
II. Title.

E141.V3 2008
970.01—dc22   2008020714

www.ingramcontent.com/pod-product-compliance
Lightning Source LLC
Chambersburg PA
CBHW061343300426
44116CB00011B/1970